The New York
New Haven
and Hartford
RAILROAD CO.

The New
England
Steamship
COMPANY

New Bedf'd
Marthas
Vineyard
and
Nantucket
STEAMBOAT CO.

# Splendor Sailed the Sound

## George H. Foster & Peter C. Weiglin

The New Haven Railroad and The Fall River Line

This work is dedicated
To the Memory of

# Dorothy Hoagland Foster

Mother, single parent, teacher,
supporter, challenger, friend.

and

To

# Jeanne Tilson Weiglin

*sine qua non.*

Publishers:

Potentials Group, Inc.
608 S. Railroad Avenue
San Mateo CA 94401

Mid-State Associates
7241 E. 28th Street
Tucson AZ 85710

Library of Congress Catalog Card Number: 89-92281
International Standard Book Number: 0-96246-740-5

Manufactured in the United States of America

# Foreword and Acknowledgements

More than fifty years have passed since a Fall River Line steamer slipped its lines and pulled out into Narragansett Bay, the North River, or Long Island Sound, carrying a group of passengers on what was described as "a little voyage of enchantment," a whiff of the splendors of a bygone age

Indeed, about twenty years have passed since the company that owned those boats, the New York New Haven and Hartford Railroad, itself went out of existence, merged and submerged into something called the Penn Central. For the last years of its life, "splendor" was not a word used to describe the New Haven Railroad, with its angry commuters, frustrated shippers, and rueful employees. But in years past, the NYNH&H offered as good a transportation service to its region as could be found anywhere in the nation. And as we shall see, it included splendor in abundance.

And some vestiges of those days remained. The island boats to Martha's Vineyard and Nantucket, although severed from the railroad in 1945, kept memory alive. And as recently as the early 1980s, one of your authors rode Martha's Vineyard (II) between Bridgeport and Port Jefferson, a familiar route made all the more pleasant by knowledge of the vessel's history and background.

This book has been in preparation for a quarter of a century, since George Foster first heard a rumor that there had been railroad steamboats on Long Island Sound, during the course of his research on a book covering the Long Island Rail Road. The process of gathering information was akin to peeling an onion; layer after layer of data was revealed, and many fine people were met along the way.

Peter Weiglin joined the project ten years ago, improbably discovering a common interest in the Sound while 2,500 miles away in Tucson, Arizona. You hold the result of a long and painstaking collaboration in your hands.

Along the way, it became necessary to redefine the scope of this volume to include the Sound operations of the NYNH&H and their predecessors as well as the related Island services. But the NYNH&H owned or controlled more than these maritime interests at one point in its history; control of the Boston and Maine Railroad brought with it control of a fleet of steamboats operating generally up the coast out of Boston. Ownership interests in Merchants' and Miners Transportation Co. and Eastern Steamship Co. meant that the railroad was involved with quite a few coastal shipping vessels. Control of the New York Ontario and Western Railroad caused the New Haven to own a fleet of coal barges that traversed the Sound on a regular basis. To keep the volume within bounds, we elected to concentrate on the Sound and Island services, with the others playing only supporting roles. Even thus limited, the material fills this volume.

Special thanks must go to our three readers, experts in steamboat lore, who provided some fascinating correspondence and some vital facts and corrections. They were William T. Greenberg Jr., George King Sr. and James T. Wilson. Mr. Wilson, sad to say, passed away just as this volume went to press; we're hopeful and confident that there are steamboats, trains, and other objects of pleasure where he is now.

If there be further sadness, it is in knowing that even after more than 380 pages, there was still much more material that we would have liked to have shared with you. The most difficult part of this project has been the deciding, what stays and what goes. This process is made more difficult when two authors assign different values to a given item. So if there is not enough Nobska, or not enough Priscilla, or not enough locomotives, or not enough whatever, be it known that we agree.

We also acknowledge the help of Helen C. Foster, whose eagle eye and sharp pencil freed the manuscript from typographical errors. As a general rule, with regard to any deficiencies, errors, emphasis or insight relative to that of the reader, each of the authors is only too happy to place full responsibility on the other one.

Should your appetite be whetted for more, we urge you to contact and join the Steamship Historical Association. Their address is: 345 Blackstone Blvd., H. C. Hall Bldg., Providence RI 02906

The annals of the New Haven Railroad are being compiled on a continuing basis by a group of people banded together as the New Haven Railroad Historical and Technical Society, Inc.; write to Box 412, Grafton MA 01519.

The Friends of Nobska are restoring that vessel; you can aid them in that effort by writing 128 Ocean Ave., Cranston RI 02905.

Those are present day activities and efforts. For the moment, however, let us journey to the past, to visit a very different New England and a very different New York. As you turn the pages and read of the efforts of literally thousands of people who participated in the New Haven's unified system, its predecessors and competitors, perhaps you will come to agree with us that the true splendor of the Sound was those people who made it all happen.

This is their story.

G. H. F.
Tucson AZ

P. C. W.
San Mateo CA

---

We pause here to acknowledge the assistance provided by the following individuals and organizations:

**Individuals:**

John Ackerman
Ralph Albright
Edith G. Blake
Laura Brown
John Burnes
Martin J Butler
Joseph Caprilozzi
Norton D. Clark
Harry Cotterell
William King Covell
Jim Crew
Dr. & Mrs. Kurt P. Cronheim
Dr. Connie E. Cronin
Kenneth L. Douglas
Wayne Drummond
Mr. & Mrs. William Ewen Jr.
Rex & Elise Fletcher
Barry Garland
R. Loren Graham
Howard F. Greene
C. B. Gunn
Ken Hall
Mr. & Mrs. Robert Havens
Ken & Jean Haviland
George W. Hilton
Melancthon W. Jacobus
Miss Faith Jennings
Mr. & Mrs. George King Sr.
Mr. & Mrs. Henry Kuhlman
Steven Lang
Paul E. Levasseur
Charles O. Lawesson
Mr. & Mrs. Seth Linthicum
John L. Lockhead

Roger W. McAdam
Henry R. Palmer
Mr. & Mrs. Ludwig H. Pannenborg
Mr. & Mrs. James Payer
Alice Ramsdell
Chuck & Muriel Rochon
Charles F. Sayle Sr.
Carolyn Staggs
Mr. & Mrs. Leon Steinberg
Thomas Stevens
E. Tone
Loren Wilcox
Jim & Alice Wilson
Ron Ziel

**Organizations:**

The Railway & Locomotive Historical Society
California Museum of Photography
    University of California
The California State Railroad Museum Library
The National Museum of American History
The New Haven Railroad Historical & Technical Association
The Steamship Historical Society of America
Baker Library, Harvard University
Society for the Preservation of New England Antiquities
Mariners Museum
Greene Library, Stanford University
Nantucket Historical Society
American Antiquarian Society
Essex Institute
National Archives
Peabody Museum
Library of Congress
Fall River Historical Society

# Table of Contents

*Chapter One*

# Introduction

On an American arm of the sea named Long Island Sound, a neighbor of the Hudson River artery, sailing vessels had been operating since the 1600s, mostly carrying freight. The variability of schedule displayed by a vessel at the mercy of wind and tide tended to reduce the sailing packet's attractiveness as a passenger carrier. No one could accurately predict the arrival of any sailboat at any given port, given the possibility of calm, or the necessity to tack for hours to achieve a short distance against the wind. But even the relatively slow sloops of the era were preferred to the stark and spine-shattering stagecoaches that travelled at a relative snail's pace over the rutted paths between New England and New York.

In an era when people vent their anger against an insensitive Congress which had the temerity to reduce the maximum highway speed limit to 55 miles per hour, it is not easy to visualize the state of overland transportation in the early 1800s. First, the majority of people walked. Everywhere. Any other means of transportation was likely to be beyond the means of the average citizen. This had the interesting side-effect that during their entire lifetimes, most people never travelled or relocated more than fifty miles from the place of their birth.

The early Fall River Line steamer *Empire State*, built in 1848, is shown in her element; taking on a crowd of passengers. This old photograph was a time exposure; note the rowboat and the flag not cooperating for the photographer. The walking beam of her engine towers above the folks on deck, and we can clearly see the outboard boilers on her guards, just ahead of the paddle wheels. Photographs of early boats are rare, because the early films and processes were not fast enough to capture moving objects successfully.

Travel, then, was an activity undertaken by a small fraction of the population; those who possessed both money and an adventurous spirit in above-average quantities. For those who did not own horses (with or without carriages), commercial land transport was provided by stagecoaches with primitive springing and suspension systems. Freight transportation vehicles were animal-drawn wagons, driven by teamsters, and dwarfed by today's tractor-trailer trucks.

But if the vehicles were primitive, the roads were even less developed. The average Boy Scout camp today has better-developed roads and paths than were the norm in Thomas Jefferson's America. Pavement was a faraway dream, leveling and grading an infant science, and directness of route more the result of accident than design. (We forget that most of the Interstate highway system was not begun until the 1950s.)

Given these conditions, overland travel between New York and Boston took four days, punctuated by three nights of uncertain accommodations about which the only constant seemed to be the exorbitance of their prices. Under these circumstances, the waterways became the avenues of commerce in America; the sailboats, however unreliable, were preferable to land travel.

The rivers in America, notably the Hudson, Connecticut and Delaware, quickly became primary transportation arteries. A protected arm of the sea east of New York City developed into a vital connecting link.

## Long Island Sound

The Sound is a 120-mile long, 20-mile wide body of water, bounded on the north by the state of Connecticut and on the south by Long Island, part of New York State. The protection offered by Long Island makes for more gentle wave and current

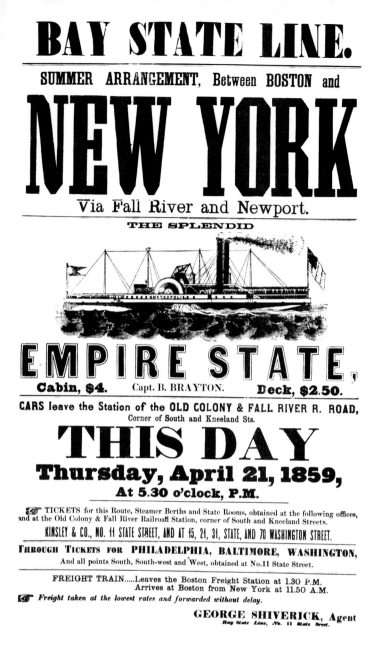

## BAY STATE LINE.

### SUMMER ARRANGEMENT, Between BOSTON and

# NEW YORK

### Via Fall River and Newport.

**THE SPLENDID**

# EMPIRE STATE,

**Cabin, $4.**   Capt. B. BRAYTON.   **Deck, $2.50.**

**CARS** leave the Station of the **OLD COLONY & FALL RIVER R. ROAD,**
Corner of South and Kneeland Sts.

# THIS DAY

## Thursday, April 21, 1859,

### At 5.30 o'clock, P.M.

☞ TICKETS for this Route, Steamer Berths and State Rooms, obtained at the following offices, and at the Old Colony & Fall River Railroad Station, corner of South and Kneeland Streets.

**KINSLEY & CO., NO. 11 STATE STREET, AND AT 15, 21, 31, STATE, AND 70 WASHINGTON STREET.**

**THROUGH TICKETS FOR PHILADELPHIA, BALTIMORE, WASHINGTON,**
And all points South, South-west and West, obtained at No. 11 State Street.

FREIGHT TRAIN.....Leaves the Boston Freight Station at 1.30 P.M.
Arrives at Boston from New York at 11.50 A.M.
☞ *Freight taken at the lowest rates and forwarded without delay.*

**GEORGE SHIVERICK, Agent**
*Bay State Line, No. 11 State Street.*

An early Bay State (Fall River) advertising poster, showing connecting service via the "Old Colony & Fall River R. Road." The train-boat transfer is captured in the engraving below.

Note that the woodcut is of *Metropolis*, while the poster advertises *Empire State*. There was no sense wasting good money on anything more than a "generic" woodcut.

---

tion; the most difficult route of all is the "outside route" around Cape Cod to Boston.

Summer was (and still is) the busy season for maritime activity on the Sound; many ports, anchorages and beaches line both shores. Winter brings many hazards, however; in the early years, many steamboat lines suspended operations altogether during the winter months; chunks of ice in the water were hazardous; indeed, during some winters, eastern portions of the Sound were frozen over. The longest continuous freeze during the steamboat era was 39 days, between January 17 and February 24, 1857. It was not until the 1870s and 1880s, after large steel-hulled boats became the norm, that year-round schedules were a matter of course.

### Hell Gate

Hell Gate in particular was a legendary danger. Swift and swirling currents coupled with many submerged rocks and reefs meant disaster for the unwary pilot. The current was quite capable of overpowering a boat's propulsion and steering, carrying the vessel helplessly to a submerged rock, or into collision with another boat. Listen to Washington Irving's contemporary description of the notorious channel before improvement:

action in the Sound than is present in the open ocean nearby. While the Sound is wide enough for most of its length, navigable channels constrict to dangerously narrow outlets at both ends. On the east, there is The Race, between Fishers Island and the Connecticut coast near New London. Rocks and shoals limit the areas through which a boat of any size may safely pass. On the west, an even more formidable barrier exists; the aptly named Hell Gate, a roiling and rocky stretch of conflicting currents at the north end of New York's East River. (Note: the East and Harlem "Rivers" in New York are in fact straits connecting other bodies of water; they are not true rivers.)

East of Long Island Sound, if you're going to Providence or Fall River on Narragansett Bay, you have to round Point Judith; the waters and winds there are ferocious to the point of legend. The unprotected Atlantic Ocean is no friend to naviga-

"Being at the best of times a very violent and impetuous current, it takes these impediments in mighty dudgeon; boiling in whirlpools; brawling and fretting in ripples; raging and roaring in rapids and breakers, and in short indulging in all sorts of wrongheaded paroxysms. At such times, woe to any unlucky vessel that falls within its clutches. At low water it is as pacific a stream as you would wish to see. At half-tide it roars with might and main, like a bull bellowing for more drink; but when the tide is full it relapses into quiet, and for a time sleeps as soundly as an alderman after dinner."

Between 1852 and 1896, the city, state, and federal governments spent about $5 million on efforts to dredge, blast and drill rocks and shoals, toward the goal of providing a channel 26 feet deep at low tide. Still, the 1980s maritime charts carry this warning:

"CAUTION : STRONG TIDAL CURRENTS OF UP TO 5 KNOTS, HEAVY SWIRLS AND HEAVY TRAFFIC IN HELL GATE REQUIRE EXTRA CAUTION ON THE PART OF THE MARINER TO AVOID ACCIDENT OR COLLISION."

## The Competent Mariners

Our literature overflows with thrilling tales of gallantry and heroism on the high seas, particularly in the era called the days of wooden ships and iron men. But sometimes sheer courage and amazing competence get taken for granted, merely because they occur on a daily basis, in a relatively humdrum setting. Mark Twain made the Mississippi steamboat captains and pilots immortal for their capacity to memorize every inch, every twist, every turn, every landmark, every trick of the river, to make a trip successfully.

But the Mississippi is not, we submit, the most severe test of an American steamboater's skills; that dangerous honor goes to Long Island Sound. For more than 120 years, from 1815 to World War II, steamboats operated between New York City and various points on the Connecticut, Rhode Island and Massachusetts shores; a couple of thousand travelers each day used the boats and connected with trains to Boston and other New England points. The steamboats also got tons of freight, including Fall River textiles and other goods, to manufacturer and to market.

In the steamers' heyday, from the 1880s to the 1930s, ten to twenty fairly large steamboats made the trip to and from New York every day, the skipper traversing Hell Gate, then the Sound, finding The Race's narrow passage, and then rounding P'int Judy. Or the reverse. And they weren't crawling either; good service and competition required 15 to 20-knot speeds.

It took a special breed of seafarer to do that; on the bounding main at least, you're not in constant danger of crashing into something. Navigation by dead reckoning isn't easy. It was more difficult because the Sound was quite often fogged in at one end or the other. But the full impact of these captains' daily achievement comes when you realize that the majority of schedules over the years called for the boats to leave their docks between 5:00 PM and 7:00 PM in the evening, and to dock between 3:00 AM and 6:00 AM the next morning. That's right; these Sound seafarers navigated in the fog, at night, night after night, before radar was invented and even before radiotelecommunications came into use.

Given the opportunity for catastrophe, the miracle is that there were not many more mishaps. As Roger Williams McAdam reported in his light-hearted treatments of the Sound steamers, the Coast Guard compiled (apparently in 1935) a list of the early major American maritime disasters resulting in great loss of life. Only seven occurred in connection with the Sound services.

New England 1833, boiler explosion
Lexington (I) 1840, fire
Atlantic 1846, stranding
Metis 1872, collision
Narragansett 1880, collision
Larchmont 1907, collision
Lexington (II) 1935, collision

That the list is not considerably longer is a tribute to the men* who did the work, and to the managers who trained them.

## The First Steamboats

There is some question as to who was the first person to operate a boat under power of steam in the United States: John Fitch or Samuel Morey. (No, the honor does not belong to that well-financed Bobby-come-lately, Robert Fulton). The available evidence tilts toward Morey, whose initial experiments were carried out on the Connecticut River, at Orford, NH in the 1780s. John Fitch, a Connecticut native, first tested his new steamboat in August 1787, on the Delaware River near Philadelphia. In that year, the New York legislature granted to John Fitch ". . . the sole right and advantage of making and employing the steamboat by him lately invented. . . ."

Unfortunately, the first Fitch boat moved at only three miles per hour, but by 1790, the breath-taking speed of eight miles per hour had been attained. Financial and organizational difficulties prevented these and later experiments from bearing fruit; Mr. Fitch committed suicide in 1798.

Elijah Ormsbee of Providence is alleged to have made a few primitive trials on the Providence River

NEW LINE BETWEEN BOSTON AND NEW YORK, VIA NEWPORT AND FALL RIVER.

Consisting of the New Steamers

**BAY STATE, EMPIRE STATE AND STATE OF MAINE.**

Bay State and Empire State each 1600 Tons and State of Maine 900 Tons burthen, all built expressly for the outside route and are in every respect sea going Steamers

in 1792 with a steam engine propelling a small boat by means of "goose-foot paddles", but nothing came of it.

Samuel Morey it was who produced the first practical long-distance steamboat; in 1794 his bow-wheeler made the trip from New York to Hartford, thus becoming the first steamboat on Long Island Sound. In fact, it was the first steamboat on any arm of the sea, anywhere. Mr. Morey's 1795 patent was signed by President George Washington. The Rev. Cyrus Mann, who conducted intensive historical research in the 1850s into the origin of steamboats, stated (none too kindly) that Robert Fulton had built upon the work of Morey and others. Put a bit more bluntly, the charge is that Robert Fulton and his wealthy backer, Robert Livingston, led Mr. Morey along with promises of money, learned what they could about steamboats, and coolly stole his ideas and designs without compensation. Remember for a moment that the victim was a Connecticut man, who remained active in steamboating and things mechanical.

Oliver Ellsworth of Pennsylvania first applied high-pressure steam engines to boats, building a dredging scow for the City of Philadelphia. in 1804. He had been experimenting with steam power since 1787 also, with the help of the Pennsylvania legislature.

Yet all of these became overshadowed in the public mind by Robert Fulton. Mr. Ellsworth later commented, ". . . had I been patronized, as Mr.

Consider, if you will, the contrast between the largely open-air *State of Maine*, built in 1848, and the opulent two-story Grand Saloon of the 1889 steamer *Puritan*, operating between New York and Fall River. The Fall River Line had a patent on the carpet design used in her later boats. The stern-visaged portrait at the head of *Puritan*'s grand staircase was a likeness of John Endecott, Governor of the Bay Colony for most of the time between 1640 and 1665.

---

Fulton was by the State of New York, with the exclusive right for thirty years, and by a Mr. Livingston with thirty thousand dollars, to make the experiment, I might have shown steamboats in full operation before Mr. Fulton began his boat, which was finished in 1807. . . ."

### Fulton, Livingston, Gibbons and Ogden

Mr. Fulton's support was considerable. In 1798 (just before John Fitch's suicide), Robert R. Livingston, a prominent New Yorker, persuaded that state's Legislature to repeal its earlier grant to John Fitch and to issue a thirty year monopoly arrangement to himself for the operation of steamboats in "New York State waters", as an incentive to technological and financial advancement. Livingston was working on a steamboat at the time, with Nicholas Roosevelt and John Stevens. The boat proved to be unsuccessful, and experiments ended in 1800 when President Jefferson appointed Livingston as Minister to France.

In France, Livingston met Robert Fulton, who was experimenting with steamboats on the River Seine, and a funding arrangement was reached. Fulton returned to America in 1806, and by August 1807 his boat was ready for a trial trip. The "North River Steamboat of Clermont" was her name, Clermont being Robert Livingston's home town on the Hudson River. As every schoolchild knows, the Clermont was a success, and the monopoly, named the North River Steamboat Company of New York, was in business. (Note: the Hudson River was known to the citizens of the colony of Nieuw Amsterdam, later to be New York, as the "North" River; the corresponding "South" River on the old maps was the one we know as the Delaware.)

The Clermont's first voyage in August 1807, between New York City and Albany on the Hudson River, ushered in a new era in water transportation. With steam power harnessed to propel a boat, the unreliability of sails could be avoided . . . and with

*Priscilla* rests at Pier 14 North River, above, as horse-drawn wagons carry the goods to their destinations. This was commerce on West Street on New York City shortly after the turn of the century. At the height of the season, more than a thousand people per day would pass through those pier gates to travel to their different New England destinations. But there's still time for another drink at Wallach's Restaurant (lower right of photo) before departure.

Almost simultaneously, in the photo at the right, 200 miles and a few light-years away, at Siasconset on Nantucket Island, three youngsters look out toward the sea, ignoring the narrow-gauge 4-4-0 behind them.

Pier 14 and 'Sconset represent the two extremes of the New York, New Haven and Hartford Railroad's steamboat system in many more ways than can be shown on a map.

such reliability enabling regular schedules came greater opportunity for profit to shipowners. Steamboat service on Long Island Sound was a natural extension, in response to a well-defined demand, through a well-defined transportation corridor connecting New York City and many bustling New England cities.

But the Livingston monopoly pinched the development of steamboat commerce until 1825 when a landmark U. S. Supreme Court decision in the case of Gibbons v. Ogden established the rules of interstate commerce and began to define Federal power as compared to that of the states. Behind that legal case lay a boiling feud, a ruined fortune, politics as usual, and the entry onto the stage of the man who would dominate the first thirty years of Long Island Sound steamboating.

Under the terms of the New York monopoly grant to Livingston and Fulton, no one could operate a steamboat in or to New York without paying their firm for a license to operate. The New Jersey Legislature retaliated by authorizing any Jersey steamboat operator whose boat was seized under the Livingston monopoly grant, to seize any New York boat found in "New Jersey waters." The dispute was enhanced by conflicting claims as to boundaries; New York claimed jurisdiction all the way across the Hudson to the Jersey shoreline; hence, New Jersey boats, they claimed, could not even leave ports like Hoboken without New York permission.

In 1813, New Jersey granted a similar steamboat monopoly to a former New Jersey governor, Aaron Ogden of Elizabeth. Interstate commerce using

steamboats stopped cold. Ogden's opponents got the New Jersey monopoly grant repealed in 1815. As public opinion in all states was reacting against the Monopoly, Livingston was concerned that New York's legislature might not remember his earlier arguments and persuasions. He issued Ogden a license to quell the lawmakers' concerns about impaired commerce. Other steamboat operators remained in the cold. They either paid the fees (if Livingston liked them), avoided New York, or operated illegally on a "catch me if you can" basis.

A notable renegade operator was another Elizabeth New Jersey lawyer named Thomas Gibbons, former partner and current enemy of Aaron Ogden. Unable to gain a license because of Ogden's opposition, Gibbons bought a steamboat and placed it into service between New York's Battery and Elizabeth. He found a daring and resourceful young captain for his vessel: young Cornelius Van Derbilt (as he spelled it then) of Staten Island. For the next five years, Van Derbilt outmaneuvered the monopoly's agents in New York's sacred currents, while a continuing legal battle was waged between Gibbons on one side, and the monopoly and Ogden on the other.

In 1819, Mr. Gibbons secured an injunction keeping Livingston and Ogden steamboats out of New Jersey waters. Mr. Ogden sued and obtained a court injunction preventing Mr. Gibbons from operating a steamboat in New York. Mr. Gibbons appealed the New York injunction, and the New York Court of Errors upheld the Monopoly. Appeal was made to the United States Supreme Court, Gibbons arguing that the New York Legislature's

monopoly grant was contrary to the concept of interstate commerce as set forth in the Constitution.

To handle the appeal, Mr. Gibbons retained Daniel Webster; Cornelius Van Derbilt went to Washington with the retainer fee and impressed the distinguished orator and attorney. The case was not heard until 1824. During that interim period much public agitation against New York ensued; we shall explore Connecticut's reaction in the next chapter.

Chief Justice John Marshall wrote the decision, one that helped to define the federal government and its powers. But, for the non-attorneys of the world, the decision was that the Monopoly violated the concept of interstate commerce, and was therefore unconstitutional. Gibbons had won; he and others began operating increased service to New York amid public celebrations of welcome. Shippers and the public in all states rejoiced. Customers deserted the Monopoly in droves, emphatically, purposefully, and "on general principles." Mr. Ogden's fortune was gone in legal fees and lost business. And Cornelius Van Derbilt prepared to start his own steamboat operation, first to New Jersey, then to Long Island Sound. He would be a major presence there until 1850.

Repeal of the monopoly meant instant and intense competition, as new lines came on stream charging lower fares. The old companies responded with cuts of their own, with fares sometimes reaching ridiculous levels, as for example, New York to Fall River for $1.00. But before we shed a tear for the steamboat companies, we should remind ourselves that the revenues from the bars and food services in the steamships (particularly the bars) quite often made up for the revenue lost in fare cutting. From the earliest days, even the smallest passenger steamships featured a bar, where beverages of varying potency could be had during the trip. In the first twenty years of Sound steamboating, public drunkenness did not carry the social stigma that it would have after the Anti-Saloon Leagues got going in the 1840s and 1850s. In the later years, fine cuisine and spirits enhanced both the ambience of both the ride and the revenue stream.

New York's Legislature repealed even the Livingston intrastate monopoly in 1826; New York was now open to all, even for intrastate commerce. The Livingston-Fulton firm soon went out of business under the weight of competition and bad public memories.

But while the waters were open to all, there was still the problem of landing places and landing rights. While the historical focus of this and other volumes is on the boats, economic control of the steamboat lines most often centered on the piers at which the boats called. No competitor would be allowed to land at a private company's wharf, except in an emergency. Acquisition of dock space was seen as the critical necessity to start a steamboat line, and it was not always possible. Even space at the "public" docks was limited, and was regulated by public officials whose approval had somehow to be gained. In many cases, the memories of these public gatekeepers had to be periodically refre$hed. Thus Company A often bought out Company B not so much to acquire the boats or the business, but rather to obtain Company B's wharf and dock property or landing rights to use themselves or to insure that they could not be used by a potential Company C.

Competition was fierce, especially for precious landing space. An extreme example: young Oliver Vanderbilt attempted to compete against older and richer cousin Cornelius on Staten Island; one morning Oliver found his landing blocked by a boatload of gravel, dumped there by orders of his relative in the belief that family relations had nothing to do with cutthroat business. (We should also note that Oliver survived by whipping up public interest against Cornelius' "monopoly," neatly turning his wealthier cousin's tactics against him.)

## The Railroads

It is impossible to describe the steamboats on Long Island Sound without also including some information about the railroads with which the vessels and their operators intertwined throughout their history. While the steamboats came first, after the 1840s the railroads provided overland connections to the port cities. The businessmen of each port city sought a competitive advantage through their boat and rail connections. Most of the passengers and freight shipments traveled by both boat and rail to get where they were going. For longer-distance travelers, particularly those travelling between New York and Boston, the consumer choice among competing steamship lines was a question of how much of the trip to take by boat and how much by a connecting train, considering speed, service and comfort.

While the steamboat services were highly competitive after the breakup of the Fulton-Livingston Monopoly, the railroads were able to achieve a greater economic strength over time because of a "physical monopoly;" they owned their roadbeds, and the price required for a railroad competitor to enter the market was considerably higher than for steamboaters. Thus the railroads usually (but not always) had the upper hand in dealing with their steamboat connections. Sometimes the steamboat companies were relatively stronger, in cases where their prime assets were their land locations rather than their vessels.

In the beginning of the steamboat era, the faster trips involved longer water segments because land travel was painfully slow; the pendulum swung with improvement of railroad routes and comfort.

Today's trains make the New York-Boston run in about five hours; more significantly, the trip by private automobile takes about a half-hour less.

In the last decade of the nineteenth century and the early part of the twentieth century, an overnight train "sleeper jump" between cities was the preferred way to travel in America, particularly on business. Such nocturnal travel featured the Pullman sleeping car, even for comparatively short distances. If a passenger boarded his train in the evening after the close of business, he was assured

of a good meal in the diner, congenial company in the lounge or a place to work quietly as he desired, and a reasonably comfortable Pullman bed until morning. The actual time of arrival of the Pullman car in the destination city made little difference; many such cars sat on station sidings after a 4:00 or 5:00 AM arrival, until the sleeping passengers were awakened at 6:30 or 7:00 AM.

But the space on a train was limited, the locomotives belched shirt-staining smoke and cinders, and rail roadbeds were nowhere near as smooth as the Sound. So the heavily travelled "corridor" between New York City and New England points, particularly Boston, was an exception. The trains could not compare with the relative luxury, quiet, and natural air-conditioning of the night steamboats. The boat schedule was similar to the Pullman: departure from New York at or shortly after 5:00 PM, an excellent dinner on board the steamer, an evening band concert, and a berth in a stateroom which, while not large, provided a bit more room than a Pullman berth. The next day began with arrival in say, Fall River, MA at 6:30 AM, with a fast "Boat Train" ride to Boston in time for the day's

Here's one of the unsung heroes of New England steamboating, *General* of the Newport-Wickford ferry operation across Narragansett Bay. With its rail connection at Wickford Junction, the ferry allowed people coming from the west to avoid the circuitous trip all the way around Narragansett Bay through Providence to reach Newport. No orchestras, no fancy meals, just transportation.

business meetings or social activities. For many, the elegant steamers were the only way to travel. And the network of railroad connections extended the "reach" of the steamboats inland, beyond the coastal cities.

The ultimate boat/rail relationship, of course, came about when the New York, New Haven and Hartford Railroad bought most of the steamship lines on Long Island Sound. The NYNH&H also bought most of the street and electric railways in its service area, with the avowed intent of creating a transportation monopoly. Some of the results and effects of that policy are also considered in this volume.

## Some Preliminary Notes

Throughout this volume, we refer to the controlling corporate entity known formally as the New York, New Haven and Hartford Railroad as the "NYNH&H." This was done to avoid confusion with predecessor railroads and the Connecticut City, and to save space. We have accorded similar treatment to the Hartford and New York Transportation Company ("H&NYTCo"), the New England Steamship Company ("NESS"), and the New York and New England Railway Company (NY&NE) for the same reasons.

A few other points: first, the ancient question of how big a "boat" must be before it is called a "ship" rages on. It's clear that especially in later years, the Sound steamers were as large as many ocean-going vessels. Yet, their masters and crews called them "boats", not "ships." We will do these intrepid mariners the honor of following their custom.

The term "Captain," in popular usage, refers to the commander of a vessel. Yet, commercial steamboat pilots and masters are licensed; many licensed "Captains" do not command vessels. For this reason, the Old Colony Steamboat Co. took to using the title "Commander" when designating the person in charge of a boat. This usage fell from favor in the early 1900s, with the more popular but less precise "Captain" being the term of choice.

Roman numerals in parentheses following a boat's name are our attempt to keep the chronology straight where a name was used for more than one vessel. The numerals were not applied to the boats or used by the owners, because there rarely was more than one boat with a given name operating at the same time. The reader should not confuse our informal attempt at clarification with the yachtsman's practice of adding a roman numeral as part of a boat's name, as for example, a well-known bankruptcy attorney's Chapter XI.

A glossary is provided at the back of this book to define other nautical terms with which the reader may be unfamiliar.

With her sister ship *Bristol*, Jim Fisk's *Providence* (II), the second of three vessels to carry that name, put the Fall River Line on the map. Only one wooden Sound liner ever exceeded her in size, and none excelled her in providing first-class service during the years between 1868 and 1882. Operated as a spare boat thereafter, *Providence* survived until 1901.

## Is It All True?

While there is no way at this late date that we can be absolutely certain of the historical accuracy of all of the facts and events as they are described herein, we have made every attempt not to write beyond the headlights of our research. This project has consumed years of digging, checking and cross-checking against and between sometimes conflicting sources. Gradually, the historic mosaic was assembled from published books and periodicals, newspapers, museum and private collections, company and family memorabilia, and government documents (one instance in which we did not begrudge the various levels of government their massive consumption of paper).

The task was all the more difficult because the NYNH&H, its attorneys and its financiers actively worked to conceal the true nature and extent of the transactions that led to control by the NYNH&H. They used a number of subsidiaries and intermediaries, personal and corporate, to shield the nature of its transactions from prying eyes, including those of government zealots who sought to enforce the provisions of the Sherman Anti-Trust Act. Even while they were happening, these activities and transactions were stoutly denied by all concerned. Accurate information was more easily restricted to insiders in those days, which preceded the Securities and Exchange Commission and disclosure laws. Many facts did not emerge until years later, and some accompanied the principal actors to their graves.

Through it all, we kept in mind that the boats did not run themselves. Like plows, lathes, rifles or looms, the steamboats, and their corporations, were only tools, used by men* to achieve their designs and purposes. We must also note that the corporate shuffling and reshuffling had comparatively little effect on the actual operation of the steamboat services. With relatively few exceptions, the boats were run well, and the NESS lines collectively became known as the finest steamboat operation in America.

*Note: the use of any word other than "men" here would likely have caused bemused contempt among the steamboat crowd of long ago. Neither the language nor the profession was inclusive of the Opposite Sex, with *very* rare exceptions.

# Chapter Two

# In the Beginning, There Was New Haven

E ight years after the North River Steamboat's initial voyage, in March 1815, *Fulton*, under the command of Captain Elihu S. Bunker, and owned by Robert Fulton's North River Steamboat Co. of New York, braved Hell Gate and steamed to New Haven. Actually, *Fulton* was completed and ready for service in 1814, but there had been a war on since 1812, and the presence of British warships enforcing a blockade of American shipping at the east end of the Sound necessitated a discretionary delay for the safety of all concerned.

The Fulton company began regular steamboat service on Long Island Sound in 1817, three days a week between New York and New Haven, using *Connecticut* (I). Thus, *Connecticut* was the first of the Long Island Sound steamers. The smaller *Fulton* under Captain George Law, provided a connecting service between New Haven, New London and Norwich CT. It was deemed prudent to split the line, rather than to attempt the greater distance between New York and Norwich with one boat.

Neither of these boats could be called luxurious; they had no staterooms, no dining rooms, no orchestras, no plush decor, no hurricane decks. In contrast to the sailing ships, the steamboats concentrated on passenger traffic, at $6.00 and up per head. The firewood required to fuel the primitive boilers for these long voyages consumed so much space that there was little room for freight.

As we noted in Chapter One, the New York State Monopoly on steamboating restricted commerce, and rankled those in the Nutmeg State; Connecticut mariners were constrained from operating regularly scheduled service to New York City without paying tribute to Mr. Fulton. In 1822, Connecticut's legislature passed a "Retaliatory Law" to prevent any boat of the New York Monopoly from operating in "Connecticut waters." Exit *Fulton* and *Connecticut*, which began braving the distance from New York to Newport and Providence, in more hospitable Rhode Island.

In November 1822, New Haven interests formed the Connecticut Steamboat Company, and purchased *United States*, a New Jersey steamboat which had been enjoined by New York courts from operating on the Hudson River in competition with the monopoly. They entered her into New Haven and New York service. The New York law was circumvented with the aid of a sailboat named *Huntress*. In New York waters (including Hell

For most of its life, the New Haven Steamboat Co. operated from New York's Piers 25 and 26, East River. The photo above was taken looking south from the deck of the then-new Brooklyn Bridge, and shows *Richard Peck* sharing Pier 25 with the smaller *Hartford* (I). An empty coal barge (foreground) is leaving the slip after fueling the Sound Flyer.

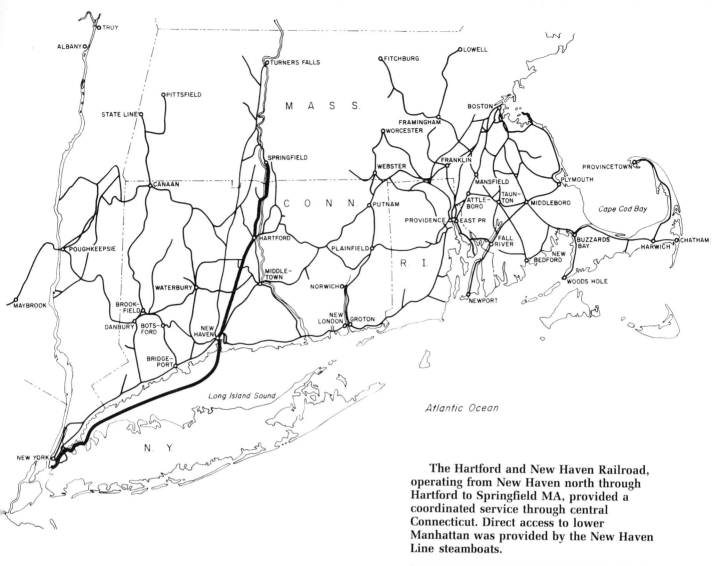

The Hartford and New Haven Railroad, operating from New Haven north through Hartford to Springfield MA, provided a coordinated service through central Connecticut. Direct access to lower Manhattan was provided by the New Haven Line steamboats.

Gate), *Huntress* towed *United States*, so that the steamer was not operating under its own power in New York waters. As the state line was passed, the positions were reversed; the steamboat towed the sailing ship. An alternate plan was put into effect in June 1823, with *United States* operating between New Haven and Byram Cove CT, just east of the New York border. Stagecoaches carried its passengers through twenty-five miles of Empire State to the City.

Such foolishness was ultimately made unnecessary by action of the U. S. Supreme Court in 1824. With the legal restriction removed, *United States* immediately began operating directly to a pier at the foot of Maiden Lane, New York under its own power all the way. The Connecticut Steamboat Co. stockholders reorganized their company as the New Haven Steamboat Co., to prepare for the bright new non-monopoly future.

At that point began a characteristic of Sound steamboat operations that was to last well into the twentieth century: competitive battles between steamboat owners. The Fulton company returned *Connecticut* and *Fulton* to "Connecticut waters" soon after the New York monopoly (and the legal basis for Connecticut's retaliation) evaporated. But

in late summer, these boats were withdrawn; it appears that there was residual animosity toward the Livingston Monopoly behind the low Connecticut patronage. Another characteristic of the steamboat years showed itself: New Englanders preferred to use boats operated by "local" firms to those from New York.

Despite tales of heroics, steamboating on the Sound was not a recommended practice in wintertime, and operations were seasonal. *United States* was laid up for the winter in 1824, per custom. One Jonathan Peck, whose descendants were to swarm over the steamboat world, placed a new steamer, *Linnaeus*, in winter service to fill the void. Alarmed, the New Haven Company refloated *United States* for winter operation. By the next year, prospects looked good enough to allow the purchase of another boat, *Hudson*, which, with *United States*, allowed institution of daily service between New Haven and New York. Yet another opposition boat, from a third company, entered the service between New Haven and New York in 1825. This was the steamer *Providence* (locally known as the "Little Providence"); in a move which was later to be carried to extremes, the New Haven Company bought out this new competitor.

*Superior* was added to the fleet in 1831, and *United States* was sold that year. *Splendid*, a larger boat than *Superior*, was built in 1832; these two boats carried passengers and mail sacks with clockwork regularity between New Haven and New York. Each boat made one trip each way each day. In contrast to later practice, they ran as day boats, leaving New York at 6 AM and New Haven at 1 PM.

These two were thought to be the finest boats on the Sound, but in 1835 the New Haven Company upgraded its fleet by selling *Superior* and adding a new boat, *New Haven* (I). *New Haven* was the first of the Company's boats to use the "walking beam", a rhombic overhead structure that provides a brute force method of transmitting power from the engine to the paddlewheels.

A much larger boat, *New York*, was built in 1836 and placed in operation under the command of Captain B. Stone. His brother, Captain J. Stone, commanded *New Haven*, which "ran opposite" *New York* between their namesake cities. Travel was still a rugged process then, with some uncertainty about quality of personnel; the New Haven

The steamer *Elm City* entered New Haven–New York service in 1855 and served there until 1895, with the exception of a stint in Federal service as a hospital transport during the Civil War. Her first recorded mishap was a grounding in 1856, in Hell Gate. On the foggy morning of April 22, 1868 she collided with the steamer *Electra*, causing minor damage. Investigators blamed the fog, rather than either Captain.

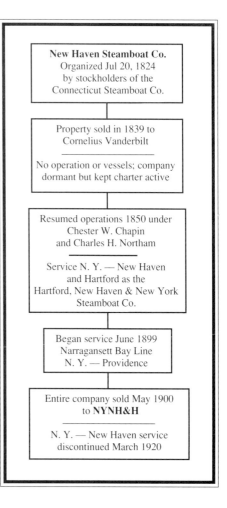

**New Haven Steamboat Co.**
Organized Jul 20, 1824
by stockholders of the
Connecticut Steamboat Co.

Property sold in 1839 to
Cornelius Vanderbilt

No operation or vessels; company
dormant but kept charter active

Resumed operations 1850 under
Chester W. Chapin
and Charles H. Northam

Service N. Y. — New Haven
and Hartford as the
Hartford, New Haven & New York
Steamboat Co.

Began service June 1899
Narragansett Bay Line
N. Y. — Providence

Entire company sold May 1900
to **NYNH&H**

N. Y. — New Haven service
discontinued March 1920

Company disclaimed any liability for loss of packages unless the passenger personally entrusted them to the Captain. *Splendid* became the spare boat, and business went quite well at a $2.00 fare.

## The Railroad Arrives

In December 1838, railroad trains of the Hartford and New Haven Railroad began operating from New Haven to Meriden, and within a year to Hartford. The December opening, by the way, was orchestrated to occur as the Connecticut River iced over, curtailing Connecticut River steamboat operations for the winter (See Chapter Four). The railroad thus insured itself of a head start in traffic generation until spring. Another marketing step was entering into a secret contract with the New Haven Steamboat Co. to coordinate schedules and through rates.

The steamboat connection was valuable to the Hartford and New Haven; east-west land travel to and from New York was still difficult because of the many bays, inlets and swamps along the Connecticut coastline. There was nothing inherently illegal about that agreement then, but when word leaked out there was outrage against the "secret monopoly." It was not the last time that phrase was to be used in connection with that railroad and its successors.

But for the moment, the outraged competitor was the Connecticut River Steamboat Co., and Cornelius Vanderbilt, operating steamboats between New York and Hartford. They saw themselves being bypassed. The Connecticut River company threatened to establish a stop at New Haven for its boats, in direct and venomous competition with the financially weaker New Haven line.

The New Haven Steamboat Line's resistance vanished when disaster struck on March 22, 1839; *New York* burned while she was docked at New Haven, causing a great financial loss. Shortly afterward, the assets of the company were sold to the Connecticut River Steamboat Co., which immediately set about protecting the River steamers by throwing a 120-foot wrench into the agreement between the New Haven Steamboat Co. and the Hartford and New Haven Railroad .

The "wrench" took the form of an old former Staten Island ferryboat named *Bolivar*, which Mr. Vanderbilt put in service in place of *New York*. *Bolivar*'s lack of speed was well-known; the legend was that a New Haven man won a bet by travelling over the swampland to New York in less time than that taken by the underpowered *Bolivar*.

Such a poor service level was obviously designed to impair the railroad while grazing the letter of the contract. *Bolivar* and Vanderbilt earned almost instant animosity among the citizens, which

was characteristically disregarded. But criticism was followed by competition; it came in June 1841, in the form of the Citizen's Line, a New Haven firm operating *Telegraph*; and another New Haven figure, Captain Curtis Peck, Jonathan's brother. Captain Peck owned the popular local steamer *Belle*, for which Belle Dock in New Haven was named. Jonathan's son (and Curtis' nephew) Richard Peck began his career here, rising to command of *Belle*. The competition between Vanderbilts and Pecks was intense, with fares dropping as low as one shilling (12-1/2 cents) at times on the Vanderbilt line. But the local *Belle* was the winner over the New Yorkers, carrying most of the freight and passenger traffic at a $1.00 fare. *Telegraph* charged as low as 50 cents; after a negotiated truce, its Citizen's Line was consolidated with the Vanderbilt company in 1842.

By 1845, Mr. Vanderbilt made up for the *Bolivar* debacle with *Traveler*, a new and much faster vessel than the run-of-the-Sound steamboats of the era. The 225-foot long *Traveler* was the last boat to carry mail between New York and New Haven, doing so until 1848. She ran as a day boat, then was switched to night service in 1849, despite her daytime popularity.

| | | | | | |
|---|---|---|---|---|---|

## NEW HAVEN STEAMBOAT CO.
### AND CONNECTICUT RIVER R.R. LINE.
DEPOT—PIERS 25 and 26, EAST RIVER, NEW YORK.

E. F. DE YOUNG, Gen. Passenger Agent, New York.

Fast Steamer Service between New York and New Haven, daily, Sundays excepted, arriving in time for all early express trains north and south.

| GOING NORTH. | | *March 15, 1899.* | GOING SOUTH. | |
|---|---|---|---|---|
| 3 00 P.M. | 12 00 N'HT | Leave...**New York**...Arrive | 5 30 A.M. | 3 30 P.M. |
| 8 00 P.M. | 5 00 A.M. | Arrive.**New Haven** [1] Leave | 12 30 N'HT | 10 30 A.M. |
| | | (Via N.Y. N.H. & H.R.R.) | A.M. | A.M. |
| 8 00 P.M. | 6 40 A.M. | Leave...**New Haven**..Arrive | 11 17 P.M. | 9 30 9 15 |
| 8 26 » | 7 05 » | Arrive...Wallingford...Leave | 10 51 » | .... 8 48 |
| 8 40 » | 7 21 » | Arrive....Meriden....Leave | 10 40 » | 9 01 8 35 |
| 8 54 » | 7 37 » | Arrive.....Berlin.....Leave | 10 25 » | .... 8 20 |
| 9 05 » | 7 48 » | Arrive. New Britain..Leave | 10 13 » | .... 8 08 |
| 9 20 » | 8 04 » | Arrive....Hartford [5]...Leave | 10 05 » | 8 33 8 00 |
| 9 35 » | 8 18 » | Arrive.....Windsor....Leave | 9 47 » | .... 7 42 |
| 9 46 » | 8 29 » | Arrive.Windsor Locks..Leave | 9 36 » | 8 12 7 31 |
| 9 51 » | 8 34 » | Arrive.Warehouse Pt..Leave | 9 31 » | .... 7 26 |
| 10 00 » | 8 44 A.M. | Arrve.Thompsonville..Leave | 9 21 » | 8 02 7 16 |
| 10 16 P.M. | 9 01 A.M. | Arrive.**Springfield** [3] Leave | 9 05 P.M. | 7 50 7 00 |
| | | (Via Conn. River R.R.) | P.M. P.M. | A.M. A.M. |
| 10 15 P.M. | 9 15 A.M. | Leave..**Springfield**...Arrive | 6 18 8 28 | 7 30 6 38 |
| 10 34 » | 9 32 » | Arrive....**Holyoke**....Leave | 6 05 8 13 | 7 15 6 20 |
| 10 51 P.M. | 9 50 » | Arrive..Northampton..Leave | 5 48 7 53 | 6 55 6 00 |
| | 10 22 » | Arrive...Greenfield [4]...Leave | 5 20 P.M. | 6 20 A.M. |
| | 10 45 » | Arrive. South Vernon..Leave | 4 55 | 5 50 |
| | 11 55 » | Arrive.....Keene.....Leave | 2 45 | .... |
| | 11 06 A.M. | Arrive.. Brattleboro...Leave | 4 34 | 5 28 |
| | | (Via Central Vermont R.R.) | P.M. | A.M. |
| | 11 56 A.M. | Arrive.**Bellows Falls** [5]..Leave | 3 55 P.M. | 4 45 A.M. |
| | 1 00 P.M. | Arrive. ...Windsor....Leave | 3 08 P.M. | 3 55 » |
| | 1 25 P.M. | Arrive.White River Jn [6]..Leave | 2 40 P.M. | 3 25 A.M. |
| | 5 40 P.M. | Arrive....**St. Albans**...Leave | 11 10 A.M. | 10 55 P.M. |
| | | (Via Passumpsic R.R.) | | |
| | 2 31 P.M. | Arrive.......Ely......Leave | 10 48 A.M. | .... |
| | 3 25 » | Arrive..**Wells River** [7]..Leave | 9 55 A.M. | 1 25 A.M. |
| | 4 22 » | Arrive.St. Johnsbury [8]..Leave | 9 00 A.M. | 12 35 N'HT |
| | 6 20 P.M. | Arrive....**Newport** [9]....Leave | 7 00 A.M. | 10 50 P.M. |
| | 5 00 P.M. to 5 40 P.M. | (Via Con. & Mont. R.R.) ....**White Mountains**.... | 9 00 A.M. to 7 30 A.M. | |

At this season of the year passenger trains do not connect at steamboat wharf. Electric cars to and from railroad depot at New Haven.

CONNECTIONS. — [1] With railroads diverging. [3] With N.Y. N.H. & H.R.R. [3] With Boston & Albany R.R. [4] With Fitchburg R.R. [5] With Cheshire Div. Fitchburg R.R. [6] With Northern Div. B. & M R.R. [7] With Boston & Maine, and Montpelier & Wells River R.Rs. [8] With Boston & Maine R.R. [9] With Canadian Pacific Ry.

# NEW HAVEN STEAMBOAT COMPANY.

No.                              New Haven,                              18

STATE OF CONNECTICUT.

It is hereby certified, by the President and Directors of the New Haven Steamboat Company, that                              of

is entitled to                              share     of stock of said Company, and to all

dividends that may arise thereon; which share     transferable at the office of said Com-

pany, agreeable to the rules and forms instituted for that purpose     But the said share

not to be transferred while the said                              is indebted to said

Company, but to remain as security for the payment of such debt.

President.

Secretary.

Above, a blank early stock certificate form for the New Haven Steamboat Company.

Below left, a timetable extract showing the railroad connections available to passengers on New Haven Line steamboats, to all parts of New England. The New Haven Line made the best of their situation as compared to the lines operating farther east; note that they feature northern points rather than Boston.

*New Haven* (II) was among the first propeller-driven boats on the Sound, operating as a relatively unsung freighter between 1866 and 1895. In that, she was more typical than the "floating palaces" that captured public attention during her life.

When retirement came, she was sold at auction, along with *Elm City*, to M. H. Gregory of Great Neck NY in August 1895. She fetched $1433.

One of the more famous steamboats in Long Island Sound service was the hardy trouper *C. H. Northam*. Built in 1872-73 in Greenpoint, which was then a city separate from Brooklyn, she survived until 1907. From the day of her trial trip on June 3, 1873, her owners knew they had something special. On that first day, *C. H. Northam* left her pier at the foot of 12th Street on the East River in New York at 9:15 AM with some 1,000 excursionists bound for New Haven. Arriving in New Haven at 2:15 PM, the passengers were landed. *C. H. Northam*'s crew thereupon took another thousand souls for a trip on the Sound, returning at 5:30 PM. To end the day, at 8:00 PM, *Northam* left New Haven for New York, taking her New York passengers home. Not bad for a first day's work.

Her namesake and part owner, Charles H. Northam, was also known for hard work. He was president of the Connecticut River Steamboat Company, operating *Oliver Ellsworth* and *Chief Justice Marshall* (gratefully named for the man who wrote the Gibbons v. Ogden judicial opinion). Mr. Northam and Chester W. Chapin were the major owners of the New York & New Haven Steamboat Co.

But *C. H. Northam* did not have an easy time on the Sound; she was plagued by mishaps throughout her 34-year life. Long Island Sound service was a not a calling for the weak of heart. Herewith we present a few examples:

June 16, 1874: A collision between *Northam* and *Acushnet* in the East River. No lives lost, no injuries, very little damage to *Northam*, more severe damage to *Acushnet*. The Investigating Board held *Northam*'s master blameless.

May 8, 1875: A collision, wherein *Northam* did "considerable" damage to the steam yacht *Signet*.

October 17, 1875: A breakdown, with *Northam* towed in by two tugs (*J. Birkbeck* and *Seth Low).*

November 4, 1877: A broken crankshaft. Towed in to the John Englis shipyard for heavy repair.

November 27, 1877: A fire; *Northam* burned to the water's edge while laid up for repairs (see previous item) at the foot of Seventh St. East River. (The boat wasn't even safe at the repair dock.) Three lives were lost in the blaze; colored workmen trapped in her hold. *C. H. Northam* had cost $500,000 new; the fire caused $200,000 worth of damage. But the boat was rebuilt and was re-launched seven months later, June 29, 1878.

December 27, 1881: A post-Christmas grounding in a thick fog on Blackwell's Island (later Welfare Island, later Roosevelt Island) in New York's East River. *Northam* had left Peck Slip for New Haven at 3:00 PM Her forty passengers were removed, but the boat wasn't refloated until January 2. *Traveler* was called out to substitute and to ring in the new year.

April 1886: Heavy repairs needed after her winter layup, to be performed at the John Englis yard.

November 27, 1886: Back in service after a recent collision, this time with a tugboat, *W. A. Levering*.

May 28, 1887: A newspaper item, announcing that Capt. Fred Peck (son of Captain Richard Peck), commanding *C. H. Northam* for the past few years, "has given up steamboating and bought a cattle ranch out West."

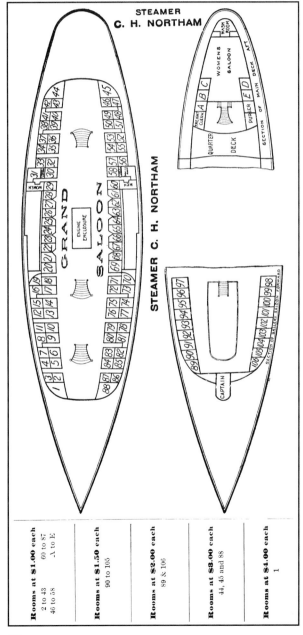

STEAMER
C. H. NORTHAM

STEAMER C. H. NORTHAM

GRAND SALOON

ENGINE ENCLOSURE

WOMEN'S SALOON

QUARTER DECK

SECTION OF MAIN DECK FORWARD

WASH ROOM

SECTION OF GALLERY SALOON FORWARD

CAPTAIN

**Rooms at $1.00 each**
2 to 43    60 to 87
46 to 58    A to E

**Rooms at $1.50 each**
90 to 105

**Rooms at $2.00 each**
89 & 106

**Rooms at $3.00 each**
44, 45 and 88

**Rooms at $4.00 each**
1

July 28, 1888: Another breakdown, off Riker's Island near Hell Gate with a Sunday crowd aboard. Towed in for repairs by tugs *Indian* and *Cheney* (not the *Levering*).

August 10, 1889: A fire in her kitchen as *Northam* lay in her East River pier; $300 damage.

November 7, 1889: A collision in the East River, with *Northam* striking the schooner *Rudolph*, being towed by a tug at the time.

September 8, 1890: A collision in the East River between *Northam* and *Continental*; several persons injured, damage to *Northam* between $5,000 and $10,000.

June 7, 1899: A serious collision off Norwalk CT in another early-morning dense fog, this time with the steel-hulled *Richard Peck*. The wood-hulled *Northam* was described as "nearly having her bow cut off." She was beached and later refloated, limping to her "second home", the John Englis repair yard. Twenty days later, she was back in service, after considerable frontal surgery. One oddity: Capt. Aaron Hardy was commanding *Northam* that night, while his brother Edgar was in command of *Richard Peck*. That is believed to be the only instance on the Sound of a collision between steamboats of the same line, commanded by brothers. Legend has it that the brothers did not speak to each other after the accident.

By the turn of the century, *C. H. Northam* was the last of the "old-time" steamboats, with her boilers "outboard" on her guards, in regular service. Whatever her troubles, *Northam* was a survivor!

## The New York and New Haven

Why the timetable change? Because the New York & New Haven Railroad opened its rail line to Gotham early in 1849. This rail segment had been slow to open because of the difficulties of coastal railroad construction, and the Connecticut firm's difficulties in obtaining permission to build in New York. The contractor, one Alfred Bishop of Bridgeport, accepted stock as well as cash in return for his work, which established him and his sons as major players in New England rail development.

The NY&NH found it desirable to acquire trackage rights over the New York and Harlem Railroad from Woodlawn into New York City. The Harlem dictated the terms, and for more than a century, "Yankee" trains polished New York Central rails between Grand Central Terminal and Woodlawn NY, as long as the companies and their successors (the New York Central and the NYNH&H railroads) remained separate. Bi-state commuter trains from Grand Central follow the route to this day.

More contracting: to protect its position, the New York and New Haven Railroad agreed to pay Cornelius Vanderbilt's steamboat company $20,000 per year for five years if he would close down the day steamboat line, forcing passengers to the new railroad. One wonders whether such affluence on the part of the railroad helped to convince the Commodore that railroads could be profitable; he did achieve some success in that field in later life, after becoming almost accidentally involved with the New York and Harlem Railroad in 1850.

## THE STEAMER *RICHARD PECK*

*Richard Peck* was rightfully known as the "Greyhound of the Sound." Named for the New Haven Line's famous Commodore, she was designed by A. Cary Smith, who had been best known for some sleek yacht designs. The 1892 general views survived, and are reproduced above. There was some question about whether Cary Smith could successfully design a boat of this size; her performance decisively ended all speculation.

On her trial trip, August 18, 1892, she attained a speed of 23.5 miles per hour, which put her in contention for the Sound speed sweepstakes. *Richard Peck*'s speed was combined with a comfort level unknown on the New York-New Haven run until her appearance. Narrower than most Sound steamers, *Peck* was expected to roll with the seas, but her stability was not substantially different from her wider competitors. While she was designed for the relatively calm waters of Long Island Sound, *Peck* handled service assignments to Narragansett Bay with relative ease.

*Richard Peck* often made the run between New York and New Haven in just under four hours, almost one hour less than had been required by *C. H. Northam* on her trial trip. And when, in 1893, the management tested her with only four of her six

boilers in operation, her time to New Haven was four and one half hours.

*Richard Peck* also represented a formidable challenge to the Connecticut River steamers; from Belle Dock, the rail connection between New Haven and Hartford provided a more direct route than the all-water service via Saybrook and Middletown.

From the hardwood-floored social hall to the Wilton-carpeted Ladies' Saloon, the atmosphere was one of elegance. Entering on the Main Deck, one ascended a mahogany stairway to the Saloon Deck. The Main Saloon was 215 feet long and 22 feet wide between the rows of staterooms on each side. Large mirrors of French plate glass highlighted the gold-trimmed pastel decor.

Another staircase up to the Gallery Deck from the forward part of the Main Saloon, led to the frescoed dining room, with food to match the fine ambience. *Richard Peck* was lighted through domes by day, and with more than 600 incandescent lights by night; this at a time when relatively few structures on land had yet been wired for electricity.

More than any other vessel, even *Belle*, *Richard Peck* was New Haven's favorite, a worthy namesake for a well-regarded steamboatman.

The Commodore's happy accident had its origin in the building of the New York and New Haven Railroad. That company's first president was one Robert Schuyler, a scion of one of New York's premier families. Robert Schuyler and his brother George were grandsons of a Revolutionary War general; they were nephews of Alexander Hamilton. They were also partners in a successful stockbrokerage firm, impeccable and beyond suspicion.

The financial community was stunned to discover in 1853 that Robert Schuyler had been looting the NY&NH almost from Day One. As one example, almost $2,000,000 in NY&NH stock had been sold by Mr. Schuyler; problem was, it had never been authorized for issuance. The legal complications as the courts sought to untangle the

pile of defrauded stockholders, banks, and other financial institutions, kept the railroad in difficulty for years. Schuyler was never arrested, but he did leave the country.

Cornelius Vanderbilt had loaned money to Schuyler, with some of the suspect stock as collateral. The settlement involved the Commodore in the New York and Harlem; for the steamboat pioneer it was then but a short step to preeminence in the railroad field. One result was that Commodore Cornelius Vanderbilt sold out his steamboat interests and left the Sound.

## Peck, Chapin and Northam

Meanwhile, Captain Peck and the original Connecticut Steamboat Company briefly placed into New Haven service a new *Connecticut* (II) in 1849. At 282 feet long, she was among the largest boats on the Sound, if not the largest of the period. This second *Connecticut* could make the run from New Haven to New York in just over four hours.

Late in 1850, the Vanderbilt New Haven interests were purchased by Chester W. Chapin (Sr.) and Charles H. Northam. Northam was President of the Connecticut River Steam Boat Co. (see Chapter Four). Mr. Chapin, a Springfield, MA stagecoach line owner and banker, also had an interest in the Valley Railroad. He was a Vanderbilt confidant and advisor, and was later to become the President of the Western Railroad (Boston and Albany) in addition to his steamboat interests.

Known as the Hartford, New Haven and New York Steamboat Co., the revived firm continued to operate *Traveler* as a night boat between New Haven and New York, with *Champion* operating between New Haven and Hartford. Apparently this service was operated under the original New Haven Steamboat Co. charter; after selling the assets to Vanderbilt in 1839, the company's shareholders continued to hold annual meetings and kept the company's charter alive.

Richard Peck became the Commodore of the New Haven line, managing operations and supervising the construction of the company's new boats. *Elm City*, honoring New Haven's nickname, joined the fleet in 1856; *Continental* arrived in 1861. Day service was re-instituted, and by 1866 the two boats (with *Traveler* as a spare) were each making 1-1/2 daily trips, with scheduled departures from New York and New Haven at 11 AM, 3 PM and 11 PM.

*Northampton* and *New Haven* (II) were built in New Haven in 1866 for another new competitor. This service ran from New York to the Canal Dock in the basin of the New Haven-Farmington Canal, where connections were made with trains of the New Haven and Northampton Railroad. *Northampton* and *New Haven* (II) were unusual in that they had screw propellers rather than the huge side

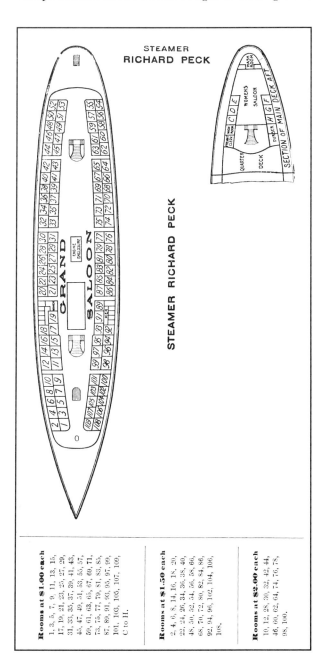

paddle wheels characteristic of Sound steamers up to then. This new technology was not appreciated by the New York and New Haven Steamboat Company until after the competing company was absorbed by the New Haven Steamboat Co. in 1879.

Another competitor, the Starin New Haven Line, grew out of an 1870s towing line, perhaps best known for its work for the Lackawanna Railroad in New York harbor. The freighters *John H. Starin* and *Erastus Corning* began service between New York and New Haven in 1873, connecting with the New Haven and Derby Railroad to inland points.

In 1873 the New Haven Steamboat Co. placed *C. H. Northam* in service; the big side-wheeled boat operated until 1877 when, while laid up for machinery repairs, she burned to the water line. *C. H. Northam* was rebuilt and improved, but continued to suffer more than her share of fog-related mishaps; she was the last paddle-wheel steamer bought by the New Haven line. A propeller-driven freighter, *Eleanor F. Peck*, was added to the fleet in 1884.

Harlan and Hollingsworth of Wilmington DE built the steel-hulled, twin-screw *Richard Peck* for the company in 1892. She was the New Haven company's first departure from the "standard" wooden hull side-wheel boats. This latest of the Peck family namesakes measured 303 feet in length and immediately became known as one of the fastest boats on the Sound. She ran between New York and New Haven for almost thirty years, most of them under the command of Captain Edgar Hardy. The story is told but unproven that Hardy, while a young bow watchman, one day jumped overboard to save Nellie Peck, the Commodore's daughter; he was rewarded by rapid promotions. Hardy more likely advanced through competence than gratitude; after all, while females were not encouraged to swim in those days, what Commodore would not teach even a daughter to swim at an early age?

The New York and New Haven Railroad had now been in place since 1848, more than 40 years, yet the steamboat business was quite good, because the boats were a bit faster and considerably more comfortable than the trains. But competition between boat and train became increasingly fierce, particularly since Mr. Chapin had enlarged his Massachusetts railroad interests, eventually becoming President of the Boston & Albany Railroad, arch-rival of the New Haven railroad.

After Mr. Chapin's death in 1883, his estate was managed by his son, Chester W. Chapin Jr., who was no less active with the Boston and Albany, the Central New England, and the steamboats, and maintained their interests in the face of the growing NYNH&H monopoly presence. In the early '90s, Mr. Chapin complained to the NYNH&H railroad's president about some freight that had come down to New Haven by rail with plain instructions to be transferred and shipped by steamboat to New York. A "fresh young freight clerk" had calmly diverted the shipment to an all-rail route, depriving the steamboat company of revenue intended for it. The personality description of the "clerk" (actually a rising executive in the traffic department) is consistent with later events; his name was Charles Sanger Mellen, and he was to have more to do with steamboats a few years hence.

The comparative advantage of the steamboat in that era was particularly true over the longer distances to points east of New Haven; the railroad saw less reason to cooperate with steamboat operators outside the "family," over the comparatively shorter hauls to Bridgeport and New Haven. Thus, the railroad enraged the younger Mr. Chapin in 1899 by abruptly ceasing to run its connecting trains and trolleys to Belle Dock.

How enraged was Mr. Chapin? Early in 1899 an "unknown party" leased dock space in Providence, RI. In June, a new line was established, extending steamboat service to Providence from New Haven and New York, in competition with the railroad and its boats. The new "Narragansett Bay Line" was operated using the speedy *Richard Peck* and two chartered vessels, *Shinnecock* and *Lincoln*. There was some speculation that the upstart service was a project of Chapin's New York and New Haven Steamboat Company. The NYNH&H was both surprised and chagrined by this turn of events.

All speculation about the Narragansett Bay Line's true ownership vanished with the addition of the line's newest twin-screw steamer; she was named *Chester W. Chapin*. The new *Chapin* and the faithful *Richard Peck* were fast and well-regarded boats, with elegant decor and courteous service on board. They gave the New Haven-owned Fall River and New London steamers a considerable run for their money. Their reward was an increasing share of the Boston boat-rail passenger and freight business through the Providence gateway, as well as serving the Rhode Island capital directly.

The New York and New Haven Steamboat Company emerged as a major competitor to the NYNH&H, and showed a profit doing so. Mr. Chapin was even seeking bids on construction of a sister ship to his father's namesake. The people of Provi-

---

**The America's Cup yacht races at the turn of the century were spectator events. For those who did not have access to a private yacht, the steamboats provided the floating grandstands. *Richard Peck*'s 1893 passenger list for the races included the sedate and substantial members of the Union League Club, who felt quite at home aboard the Sound flyer. There was no more comfortable way to view the yachtsmen's exploits than from the Gallery Deck, never far from the faithful and efficient purveyors of liquid spirits and bountiful light snacks.**

Sometimes, the spectators became part of the race, as *Richard Peck* and other steamboats engaged in a bit of competition of their own on the way to or from the yacht races. In 1893, *Peck* and New Jersey's *Monmouth* raced all the way back to New York harbor. *Monmouth* had a head start, *Peck* was catching up, and the Union League Club members were getting some unexpected excitement.

Of course, nobody actually raced, you understand, because racing was against the United States maritime regulations. Still, if two steamboats just happened to be going in the same direction at roughly the same time, and they happened to be testing their engines, who was to say that it was more than coincidence?

Two such "coincidences" pitted *Richard Peck* against the Fall River Line boats *Priscilla* and *Puritan* in that Autumn of 1893, with no clear winner emerging. More was to come.

On the opposite page, the sailing yacht *Shamrock III* is shown at the finish line as the crowd aboard *Richard Peck*, extreme right, looks on in comfort. The photo was taken during the 1903 races.

Below, we're looking across the East River toward Brooklyn in the late 1890s, as *Richard Peck* approaches her slip. The trolleys on the bridge and the East River ferries are long gone, and the *Peck* outlasted them all.

dence welcomed the competition, believing that it improved the honesty and fairness of the railroad (not to mention the average level of passenger and freight rates). The Chapin firm withstood the competition, and by promoting the Boston and Albany Railroad as an alternate gateway to the west, gave the NYNH&H management severe palpitations.

By October 1899, the apprehensive railroad gave up its competitive stance and was offering to buy out the Chapin steamboat interests in New Haven and Providence. J. P. Morgan and C. W. Chapin met aboard a yacht. It is perhaps indicative of Mr. Morgan's and Mr. Chapin's relative positions in their negotiations that the yacht was not Mr. Morgan's *Corsair*, scene of many such talks; but Mr. Chapin's *Iroquois*, to which Mr. Morgan was brought by launch from *Corsair*. Subsequent negotiations were punctuated by the railroad's threat to evict Chapin from Belle Dock, and by Chapin's attempts to obtain the railroad's considerable fresh fish business between Fall River and New York.

The deciding move in the chess game appears to have been Mr. Chapin's. Early in 1900 he announced the imminent startup of a steamboat line on the Hudson River between New York and Fishkill. What riveted Mr. Morgan's attention was the realization that such a line, connecting with the railroad there, would provide a viable alternate route between Boston and New York. The numbers increased in size, agreement was reached in April 1900, and by May the New Haven steamboats were "in the railroad basket." Mr. Morgan had met Mr. Chapin's price.

The sale came as an unpleasant shock to the Providence merchants and civic leaders, and to those in New Haven as well. As we noted, the NYNH&H was not universally loved, and independent companies were the best protection against what they called a monopoly's "excesses." Other competition on the Providence run was to come, as we shall see, but it was not as elegant as that which ended in April 1900. It should also be noted that Commodore Richard Peck died suddenly of a heart attack on the day that the sale was announced.

In his later years, Chester W. Chapin was quoted as saying, "Mr. Morgan debated with me how foolish it was to divide a dollar. I know now that I made a mistake selling the line, and perhaps the railroad made a mistake in buying me out. I could have made much more money continuing the service I had started to Providence, as was proved by those who came later."

The chapters to come will explore the wisdom of that statement.

Above, this extract from the *Travelers' Official Guide* shows the features of the new Narragansett Bay Line. Note that this schedule called for the Providence boats to make a stop at New Haven, presumably after the musical programme was over. The reference to "daylight views" is seasonal; this ad appeared in the July, 1899 issue, four months after the service started.

*Richard Peck* was best known as a New York–New Haven boat, although at one time or another she ran to every NYNH&H port. In this more or less typical photo of a gray day on the Sound (right), we see small groups of passengers, bundled up against the chill, under the wheelhouse on the gallery deck and, one flight down, seated under the canopy on the saloon deck. We'll be in New Haven in less than four hours!

# THE STEAMER *CHESTER W. CHAPIN*

*Chester W. Chapin* is shown under construction at Sparrows Point, Maryland in the photo above. Her July 1899 launch was a festive occasion, with company officials traveling to Baltimore in a private railroad car. After the launch, the party repaired to the shipyard's mould loft for an elaborate and festive luncheon.

The *Chapin* made her first appearance on the Sound in December 1899, running from New York to New Haven and Providence. The Rhode Islanders welcomed her as something of a Christmas present. On the opposite page is a relatively rare photograph of *Chapin* as she looked in her New Haven Steamboat Co. livery, in the days before she became part of the NYNH&H fleet. The photo was taken at yet another America's Cup defense.

Like *Richard Peck*, *Chapin* was designed by A. Cary Smith, and many of *Peck*'s amenities were repeated on the new vessel. Her interior decor was more Edwardian than Renaissance, featuring ivory and rose walls with gilded trim, and elegant and durable Persian style carpets.

*Chester W. Chapin* led a relatively easy life, mostly free from mishap. She grounded in Narragansett Bay in April 1901, and her passengers were placed aboard a train for New York without injury. She was refloated, repaired, and placed back in service in a few weeks.

A more serious mishap occurred while Captain Thomas Rowland was in command on a morning in August 1928, when *Chapin*, on her way down the East River near Hell Gate, altered course to avoid a tow coming from Harlem River (presumably NYNH&H car floats being shepherded by a Transfer tug). Another tug, *Volunteer*, misunderstood and steered into the *Chapin*'s path. *Volunteer* sank, and *Chapin* was pushed onto a sand bar to be refloated later that day.

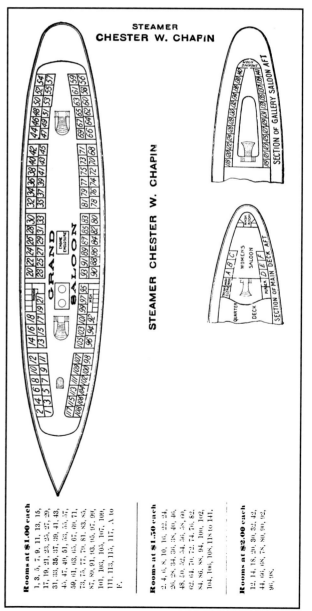

STEAMER
CHESTER W. CHAPIN

STEAMER CHESTER W. CHAPIN

**Rooms at $1.00 each**
1, 3, 5, 7, 9, 11, 13, 15, 17, 19, 21, 23, 25, 27, 29, 31, 33, **35**, 37, 39, 41, 43, 45, 47, 49, 51, 53, 55, 57, 59, 61, 63, 65, 67, 69, 71, 73, 75, 77, 79, 81, 83, 85, 87, 89, 91, 93, 95, 97, 99, 101, 103, 105, 107, 109, 111, 113, 115, 117, A to F.

**Rooms at $1.50 each**
2, 4, 6, 8, 10, 16, 22, 24, 26, 28, 34, 36, 38, 40, 46, 48, 50, 52, 54, 56, 58, 60, 62, 64, 70, 72, 74, 76, 82, 84, 86, 88, 94, 100, 102, 104, 106, 108, 118 to 141.

**Rooms at $2.00 each**
12, 14, 18, 20, 30, 32, 42, 44, 66, 68, 78, 80, 90, 92, 96, 98.

# Chapter Three

# Bridgeport and the Industrial Valleys

W hile steamboats had been reported operating to Bridgeport since the breakup of the Fulton-Livingston monopoly in 1824, the first specifically identified Bridgeport steamboat was *Lafayette*, built in 1828 and operated by Henry Eckford. It is possible that those earlier steamboats may have used Bridgeport as a way stop on the way to or from New Haven. Possible, but difficult. The physical conditions were such that Bridgeport could never rival New Haven as a trading port or shipping center, even in the days before steamboats.

Before 1836, Bridgeport harbor was limited to boats with no more than 5-foot draft (depth of the hull in the water) because of sand bars. The sand at the bottom of Long Island Sound is kept agitated by the waves and tides; it has been drifting westward for centuries, and is continually being deposited across the mouths of the rivers that empty into the Sound. This requires regular dredging to keep shipping channels open. The sand bars at Bridgeport severely limited water commerce. In 1836, Congress appropriated funds for an "internal improvement;" namely dredging at Bridgeport, yielding an eight-foot deep channel by 1838. The channel filled somewhat, and had to be re-dredged in the 1850s. In the 1870s, stone breakwaters were installed to retard the sand shifts, which has allowed maintenance of an 18-foot deep channel.

That channel was helpful and necessary, because Bridgeport became an important transportation gateway despite (or perhaps because of) its relative proximity to New York City. Bridgeport lies on the Sound's north shore at the mouth of the Housatonic River, less than 60 miles northeast of New York City and 17 miles west of New Haven. The city is known to some as "Brassport," in grudging tribute to its metallurgical economy.

Western Connecticut was and is known as a region of precision metalwork and mechanical device manufacturing. The Housatonic and Naugatuck river valleys are dotted with towns rich in the heritage of legendary American "tinkerers," from whose early efforts grew industries such as precision tools and bearings (e. g. Torrington), firearms (both Colt and Remington), sewing machines (Elias Howe's plant was in Bridgeport), clocks (Thomaston CT is named for clockmaker Seth Thomas) and other light industrial goods.

Unlike the Connecticut River, the Housatonic and Naugatuck rivers are not navigable by boats of any size. While there was an early effort to promote a canal along the Housatonic River in the 1820s, the canal projects were abandoned in favor of railroads following the riverbanks in the Housatonic and Naugatuck valleys to bring raw materials in and finished goods out, to the north and the south. Bridgeport became the collecting point and the connecting point for boats to New York.

Bridgeport became the collecting point largely due to the efforts of local contractor Alfred Bishop, whose firm built the Housatonic and Naugatuck railroads, and most of the New York and New Haven trackage as well. The Bishop family was never far from railroad affairs, and was involved in many large-scale construction projects in New England and the Mid-Atlantic states.

---

The photo on the preceding page shows the steamer *Allan Joy* with a "Bridgeport Line" identification on her bow, passing beneath the Williamsburg Bridge on a festive day celebrated with flags and bunting. The occasion is unknown, but apparently required security measures; notice the policeman in the truss structure at the left edge of the photo. Or perhaps he's just enjoying the view.

There is one anomaly: the 48-star American flag did not appear until July 4, 1913. Yet, *Allan Joy* was renamed *Naugatuck* in 1905.

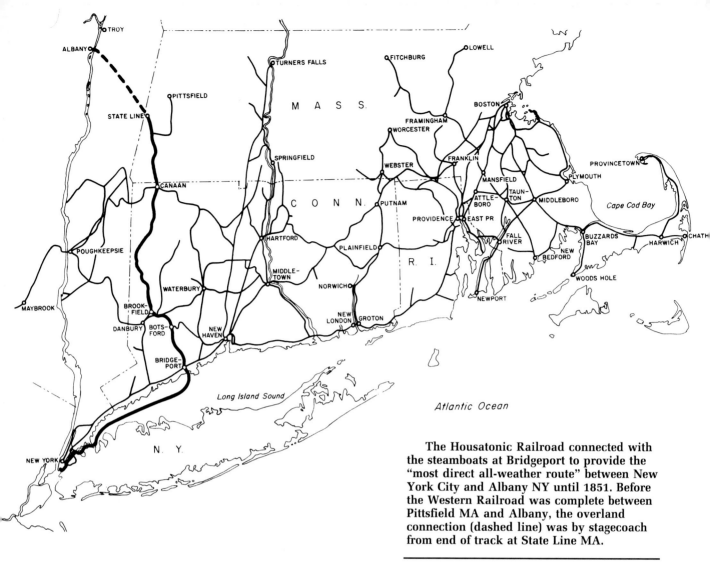

The Housatonic Railroad connected with the steamboats at Bridgeport to provide the "most direct all-weather route" between New York City and Albany NY until 1851. Before the Western Railroad was complete between Pittsfield MA and Albany, the overland connection (dashed line) was by stagecoach from end of track at State Line MA.

The Housatonic Railroad was the first rail line to open in Connecticut, between Bridgeport and New Milford in 1840 and from New Milford north to State Line MA in 1842. A small railroad was built and leased to complete the route to Pittsfield MA in 1850. At both Pittsfield and State Line, rail connections were made with the Western Railroad (later part of the Boston and Albany). It should be noted that the Western Railroad was also the only through rail route between Albany NY and Boston MA.

Because the first of the more direct New York Central lines up the Hudson valley was not completed until 1851, the Housatonic, with its steamboat connection between New York City and Bridgeport, enjoyed a nine-year period, between December 1842 and October 1851, as the primary wintertime connecting link between New York City and the west. The winters were significant because the Hudson River steamboats were prevented by excessive ice from reaching Albany. In prior years, that winter blockage severely limited commerce, but beginning with the winter of 1842-43, transportation would never again be the same. An example of change was *Roger Williams*, normally a Hudson steamboat, which advertised as providing winter service via Bridgeport instead of Poughkeepsie.

On the Bridgeport end, the steamboat *Nimrod* had been running to New York since the mid 1830s. The new Housatonic Railroad contracted with the steamboat line to forward freight and passengers to and from New York, connecting with the railroad under an agreement reached in November 1843. The contract was to expire in November 1850. *Nimrod* was a former Vanderbilt Hudson River boat. Commanded by Capt. John Brooks, she ran as late as 1848. The Housatonic Railroad invested in wharf facilities as early as 1846, to facilitate the connection. The boat trip between Bridgeport and New York was scheduled to take about five hours.

Those early services were, by and large, daytime sailings. Bridgeport's advantage was that overnight steamer travel was not required (although night boats sailed, primarily for freight). In steamboating's adolescent era, nocturnal travel was less than pleasant. Sleeping accommodations were primitive in quality and insufficient in number. A commentator wrote of the futility of trying to get some sleep aboard a boat "filled with mingled associations of groaning machinery, bawling commands of Captain and Pilot, the crying of children, the endless thumping of logs on their way to the furnace . . . ." The palace steamers that would make

Bridgeport a less important destination were years in the future.

On December 27, 1848, the picture changed, as the New York and New Haven Railroad opened for traffic between New Haven, Bridgeport and New York City. The newcomer found the Housatonic Railroad committed to the steamboat company by contract, and solved the problem by entering into their own contract with the steamboat company to divide all revenues generated by their mutual activities. This arrangement was made all the easier, according to one commentator, by the fact that the President of the New York and New Haven and the President of the steamboat line were brothers.

The second valley railroad, the Naugatuck Railroad Company, was completed from Devon to Winsted in September 1849. Through Alfred Bishop's efforts, the Naugatuck reached Bridgeport from Devon by trackage rights on the New York and New Haven, and shared terminal facilities in Bridgeport with the Housatonic Railroad until 1863.

---

The steamer *Stamford* was built in 1863 at Williamsburg NY, and was operated as a spare boat in Bridgeport service between 1865 and 1870.

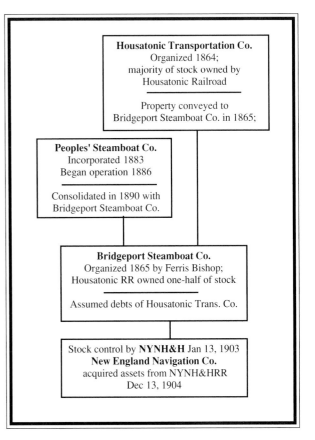

**Housatonic Transportation Co.**
Organized 1864;
majority of stock owned by
Housatonic Railroad

---

Property conveyed to
Bridgeport Steamboat Co. in 1865;

**Peoples' Steamboat Co.**
Incorporated 1883
Began operation 1886

---

Consolidated in 1890 with
Bridgeport Steamboat Co.

**Bridgeport Steamboat Co.**
Organized 1865 by Ferris Bishop;
Housatonic RR owned one-half of stock

---

Assumed debts of Housatonic Trans. Co.

Stock control by **NYNH&H** Jan 13, 1903
**New England Navigation Co.**
acquired assets from NYNH&HRR
Dec 13, 1904

The Housatonic Railroad's steamboat connection, known as the Naugatuck Transportation Company, replaced *Nimrod* with *Niagara* in 1848, and ran her until 1853. Her deep draft caused problems in Bridgeport's shallow harbor. About 1851, *Ansonia* began running between New York and Bridgeport. An opposition line started in 1851 with *Cataline*, a former Hudson River vessel. By 1852, an agreement had been reached between the two companies that had *Cataline* and *Ansonia* operating on alternate days. *Bridgeport* (I), built in 1857 at the Brooklyn shipyard of Samuel Sneeden, replaced *Cataline* in regular service; *Bridgeport* ran until 1889.

*John Brooks*, named for *Nimrod*'s master, joined the fleet in 1859. *John Brooks* was a fast boat; best time 3 hours 1 minute. She was fast enough for the line to place her in daily service, departing Bridgeport at 7:40 AM and New York at 1 PM. *Ansonia* and *Bridgeport* were operated every other day for freight only, leaving Bridgeport and New York at 10 AM.

*John Brooks* was chartered by the United States Government for Civil War duty in 1862. Evidence shows that *Bridgeport* was given the daily service assignment, and *Cataline* was returned to alternate day service running opposite *Ansonia*. *John Brooks* went to Maine after the war.

The Housatonic Railroad formed its own steamboat company in 1864, running *Captain A. H. Bowman* and *Stamford*. The *Bowman* was sunk, and some costly claims followed. Faced with losses and heavy competition, the Housatonic Transportation Co. was in poor shape.

They were thus only too willing to have their property taken over in 1865 by a new company, the Bridgeport Steamboat Company, in which the Housatonic Railroad would have a 40 per cent interest. The Naugatuck Railroad also became a part owner of the new company, which is not surprising since the new firm was promoted by Ferris Bishop, son of Alfred, who had promoted and built the Naugatuck Railroad. The new company bought *Bridgeport* and *Stamford* in 1866, and built *James B. Schuyler* in 1867. *Stamford* was declared surplus and sold to a Massachusetts company in 1870.

---

**Rosedale (below), built in 1877, was introduced in 1879 as a competitor to the Bridgeport Steamboat Co., and she quickly made off with a profitable share of the market. People would pay a premium fare to ride on her, which contributed to the Old Line's decision to buy the Peoples' Line in 1890. Like *Belle of New Haven*, *Rosedale* had her dock named for her; the Rosedale Dock lasted until 1927. *Rosedale* herself lasted only until 1922, when she burned at her dock in Norfolk VA. She had left Bridgeport service in 1904.**

**Crystal Wave (upper right) operated to Bridgeport for the "Old Line" between 1882 and 1889, but not consistently. During the summers of 1886 and 1887 she was chartered to the Central Railroad of New Jersey for service between New York and Sandy Hook NJ. Sold to Washington DC interests in 1889, *Crystal Wave* was on her way to the Potomac when she collided with *Cleopatra* off the Delaware coast. Both ships were lost.**

The Bridgeport Steamboat Company, although itself dating back only to 1865, became known as the "Old Line," most likely because of its railroad-related antecedents. In 1870 the Old Line chartered *Granite State* from the Hartford Line for a short time. The iron-hulled *Laura* (built in 1867) was purchased in 1872 to augment the fleet. The service had increased to two passenger round trips each day, daily except Sunday, plus freight trips as needed, apparently during the night hours.

We have noted that competition was never far off in the steamboat world. In the Bridgeport case it was brought about only in part by an increasingly attractive market. The precipitating cause was an argument over service. A leading citizen of Bridgeport was engaged in a dispute with the Old Line over transport of his circus from its winter quarters at Bridgeport. The outraged customer was Phineas Taylor Barnum, father of many modern marketing techniques and Mayor of Bridgeport for part of the 1870s. Mr. Barnum owned some wharfside property in Bridgeport, and turned up as one of the backers of the People's Steamboat Co., which started competitive operation in 1872 with the *Wyoming* and the *Artisan*. The line was suspended after two years.

In 1879, Capt. Anning Smith began operating *Rosedale* in opposition to the Bridgeport Steamboat Co. *Rosedale* was superior to any boat the Old Line had, and held her own despite the Old Line's undercutting of her fares. The Old Line countered the *Rosedale*'s better service with the chartered *John Sylvester* in 1880, and then with *Crystal Wave*

(chartered in 1880, purchased in 1882) in an effort to keep up with *Rosedale*. *Laura* was rebuilt in 1884, emerging as *Waterbury*.

Mr. Barnum and other Bridgeport merchants bought the opposition line in 1886, revived the People's Line name, and named Anning Smith to be General Manager. *Josephine* was added to the New Line in 1886. *Rosedale* and *Josephine* gave the Old Line fits by providing a better quality service. Unlike the normal situation, it was the new company that was running the better boats and charging the higher fares. To ride *Rosedale* cost 65 cents one way, $1.00 for a round trip. The Old Line charged 35 cents one way, 50 cents round trip. The amenities meant less for freight, however, and competition between the companies was intense; it was the kind of battle Barnum relished.

But profit, and not the battle, is the goal of sane businessmen. So, a year later, the two companies quietly agreed on an amicable division of the 1000 passengers or so per day that used the steamboats between New York and Bridgeport. For carrying freight, *City of Bridgeport* and *Vulcan* were added in 1886.

*Bridgeport* ran aground at Riker's Island near Hell Gate in 1888 and was broken up. *Crystal Wave* was sold in 1889 to a Potomac River operator, but she never made it, being lost in a collision with *Cleopatra* on her way to her new assignment.

In 1890, the Bridgeport Steamboat Co. owners quietly purchased a controlling interest in the People's Line and merged the operations, a move

that came as a surprise to some of the People's Line directors. Feeling that they had been "ambushed," the People's Line board sought to block the merger; they were unsuccessful. The combined companies' greater financial strength led to construction of a new boat, *Nutmeg State*, in that year to run with *Rosedale* and replace *Waterbury*.

*Nutmeg State* was lost on the morning of October 14, 1899 by fire while en route from Bridgeport to New York. About 60 passengers and 55 crewmembers were on board when *Nutmeg State* left Rosedale Dock at 3:00 AM that Saturday. At about 6:00 AM, the fire was discovered, near Execution Light. Captain Charles Brooks ordered the helmsman to turn toward shore at Sands Point NY, to beach her. The vessel burned to the water's edge in minutes, owing to the large quantity of textiles on board. She was also reported to be carrying a large quantity of cartridges from a Connecticut manufacturer; the explosions increased both the degree of flammability and the level of terror. All of the passengers were saved, but seven of the crew lost their lives. To replace *Nutmeg State*, the company first chartered *Mount Hope* from the Fall River & Providence Steamboat Company for an interim period, and then purchased *Allan Joy* from the Joy Line just before the new year.

*William G. Payne*, named for the Bridgeport Steamboat Co.'s Vice President, was a Harlan and Hollingsworth product, built in 1902. She was one of the last sidewheel boats built for the Sound. Those sidewheels were unusual in that they were significantly smaller than normal, in proportion to her size; but they revolved at 48 to 50 RPM, a bit more than twice as fast as the Fall River Line paddlewheels. She had been guaranteed by her manufacturers to make an 18-knot speed, achieved a 21-knot speed on her trial trip, and regularly cruised at 19 knots. *William G. Payne* was in fact called "the fastest sidewheeler in America."

In one of those "accidental" encounters shortly after she entered service, the *Payne* tested her speed against that of the champion, the propeller-driven *Richard Peck*. As usual, it looked like a race, but this was solemnly denied by company officials. The result was very close; both sides claimed victory.

The NYNH&H renamed her *Bridgeport* upon acquisition of the Bridgeport Steamboat Co. in 1903; the railroad removed personal names from some of its boats. As *Bridgeport*, she continued to operate until about 1914, when she was sold to the McAllister Steamboat Co. for Hudson River operation under the names *Highlander* and (in 1925) *Bear Mountain*.

Bridgeport Steamboat Company's last boat was the *William G. Payne,* built in 1902. *Payne* was known as a speedy boat, and business continued to increase. At the peak of the season, the *William G. Payne* carried some 2,000 passengers per trip. If this number seems large, remember that the Bridgeport run was a short one, without the necessity for sleeping accommodations. *William G. Payne* represented the advance of sidewheel technology; smaller, faster wheels with "feathering" buckets, equipped with linkages that lessened their resistance in the water when not actually pushing.

None of this had escaped the notice of the NYNH&H, which leased the Naugatuck Railroad in 1887 and the Housatonic Railroad in 1892 (see Chapter Nine). The Bridgeport Steamboat Company, a separate entity although not entirely independent of the two local railroads, was not purchased by the NYNH&H until February 1903. The property included the Bridgeport wharf land and buildings, and the steamers *Rosedale, Allan Joy,* and *William G. Payne. Rosedale* was sold to her former owner, Capt. Anning Smith, in 1904. Mr.

Smith knew better than anyone how good a boat *Rosedale* was.

Under NYNH&H ownership, the two main Bridgeport boats were renamed, with *Allan Joy* becoming *Naugatuck,* and *William G. Payne* becoming *Bridgeport.*

---

**Bridgeport was a comparatively short-haul service, ideal for smaller boats like *Rosedale*. Here's another look at her, with a tug shepherding a lighter at the left.**

*Mount Hope* **was built in 1888, relatively late for a wooden-hulled ship. She was an occasional visitor to Bridgeport as a charter replacement. When** *Rosedale* **collided with** *Oregon* **in September 1896 and was sunk,** *Mount Hope* **filled in.** *Rosedale* **was later raised and repaired. Then, when** *Nutmeg State* **burned in 1899,** *Mount Hope* **again was borrowed by the Bridgeport Line. Her more normal place was Narragansett Bay, where she ran on cross-Bay lines between Fall River and Providence.**

# Chapter Four
# Hartford and the Connecticut River

The Connecticut River (named *Quinneh-ta-cut* by the Mohican Indians, meaning "beside the long tidal river") flows southward from the Canadian border, serving as the boundary between New Hampshire and Vermont, then through Northampton and Springfield, MA; continuing past Hartford and Middletown CT to reach Long Island Sound thirty miles east of New Haven at Saybrook. It is indeed a "long tidal river;" a tidal change of about six inches is felt at Hartford, some forty miles upstream from the Sound.

The water route from New York City to Hartford is something of a "hook shot;" a boat sails first out east on the Sound to Saybrook, within thirteen miles of the Thames River mouth at New London; then back northwest, upriver to Hartford, passing (or stopping at) Middletown and a number of smaller river landings.

Even before the steamboat, the Connecticut was a busy commercial waterway. The vessels were sailboats, poled boats, and rafts. In 1788, a group of Hartford citizens petitioned the Legislature for permission to dredge a ten-foot deep channel, to be funded by tolls. That petition was not approved, but in 1800 the Union Company was approved and incorporated ". . . for the purpose of removing the obstructions in Connecticut River from Hartford to the Sound . . . to dig, cleanse, and remove obstructions . . . ." Upon completion of a suitable channel, the Union Company would be entitled to collect tolls for sixty years.

The toll schedule varied from six dollars for a boat drawing six and one-half feet of water to thirty-

---

No, this is not the Connecticut River. We are on a rooftop in Brooklyn Heights, looking toward Manhattan, shortly after the turn of the century. The East River was the center of commerce, with America's largest city, New York, on one shore; and America's third largest city, Brooklyn, on the other. The two cities became one in 1898.

The Brooklyn Bridge had opened in 1883, but the Fulton Ferry, one of five such ferry lines operated by the Union Ferry Co., was still running across the East River. The connecting elevated train (lower left) made transfers easy; even then, rush hours were a wonder to behold.

The two steamboats at the left of the picture are *Hartford* (II) and *Richard Peck*, awaiting their departures to Hartford and New Haven respectively. Predecessors of those boats had occupied those slips for almost 70 years before the bridge opened.

Note the Long Island Rail Road freight terminal on the Manhattan shore at the right. The NYNH&H operated a similar facility a few piers to the north, using the same type of two-track car floats with center platforms, described more fully in Chapter 15.

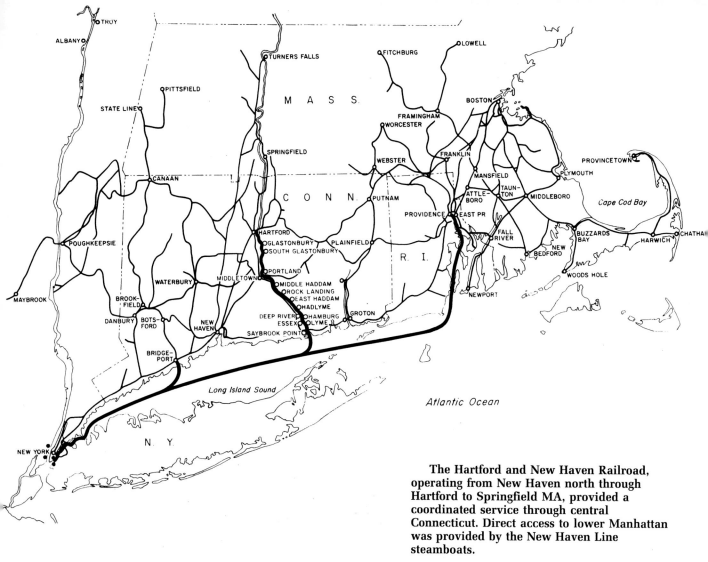

The Hartford and New Haven Railroad,
operating from New Haven north through
Hartford to Springfield MA, provided a
coordinated service through central
Connecticut. Direct access to lower Manhattan
was provided by the New Haven Line
steamboats.

eight dollars for a boat drawing ten feet of water.
The Union Company set about its work, and by
1806 had dug, cleansed and removed sufficient
obstacles to create a seven and one-half foot channel. That qualified the Company to begin toll collection, and touched off instant public opposition
to the tolls. The Union Company hung on, resisted
the ungrateful public, and collected its rightful
tolls for the full sixty years; the business was
wound up in 1864.

### The First River Steamboats

Captain Elihu Bunker ran *Fulton* up to Hartford
on the Connecticut River as an adjunct to at least
one of his New Haven trips in 1815. The people of
the city turned out *en masse* to see this marvel of
technology; but there is no record of *Fulton* or any
other steamboat operating on the Connecticut River
for the next three years.

In 1819, the first steamboat to be built in Hartford was launched; she was *Enterprize*, a towboat,
designed to carry passengers while assisting other
vessels on the journey between Saybrook and
Hartford. Her engine design derived from an 1815

patent issued to Samuel Morey, who was still
active, recognized, and commercially rewarded in
Connecticut if not in New York.

Steamboat service on the Connecticut River was
the purpose of the Connecticut River Steamboat
Company, formed in 1819. A secondary purpose
was a connecting service via the Sound between
Connecticut and New Jersey, bypassing the Livingston-Fulton monopoly in New York. The stockholders' meeting was held at the Exchange Coffee
House on the north side of State Street in Hartford,
an establishment owned and operated by one Joseph Morgan. Mr. Morgan was also active in local
politics, banking, and the first insurance companies to be founded in Hartford. And one of Mr. Morgan's grandchildren, John Pierpont Morgan, born
in 1837, was to have his own impact upon transportation in New England some years hence.

The Company's first service was on the river,
with smaller flat-bottomed boats working the upper
section from Hartford north to Springfield MA, and
larger vessels in the wider and deeper lower portion of the river between Hartford and Saybrook.
The upper-river boats were mostly sternwheelers,

because that configuration allowed maximum hull width going through the narrow upriver locks.

The more normal sidewheel configuration was used on the lower river and Sound. By 1823, *Enterprize* was running between Hartford, Saybrook and even New London (which, you remember, was only thirteen miles from Saybrook). With apologies to Mr. Morey's memory and achievements, *Enterprize* was not a very reliable boat, and the company's first years were not very prosperous.

As noted in Chapter Two, Connecticut passed its "retaliatory law" against Fulton's New York steamboat monopoly in 1822. The Connecticut Steam Boat Company was the instigator of that legislation, no doubt citing the example of Samuel Morey's treatment at the hands of the New Yorkers as well as arrogant restrictions to commerce. The law was passed, vetoed by Governor Wolcott, and enacted upon an overwhelming veto override vote in the legislature. Connecticut would not be trampled by any monopoly.

In 1823, the Connecticut River Steamboat Co. was formed by Col. Charles H. Northam and Mayor Philip Ripley of Hartford, presumably with Joseph Morgan's approval. Northam, only 26 at the time, was well on his way to becoming a pillar of the Hartford community. He had been in the grocery business and had been involved with East India trading. When C. H. Northam died in 1881, his

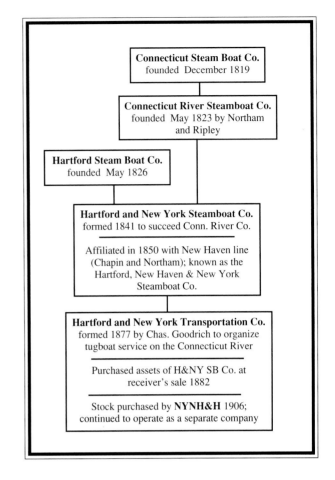

**Connecticut Steam Boat Co.**
founded December 1819

**Connecticut River Steamboat Co.**
founded May 1823 by Northam and Ripley

**Hartford Steam Boat Co.**
founded May 1826

**Hartford and New York Steamboat Co.**
formed 1841 to succeed Conn. River Co.

Affiliated in 1850 with New Haven line (Chapin and Northam); known as the Hartford, New Haven & New York Steamboat Co.

**Hartford and New York Transportation Co.**
formed 1877 by Chas. Goodrich to organize tugboat service on the Connecticut River

Purchased assets of H&NY SB Co. at receiver's sale 1882

Stock purchased by **NYNH&H** 1906; continued to operate as a separate company

---

*Granite State* was built in 1853, and spent most of her thirty-year life in Connecticut River service. The Connecticut *Courant* described her as having an upper deck with "a long saloon, beautifully carpeted and furnished with settees, easy chairs, marble top tables, and all the other etceteras desirable in a first-class boat. Opening from the saloon are forty staterooms with all the comforts one can ask for . . . ."

The end for *Granite State* came on May 10, 1883, in the River at East Haddam. A fire started in her engine room and quickly enveloped the boat. Most of the passengers and crew scrambled to safety; only two lives were believed lost. The East Haddam ferry and other small boats performed the rescue missions while the *Granite State* burned to the waterline.

reputation for the highest integrity was unsullied, a condition which was by no means universal in the steamboat business.

## Oliver Ellsworth Arrives

The company's first successful steamboat was *Oliver Ellsworth*, built in 1824, named for a Windsor resident who had been the first Connecticut man to serve on the U. S. Supreme Court, as the third Chief Justice (1796-1799). Her Captain was Daniel Havens.

*Oliver Ellsworth* was 127 feet long, 230 tons, and featured the first cast iron boiler on the Sound, sixty-two berths and a dining cabin. Although a steamboat, she carried a full set of sails in schooner rigging. Her schedule at first was uncertain, and arrivals were announced by firing a cannon. Until the invention of the steam whistle (see Chapter Seven), a cannon was the most practical long-distance signal for a vessel.

After the New York monopoly was demolished by Justice Ellsworth's successors, the company began direct service to New York. It is said that on one trip in 1826 *Oliver Ellsworth* carried about 400 passengers between Hartford and New York in

As *State of New York* or *City of Springfield*, this boat was both the largest and the unluckiest vessel to provide service between New York and Hartford. She had 160 staterooms when she was new, including two bridal chambers "fitted up with Oriental magnificence." Her main saloon was 250 feet long, and featured plate glass mirrors, rich carpets, overstuffed furniture and chandeliers. She had gas lighting and improved plumbing; the paddle wheels kept water splashing into two cisterns which supplied water to lavatories and toilets.

But the *State of New York* had more than her share of troubles; she hit a granite block destined for a breakwater, she foundered in Hell Gate, she collided with the *City of Boston*, she rammed her East River dock and, in 1881, she hit a snag and sank in the Connecticut River above East Haddam. After a $40,000 refitting, the company changed her name to *City of Springfield*. But before her retirement in 1896, she suffered a broken walking beam, a broken main shaft, another gash in her hull, and a lost roof section in a high wind. But they loved her in Hartford (that is, everybody loved her except the insurance folks, it seems).

about 18 hours, with the *Experiment*, built in Middletown, providing a connecting service between Saybrook and New London. The agents in Hartford were Messrs. Chapin and Northam.

In March 1827, while *Oliver Ellsworth* was off Saybrook on her way to New York, her innovative

boiler exploded, scalding many on board. One passenger and one crew member died in the accident. The news was of sufficient importance to warrant an interruption of the Legislature's deliberations at Hartford; a flustered Capital messenger alarmed the solons with the excited statement that the "Elliver Olsworth had biled her buster." The boat was repaired, improved and placed back in service, to run until 1833.

The "normal" passenger fare between Hartford and New York in those days was $4.50; but competition often wrought changes. Competition on the River first arose in 1826 in the form of *MacDonough*; named for the victor in the 1814 Battle of Lake Champlain. She was operated under Capt. William Beebe by the new Hartford Steamboat Co. until 1834 when she was sold to Maine interests. In 1832, *Chief Justice Marshall* (in honor of the monopoly-breaking jurist) joined the Hartford-New York run for three years, until she was destroyed by a gale in 1835.

It wasn't too long before the rival companies reached a mutually satisfactory agreement to divide and rationalize the service, rather than cut each other's throats. The three rival companies split the week as follows:

| Boat | Lv. New York | Lv. Hartford |
| --- | --- | --- |
| *MacDonough* | Monday | Wednesday |
| *Oliver Ellsworth* | Tuesday | Thursday |
| *Ch. Justice Marshall* | Wednesday | Friday |
| *MacDonough* | Thursday | Saturday |
| *Oliver Ellsworth* | Friday | Monday |
| *Ch. Justice Marshall* | Saturday | Tuesday |

Interline charters were not uncommon between Sound steamboat lines, even before the NYNH&H provided a unifying influence. *City of Lawrence*, above, was normally a Norwich Line boat, but she was chartered twice by the Hartford line. In 1884 she filled in for the *City of Springfield* during one of the latter's many trips to the shops. In 1899, the *Lawrence* "held the fort" during the period after *Hartford* (I) went to war, and before *Hartford* (II) arrived.

The Connecticut River panorama below shows *Middletown* in her element; among a group of smaller boats. The Connecticut river was a difficult waterway in which to navigate; for years, the Hartford and New York Steamboat Co. financed the dredging and navigation light maintenance necessary to keep its boats moving safely. Many others benefitted from these efforts.

The timetable listing above showed the service pattern on the Connecticut River in the closing years of the nineteenth century, complete with intermediate stops and NYNH&H connections. The service continued until 1931, with the Hartford line retaining its operational autonomy.

The Vanderbilt interests reached over from the Hudson to put *New England* into Hartford service in 1833, and *Water Witch* in 1834. These were operating on truly competitive schedules, against the Connecticut and Hartford companies. While a round of rate-cutting was favorable in the short term (with that normal $4.50 fare reduced to $1.50 at times), others warned that this invasion by New Yorkers would hurt local interests. The spirit in which the retaliatory laws had been passed had clearly not dissipated.

During the evening of October 9, 1833, *New England*'s boilers exploded while the boat was off Essex. Many passengers and crewmembers were scalded, and about fifteen of the seventy passengers on board were killed. Some of the injured travelers were on their way to an Episcopal Church convention as delegates; it was said that the future of that church in America was significantly changed because the members' absence caused the lack of a quorum for some important votes.

This serious boiler accident, and the subsequent thorough investigation into its causes, led to the modification of steamboat boilers by installing safety pop valves which automatically let go if the boiler's internal pressure exceeded safe limits. *New England* was rebuilt and operated on the River until 1837, when she was sold to a company operating between Boston and Portland ME.

*Lexington*, Captain Jake Vanderbilt commanding, joined the Hartford-New York fray in 1835; the fare was cut to $2.00. The fare was flexible: it was lowered to $1.00 on the days when a competitive boat was also at that end of the line. Lexington was the fastest boat on the Sound, and Jake Vanderbilt one of the legendary captains. This was the same *Lexington* that was destined for disaster less than four years later, in 1840. In 1837, another Vanderbilt boat, *Cleopatra*, was added to the service, where she ran for six years before moving on.

The locals responded with *Bunker Hill* (I) in 1835 and *Charter Oak*, commanded by Captain Mem Sanford, in 1836. The competition between Capt. Jake Vanderbilt and Capt. Mem Sanford provided much fodder for discussion and argument all along the River and the Sound; here were two nautical giants squaring off, each with their enthusiastic cheering sections. By 1839, the schedule showed four boats making the Hartford-New York run, with a stop at New Haven: *Bunker Hill* and *New Haven* operated day trips, with *Charter Oak* and *Cleopatra* making the night run. Such was the pattern until the railroad came.

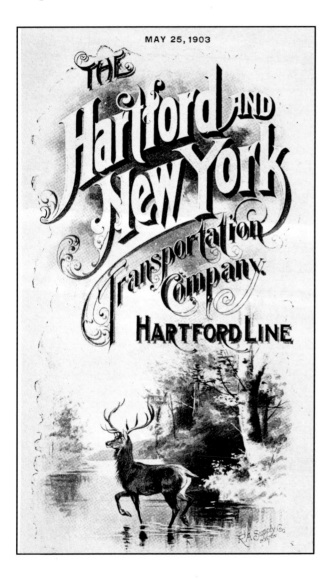

MAY 25, 1903

THE Hartford AND New York Transportation Company HARTFORD LINE

R.A. Supply Co.

This ornately engraved folder shows the turn of the century style of advertising. Note that the line did not experience much turnover among its executives (see previous page). Note also that New York departures were now from Pier 33 (New). The City had renumbered the East River piers about 1900; Pier 33 (New) was, in fact, Pier 24 (Old).

## Steamboats Upriver

Steamboat service on the Connecticut River above Hartford was difficult; Hartford had been the head of navigation in sailing days. With the aid of dredging and some short canals, smaller steamboats operated regularly between Hartford and Springfield beginning in 1830. Still smaller boats, mostly sternwheelers rather than sidewheelers, were known to operate as far north as Bellows Falls, VT. The Hartford-Springfield steamboats were intensely rivaled by the parallel stage line, owned in part by Chester W. Chapin, who controlled both land and water transport in that corridor for twelve years. Passenger boats operated until the railroad went through to Springfield in 1844; some freighters continued operation for a few years thereafter.

## The Railroad Arrives

The spotlight on traffic between New Haven and Hartford shifted to the railroad in 1839, when the Hartford and New Haven railroad line between the two cities was completed. The new trains connected with steamboats from Belle Dock to New York. The New Haven and Hartford steamboat lines came under control of the Connecticut River Steamboat Co.

But by 1846, railroad or no, Hartford was a thriving port, with regular steamboat and packet services to New London, Providence, Boston, eastern Long Island, New York City, Philadelphia and Albany. *Champion*, *Globe*, and *Hero*, among others, operated to points down the river and beyond. In 1852, two landmark boats appeared: the 274-foot *City of Hartford* and the 265-foot *Granite State*. These two boats were larger and more opulent than anything on the Sound before their arrival. One consequence was that they could no longer make all of the Connecticut River stops owing to their deeper draft; smaller boats filled in the gaps. This was an impressive showing, despite the standing joke about the shallowness of the river (perpetrated, it is believed, by jealous New Haven folk); "The problem with steamboating to Hartford is that the paddle wheels kick up too much dust!"

In 1850, Messrs. Chapin and Northam acquired control of the Connecticut River Steamboat Co. as well as the New Haven steamboat lines; Commodore Vanderbilt departed the area. The whole enterprise became known as the Hartford, New Haven and New York Steamboat Co. (see Chapter Two). The Connecticut River assets were grouped under the Hartford and New York Steamboat Co., but boats served both lines. In some cases, the service was from New York to Hartford with a stop at New Haven.

Completion of a railroad between New London and New Haven, the Shore Line Railroad, was an 1852 event. The rail line supplanted stages operat-

ing along shore roads, and connected with both steamboats and the New York and Hew Haven rail line opened three years previously. The steamboats yet retained their coastwise time advantage, however, because the railroad was obliged to use a carferry, *Shaumpishuh*, to cross the Connecticut River between Lyme and Saybrook. It was not until 1870 that a drawbridge was built to carry trains across the river.

The next landmark vessel was *State of New York*, built in 1865 for the Hartford & New York Steamboat Co. by the Greenpoint firm of C & R Poillon. The *New York* packed accommodations for 800 passengers into its 286-foot length; it was the largest boat to run on the river. Plagued by a

Bridges, of course, sometimes became a hazard to navigation. The *City of Hartford* figured in a famous March 1876 collision with a railroad drawbridge one dark night at Middletown; a white bridge marker light was out, and a white light in the town was mistaken for the marker. The boat missed the open draw span, and carried an adjacent section of the bridge away from its piers. We present here two views of the result. The remarkable fact is that no one was killed. From this accident came the Federal requirement to mark all bridge draws with red lights, to distinguish them from lights on shore.

*City of Hartford* was rebuilt and renamed *Capitol City* in 1883. In 1886, she went aground at Rye Beach NY, and broke up on the rocks.

series of non-fatal accidents, the large boat was considered a mixed blessing by its owners.

Economically, the Connecticut River run became less and less profitable as time went by and operating costs increased. True, larger boats could operate on a scale sufficient to offset rising labor costs. But river navigation at low water led to problems that worked against such larger vessels. *State of New York*'s costly string of accidents, and its high total operating costs, contributed to the poor financial condition of the Hartford & New York Steamboat Company, which went into receivership after its then owner, William Goodspeed, died in 1882. *Granite State*, *City of Hartford*, and *State of New York* were sold by the U. S. Marshal at New London to the Hartford & Connecticut Valley Railroad Company. They changed the name of *State of New York* to *City of Springfield* and began a rail-boat service from Hartford to New York, with the steamers operating between New York and railroad-owned docks at Saybrook.

The rail-boat service via Saybrook may or may not have been prosperous; remember that operating from Hartford via Saybrook to New Haven or New York was not a direct route. It did, however, attract the attention of the NYNH&H because, with its connections, it was a real or potential competitor. The real danger was that the Boston & Albany or another connecting railroad might buy it, and use its parallel routing as leverage in rate division discussions. The NYNH&H bought the Hartford and Connecticut Valley late in 1882.

In 1882, the boats were sold by the railroad to Charles Goodrich's Hartford & New York Transportation Co. (H&NYTCo), a company that was operating a towboat service on the river for coal barges and other craft. The Goodrich people found themselves financially taxed when *City of Springfield*'s walking beam broke, necessitating costly repairs. (Remember, this was the luckless old *State of New York*, living down to its reputation.) More trouble came in March 1886. *City of Hartford*, renamed *Capitol City* to honor Hartford's status, ran aground at Rye Beach in the fog; she was a total loss. Chartered and leased boats filled in the service gaps, along with *City of Richmond*, built in 1880, and purchased by the H&NYTCo about 1885. *Granite State* lasted until May 1883, when she burned beyond repair.

That there was some co-operative relationship between the NYNH&H and the H&NYTCo is beyond question, although the year-to-year details are not known. In fact, it is quite likely that the NYNH&H was supporting the H&NYTCo's operations as far back as 1884, when the first arrangement was made to transfer and operate the boats. As we will see, Mr. Goodrich himself testified to arrangements between his company and the railroad, but these contracts were not public documents.

An 1899 advertising flyer from the H&NYTCo describes the service offered to all landings on the Connecticut River by the line. Of course, the larger vessels used in later years meant fewer landings were accessible. We can only wonder about the accuracy of the claim for "refreshing sleep," if that sleep were attempted while the boats were loading and unloading at those intermediate landings.

We can guess, however, that an agreement (or, more likely, a series of agreements) between the H&NYTCo and NYNH&H would have called for some percentage split of the total railroad and steamboat passenger and freight revenue attributed to transportation between New York and Connecticut River points, with the NYNH&H subsidizing operating and/or capital expenses, and H&NYTCo agreeing to a maximum profit from passenger and freight operations. NYNH&H also probably had approval rights on routes and schedules. In that way, the NYNH&H would insure itself against competition, while the H&NYTCo was protected against financial loss. During those months when the river was frozen, the railroad carried all traffic.

The towing and barge service seems to have remained separate, and was always a profitable and well-regarded service on the river.

H&NYTCo bought two more boats in the 1890s: first came *Hartford* (I), 1892, a twin-propeller boat with 65 staterooms and capacity for much freight. In 1895, *Middletown*, 245 feet, came from the same builders. The U. S. Army bought *Hartford* (I) in 1898 for transport service in the Spanish-American War; she was renamed *General Terry* by the military. In 1899, a second *Hartford*, about the same size as *Middletown* but with two smokestacks, arrived on the scene.

*Hartford* (II) and *Middletown* were the final two boats in service between Connecticut River points and New York City, alternating each day, uneventfully, week after week, with the number of mishaps during the next 32 years counted on the fingers of one hand, and none of them serious. The design and construction of these two boats, built in the late 1890s, along with modern navigational aids, had removed the adventure that had characterized steamboating's early days. It was, however, a kind of "adventure" that any steamboat company manager would have told you he could well do without.

**Shaumpishuh** **was the old ferry which operated across the Connecticut River between Old Lyme and Old Saybrook, for the New Haven and New London Railroad, built about 1850. Railway cars were shuttled across the river a few at a time, and trains were then reassembled to continue on their journeys. The ferry was replaced by a drawbridge in 1870.**

The capital stock of the H&NYTCo was purchased by the NYNH&H subsidiary New England Navigation Co. on October 9, 1906. Mr. Goodrich and the other owners received stock in the NYNH&H, not cash. That transaction marked formal and legal ownership by the NYNH&H; but, as noted, the time when "control" was first established was some time earlier.

The H&NYTCo continued as a separate operating entity, with subsidiaries of its own, which will be detailed in later chapters. The arrangement lasted until 1930, when the H&NYTCo was merged into the New England Steamship Co. (NESS), the major NYNH&H steamboat subsidiary. Connecticut River steamboat service stopped on October 31, 1931, and the tug and barge operations were sold to the Blue Line Navigation Co. of New York.

## Hartford (I) and Hartford (II)

*Hartford* (I), built in 1892, was the first twin-screw propeller vessel built for Hartford service. She had only 65 staterooms, but had a large freight-carrying capacity. As such, she was one of the less glamorous "workhorses" that carried freight between Connecticut points and New York. That mundane task was the primary reason for the boats' existence.

In December 1898, *Hartford* (I) was sold to the U. S. Army Quartermaster Department to serve in the Spanish-American War, after being renamed *General Terry*. Her activity consisted of transport duties in Cuban waters. After the war, the boat was sold into Great Lakes service on Lake Michigan and later Lake Superior. She operated under the names *Charles H. Hackley* and later *Carolina*. Her registration was active until 1960.

*Hartford* (I) was replaced within a year by *Hartford* (II), shown on Page 327. These two boats have been confusing to historians because of the similarity of their registration numbers: *Hartford* (I) bore 96172, while *Hartford* (II) carried 96472. Particularly when looking at faded documents, the interpretation requires much care. We present both of the *Hartfords* in this volume for your personal comparison; there were indeed two boats, they were not identical, and the serial numbers, similar by coincidence, are not a misprint or clerical error.

*Hartford* (II) was slightly larger than her predecessor (243 feet vs. 220 feet long, 1488 gross tons vs. 1337). She was built in 1899, shortly after *Hartford* (I) went to war, and went into service on the Connecticut River as companion boat to *Middletown*.

In 1916, *Hartford* (II) grounded on the rocks at Watrous Point in the River; her engine room was flooded. The tugs that rescued her took off her 100 passengers, and towed her to dry dock. The only other major mishap in her career was being trapped in the winter ice, again near Essex, in January 1928. She was scrapped in 1938.

## SOUTH STREET SCENES

A tour of South Street fronting on the East River at the turn of the century would probably be as confusing to your nose as to your other senses. At the upper left, wagons pick up and deliver in the area of Pier 16, just to the south of the New Haven Line and Hartford Line piers. We get a better perspective in the photo at the lower left, in which the same pier appears at center left. Sailing ships still mixed with steamers in 1901, and the wooden barrel was the container of choice for a wide range of commodities.

The seaport is people and horses as well as ships; the atmosphere of the steamboat freight world at the turn of the century is captured in the photo above. Electric trucks and containerization are years in the future.

Finally (lower right), we look back at Brooklyn from atop a building in lower Manhattan; compare the view from this vantage point with the photo that opened this chapter. The time period is a bit different; the shed on the B&O pier is being rebuilt. What appears to be *Hartford* (I) is in the slip.

# Chapter Five

# Norwich and New London

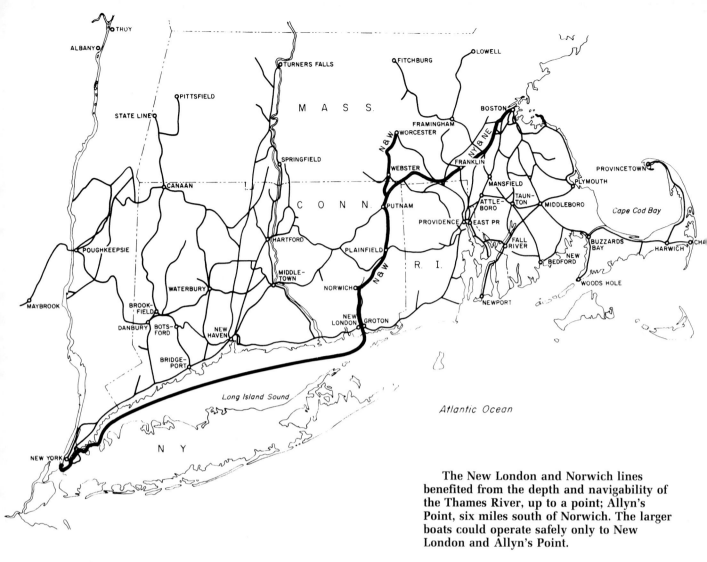

The New London and Norwich lines benefited from the depth and navigability of the Thames River, up to a point; Allyn's Point, six miles south of Norwich. The larger boats could operate safely only to New London and Allyn's Point.

---

## A QUIET DAY AT NORWICH HARBOR

The photo on the preceding pages shows the Norwich CT harbor in all its glory on a summer day. The spire of the Congregational church dominates the skyline, and the large freight house of the Norwich & Worcester Railroad dominates the wharf at the confluence of the Yantic River (entering from the left) and Shetucket River (entering from the top), which join to form the Thames River (exiting toward the Sound to the right).

The Norwich Line steamer *City of Lawrence* is taking on freight at the freight house. Across the Shetucket at the base of Laurel Hill, the local boat *Ella*, and the Norwich Line's relief boat *City of Norwich* are moored. The Norwich & Worcester Railroad's freight yard is behind *City of Norwich*. Present your ticket or a pass if you have one; *City of Lawrence* will depart early this evening.

At right, *City of New York* churns through the Sound on her way to New London and Norwich. Note the boilers on her guards, outside the main hull. *City of New York* and *City of Boston* were the first "large" steamboats bought by the Norwich Line, in 1862, to compete for the through trade to Worcester, Boston and other New England points. The two boats operated until 1895.

New London and Norwich are located on the Thames River, which empties into Long Island Sound some fifteen miles east of the Connecticut River, and thirty-five miles west of the entrance to Narragansett Bay in Rhode Island. New London is located on the west bank of the Thames, about three miles upriver from the Sound, with Norwich on the east bank another twelve miles upstream to the north.

The first steamboat to reach Norwich was *Connecticut* (I) under Capt. Elihu Bunker's command, on October 15, 1816. Regular service began in 1817, as an extension from New Haven (See Chapter Two), using *Fulton*.

### A Presidential Visit

A home-grown Norwich boat, *Eagle* (also known as *John Hancock*), built by Gilbert Brewster, was launched in 1817. She was a small boat, used for local excursion service on the Thames. On a certain festive day in 1817 a great honor befell New London: recently inaugurated President James Monroe was arriving on *Fulton*, paying the city a visit as part of a New England tour. The little *Eagle* carried a group of excursionists from Norwich down the river to welcome the distinguished visitor. All 51 passengers and crew members aboard hurried to the deck to catch a glimpse of the president. Unfortunately, as President Monroe arrived, the back end of *Eagle*'s boiler blew out, slightly injuring one crew member. The cabin which they had all hastily vacated to go on deck was destroyed. The investigation disclosed the startling fact that Mr. Brewster had made *Eagle*'s boiler of wood! Rebuilt and fitted with a proper boiler, she returned to service. A short time later, *Eagle* was relocated to Boston, where she operated for a number of years.

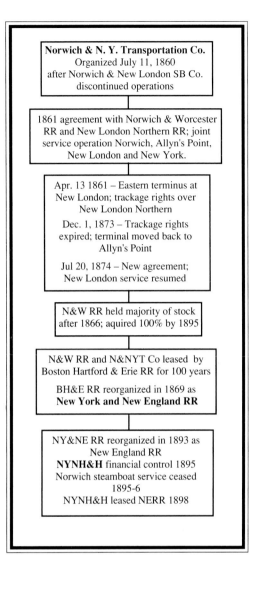

**Norwich & N. Y. Transportation Co.**
Organized July 11, 1860
after Norwich & New London SB Co.
discontinued operations

1861 agreement with Norwich & Worcester RR and New London Northern RR; joint service operation Norwich, Allyn's Point, New London and New York.

Apr. 13 1861 – Eastern terminus at New London; trackage rights over New London Northern

Dec. 1, 1873 – Trackage rights expired; terminal moved back to Allyn's Point

Jul 20, 1874 – New agreement; New London service resumed

N&W RR held majority of stock after 1866; aquired 100% by 1895

N&W RR and N&NYT Co leased by Boston Hartford & Erie RR for 100 years

BH&E RR reorganized in 1869 as **New York and New England RR**

NY&NE RR reorganized in 1893 as New England RR
**NYNH&H** financial control 1895
Norwich steamboat service ceased 1895-6
NYNH&H leased NERR 1898

CITY OF NEW YORK

Regularly scheduled steamboat service from Norwich and New London to New Haven, three times a week, began in 1817. Captain George Law commanded *Fulton*, operating between the Thames River and New Haven. *Connecticut* operated between New Haven and New York, providing the connecting service. This service was ended by passage of the Retaliatory laws.

After the end of the New York monopoly, the steamer *Henry Eckford* began operating between Norwich and New York twice each week. She was named for a prominent New York shipbuilder, the man whose firm had built *North River* (Clermont), in fact. The stagecoach operators met the boat to carry passengers to Boston and Providence. Even at a total Boston-New York fare of $11 ($5 for the steamboat run), *Henry Eckford* proved to be too small, and was replaced by *Fanny* in 1827.

Captain W. W. Coit, a New London native and former sailing packet commander, was the most prominent figure in early Thames steamboating. He commanded *General Jackson* (named for Andrew, hero of the Battle of New Orleans and President of the United States from 1829 to 1837) on a direct Norwich-New York run between 1834 and 1836. *General Jackson* is reported to have been the first Sound steamboat to use coal for fuel, rather than wood. Captain Coit was involved in building steamboats at nearby Mystic CT (site of a large maritime museum today). He also operated steam-

boats in Gloucester MA; and in Greenport NY, at the eastern tip of Long Island's North Fork. His *Norwich*, *Huntress*, and *Worcester* were popular boats wherever they ran.

*Norwich*, built in 1836 by Lawrence & Sneeden of Greenpoint NY, was small by later standards, being 160 feet long. She was, however, a good-sized vessel for her time, and the quality of her accommodations reflected Captain Coit's desire to provide good service. *Norwich*, in March 1840, had the distinction of carrying the first through passengers to New York from a connection with a new railroad, the Norwich & Worcester.

### The Railroad Connection

Worcester MA is decidedly not a seacoast city; yet a steamboat launched in 1842 bore her name because of that railroad connection. As was so often the case in those days, the drive to build a connecting transportation link began as a project to build a canal. This one was to run from Norwich north to Worcester, and was promoted largely by

The *City of Boston* waits for her departure time at the Norwich freight house. An 1861 product, *City of Boston* represented the Norwich Line's attempt to compete with Providence and Stonington boats. Despite the boat's speed and comfort, the line had a built-in drawback: the early morning transfer time.

**Norwich & New York Transportation Co.**

Be it Known, that _____ the
Proprietor _____ Shares of the
Capital Stock of the NORWICH & NEW YORK TRANSPORTATION COMPANY, on
which has been paid Twenty-five Dollars per share, subject to a Statute Law
of the State of Connecticut, entitled "An Act relating to Joint Stock Corporations,"
and is transferable on the Books of this Company, by the surrender
of this Certificate by said Proprietor or h Attorney.
Dated at Norwich, this _____ day of _____ 18___

Stewart Harting & Warren, 170 Broadway N.Y.

Secretary.                          President.

Norwich businessmen. The switch from canal to rail technology was also a familiar occurrence in the 1830s, and so the Norwich & Worcester Railroad was opened between its namesake cities in March 1840. Arrangements were made with Captain Coit for the steamboat connection to New York. At first, *Norwich* ran the connecting service three times a week; one round trip every two days. *Norwich* was quickly overburdened by the railroad traffic, and Captain Coit chartered two larger boats to operate the service: *Charter Oak*, and *Belle*. By 1841, Captain Coit's new boat, *Worcester*, was ready. After only 15 years on the Sound, *Norwich* was sold to new owners on the Hudson, where she operated until about 1916 as a towboat. Not many steamboats lasted eighty years.

The Norwich steamboat-rail connection between New York and Boston was rivaled only by the similar route via Stonington, which had started three years earlier. The Norwich and Worcester Railroad trumpeted its superior service to that of the Stonington line, which required a relatively inconvenient rail-ferry-rail transfer across Providence. Both Norwich and Stonington were preferable to cities farther west as boat-rail transfer points; indeed, they were superior even to New London. It must be remembered that New London lies on the west shore of the Thames River, and that no bridge crossed the Thames at New London until 1889. Thus, Norwich on the east shore of the Thames was far closer to eastern Massachusetts than New London

on the west shore, and the Norwich Line became popular with some Boston-bound folks. More importantly, the Norwich line became popular with the increasing number of travelers headed not to Boston itself but to other points west of Boston, more easily reached via Worcester, a rapidly-growing area with much commerce and industry.

The railroad had built a large steamboat dock at Norwich, but the Thames River often iced solid at Norwich in wintertime. Also, the river at Norwich was not wide or deep enough to handle the larger steamboats which the company believed it required. In 1843 the railroad was extended down the Thames' east shore to somewhat warmer waters at Allyns Point, about half way to Groton, the city opposite New London. Passenger and freight transfer between trains and steamboats at Allyns Point was relatively convenient.

The steamboat service to the rival port of Stonington was operated by Commodore Cornelius Vanderbilt; but in 1842, he was having a minor disagreement with the Boston and Providence Railroad, over the division of through ticket revenues between steamboat and railroad companies. With the tact and diplomacy so typical of the man, Vanderbilt left the Boston and Providence high and dry. The Commodore made a deal with the Norwich and Worcester and Captain Coit to buy Captain Coit's line and operate to Norwich in co-operation with the N&W railroad. Daily service began almost at once, using *Worcester* commanded by brother Jacob Vanderbilt; and *Cleopatra*, under Captain Isaac K. Dustan.

Dustan had moved to Norwich service with Vanderbilt, having been promoted to Captain from First Pilot after proving his courage in exciting circumstances. In 1836, while in Providence service (see Chapter Six), *Lexington*'s rudder control ropes broke during a heavy storm. First Pilot Isaac Dustan volunteered, and was lowered over the side in the gale to splice the ropes. His reward for this extraordinary service was to have tragic consequences.

It was around this time that the Long Island Rail Road was promoted, not as a commuter line, but as the southwestern link in a rail-water-rail combination via Greenport NY and Norwich. The Long Island opened to Greenport in 1844. Vanderbilt and Stonington Line owner George Law were both named to the LIRR Board of Directors, having purchased stock in the line; Vanderbilt sold the railroad the trio of *Worcester*, *Cleopatra* and *New Haven* for a reported $225,000. As a spare, the LIRR bought an older Vanderbilt boat, *Traveler*. From 1844 to 1846, the Long Island Rail Road operated the New York-Norwich boats, as well as routes between Greenport and Norwich, Greenport and Providence, and even (for two weeks) between Greenport and Fall River MA. Business was not bad; a summer trip from New York to Norwich might have 500 to 800 passengers, plus freight.

In June 1846 the Norwich and Worcester Railroad bought out the Long Island's Norwich steamboat operations, including *Worcester* and *Cleopatra*; the boats' price was $150,000. Jacob Vanderbilt was made the agent for the new "Norwich & New London Steamboat Co."

In response to George Law's new *Oregon* on the Stonington run, the Norwich Line launched *Atlantic* in August 1846. The railroad hired Cornelius Vanderbilt to supervise the design and construction of *Atlantic*, built at the Bishop & Simonson yard in New York for $160,000. *Atlantic* was the first sound steamer to be lit by gas, having the capability of manufacturing illuminating gas on board. She was considered to be the finest boat on the Sound at that time.

Tragically, *Atlantic*'s career lasted little more than three months; on November 27, 1846, Thanksgiving Day, she lost her propulsion when a steam pipe blew. A howling gale was raging, and her anchor chains snapped from the strain. She was blown ashore to Fishers' Island. The helpless *Atlantic*, her bell clanging throughout, splintered on the rocks, and was a total wreck. More than forty people were killed, including Captain Isaac Dustan. For days afterwards, her bell, still attached to a piece of wreckage, continued to toll periodically as water moved it. The eerie sounds inspired awe and poetry; the effect was reported to be sufficient to cause people to take the Pledge.

*Cleopatra*, *Worcester*, and *Mohegan* held down the service for the railroad through the late 1840s, but the losses from the *Atlantic* disaster crippled the railroad. The steamboat operations were sold to the newly-formed Norwich and New London Steamboat Co. as of September 1, 1848. The new company included among its owners Captain W. W. Coit and Henry B. Norton. In 1850, *Connecticut* (II) joined the fleet; she outran every boat on the Sound during the next few years.

But the boat that captured people's attention was *Commonwealth* (I), new in 1855. The Norwich Line built her under the requirements of a new contract with the railroad, which called for a new luxury steamer to be provided. *Commonwealth* (I) operated on the Norwich-New York run through 1858, becoming known as the state of the art in passenger accommodations for that decade.

A view westward across the Thames estuary from Groton discloses this scene at New London. Steamers sailed from here to New York, Norwich, Block Island, Fishers Island, Greenport and other points on Long Island, and, occasionally, other destinations. Modern services survive to the closer islands and to Greenport (Orient Point), but they are utilitarian ferries.

Below, three Norwich Line boats are at rest in Norwich harbor, with the iron-hulled *City of Lawrence* closest to the camera, moored at the freight house. It appears that *City of New York* is at *Lawrence*'s side, while *City of Boston* is at the coaling dock, left. Side-by-side mooring often aided freight loading, across one boat to the other.

At that point, the problem of dividing the through ticket revenues again reared its head. The division had been 55 per cent to the railroad, 45 per cent to the steamboat company, which was more favorable to the railroad than most of the Sound arrangements of the era. The Norwich and New London Steamboat Company wanted a 50-50 split, and didn't get it. The contract expired December 31, 1858; the Steamboat Company sent *Commonwealth* to the Stonington run and went out of business.

The Norwich & Worcester Railroad again organized its own steamship line to New York from Allyns Point and from New London (by rail connection with the New London Northern Ry.), taking a 40 per cent ownership interest for itself. The new Norwich and New York Transportation Company purchased the Steamboat Company's old vessels, and added two new boats built at Greenpoint by Sneden & Rowland. These were *City of Boston* (launched 1861) and *City of New York* (launched 1862). Just over 300 feet long, with paddle wheels almost 38 feet in diameter, they represented an unabashed bid for the fast through traffic between New York and Boston. They also became the new Sound steamer speed champions;

The photo montage above contains formal portraits of the officers of the second *City of Norwich*. Captain Joseph Reynolds occupies the position of prominence, flanked in the top row by his First and Second Pilots, Sam Geer and Peter Holm. Other identified officers include First Engineer Henry Avery, top left; and Fred Burns, Purser, top right. Such displays were used for advertising as well as keepsakes; the quality and personality of a boat's officers had a great deal to do with that vessel's attractiveness to passengers.

At right, this advertisement from an 1881 Travelers' Official Guide sings the praises of a journey via New London, perhaps on the (IRON) *City of Lawrence*. Note the 2:00 AM transfer, to the trains, one of which went through to Maine. (Imagine a train ride between New London and Portland taking more than eleven hours.) The line's Superintendent was Capt. Stephen A. Gardner, later to run the Old Colony (Fall River Line) operations. Capt. Gardner's son Howland was 10 years old at the time of this ad.

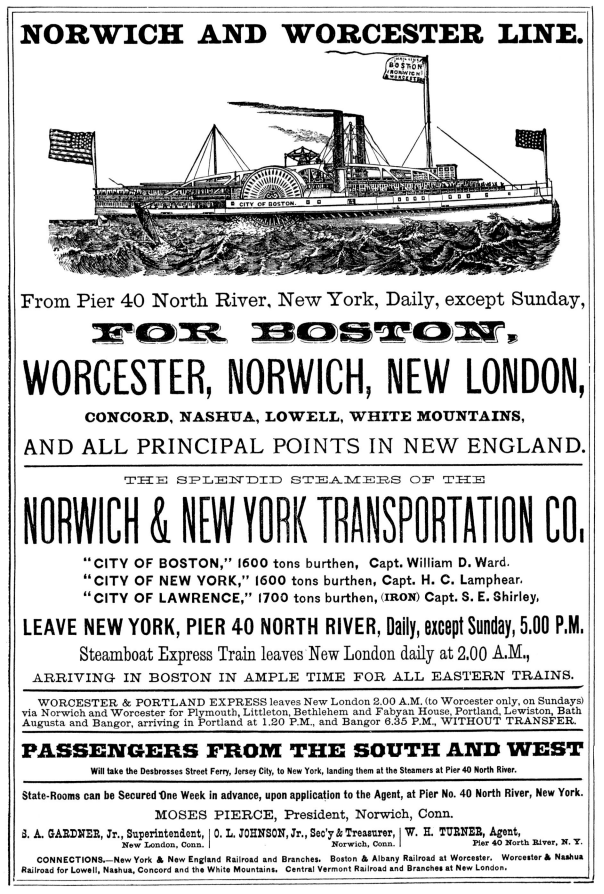

# NORWICH AND WORCESTER LINE.

From Pier 40 North River, New York, Daily, except Sunday,

## FOR BOSTON,

## WORCESTER, NORWICH, NEW LONDON,

### CONCORD, NASHUA, LOWELL, WHITE MOUNTAINS,

## AND ALL PRINCIPAL POINTS IN NEW ENGLAND.

THE SPLENDID STEAMERS OF THE

# NORWICH & NEW YORK TRANSPORTATION CO.

"CITY OF BOSTON," 1600 tons burthen, Capt. William D. Ward.
"CITY OF NEW YORK," 1600 tons burthen, Capt. H. C. Lamphear.
"CITY OF LAWRENCE," 1700 tons burthen, (IRON) Capt. S. E. Shirley,

## LEAVE NEW YORK, PIER 40 NORTH RIVER, Daily, except Sunday, 5.00 P.M.

Steamboat Express Train leaves New London daily at 2.00 A.M.,

ARRIVING IN BOSTON IN AMPLE TIME FOR ALL EASTERN TRAINS.

WORCESTER & PORTLAND EXPRESS leaves New London 2.00 A.M. (to Worcester only, on Sundays) via Norwich and Worcester for Plymouth, Littleton, Bethlehem and Fabyan House, Portland, Lewiston, Bath Augusta and Bangor, arriving in Portland at 1.20 P.M., and Bangor 6.35 P.M., WITHOUT TRANSFER.

## PASSENGERS FROM THE SOUTH AND WEST

Will take the Desbrosses Street Ferry, Jersey City, to New York, landing them at the Steamers at Pier 40 North River.

State-Rooms can be Secured One Week in advance, upon application to the Agent, at Pier No. 40 North River, New York.

MOSES PIERCE, President, Norwich, Conn.

| S. A. GARDNER, Jr., Superintendent,<br>New London, Conn. | O. L. JOHNSON, Jr., Sec'y & Treasurer,<br>Norwich, Conn. | W. H. TURNER, Agent,<br>Pier 40 North River, N. Y. |

CONNECTIONS.—New York & New England Railroad and Branches. Boston & Albany Railroad at Worcester. Worcester & Nashua Railroad for Lowell, Nashua, Concord and the White Mountains. Central Vermont Railroad and Branches at New London.

73

*City of Boston* set a record of 6 hours 5 minutes for the 120-mile trip from New York to New London.

The two large boats operated no farther up the Thames than New London. Two smaller boats, *City of Norwich* (I) and *City of New London* were added in 1862, primarily for freight but with some passenger-carrying capacity. These smaller boats, costing about $150,000 each, were intended to provide direct service upriver to Norwich. *City of New London* figured in a tragedy in November 1871 while fogbound on the Thames en route to Norwich. Seventeen passengers and crew members were killed when a fire broke out in the galley and spread to cotton bales being carried to a textile mill.

*City of Norwich* had its share of mishaps after returning from the Civil War, during which she had been chartered for army transport service. In April 1866, she burned to the waterline and sank in the East River, killing 13 people and one horse. Refloated and rebuilt, she was back in service by

September. Two years later, she burned to the waterline again, off New Haven this time; 11 people died. She was raised and rebuilt again, running until 1879 when she was converted into a barge.

*City of Boston* acquired the reputation of a dangerous boat to be near, suffering more than the normal share of mishaps during her 35-year life. Curiously, one encounter was with a similarly afflicted vessel we have met earlier, the Hartford Lines' *State of New York*. In July 1868, *City of Boston* collided with *State of New York* off Saybrook. Previously, on a trip up the Hudson, City of Boston had sunk the steamer *Oregon*.

Fate was not finished with *City of Boston* after the *State of New York* incident; in April 1874, while rounding the Battery en route from Pier 39 North River to New London, she was rammed by a Providence Line boat, *Electra*. The captain of a nearby tugboat swerved to avoid that collision; in so doing, he hit and sank another tugboat that was

The railroad extension to Groton opened in June 1899; here is a photo of the first train from Groton at the Laurel Hill yard in Norwich. The flag decoration attests to the festive nature of the occasion. The stone bridge pier supported the former railroad bridge built in 1843 across the Shetucket River. The location is behind the steamer *Ella* in the photo at the opening of this chapter.

Music was part of the difference between ordinary travel and the first-class accommodations possible aboard a Sound steamer. Here we meet Tubbs' 21-piece band, one of many organized to emulate Patrick Sarsfield Gilmore's successful Boston group. The Tubbs aggregation played aboard the Norwich line excursion steamers. Band music was a popular form of entertainment in every American town after the Civil War. We should note that Mr. Tubbs formed his band in 1872, twenty years before John Philip Sousa resigned from the U. S. Marine Corps to form his traveling band.

The Fall River Line was best known for its waterborne orchestral entertainment on its regular overnight trips, made easier by the later transfer time. The size of the orchestras decreased as business fell off after 1912.

innocently passing by. The most frustrating damage to *City of Boston* occurred at a time when such a boat might be considered in the safest position: the boat fell off a dry dock in the East River in May 1882. Most of her bottom had to be replaced.

In 1867, the company's first iron-hulled steamer, *City of Lawrence*, was delivered from the Harlan & Hollingsworth shipyard in Delaware. The passenger accommodations included 78 staterooms with accommodations for 225 persons. Many more passengers could be carried, enjoying the velvet carpeted saloon and restaurant; most passenger loads ranged between 300 and 500.

While the Norwich and New York Transportation Co. was a separate corporation, the fate of the Norwich and Worcester Railroad affected its fortunes to a considerable extent. In 1869, the N&WRR was leased by the Boston Hartford and Erie Railroad, an early consolidated line reaching eastward from Boston. A connection to steamboats (the main line of the BH&E crossed the N&W at Putnam CT) was considered sufficiently desirable to yield a 10 per cent lease payment from the BH&E, in a time when the usual payments were between 6 and 8 per cent. Given its propensity for paying premium prices, does it surprise you to learn that the BH&E went bankrupt in 1870? It became a major component of the New York and New England system.

## THE STEAMER *CITY OF WORCESTER*

The Norwich & New York Transportation Company was serious about its competitive position in the Long Island Sound marketplace. *City of Worcester* made her debut in September 1881, fresh from Harlan & Hollingsworth. The customary hog frame trusses are missing; this was the first large steamboat on the Sound built with a steel hull, following up on the success of the smaller iron-hulled *City of Lawrence*. *City of Worcester* was the first boat on the Sound to have electric lights (although oil lamps were also installed "just in case"). Although not quite as fast as the *Cities of Boston* and *New York*, she was the finest boat on the Sound for two years, until the Fall River Line's *Pilgrim* appeared.

The photo above is believed to date back to 1896; the 45-star flag helps to confirm that. Note the side-by-side stacks, a configuration shortly to be outmoded. The design at the hub of her 38-foot diameter paddlewheels is the seal of the City of Worcester MA.

The *City of Worcester*'s steel hull served her in good stead in January 1890 when she grounded on Bartlett Reef, near New London's harbor. Four of her six watertight compartments were opened up. Passengers were removed, divers called, and in a week she was on her way to dry dock for repair.

One other accident, in May 1898, deserves mention; the *City of Worcester* sank in New London harbor after a reef acted as a can opener. For three days she sat in water up to her main deck, an unusual sight indeed. But the photo at right, which appears to be a trial run, shows the *City of Worcester* as her designers expected to see her.

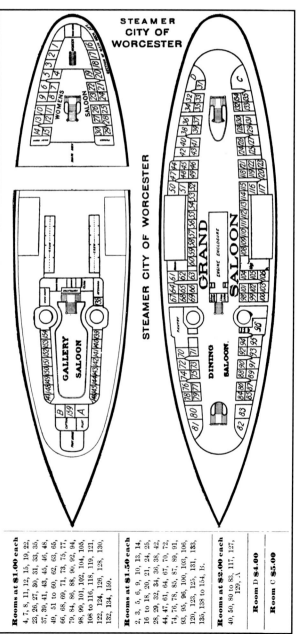

STEAMER CITY OF WORCESTER

**Rooms at $1.00 each**
4, 7, 8, 11, 12, 15, 19, 22, 23, 26, 27, 30, 31, 33, 35, 37, 39, 41, 43, 46, 48, 49, 51 to 60, 62, 63, 65, 66, 68, 69, 71, 73, 75, 77, 79, 84, 86, 88, 90, 92, 94, 98, 99, 101, 102, 104, 105, 108 to 116, 118, 119, 121, 122, 124, 126, 128, 130, 132, 134, 159.

**Rooms at $1.50 each**
2, 3, 5, 6, 9, 10, 13, 14, 16 to 18, 20, 21, 24, 25, 28, 29, 32, 34, 36, 38, 42, 44, 47, 61, 64, 67, 70, 72, 74, 76, 78, 85, 87, 89, 91, 93, 95, 96, 100, 103, 106, 120, 123, 125, 131, 133, 135, 138 to 134, B.

**Rooms at $2.00 each**
40, 50, 80 to 83, 117, 127, 129, A.

Room D $4.00

Room C $5.00

At left, we're looking at The Parade, toward the wharf at New London in 1881, as the brand new *City of Worcester* passes by, the center of attention. For local travel across the Thames River to Groton, the small ferry *Uncas* is in her slip at the left, and the railroad ferry *Thames River* is visible at the right center, behind the fish wholesaler. The railroad station is the building at the far right of the picture. The Norwich Line quay is out of the picture to the left; *City of Worcester* appears to be departing. Note the passengers standing on top of the clerestory dome above the boat's dining room, behind the pilothouse.

*City of Worcester* was also featured on the 1891 Norwich Line flyer shown below. The Norwich Line was indeed after the trade to Boston as well as Worcester and other points.

THE Norwich Line 1891

BETWEEN NEW YORK, BOSTON,

WORCESTER, AND ALL POINTS NORTH AND EAST.

TOURS

THOMAS CLARK, PRESIDENT, NORWICH CONN.
GEO. W. BRADY, AGT. PIER 40 N.R. NEW YORK
O.L. JOHNSON, JR. SEC'Y & TREAS. NORWICH CONN.

## THE STEAMER *CITY OF LOWELL*

While similar to *Richard Peck*, and indeed often teamed with *Peck* during her lifetime, the twin-screw *City of Lowell* was the first steel-hulled steamboat to be built in Bath ME, in 1893. She was designed by A. Cary Smith, who had designed *Peck*, but carried a full gallery deck.

Her first trip to New York was made in July 1894; she was booked to capacity with all 146 staterooms taken. (1 to 141, A through F, no Number 13.) She was fast; speeds of 22 knots were not uncommon, putting her safely in the same speed range with *Richard Peck*, *William G. Payne*, and *Priscilla*. As you might expect, *City of Lowell* set the speed record for her route from New York, five hours and thirty-five minutes to New London. *City of Boston*, the previous titleholder, could do no better than six hours and five minutes. We view on these pages two photos of *City of Lowell* in her element, flying (among others) the Maltese Cross flag of the NY&NE Railroad.

Her life was surprisingly free from accidents, although she did sink one of the Union ferryboats, *Columbia*, in the East River on a foggy day in November 1904. In February 1905 she trashed the schooner *Oakwood* off Whitestone, and in July 1907 she collided with a railroad car float. *City of Lowell* was singed in the 1906 fire that destroyed *Plymouth*'s superstructure, but not structurally damaged.

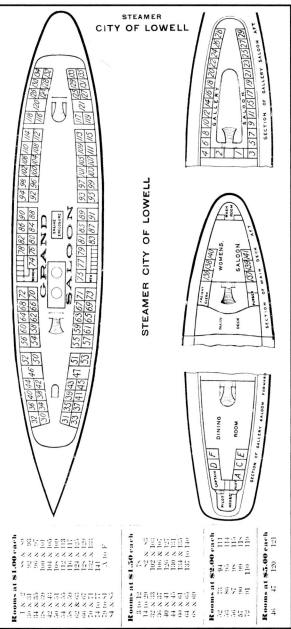

The railway's financial troubles were due to overexpansion, not lack of business. The 1870s proved prosperous for the railroad and the Norwich steamboats; extra trips and excursions kept the crews fully employed. In 1880, the need for another steamboat was seen and an order placed.

The 1881 *City of Worcester*, also built by Harlan & Hollingsworth, was the first large steel-hulled passenger boat on the Sound. *City of Worcester* had 193 staterooms and 164 berths, and was the first boat with separate gangplanks for her 500 passengers and 110 tons of freight, to allow for more efficient loading.

A second boat received in 1881 was *City of Norwich* (II), a clumsy freighter with an unseemly appetite for fuel. She immediately became the relief boat, not to be used except as a last resort; the company lost money with every revolution of her hungry engine. Clearly, Captain Reynolds had been handed an albatross, but he made the best of her. *City of Norwich* was unceremoniously scrapped in 1913 after her boilers were declared unsafe by government inspectors.

The last major passenger vessel to come from the New London operation was one of the acknowledged speedster steamboats to run the Sound. The Norwich Line asked A. Cary Smith, who had designed the surprising *Richard Peck* for New Haven service, to design its new boat. The resulting *City of Lowell* was built and placed in service in 1894. Under the command of Captain J. Cleveland Geer, she beat, or at least tied, all comers in the parallel, independent and purely coincidental speed tests (never "races") that often took place whenever competing steamers found themselves near the new *City of Lowell*. Her best time between New York and New London was five hours and thirty-five minutes.

Of course, this preoccupation with speed was largely unnecessary for the overnight service; a fast calculation based on the post-1900 timetables shows that a 5:00 PM departure followed by even a seven hour running time put the steamer in New London at 12:00 Midnight. Connecting trains left for inland points between 5:00 and 7:00 AM, which meant that the passengers would snooze peacefully while the steamer did likewise, at the New London wharf. (Passengers on the Fall River steamers could sleep about an hour longer.) Of course, those who lived in or near New London would be able to sleep in their own beds. But the concern with speed was more than a matter of prestige; for daylight runs or excursions, which were popular in the pre-1900 days when most of the shipbuilding decisions were made, speed was important; and it also attracted the customers.

In 1893, the Norwich & Worcester Railroad, which had a minority interest in the steamboat line, bought out the remaining shares. At that time, three steamboats were operating: *City of Lowell*, *City of Worcester*, and *City of Lawrence*. The *Cities of Boston*, *New York*, and *Norwich* were retired, but still on the property. As noted, the N&W became part of the New York and New England Railroad system, of which more in Chapter Nine.

---

*City of Lowell* stern view upper right; she's flying short flags with abbreviations on this windy day. (No, the picture is not reversed; the flags were customarily flown to "read right" from the port side of the boat, with a headwind.) The photo was apparently taken from another vessel during a celebration. At bottom right, a silhouette view from inside *City of Lowell*'s wheelhouse.

Below, the Long Island & New London Steamboat Co.'s *Long Island* noses in from left to carry the mail in this 1899 photo, as *City of Lowell* and *City of Lawrence* await departure at New London.

## THE LAST LAND LINK

New London did not have a rail connection until 1850, quite late in the game. Frankly, they didn't miss it, until the whaling industry declined in the late 1840s and the depressed town felt the need to diversify. The Norwich & Worcester was unwilling to build to New London because of New London people's past indifference to that line, and because it might hurt Norwich.

So the New Londoners financed their own railroad, a line north to Willimantic and Palmer. Local merchants and government were only too willing that the railroad come through town, along the waterfront. This line became the New London Northern Railroad.

The second rail connection came in 1852; it was the New Haven & New London Railroad, operating to the west along the Sound shore. In 1858 the eastward link was opened; The New London & Stonington railroad began operation of a rail carferry across the Thames, connecting with a new rail line from Groton to Stonington. From there, connections could be made to Providence.

The NYNH&H took over the lines between New Haven and Stonington in 1870, the year that the Connecticut River was bridged at Saybrook. The Thames, however, remained unconquered by steel through the 1870s and 1880s. Ferries such as *Groton* and *Thames River* shuttled cars across the river.

The Thames River represented the last physical gap in an all-rail route between New York and Boston, and many plans for bridging the river were made, as early as 1881. But there were obstacles. Norwich interests bitterly opposed the bridge, and had sufficient influence to delay the Legislature.

The U. S. Navy was opposed, because such a bridge might block access to its shipyard. The Thames was a strategic waterway, and any bridge, if built, would have to clear the largest ships afloat now and in the foreseeable future. What had started as a relatively simple project turned into a bureaucratic monster, requiring approval from an array of state and federal agencies. It also became, because of the requirements those agencies imposed, the largest railroad engineering project in Connecticut during the nineteenth century. What was required was a 200-foot wide clear opening. What was built by the Stonington Railroad was a bridge containing the longest draw span in the world when it was opened.

The map at the upper left shows the location of the bridge and its approaches; the line swung around north of the New London wharf to gain altitude for the crossing.

The Union Bridge Co, of Buffalo NY won the contract to build the bridge, at a cost of $1.6 million. The 200-foot requirement was met with a swing span of 502 feet, allowing 225 feet on either side of the center pivot foundation. The fixed approach truss spans were each 310 feet in length. The whole bridge was double-tracked to handle large traffic volumes.

The first train to use the bridge crossed westward on September 15, 1889, 25 days before the formal opening ceremony on October 10. The ceremony involved special trains and dignitaries from New York, Connecticut, Rhode Island and Massachusetts, and the Cornet Band from Woonsocket RI.

Unfortunately, the bridge proved unable to handle the heavy weights of post-1900 locomotives; a new stronger structure opened in 1918 to replace the original bridge.

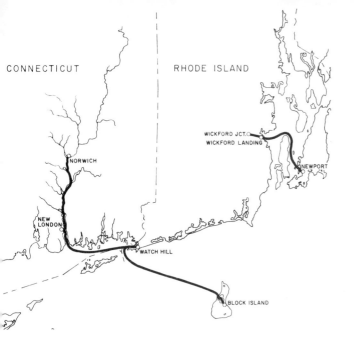

# The New London Steamboat Company

The New London Steamboat Company operated a service between New London and Block Island (a part of the State of Rhode Island), and Watch Hill RI. In addition, the Central Vermont Railroad was operating two freight steamers from New London to New York. This line formed the eastern end of a significant transportation link to the midwest, using the boats, the Central Vermont and the Grand Trunk Railway. For some commodities, notably sugar, this routing was competitive with that of the New York Central and Pennsylvania, and the tonnage was surprisingly large. Overall conditions for the railroad were not continuously favorable, however, and the Central Vermont Railroad entered receivership in 1896. It was thus unable to replace its aging steamers.

To fill the gap, the Central Vermont turned to the New London Steamboat Co., then owned by officers of the Central Vermont and its connecting railroad, the New London Northern. In 1899, the old steamers were replaced by two new freight boats, *Mohawk* and *Mohegan*, financed and owned by the New London Steamship Co. The Central Vermont Railway (a slightly different name as the firm came out of bankruptcy) entered into a ten-year charter agreement with the New London Steamboat Co. whereby *Mohawk* and *Mohegan* were operated between New London and Pier 29 East River in New York for the Central Vermont's benefit, including having the railroad's name painted on their hulls.

The service to Block Island from New London provides access to the island from the west. While a comparatively short distance, it is an interstate operation, subject to all of the regulations attendant thereto.

The steamer *Block Island* shuttled back and forth daily between points on the Thames River and Block Island.

The island is named for Adriaen Block, a Dutch explorer who, encountering it in 1614, named it for himself. (The local Native Americans had called it "Manisees.") The first settlement, New Shoreham, was founded in 1622.

The Grand Trunk Railroad, which controlled the Central Vermont, offered to buy the New London Steamboat Co. shortly after the charter period began, but the price was more than Grand Trunk President Charles Hays was willing to pay. The Steamboat Company soon found a willing buyer; in 1901, a New York shipyard and steamboat executive named Stevenson Taylor bought a controlling interest in the line. As was to prove to be the case in other instances, Mr. Taylor was acting for the NYNH&H. By September 1901, all of the New London Steamboat Company stock was in NYNH&H hands.

This put the two competing railroads in an interesting juxtaposition. The NYNH&H and the Canadian Pacific were friendly connections in a through route to the west. The CP's rival, the Canadian National, with its affiliate, the Grand Trunk, formed a parallel westward through route. The NYNH&H was operating two freight boats for the operators of a rival system. Yet, there was "friendly" interchange of freight between the Grand Trunk and the NYNH&H. The NYNH&H did make efforts to discontinue the charter, offering the Grand Trunk accommodating rates on the Norwich Line steamers, advertising on the piers, and other inducements. The Grand Trunk refused, maintaining its independence until the end of the charter period, in 1909. Its subsequent independent and competitive activity is detailed in Chapter Twelve.

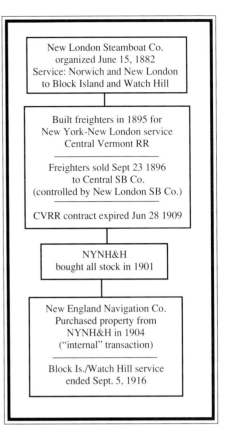

New London Steamboat Co. organized June 15, 1882 Service: Norwich and New London to Block Island and Watch Hill

Built freighters in 1895 for New York-New London service Central Vermont RR

Freighters sold Sept 23 1896 to Central SB Co. (controlled by New London SB Co.)

CVRR contract expired Jun 28 1909

NYNH&H bought all stock in 1901

New England Navigation Co. Purchased property from NYNH&H in 1904 ("internal" transaction)

Block Is./Watch Hill service ended Sept. 5, 1916

PAR VALUE $ 100.

NUMBER 92

STATE OF CONNECTICUT

SHARES

THE NEW LONDON STEAMBOAT COMPANY.

This Certifies that Geo. S. Davis is entitled to Twenty five Shares of the COMMON STOCK of THE NEW LONDON STEAMBOAT COMPANY, transferable only on the Books of the Company in person, or by Attorney on the surrender of this Certificate.

In Witness Whereof the President and Secretary have hereunto affixed their signatures this 11th day of July 1896

New London Conn, July 11 1896

SECRETARY.

PRESIDENT.

COMMON STOCK $ 500,000.

PREFERRED STOCK $ 100,000.

CAPITAL STOCK $ 600,000.

## THAMES RIVER TO BLOCK ISLAND

At left, we're back at The Parade in New London, where our busy photographer has captured *Block Island* returning from the Sound. Based upon the timetable at the right, we guess that the time is just before 5:00 PM.

That 1899 timetable shows the ferry service making all stops, including Norwich on the north and a landing at Montville, on the Thames' west bank. An interesting sidelight is that *Block Island* could have been used as a commutation mode between Norwich and New London. Perhaps it was, but the animosities between Norwich and New London probably limited the attractiveness of such an arrangement.

At the lower left, another look at *Block Island* in motion, this time in excursion service along with some of her larger sisters. Most likely, she's serving as a floating grandstand for the yacht races on the Thames.

Below, *Block Island* is at the terminal on her namesake island, approximately twelve miles south of Point Judith.

# Chapter Six

# Providence and Stonington

As we noted in Chapter One, Elijah Ormsbee's small experiment in 1792 was the first steamboating in Rhode Island. The first commercial steamboat in Providence was Fulton's *Firefly*, which operated between Newport, RI and New York during the summer of 1817. *Firefly* just wasn't fast or comfortable enough to be competitive with the sailing sloops already in New York service, and the steamer departed for good at summer's end.

In 1822, however, necessity (in the form of being bounced from the State of Connecticut) forced the Fulton boats' return to Providence, with a stop at Newport. *Connecticut* (still under Captain Elihu Bunker's command) and *Fulton* each made one round trip to New York per week in the summer; *Connecticut* continued alone, once a week, in the winter, unless prevented from doing so by ice. Running time from New York to Newport averaged 25 hours, and the fare was $10 from Providence, $9 from Newport.

Providence was the acknowledged "Gateway to New England" in that era; two dozen stagecoaches met each arriving steamboat, ready to carry the passengers to various inland destinations. The most popular of these was Boston, 44 miles distant. Even in 1817, President Monroe rode a steamboat from the scene of his explosive welcome in New London to Providence, then transferred to horseback for the trip to Boston.

Clearly, the smart traveler of the day sought to minimize the time spent in land travel and maximize use of the boats. The boats of those days might take 23 hours to travel 180 miles, about eight miles per hour. The stages traveled overland at about the same rate, but the land distances were longer and the coaches were considerably less comfortable than the steamboats. Further, meals or sleeping during land travel required stopping; the boats had the overall advantage in those primitive days of transport. The stagecoaches that ran between Providence and Boston made their intermediate meal stops in the small town of Wrentham, MA, a scant three miles from the stadium in which today's New England Patriots play football. Yesterday's rural stopover is today's suburb, thanks to improved transportation.

---

The backbone of Providence service was freight more than passengers. *Nashua* was one of the boats designed to carry freight only. These boats operated as the unsung, hardworking companions of their well-advertised passenger-carrying sisters. Their Cinderella-like status became apparent upon review of the income statments.

*Nashua*, built in 1884, had one other distinction. She was the first Sound boat to have an oscillating compound engine. It's worth remembering that *Nashua* was not constructed for the Fall River Line, but rather for the Providence & Stonington Line.

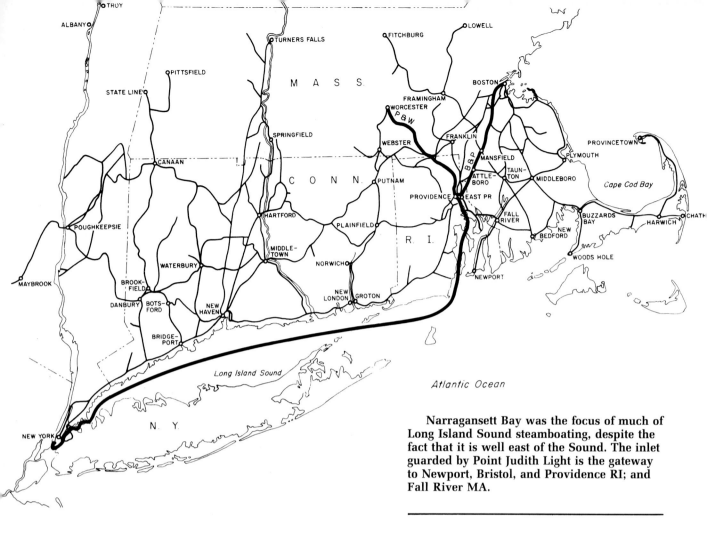

**Narragansett Bay was the focus of much of Long Island Sound steamboating, despite the fact that it is well east of the Sound. The inlet guarded by Point Judith Light is the gateway to Newport, Bristol, and Providence RI; and Fall River MA.**

There was also a cost advantage in steamboat travel. In the 1820s, when the $10 New York-Providence stagecoach fare (about 5 1/2 cents per mile) was in effect, the stagecoach fare from Providence to Boston was $3, almost 8 cents per mile. The land portion of the trip became considerably more comfortable in July 1835, when the Boston and Providence Railroad began through operation between those two cities. In fact, some scholars see 1835 as a historic dividing line: the beginning of America as we know it today; the railroads and steamboats combined to improve our mobility, and vast possibilities first presented themselves to Americans. Similar dividing lines, by the way, are said to be 1958, the first year of jet passenger plane travel; and 1975, the year the mass-market personal computer was developed.

Elihu Bunker saw these possibilities. He resigned from the Fulton company in 1825 to start his own Providence-New York operation, known as the "New York-Boston Steamship Line", an advertising slogan based on land travel connections at Providence. That firm built *Washington*, which debuted in March 1826. *Washington* was unusual in that she had two steam engines, one to drive each of the large side paddle wheels. She ran as an independent boat against the two Fulton steamers, *Connecticut* and *Fulton*.

By 1828, Providence was thriving as a transportation hub. More than 300 coaches a week connected with the growing fleet of steamboats. The newly-completed Blackstone Canal between Providence and Worcester provided an improved "land" link for passenger and freight boats and barges. *Chancellor Livingston* had joined the fleet on the Fulton side, and *Benjamin Franklin* was built for the Bunker firm. In an October 1828 match race from Providence to Newport, *Franklin* was the winner by 15 minutes.

In 1829, Captain R. S. Bunker joined his father's company; his new vessel was *President*, 160 feet. *President* was a clear statement that steamboats were practical: she was the first Sound steamer to be built without sails.

These Providence boats were sturdily built, because the trip to Providence required traversing a stretch of open ocean beyond the relatively protected waters of the Sound. The first steamboat accident in the Providence service involved a May 1831 midnight collision off New Haven between *Chancellor Livingston* and *Washington*. The latter boat sank, and one life was lost.

Capt. Mem Sanford introduced the new *Boston* to Providence service in 1831. She was commanded by Capt. William Comstock, who had been captain of *Connecticut* and *Chancellor Livingston* up to the time of the latter boat's violent contact with *Washington. Boston* was also built without sails and masts; it became generally accepted that the "insurance" of sails was no longer required.

1832 saw formation of the new Providence Steamboat Co., with John W. Richmond as President. The Providence firm took over *Boston*, and operated it with the new *Providence.* They "shared" the market with Captain Bunker's *President* and *Franklin*, operating as the "New York and Boston Steamboat Co." *Connecticut* went to Maine in 1833, and *Chancellor Livingston* to Boston, where she was wrecked in 1834. Capt. Elihu Bunker retired from active steamboating in 1835, being named Providence's Government Steamboat Inspector in that year. (Capt. Bunker died in 1847.)

During the next few years, the passenger fares fluctuated between $3.00 and $7.00, depending on the nature and extent of competition on a given day. Most of the service was overnight transportation to and from New York, with land or (slow) canal connections to Boston. Despite two months of non-operation in the summer of 1832, due to a quarantine in New York for cholera, business was good. In fact, the Providence route was preferred by New York-Boston passengers, because it offered the most water mileage. Generally, the passenger lists on all boats were full.

Completion of the Boston & Providence Railroad in 1835 further increased the size of the steamboats' market by providing an overland connection greatly superior to the stages and the canal boats. The two boat lines, however, had little respect for the railroad, mistakenly believing that it was just another connection. The rebuffed railroad officials responded to this indifference by arranging with Commodore Vanderbilt of New York to operate a connecting steamboat. He obliged with *Lexington* (I), lately in Hartford service. *Lexington* operated in day service, connecting with Boston-Providence trains, and made an immediate impression. Her first run to New York, 11-1/2 hours, set a speed record; thereafter, she bit a good-sized chunk out of the market.

By 1836, the two Providence companies had gotten together, operating *Franklin*, *President*, *Providence* and *Boston*, and three new boats of the Class of '36. The newcomers were *Massachusetts* (I) (Capt. Comstock), *Rhode Island* (I) (Capt. Seth Thayer), and *Narragansett* (I) (Capt. Coleman). The new entity was called the Boston and New York Transportation Co., later taking the corporate title of "New Jersey Steam Navigation & Transportation Co." Known familiarly as "The Transportation Company", the firm's first president was Robert

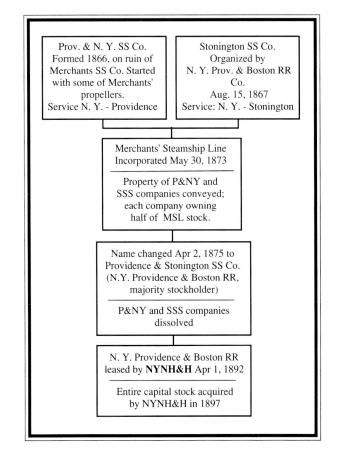

Prov. & N. Y. SS Co. Formed 1866, on ruin of Merchants SS Co. Started with some of Merchants' propellers. Service N. Y. - Providence

Stonington SS Co. Organized by N. Y. Prov. & Boston RR Co. Aug. 15, 1867 Service: N. Y. - Stonington

Merchants' Steamship Line Incorporated May 30, 1873

Property of P&NY and SSS companies conveyed; each company owning half of MSL stock.

Name changed Apr 2, 1875 to Providence & Stonington SS Co. (N.Y. Providence & Boston RR, majority stockholder)

P&NY and SSS companies dissolved

N. Y. Providence & Boston RR leased by **NYNH&H** Apr 1, 1892

Entire capital stock acquired by NYNH&H in 1897

Schuyler, not yet involved with the New York and New Haven Railroad. Under Schuyler and later under C. O. Handy, this company became a major factor in Sound steamboat operations.

Capt. Mem Sanford moved *Bunker Hill* (I) to Providence as an opposition boat operating to New York in 1836; it didn't last. The "Old Line" Transportation Company by then had gotten the message about the future of railroads: their Providence-New York steamboat service was advertised as the "Boston & Providence Railroad Line"; presumably Mr. Schuyler was able to make some mutually satisfactory arrangement with the railroad itself.

The New York, Providence and Boston Railroad, formed in 1832 and controlled in New York, extended from Providence to Stonington CT in 1837, and some steamboat traffic was diverted to the Connecticut port for reasons to be explored later in this chapter. Back in Providence, John Richmond, of the old Providence Steamboat Co., had apparently been left out in the cold by the new Colossus of Narragansett Bay. Providence interests similarly resented Stonington's place in the Transportation Company's plans. Not surprisingly, the Atlantic Steamboat Co. was formed in 1837 and began service in June 1838 with a boat named for her president, *John W. Richmond. John W. Richmond* was faster than any of the Transportation Company's boats; it embarrassed the old company, as

did Vanderbilt's *Lexington* whenever it showed up in Providence. The Railroad Line offered Commodore Vanderbilt $60,000 for *Lexington* if she could beat the upstart *Richmond* in a race. To Cornelius and Jake Vanderbilts' twin furies, *John W. Richmond* actually beat *Lexington*.

But stealth oft overcomes speed; the Transportation Company quietly bought up Atlantic Steamboat Co. stock, and disposed of its competitor by purchase. The Commodore sold *Lexington* to the Transportation Company in 1838, and arranged to amicably share the Stonington market service as well. *Richmond* was almost spitefully removed from the Sound, sold for Boston to Maine service in 1840. She burned in 1843.

### The *Lexington* Disaster

January 13, 1840 became famous in the annals of steamboating; on that below-zero winter night, the celebrated *Lexington* burned and was lost. 150 people died; only four survived.

Jake Vanderbilt was not her master that night. Capt. George Childs was in command, having departed New York at 4 PM on a run to Stonington. Off Huntington, Long Island at about 7 PM, a fire broke out amidships. It spread quickly, partially because *Lexington*'s cargo included quite a few bales of cotton. The helmsman immediately steered toward the Long Island shore as passengers rushed for the four lifeboats. The passengers panicked and jumped into the lifeboats, overloading them. All of the lifeboats were immediately swamped upon entry into the water because of the load, and because the boat was still moving forward toward the shore. Ignorance and panic killed all those

aboard the lifeboats.

Others made rafts from wreckage and sought to endure the icy waters. Despite the fiery beacon that Lexington displayed as it burned, only one ship came by to help. The sloop *Merchant* picked up three of the four survivors from amid the floating

Passes such as the one at the right were quite common before 1905; they were issued by railroads and steamboat companies to employees, large customers, officials of friendly connecting transportation companies, politicians, newspaper editors and reporters; anyone who might do the company some good. Three years later this company would merge with the Stonington Steam Ship Company.

Railroad equipment used for the boat trains was generally the best that the company had. This was particularly true of the Stonington Line, which, like the Norwich & Worcester, sought to compete on the basis of the quality of its accommodations. An unusual example of first-class passenger equipment, shown below, was this English design carriage with compartments instead of the customary American end door and center-aisle design.

The illustrations below are taken from both sides of an advertising card issued by the Providence & Stonington Railroad in the 1850s. It is one of the few such cards that featured the rail portion of the ride rather than the steamboats. The actual size of the original card is 2 $\frac{3}{8}$" x 3 $\frac{7}{8}$".

bodies and wreckage in the Sound. Even in death, *Lexington* lost none of its fame, as color lithographs of the disaster became best-sellers.

Second Mate David Crowley had the most amazing story to tell. He clung to a cotton bale for two days in the frigid Sound, drifting eastward for more than fifty miles. He came ashore, more dead than alive, near Wading River, Long Island. Crowley stumbled to a house near the shore, and collapsed on the front porch. He received care there, and lived long thereafter. He kept the lifesaving bale of cotton as a grim souvenir until the Civil War, when it was made into cloth. The "Lexington" brand of cotton goods, well-known thereafter, was named for the ill-fated steamer.

## "The Old Reliable"

Twelve miles east of New London lies the small harbor of Stonington, CT, partially protected from the ravages of the Atlantic by Fisher's Island. Stonington was and is the easternmost port on Long Island Sound's Connecticut shore. Though small, the town was known for its seafarers, whaling, and West Indies trade sailing ships. Steamboat service between New York and Stonington came about in reverse of the usual order of events: the connecting railroad from Providence was completed (in 1837) before the boats began operation.

Such a service in competition with the Narragansett Bay steamers was feasible because the Rhode-Island-bound boats ventured beyond the shelter of Long Island to the south, out of Long Island Sound and into the heavier waters of the Atlantic Ocean and Block Island Sound. More dangerously, every boat passing out of The Race and into Narragansett Bay was forced to contend with the raging waters and uncertain tides off Point Judith, at the bay's entrance. For every Hell Gate horror story told by a New Yorker, a Narragansett Bay man could relate an equally harrowing tale centered about "P'int Judy".

The Stonington service was planned from the beginning as a rail-boat combination; a steamboat would make the easy run to Stonington, and a fast train would travel the rest of the way to Providence and Boston. The Transportation Company detailed steamers *Rhode Island* (I) and *Narragansett* (I) to Stonington Service, with *Massachusetts* remaining on the Providence run.

An operating cost analysis clearly favored the port of Stonington; it cost only about two-thirds as much to operate a steamboat to Stonington as to go around Point Judith to Providence. The additional railroad mileage costs were far less than the offsetting steamboat savings. The disadvantage in terms of service was that passengers from New York were forced to arise about an hour earlier in the morning to transfer to the connecting train at Stonington.

By the early 1840's, the focus had clearly shifted away from Providence, whose harbor was too shallow for larger boats with more than twelve feet of draft. The westward drift of sand and silt operates in Narragansett Bay as well as the Sound, working against Providence on the western shore and in favor of Fall River on the eastern shore. Providence harbor was dredged out in the early 1870's, far too late to prevent the shift to Stonington and Fall River; by then they had become the ports of choice. Providence was clearly eclipsed as a New York

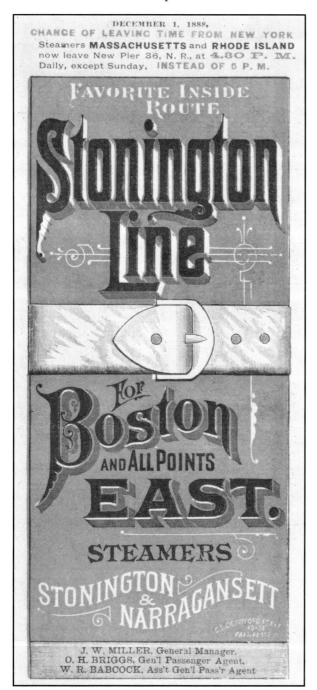

The Stonington Line flyer at left, although produced in 1888, thirteen years after the merger of the Providence and Stonington companies, treats the line as a separate entity. Note the name of Jacob W. Miller as General Manager; Capt. Miller would replace Stephen Gardner as manager of the NYNH&H merged lines to come in less than ten years. *Massachusetts* and *Rhode Island* (II) were running to Stonington because passenger service to Providence had been stopped the month before.

A Boston & Providence Railroad passenger train gets its last-minute inspection, right, before leaving Pleasant Street yard. The Boat Trains were queens of the rails, and their speed and service quality level were no less important than that of the steamboats. Note the three-way stub switch at right, and the "pointing finger" switch position indicator. We must note that pictures of trains meeting steamboats are rare, because such meetings mostly occurred at night.

passenger service terminal when regular service ceased in 1848. Independent operators with smaller vessels tried to offer passenger service at cut-rate fares during the next few years, but only freight steamers remained significant in Providence.

## Enter Drew, Law and Fisk

We have already noted (in Chapter Five) Cornelius Vanderbilt's 1842 disagreement with the New York, Providence & Boston Railroad. The railroad became vulnerable after that; financier and steamboat operator Daniel Drew and the Commodore acquired control in 1845. Drew also became the President of the Transportation Company at that time, and controlled its affairs for twenty years.

George Law placed the fast *Oregon* and *Knickerbocker* into service to Stonington. Drew responded with *C. Vanderbilt* in 1847 and *Commodore* in 1849. Cornelius Vanderbilt is likely to have been involved with both sides of this competitive situation, which was settled when Drew bought *Oregon* in 1848 and moved it to Albany NY. The older *Narragansett* and *Rhode Island* were sold in 1846.

Between 1843 and 1847, Law and Vanderbilt collaborated on a rail-boat-rail service using the Long Island Rail Road to Greenport, steamboat connections to Norwich and to Stonington, with rail service to Worcester and Boston respectively. The steamers were far from state of the art: they were *Cleopatra*, *Worcester*, and *New Haven*. But before you laugh at the service, note that they carried 150,000 passengers the first year, and won a government mail contract. The Long Island was not a "toy" railroad. The Long Island rail-boat-rail link ended only because Law and Vanderbilt desired it to. The Hartford and New Haven Railroad was completed in 1846, and the Fall River Line was in full operation by 1847, so their interests began to lie elsewhere.

*Commonwealth* (I) was moved from Norwich to the Stonington run in 1859, and *Connecticut* (II), normally a New Haven boat, also saw Stonington service. *Plymouth Rock,* built by Vanderbilt in 1854, also provided Stonington Line service until she was stranded and destroyed in 1866. *Connecticut* went to Hudson River service in 1861, but was immediately chartered by the federal government for Civil War duty.

Back in Providence in 1851, Captain William Williams and Benjamin Buffum organized the Commercial Steamship Company, which began operating a trio of small propeller ships in freight service: the *Pelican*, *Petrel*, and *Osceola*. They were the first propeller-driven steamboats in Sound

*Rhode Island* (III) is featured on the Providence & Stonington Bulletin's cover for March 1892. That place of honor would soon be taken by the new *Maine* and *New Hampshire*. The company continued its pattern of naming its large vessels after New England states, as opposed to the Norwich Line's *"City of"* series and the Fall River Line's propensity for names beginning with "P".

While the *Fall River Line Journal* became the best-known house organ in the United States in the late 1800s, the P&S efforts to keep pace were also known for ornate engraving.

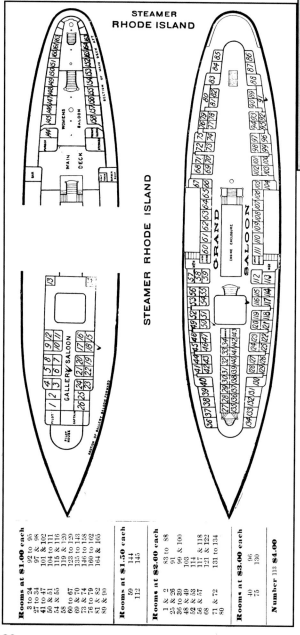

service. *Osprey* was added in 1853, *Curlew* in 1856, and six more ships between 1858 and 1861: *Albatross*, *Penguin*, *Falcon*, *Kingfisher*, *Eagle*, and *Seagull*. Most of their activity centered on Narragansett Bay, with some operation to New York. For a short time, beginning in 1855, Commercial boats operated in passenger service between New York and Stonington. Drew and Buffum made peace; Commercial got out of the passenger business, and the Transportation Company all but withdrew from Narragansett Bay freight service. Neat.

In 1860, with the New York, Providence and Boston railroad extended west to Groton, on the east shore of the Thames across from New London, the steamer-rail transfer point was moved from Stonington to Groton. The Vanderbilt and Drew interests were consolidated into the Merchants' Navigation and Transportation Co. (still known as the "Transportation Company") in 1863.

But the Transportation Company was not to go unopposed. William P. Williams and others formed the Neptune Line from Providence in 1863, taking over assets of the Commercial Line. The Neptune's 1864 propellers *Electra* and *Galatea* operated to Providence, doing much to restore some of Providence's attractiveness as a freight port. *Oceanus*, *Metis*, *Thetis*, *Doris*, *Glaucus*, *Oceanus*, *Nereus*, and *Neptune* came soon after. This was no small operation! But disaster took its toll: *Metis* was lost in an 1872 collision with a schooner, taking 70 lives

*Massachusetts* and *Rhode Island* (II) were the boats that re-instituted Providence service in 1877 after a period of dormancy; it was claimed that they were the first to have their dining rooms on an upper deck rather than in the hold.

*Massachusetts* went aground off Rocky Point, Long Island in October 1877, with $40,000 damage. *Rhode Island* was not so lucky (!) in 1881; she was wrecked at the entrance to Narragansett Bay. We see below a photo of *Rhode Island* (III), built in 1882 using the salvaged engine of *Rhode Island* (II). The hand-me-down engine was replaced in 1890.

Between 1882 and 1889, these two boats plus *Stonington*, which survived its collision with *Narragansett*, held down the service to both Providence and Stonington. That sometimes meant day-night round trips. *Massachusetts* ran aground three times during that period, with relatively minor damage. For its part, *Rhode Island* collided with the Halifax Line's *Alhambra* in July 1882, but was otherwise unharmed.

The Providence & Stonington Line indeed had more than its share of difficulties in trying to compete with the Fall River and Norwich Lines. Perhaps their new boat for 1889, *Connecticut* (III) would change their fortunes. . .

with her. The Neptune Line became part of the Merchants' company in 1866.

Meanwhile, the larger Transportation Company continued to operate the Groton service until December 1865, when a fire destroyed the Groton dock facilities and *Commonwealth* (I), which happened to be in port. That fire, which forced a return to Stonington, was the first blow in a series that crippled the Transportation Company. *Plymouth Rock* was beached and damaged in 1866. Later that year, *Commodore* suffered a similar fate. *Plymouth Rock* was repaired, but *Commodore* was a total loss. Shortly thereafter, the company suspended operations. The Stonington Railroad, which had been sold in 1864 to interests controlled by Jim Fisk, now sued the Merchants' Line for lack of service and won a $15,000 judgment.

The Merchants' Company had two steamships on order, but could not take delivery. The two sumptuous boats, which had cost the Merchants' Company almost $1.5 million, were picked up for $350,000 by financiers Jay Gould and Jim Fisk, operating as the Narragansett Steamship Company, and operated between New York and a new rail connection at Bristol, RI in 1867 and 1868. Jim Fisk emerged as head of the firm; he was to become the most spectacular figure in Sound steamboating.

The Sprague family and other Providence interests picked up some other pieces from the Merchants' failure, forming the Providence and New York Steamship Company in 1866. They also bought the rebuilt *Plymouth Rock* and a few other smaller ex-Neptune Line boats. It may also be noted here that the Merchants' Line and its predecessor Neptune Line had also been operating a direct all-water New York-Boston steamship line, around Cape Cod. When the Merchants' Line went under in 1866, Boston capitalists under Henry Whitney's leadership purchased the outside route remnants, giving birth to the Metropolitan Steamship Line.

The Stonington Railroad, its port bypassed by the Fisk move to Bristol, opened its own steamer service to New York in 1868. The Stonington Steamship Co. used two side-wheelers named *Stonington* and *Narragansett* (II). The Providence & New York Steamship Co., operating a few small freighters, was merged into the Stonington Steamship Co. in 1875 as the Providence & Stonington Steamship Co. Stonington operations continued unchanged, and in 1877, summer service between New York and the newly-dredged Providence harbor was reinstated, using *Rhode Island* (II) and the new *Massachusetts* (II). These boats were said to be the first to have their dining rooms on the main deck, rather than below as with previous vessels.

The battle of the late '70s was between the Narragansett company and the Old Colony Railroad, which is the subject of the next chapter. Suffice it to say here that for a time, the New York-Boston fare was as low as $1.00. Some folks began to think that such competition was ruinous to all; what was needed was some kind of unifying force to bring order, dignity, and profit to a chaotic situation.

The ornate P&S letterhead is shown at left in this 1880 request for a trip pass on a connecting railroad, to be paid for by the P&S. These were much more common than the annual passes, as rewards for favors and business.

*Connecticut* (III), new in 1889, turned out to be a seagoing disaster, speedy and elegant, but unreliable. The Providence & Stonington Line had depended on this fourth large boat (about the same size as the Fall River Line's *Plymouth*) to increase its share of the market in an expanding New England. As it was, the smaller freight boats were the successful and profitable part of the service.

*Connecticut* was a graceful, elegant vessel inside and out; the luxury of her accommodations rivaled those of *Puritan*, her nearest competitor. But her engine was subject to frequent breakdowns, which relegated her to relief boat status almost from the beginning of her life. We shall examine her mechanical problems in greater detail later in this volume.

The pilot house and front cabins below survived, and were turned into a two-story office building in Salem MA; they remained a curiosity for some years.

Maine and New Hampshire represented a change in the P&S operating philosophy. The two boats, new in 1892, were steel-hulled, but were smaller, not larger, than their predecessors. Further, they were configured more for freight than for passengers. The 2-1/2-deck configuration was deemed adequate, although they were only about 80 per cent the size of the Fall River Line's "small" Plymouth, and also smaller than the New Haven Line's Richard Peck.

Maine and New Hampshire appeared just before Richard Peck; Priscilla and City of Lowell came on the scene two years later, in 1894. These two P&S steamboats, therefore, represent the first of the steel propeller passenger boats on the Sound, leaving only the Old Colony/Fall River Line thinking about paddlewheels.

The people of Stonington had reason to be proud of their port area. The boat and rail facilities were considered to be a model of efficiency, compact and well-designed. The view at the lower right shows the tracks diverging toward the various piers and warehouses, and the steamers at rest. And it's all just a block from the Boston Store, a name frequently used by dry-goods merchants in many smaller cities to identify with the fashionable Hub City.

Stonington's steamboat heyday was considerable, but it happened before the turn of the century. The merger of railroads in the 1890s led to unified lines connecting at New London and Providence, making Stonington redundant. By 1904 the only occupants of her piers were boats that were laid up awaiting the call to service, or to the scrapper.

### The *Narragansett* Disaster

June 11, 1880, in a dense fog five miles off Saybrook CT, *Narragansett* was eastbound to Stonington, while her sister ship *Stonington* was westbound to New York. Suddenly, *Stonington*'s bow punctured *Narragansett*, which sank with 30 lives lost. *Stonington* was repaired and put back in service within a month. *Narragansett* was raised and rebuilt; both ships continued in service for a dozen years thereafter.

As a result of the accident, a storm of public censure descended on the Stonington company, the officers and crew, and particularly *Narragansett*'s captain, W. S. Young. In Jersey City's Trinity Methodist Episcopal Church, Pastor R. Harcourt preached on "Lessons from the *Narragansett* Slaughter." During the sermon, the outraged cleric bellowed that "the officers and crew of *Narragansett* undoubtedly are the biggest cowards in existence!" To the amazement of all, the pregnant silence that followed was broken by a deep voice saying, "You're a liar!" The shocked faithful showed their tolerance for dissent in church by hauling the dissenter to the police station, to be charged with disturbing the peace. The man was released when his identity was disclosed as Captain W. S. Young, a Jersey City resident, protecting the reputations of his men in the face of ecclesiastical slander.

More trouble for the Providence & Stonington Line was to come in 1880: *Rhode Island* was wrecked at the entrance to Narragansett Bay on November 6. Her engines were salvaged and placed into *Rhode Island* (III), built in 1882. Three years later, a new freighter named *Nashua* appeared with the first compound oscillating inclined steam engine on the Sound. As such, she was the first vessel without the characteristic walking beam transmitting power to the side wheels. At about this time, the freight boat *Thetis* was rebuilt and renamed *Pequot*. *Nashua* and *Pequot* formed the backbone freight service.

In 1889, *Connecticut* (III) was added to the fleet. Like *Nashua*, she had an oscillating inclined engine. Unlike *Nashua*, *Connecticut*'s engine was less than totally reliable; despite being the newest boat, *Connecticut* became the relief vessel, with *Rhode Island* and *Massachusetts* in regular service to Providence.

The last boats built for the Providence and Stonington Line were the smaller steel vessels *Maine* and *New Hampshire*, both propeller steamers, entering service in 1892. These boats could make the trip from New York to Stonington in less than seven hours. In that same year, the Providence & Stonington company was acquired by the New Haven Railroad.

In contrast to the block lettering that was to come, the P&S Line used relatively fancy scrollwork, as shown on *New Hampshire*'s bow in the early part of her life. And the 1873 model pass, only one year newer than the pass shown earlier in this chapter, features the Providence & New York's ornate engraved insignia.

The Travelers' Official Guide ad on the next page is from May 1897, after NYNH&H control. It shows *Maine* and *New Hampshire* operating to Stonington, with *Massachusetts* and *Rhode Island* in Providence Line service (*Connecticut* having idled in frustration because of her mechanical problems since 1896). Less than two months later, *Plymouth* and *Pilgrim* were moved over from the Fall River Line to handle summer service between New York and Providence, as the four-boat Fall River service was ended (see Chapter 7). In 1898, the NYNH&H established its Marine District to operate the Sound steamboat lines as one system. This ad, therefore, represents the end of P&S service as it had been before the NYNH&H takeover. Capt. Miller was named to head Marine District operations in 1899, and all four of the P&S vessels saw service to various ports thereafter.

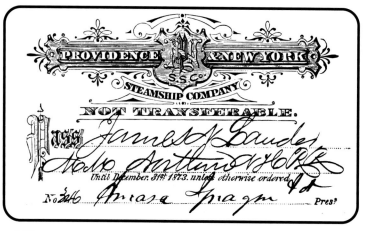

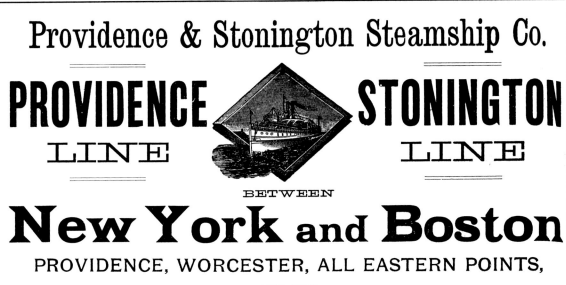

## THE NEWPORT – WICKFORD FERRY

The Newport & Wickford Railroad and Steamboat Co. built a rail spur from the NYP&B main line at Wickford to the Narragansett Bay shore at Wickford Landing, completed in 1871. *Eolus* had begun operating across the Bay between Wickford Landing and Newport in 1870. The service was popular because it allowed "short-cutting" to and from Newport, in preference to traveling all the way around the bay, through Providence. The NYP&B operated the spur as its own, sharing the revenue

with the smaller company. This arrangement was inherited by the NYNH&H when it leased the NYP&B. The line became NYNH&H property at a 1909 foreclosure sale.

*Eolus* operated until 1892, when she was replaced by *Tockwogh*. A former Chesapeake Bay steamer (Sassafras River Steamboat Co.), *Tockwogh* operated on Narragansett Bay for less than a year, burning at Wickford Landing in April 1893. The longest-lived and best known Wickford ferry was *General*, operating from 1893 until 1925.

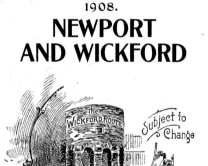

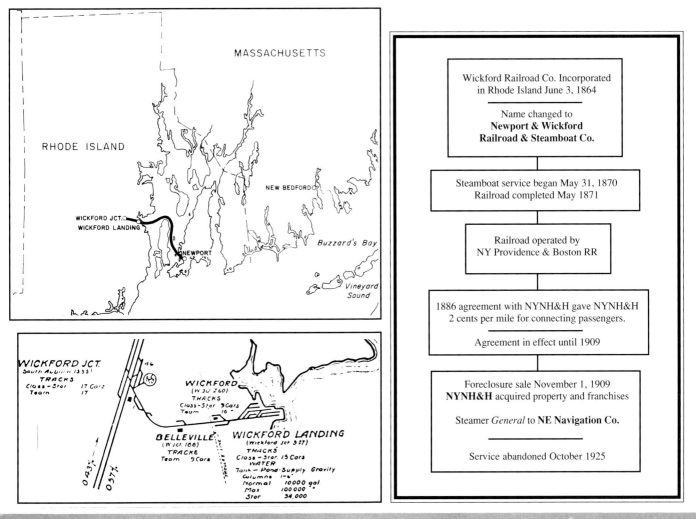

MASSACHUSETTS

RHODE ISLAND

NEW BEDFORD

WICKFORD JCT.
WICKFORD LANDING

NEWPORT

Buzzard's Bay

Vineyard
Sound

WICKFORD JCT.
South Auburn 1355'
TRACKS
Class-Stor    17 Cars
Team          17

WICKFORD
(W Jct 260)
TRACKS
Class-Stor  9 Cars
Team        16

BELLEVILLE
(W Jct 188)
TRACKS
Team   9 Cars

WICKFORD LANDING
(Wickford Jct 337)
TRACKS
Class-Stor  15 Cars
WATER
Tank-Pond-Supply Gravity
Columns  1-6'
Normal   10000 gal
Max      100000 "
Stor     34000

Wickford Railroad Co. Incorporated
in Rhode Island June 3, 1864

Name changed to
**Newport & Wickford
Railroad & Steamboat Co.**

Steamboat service began May 31, 1870
Railroad completed May 1871

Railroad operated by
NY Providence & Boston RR

1886 agreement with NYNH&H gave NYNH&H
2 cents per mile for connecting passengers.

Agreement in effect until 1909

Foreclosure sale November 1, 1909
**NYNH&H** acquired property and franchises

Steamer *General* to **NE Navigation Co.**

Service abandoned October 1925

TOCKWOGH        WICKFORD LINE

179.

That *General* should be passing familiar with the Yacht Club is no accident, as her passenger list (if she had had one) would have included many of its members. She began her life on the Hudson in 1888, joined the Newport & Wickford roster in 1893 (replacing *Tockwogh),* and was sold in 1927 to Charles Dimon of New York for excursion service to Bedloe's Island. *General* was scrapped in 1934.

## THE NEWPORT - JAMESTOWN FERRY

The ferry to Wickford was not the only cross-Bay service to terminate in Newport. *Conanicut,* built in 1886, saw regular service to her namesake island, specifically to Jamestown. The photo shows Jamestown's main street leading toward the ferry dock, in more bucolic times. Note the telegraph office for rapid off-island communications. Note too that the ferry company also operated as a coal dealer on the island, most likely from the same coal supply that fed the ferry's boilers. Highway bridges across the bay, using the island as a steppingstone, eliminated the ferry.

# Chapter Seven

# The Fall River Line

It became a generic term after 1900 for any Long Island Sound passenger steamboat, regardless of its actual destination: "Fall River Liner." But the service and the company that became symbolic of elegant transportation was only one of many enterprises. In its early days at least, the Fall River Line was not immune to competition.

In 1845, ten years after the Boston and Providence linked its namesake cities by rail, a second railroad was completed from Boston to the shores of Narragansett Bay. This was the Fall River Railroad, touching the water at Fall River MA, on the Bay's east shore, and connecting with the Old Colony Railroad at South Braintree for direct service to Boston. Jefferson and Richard Borden were among its incorporators. The Borden name was well-known in Fall River for years, even before Cousin Lizzie's alleged 1892 escapade with an ax.

Another family member, Captain Thomas Borden, who had commanded a Fall River-Providence ferry as far back as 1837, saw the benefits of rail-boat connections. Borden, by the way, is credited with installing the first whistle on a steamboat, on that local ferry. The idea (and the whistle) were borrowed from the Boston & Providence Railroad. The Borden brothers were stockholders in the Fall River railroad, and in 1845 they organized a connecting steamboat service between Fall River and New York, using a leased boat, *Eudora*.

Of all the Long Island Sound boat-rail routes, the Fall River connection had the shortest rail travel time once the steamboat portion of the journey was complete. In comfort terms, it meant that the passenger from New York could sleep latest on the Fall River Line. Even more convenient, the bleary-eyed passenger could tumble off the steamer's gangplank at Fall River and find the Boat Train to Boston right there at the wharf. Those who operate on "automatic pilot" in the mornings can readily understand the advantage. Even with the relatively small *Eudora*, 50,000 passengers were carried via Fall River during the first year of operation.

It could have been any of the Fall River Line boats in this classic pose; in this case, it's *Puritan*, new in 1889, first of the Sound four-deckers, first Sound steamer more than 400 feet long, possessor of the largest walking beam engine ever built and high enough to hide all of the vertical mechanism. Other boats came before and after, and *Priscilla* has become a sentimental favorite, but *Puritan* was the groundbreaker, the pioneer.

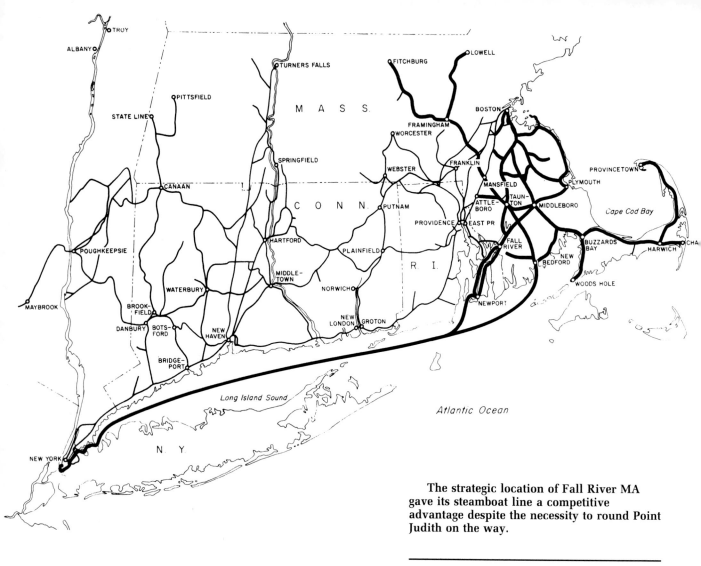

The strategic location of Fall River MA gave its steamboat line a competitive advantage despite the necessity to round Point Judith on the way.

With that level of success, the Bordens organized the Bay State Steamboat Company in 1846. The new company ordered one new boat built for them, naming her *Bay State*. They also chartered *Massachusetts* (I) from the Providence line.

It was May 19, 1847 that *Bay State*, under the command of Capt. Joseph J. Comstock, made her first trip from Fall River to New York, shortly after the arrival of the Boat Train from Boston.

With a 1500-hp engine, the 315-foot *Bay State* was the largest inland steamboat in America. She had cost $175,000 to build. She also had one of the very first steam feed pumps designed and built by one Henry Worthington, whose products and company were to become world-famous. Mr. Worthington later credited Capt. Comstock with having given the new pumps their first chance to prove themselves.

The inevitable occurred on May 20, as *Bay State* left New York. The Stonington Line's *Oregon* just happened to be going in the same direction at the same time, and they did so at the highest possible speed. Of course, this was five years before the

government prohibition of racing. *Bay State* won the race, and the Fall River Line was off to an impressive start. The service was to exist for ninety years, and was to become world-famous.

The Fall River line was very profitable in those years. With the proceeds of immediate prosperity, the Bay State Steamboat Co. contracted for a second boat of their own, to replace the chartered *Massachusetts*. The new *Empire State* arrived in 1848. In 1849, the Bordens bought *State of Maine*, which had been operating in the waters of its namesake state on the Portland-Bangor Line. *State of Maine* was placed into three-a week service between New York and Newport for that summer.

Business continued to grow; a newer, larger vessel was needed. In 1854 *Metropolis* was added to the Fall River Line fleet. Note that *Empire State*, *State of Maine* and *Metropolis* were paid for out of earnings, while the company continued to pay dividends. The idea that customers are more comfortable, psychologically as well as physically, on larger vessels, was one to which the Bordens subscribed. *Metropolis* was believed to be the first

Sound boat with the forward part of her Main Deck fully enclosed; freight was becoming important. At 342 feet long, she was the longest on the Sound, and had the largest engine. Her size was coupled with speed. On June 9, 1855, *Metropolis* made the run from New York to Fall River in an incredible eight hours, twenty-one minutes, establishing a speed record that stood for 52 years. Yet, *Metropolis* served only until 1867 as a line vessel; *Bay State* operated until 1874.

---

At just over 300 feet in length, *Empire State* was not a small boat. Built in 1847 at the Samuel Sneeden yard for the Fall River Line, she was the company's second acquisition, serving as one of the first-line vessels until 1865, when *Newport* replaced her.

Three major mishaps marred her early career. In January 1849, much of her superstructure was destroyed by fire. She had cost $200,000 new; the damage was $120,000. She was rebuilt and operated without incident until July 1856, when one of her boilers exploded while she was en route to New York with 225 passengers aboard. Three crewmembers were scalded to death, another dozen injured. But no passengers' lives were lost.

In May 1856, *Empire State* sank. It's the only time that ever happened to a Fall River boat. It was the same story; inching ahead in a fog, at night, she ran onto the rocks, this time near Sands Point Light. A few minutes later, she was on the bottom, only her saloon deck and above out of water. Ten days later she was raised. After repair, she resumed operation.

*Empire State* was a spare boat until 1876, when she was sold for excursion service. Her first assignment after the Fall River Line was operation between Providence and Philadelphia for the American Centennial. She was destroyed by fire in May 1887 at her dock in Bristol RI.

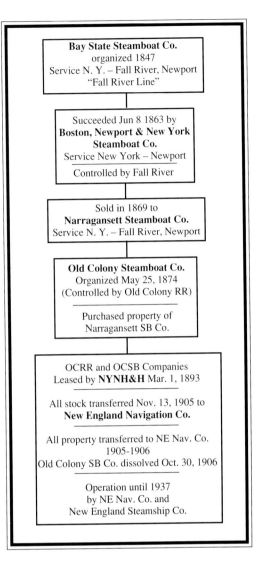

**Bay State Steamboat Co.**
organized 1847
Service N. Y. – Fall River, Newport
"Fall River Line"

Succeeded Jun 8 1863 by
**Boston, Newport & New York Steamboat Co.**
Service New York – Newport

Controlled by Fall River

Sold in 1869 to
**Narragansett Steamboat Co.**
Service N. Y. – Fall River, Newport

**Old Colony Steamboat Co.**
Organized May 25, 1874
(Controlled by Old Colony RR)

Purchased property of
Narragansett SB Co.

OCRR and OCSB Companies
Leased by **NYNH&H** Mar. 1, 1893

All stock transferred Nov. 13, 1905 to
**New England Navigation Co.**

All property transferred to NE Nav. Co.
1905-1906
Old Colony SB Co. dissolved Oct. 30, 1906

Operation until 1937
by NE Nav. Co. and
New England Steamship Co.

## The Old Colony Railroad

The connecting rail link between South Braintree and Boston was provided by the Old Colony Railroad, incorporated in 1844 to build from Boston through South Braintree to Plymouth. As small railroads gradually clumped together into larger concerns, the Old Colony was to be the major survivor in the first phases of railroad consolidation in southeast Massachusetts.

A major contributor to the Old Colony Railroad's early economic health was the Fall River rail connection with its steamboat line. The managers of the Fall River and the Old Colony railroads agreed in 1847 on a division of revenues; by 1852, the Fall River interests had come to believe that the Old Colony was getting by far

To ride the Fall River Line in the 1860s meant riding to Newport, not Fall River. *Newport*, below, was one of the two new boats to arrive during the Civil War. She was easily distinguished by her four smokestacks, one for each guard-mounted boiler.

*Newport* figured in an accident with an unusual vessel in April 1879, when she struck and sank the steamer *Fidelity* in the East River. *Fidelity* belonged to New York's Department of Charities and Corrections. Her primary daily task was making the rounds of the hospitals and prisons clustered on Ward's, Randall's and Blackwell's (Welfare) Islands, acting as a waterborne hearse.

The boats that killed the Old Colony Railroad's Newport service were James Fisk's *Bristol* and *Providence*, running to Bristol. These were the first full three-deck boats. They had been built for the Providence Merchants' Line at a cost of $1.25 million

each, with interiors modeled, it was said, after the elegant boardrooms of the Equitable Assurance Company in New York.

Records indicate that their original names were to have been *Pilgrim* and *Puritan*, but Mr. Fisk changed that. Those names were obviously still worth using, as George Peirce proved later. Jim Fisk bought the boats for $350,000 each after the Merchants' Line went under.

*Bristol* was the luckier of the two vessels during the first part of their lives; only a few minor collisions marred her elegant hull. *Bristol*'s port shaft broke in June 1882. Four months later, her starboard shaft broke.

*Bristol* was reconditioned and refurbished in 1884, including installation of Edison electric lights.

The records indicate that *Providence* was more accident-prone than *Bristol.* Here's a list of some more than trifling incidents:

July 1868: Collision with Harlem River steamboat *Sylvan Grove.*.

April 1869: *Providence* bumped *Narragansett* while both were traversing Hell Gate.

Aug 1871: collided with three schooners in the Sound, paddlebox damaged.

September 1875: collided in East River with *Bolivar*, then in service for New London & Northern.

October 1876: Rudder struck obstruction near Goat Island, broke off.

October 1882: Collided with a government scow involved with hazard removal in the East River. Severe damage; passengers were transferred to *Stonington*.

May 1884: Main shaft broke while approaching Newport dock.

June 1887: Ran aground at Dyer's Island near Bristol, was stuck for ten days. Considerable damage; engine knocked out of alignment, hog frame askew.

September 1888: Collided with and sank steam yacht *Adelaide* near Whitestone.

Clearly, Captain Ben Simmons of *Providence* had a tougher time of it than his nephew Abe Simmons, who commanded *Bristol.* Abe later commanded *Puritan*, and was *Priscilla*'s first master.

In 1885, it was *Providence*'s turn to be reconditioned and her interior refurbished and electrified, whereafter she replaced *Bristol* for winter service. *Bristol* had been running that summer. After 1883, *Bristol* and *Providence* took turns running opposite the newer *Pilgrim*.

# "POWER STEERING"

Manual steamboat steering gear involved not one but as many as three connected steering wheels in the pilothouse, with which as many as six helmsmen would struggle to hold the vessel on course. The task became very difficult in heavy weather.

In 1879, *Providence* was the testing ground for a new steam-assisted steering system, which was eventually fitted to many Sound liners and other ships. A light touch on the wheel caused a steam cylinder to move the rudder. Once the rudder stopped moving, two auxilliary cylinders filled with glycerine held the rudder in the desired position regardless of the action of the sea.

Many Sound pilots, when asked to name the greatest advances in steamboating, placed the steam steering gear at or near the top of their lists. After the *Providence* tests, it became standard equipment.

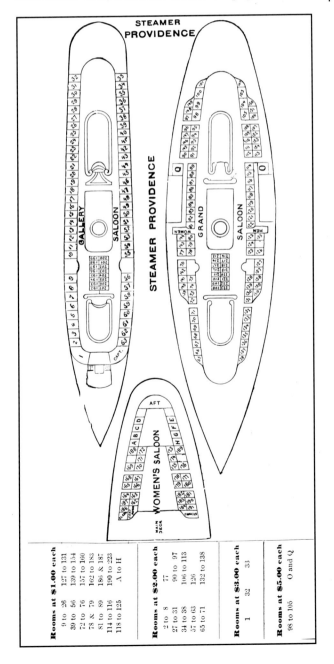

the better of the deal. The resulting dispute was settled in 1854 with the Bordens pulling out of the railroad (but not the steamship line) and the two railroads coming together as the Old Colony and Fall River Railroad.

These railroads were Massachusetts companies. In neighboring Rhode Island, the Old Colony interests funded a rail line from Newport to Fall River. Alarmed by the prospect of Fall River becoming a way station, and not too fond of the Old Colony managers in the first place, the Bordens did all they could to hinder the Old Colony's efforts to build through Fall River. The Newport line was finished in 1862, at considerably greater expense than the Old Colony had at first estimated. For one thing, the Old Colony Railroad now owned a steamboat line, having bought out the Bordens in a liberal settlement of their disputes.

The Old Colony's Boston, Newport & New York Steamboat Co. almost immediately began using Newport rather than Fall River as their steamboat terminal. Two new boats entered service in 1865, *Old Colony* and *Newport*. They replaced *Bay State* and *Empire State* as the main boats. A new rail line via Taunton was also built; it sliced fifteen minutes from the boat trains' running time. But whatever pleasure the Old Colony folks may have had in rendering the Borden's home town a way station faded a few years later in light of the realities of the marketplace.

## The "Admiral"

Jim Fisk, a onetime Brattleboro, Vermont peddler, had become by 1861 a star salesman and junior partner in the Boston dry goods firm of Jordan Marsh & Co. Anxious for larger action, Fisk ventured to Wall Street, where he gained the confidence of financier Daniel Drew, and helped to engineer a number of profitable transactions, some of them related to the Erie Railroad. Fisk achieved considerable notoriety as well as wealth. One distinction consistent with his vanity was his rank as Colonel of a New York army regiment, a rank gained not by military acumen but by meeting the regiment's annual deficits. To this he added the rank of "Admiral", not because of nautical skill but through stock ownership in the Narragansett Steamship Company.

As noted in Chapter Six, Jim Fisk and Jay Gould's Narragansett company picked up two sumptuous steamers for $350,000 from the wreckage of the Merchants' Line failure. These boats, named *Bristol* and *Providence*, operated between New York and their rail connection at Bristol RI in 1867 and 1868.

From the twin standpoints of convenience and elegance, the Fisk boats were clearly superior to the Old Colony's Newport steamers. It also became

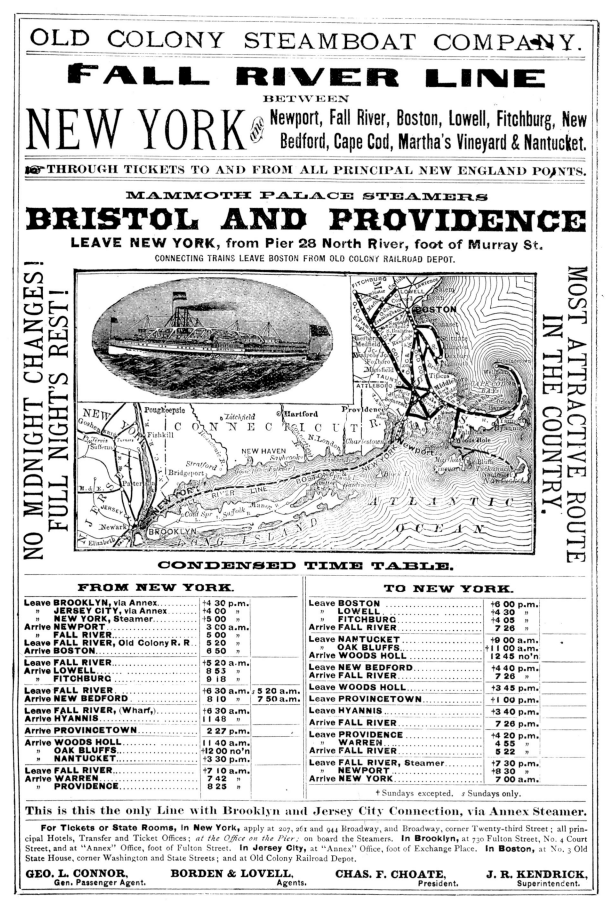

The timetable advertisement at left dates from 1881, when the "Mammoth Palace Steamers *Bristol* and *Providence*" were hailed as the finest afloat. The Old Colony Railroad provided connecting trains not only to Boston but to other points on its routes as well. The Old Colony steamers to Nantucket and Martha's Vineyard were also featured.

But note on the map the curious total absence of railroads in the states of Connecticut and Rhode Island; part of the advertising artist's skill, then as now, was not to confuse potential customers with too many facts about the competition. You may want to compare this ad with the Norwich Line insertion reproduced in Chapter Five. We should also note that even at this late date, the Borden name had not altogether vanished from the Fall River Line roster.

As the timetable notes, Fall River Line steamers departed from Pier 28 North River. Had you been at the foot of Murray Street in the 1880s or 1890s, a sight such as the one above would have greeted you. Freight is being delivered for loading aboard the steamer, workers and early bird passengers are passing the time and, as the overpowering utility pole suggests, electric lighting and telegraphy were becoming more and more popular on land as well as on the boats.

clear that the passengers considered Newport to be an unattractive transfer point, because the earlier docking time, between 3:00 and 4:00 AM, shortened their slumber on the boats before making the transfer to the train for Boston. Fisk's Bristol boats had a later transfer time, and consequently picked up an increasing share of the travelers.

Then too, *Bristol* and *Providence* were clearly superior to anything on the Sound. With 220 staterooms apiece, they could each comfortably handle more than 1200 passengers per trip, with room left over for the equivalent of 40 railroad cars of freight. Fisk's promotional talents also helped the "Palace Steamers" to become popular with travelers in a period of intense steamboat competition.

In 1867 and 1868, five different competing Sound steamer services were available to a traveler between New York and Boston, through the intermediate ports (from left to right) of Norwich, Stonington, Providence, Bristol and Newport. The first casualty was the Newport Line, and in 1869 the Old Colony Railroad sold its boats to Fisk's Narragansett firm. The agreement also called for abandonment of the Bristol connection so that the Old Colony could continue to have the rail connection traffic. A practical reason for moving out of Bristol was the fact that Bristol's channel was a relatively hazardous place for the large "palace" boats.

Fisk corrected the Old Colony's marketing mistake and moved the line's passenger terminal (but not its shops) back to Fall River in 1869. A stop at Newport continued to be made en route, however; the town was developing into a posh summer resort, and thus had become an important destination for passengers.

The Old Colony Railroad, a quite profitable firm, had made a wise decision; Fisk was the best promoter of steamboat service on the Sound, and the railroad's Fall River-Boston traffic grew. Now, in 1869, the Fisk boats *Bristol* and *Providence* became the premier boats of the reconstituted Fall River Line. The steamers had been renovated and decorated in elegant style. Their kitchen and dining operation compared well to the service in first-class hotels anywhere. Band and orchestra concerts provided entertainment during the evening hours of each voyage. The atmosphere was considerably more exciting than any available on a competing route, land or water.

The operating pattern in that era called for *Bristol* under Captain Abe Simmons, and *Providence* under Captain Ben Simmons (Abe's uncle), to run between New York and Fall River on alternate days. *Old Colony* and *Newport* supplemented the service during the summer season, operating between New York and Newport. During the winter months when only the two larger boats operated, they made an intermediate stop at Newport.

Jim Fisk's pride was evident on most evenings as the Fall River steamer prepared to depart from its New York dock. From the first time he appeared resplendent in a custom-tailored Admiral's uniform to greet "his" passengers, Mr. Fisk caused a stir. The Fall River officers and crews received smart new uniforms with appropriate badges of rank and department. The Admiral clearly understood the importance of what we today call "image" in marketing. The Fall River Line became the "only way to travel" between New York and New England.

Jim Fisk added *Plymouth Rock* to his fleet in 1870; before entering service, she was refurbished in the same elegant style, but she spent most of her time on Hudson River and New Jersey runs. Inasmuch as Fisk also controlled the Erie Railroad with its tugs, lighters and ferries, during this era, Mr. Fisk's position as master of a fleet, if not his marine knowledge, could be considered equivalent to that of any military admiral.

One uniform designed by Fisk was filled out quite differently from all the others. This provocative naval number adorned one Josie Mansfield, actress and companion to Fisk at the New York gangplank, and reportedly Fisk's companion in more congenial and private locations as well. (The lawful Mrs. Lucy Fisk was ensconced in a Boston

The trains of the Old Colony Railroad were essential to the Fall River Line's success. Even with its nine million textile spindles, Fall River MA was not a heavy travel destination.

The photo above shows a typical Boston-Fall River Boat Train consist, heavy on parlor cars with plush interiors like the one depicted at the left. The connecting trains to other points (see preceding pages) were more utilitarian.

But between 1865 and 1895, the Fall River Boat Train from Boston was best known not for locomotives like *Dorchester* No. 110, or its parlor cars. The Boat Train's prime ornament was her conductor, one Asa Porter, whose instinct for customer relations was unsurpassed. He knew the names and habits of a surprisingly large number of his customers, and they remembered him. In fact, during the more than 30 years that he supervised the Boat Train, many of the Fall River Line's passengers referred to their conveyance as "Mr. Porter's Train," because of his personality and service level.

mansion at the time.) The Admiral became known as "Jubilee Jim" Fisk, because of the stir he created at the Boston Peace Jubilee in 1869. He accompanied President Grant to the event, but his Admiral's uniform stole the show. Entertaining the mighty was a frequent pastime for Fisk, who also was liberal with largesse upon employees and others who took his fancy. In an era of skinflints, the sometimes foolishly generous and lavish Fisk belied the stereotype of his Vermont ancestry.

The Fall River Line even figured in a Jay Gould plot to corner the gold market. President Grant's brother-in-law was in on the scheme, but for the plot to succeed it was necessary to find out whether or not the Treasury would sell gold to break the corner. Messrs. Gould and Fisk royally entertained the President aboard *Providence* on a trip to Boston, but Mr. Grant disclosed nothing. Eventually, the Treasury did sell gold, and the Boys lost quite a bit of money.

FALL RIVER LINE.

MAMMOTH IRON STEAMER "PILGRIM"

COMMANDER B.M. SIMMONS

One of the Fleet forming the Fall River Line, the great Long Island Sound route between New York and Boston via Newport & Fall River

GEO. PEIRCE, SUPERVISOR OF STEAMERS

### THE STEAMER *PILGRIM*

*Pilgrim* became known as the "Iron Monarch of the Sound," as much of an improvement over her predecessors in the 1880s as the Boeing 707 was to be in the 1950s. In the print above, she is flanked by another 1883 boat, the freighter *City of Fall River*.

Ben Simmons moved up from *Providence* to become her commander, and had considerably better luck with *Pilgrim*. Her most damaging incident in early years was violent contact with a reef at 19th Street in the East River, which tore a 100-foot long hole in her outer hull. The double bottom saved her.

We mentioned the breakage of the main shafts of *Bristol* and *Providence* a few pages back; this was no small matter. For a better idea of the sizes and weights that are involved, here are illustrations of *Pilgrim*'s main shafts, to which the paddlewheels are mounted. At left, a half-shaft delivered on a flat car, almost 40 feet long and 27 inches in diameter, with a weight of 34 tons. Above, two views of the forging process.

Having conquered Boston commerce, Wall Street, the Erie Railroad, New England steamboating, and some parts of New York Society, the onetime peddler reveled in the world's limelight. But sweet Josie proved fickle, according to Those Who Knew. She began dividing her affections between Fisk and the scion of a wealthy Brooklyn family named Edward Stokes. The love triangle was the stuff on which journalists (and lawyers) thrive. It ended for Mr. Fisk in January 1872, when young Stokes came up behind the Admiral on the grand staircase of New York's Broadway Central Hotel and shot him. Jim Fisk died the next day, at age 37. His extravagant funeral was the final echo of his celebrity status, and a short-lived era, reminiscent of a financial roman candle, ended.

### The Old Colony Steamboat Co.

With Jim Fisk dead, financier Jay Gould became president of the Fall River Line. The rock-ribbed Boston-based management of the Old Colony Railroad was concerned about Gould; he had, after all, wrecked the Erie Railroad, and was considered a business partner of questionable virtue. The fact that the Ames brothers, Oakes and Oliver, members of the Old Colony Railroad board, had been involved in the Union Pacific-Credit Mobilier scandal, was brushed aside; Mr. Gould was just not thought to be a proper partner for the Bostonians.

For his part, Mr. Gould did not share the Fisk fascination for steamboats; he sold the Fall River

---

*Pilgrim* was off to an inauspicious start at her launch; on July 13, 1882 she was launched, broadside rather than with the more familiar backwards slide. The large iron hull slammed into the Delaware river; the water moved aside, but the mud did not. More than a week elapsed while the best shipbuilding minds in America figured out how to get *Pilgrim* loose.


The accompanying side and end views of *Pilgrim*'s engine provide a reasonably clear exposition of the walking beam engine used in many steamboats. Steam is admitted alternately to the top and bottom of the large cylinder (110 inch diameter or bore in *Pilgrim*) at the left of the side view causing the piston to move up and down. (Moving distance or stroke was 14 feet in *Pilgrim*.) That motion causes the diamond-shaped beam to rock, which in turn moves the other shaft at the right and turns the crank. The paddlewheels are connected to the crank by means of the thick shafts we saw on the previous pages.

The motion of the walking beam (the diamond-shaped structure, which alone weighed 33 tons on *Pilgrim*) also moves an auxiliary rod which actuates the valves that admit and exhaust steam at the top and bottom of the cylinder.

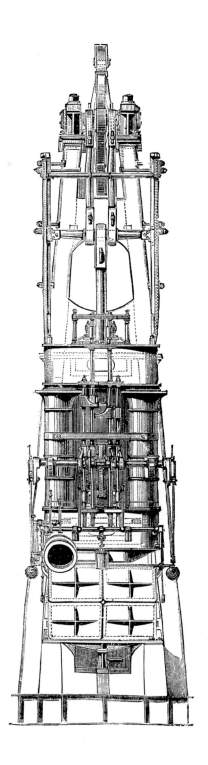

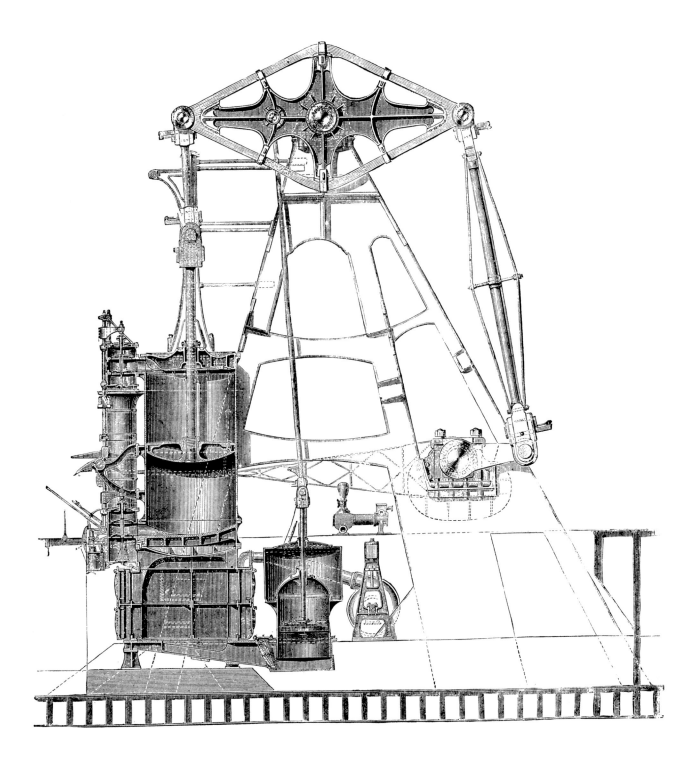

John Roach.  Walking-beam of the Pilgrim.  The Pilgrim.  The Peking.  Shipyard at Chester, Pa.

## SHIP-BUILDING WORKS OF JOHN ROACH & SONS.

John Roach became a leading citizen of Chester PA because of his Delaware River Iron Works, a pioneer in iron ship construction. He also owned the Etna Iron Works and the Morgan Iron Works, builders of steamboat engines, working closely with the firm of W. A. Fletcher. The montage at left shows his yard, two of his products *circa* 1883, and the scale of *Pilgrim*'s massive walking beam.

In later years, the yard would be known as the Delaware River Shipbuilding Co., then part of Cramp's, but it was John Roach, immigrant from Ireland, who made a shipbuilding town out of Chester; from the facility Mr. Roach started came *Pilgrim*, *Puritan*, *Priscilla* and later, *Commonwealth*.

Old Colony Steamboat Co.

Pass Mr. *G. Hoagland Foster* and Lady

ON THE TRIAL TRIP OF THE

◆✦◆ STEAMER "PILGRIM." ◆✦◆

THURSDAY, JUNE 14, 1883.

NOT TRANSFERABLE.

PLEASE SURRENDER THIS AT GANGWAY.

*J.R.Kendrick*
General Manager.

Line to the Old Colony Railroad in 1874, and the railroad formed the Old Colony Steamboat Co. to operate the fleet. The Old Colony acquired the New Bedford boats (see Chapter Eight) two years later.

The elegant service standards on the Fall River steamboats diminished only slightly with the passing of "Jubilee Jim;" the patronage continued to grow. Some 1879 figures indicate that the Old Colony boats carried an average of 400 people per night both ways. This compared favorably with the Norwich Line's 250-275 passengers. The 1879 trains carried fewer than 100 passengers, but during the next few years the trains would increase their market share as a result of (a) the bridge at New London; and (b) electric lighting on the trains.

The photo at top right shows the Newport facilities of the Old Colony steamboat operation, which was selected by the NYNH&H as the main shop facility for the consolidated lines. *Pilgrim* is currently in residence. It is also in one of these slips that *Bristol* burned on December 30, 1888, an incident detailed later in this chapter.

During the period of *Pilgrim*'s operation, 1883 to 1912, there were still many commercial sailing vessels in New York harbor. Many of these were less than stringent about displaying proper lights at night, or rules of the road; yet the law gave them the right of way over steamboats. Fall River Line captains sometimes thought of their job as "dodging schooners."

The new boat did ride a bit lower in the water than the other earlier and later Fall River Line steel boats. It was thought that this happened because *Pilgrim* was originally intended to be 25 feet longer. When the length was literally removed from the design because of concern for her maneuverability in the East River, it was removed from the middle of the hull. Since midships is the most buoyant part of a vessel, *Pilgrim* sank just a bit. Concern for maneuverability turned out to be unnecessary, as *Puritan* and later boats proved.

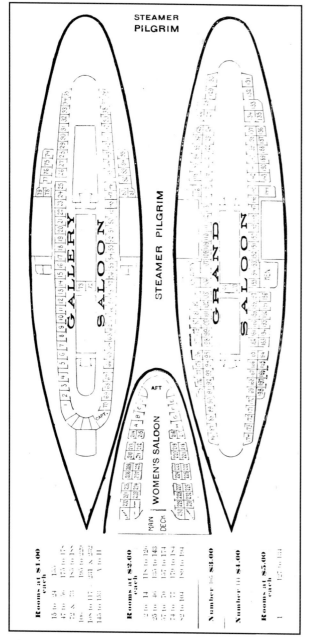

128

UNITED STATES OF AMERICA

OLD COLONY STEAMBOAT COMPANY

*This is to Certify that for value received, the Old Colony Steamboat Company will pay to _____ or assigns the sum of _____ Thousand Dollars at the Treasurer's office of said company in the City of Boston on the first day of January 1896, unless sooner redeemed under provisions set forth below with interest at six per cent per annum payable January first and July first. This Bond is redeemable at the pleasure of the Old Colony Steamboat Company at any time after the first day of January A.D. Eighteen hundred and ninety one. This Bond is authorized by a vote of the Directors of the Old Colony Steamboat Company and is transferable only at the office of its Treasurer.*

We certify that this Bond is approved, issued and recorded on the Books of the Corporation.

Boston, _____ 188__

PRESIDENT.

TREASURER.

STATE OF MASSACHUSETTS

In 1881, the Old Colony let contracts for a new steamboat, to be called *Pilgrim*. She was the first Fall River Line boat to be designed by George Peirce, the line's Superintendent of Steamers since 1878. To say that George Peirce revolutionized steamboat design is not an exaggeration; his boats contained innovations that changed the way things were done thereafter. For example, the 390-foot *Pilgrim* was an iron-hulled boat. She was not the first iron-hulled boat on the Sound (that having been the Norwich Line's *City of Lawrence*) but *Pilgrim* was the first American vessel to have a double-hull iron construction with watertight compartments to improve flotation.

When she hit an uncharted rock in 1884 and opened a 100-foot hole in her iron hull, watertight compartments and bulkheads allowed *Pilgrim* to get to port unaided, even with that serious wound. J. Howland Gardner, George Peirce's understudy and successor, was later to state, "No other American passenger or freight vessel of that date could have remained afloat under such conditions."

*Pilgrim* went into service in June 1883; she immediately became the center of much attention and wonderment. Her iron hull, and size, and elegance were significant, yes; but the greatest single attraction was Mr. Edison's miracle. Gas and oil lamps were still the means by which the world survived the night. Note, for comparison, that the White House was not wired for electricity until 1891.

While the early steamers had been paid for out of earnings, there were some Old Colony Steamboat Company bonds on the market in the 1880s to help finance the new steel-hulled vessels and other improvements. The line's profitability made them gilt-edged investments.

In the ABC Pathfinder Guide for April 1888, this Fall River Line timetable shows the two-boat service just before the summer season, with *Pilgrim* and *Providence* holding down the schedule. Note the fare reduction from the standard $5.00; were the Providence & Stonington or Norwich Line lowering rates and causing trouble?

*Bristol* and *Old Colony* would soon be joining the winter boats for the four-boat summer season. *Puritan* would be along in 1889, *Newport* had been scrapped in 1885; and although nobody knew it at the time, this would be *Bristol*'s last summer.

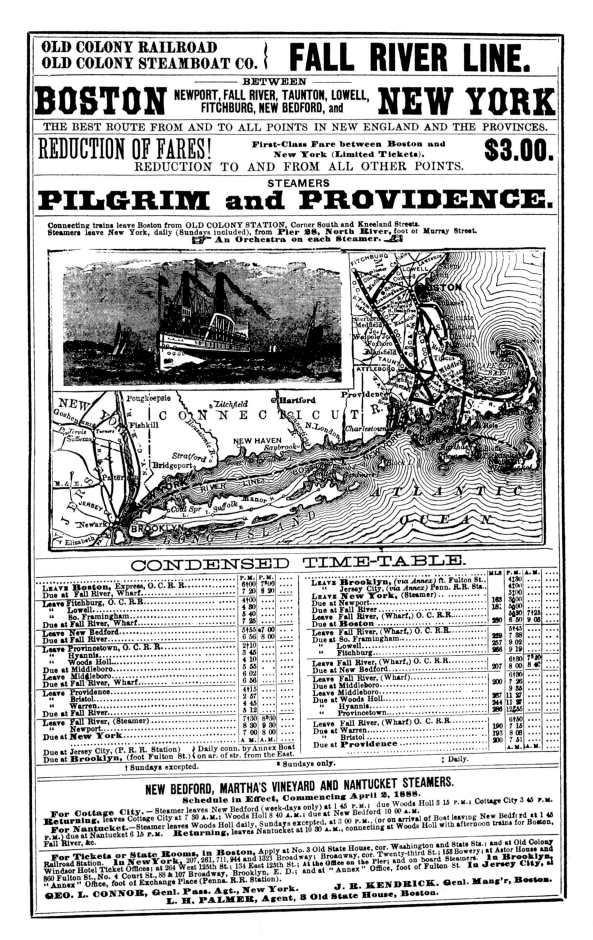

## THE STEAMER *CITY OF FALL RIVER*

The freight boats were the unsung heroes of Long Island Sound steamboating; nobody ever called one of them the "Queen of the Sound." Yet, not only were they vital parts of the service, they were also used to try out new concepts or apparatus.

The best single example of that is the freighter *City of Fall River*, built in 1883. George Peirce designed her with no less care than that lavished on a passenger steamboat, and he used her as a test site for at least two concepts being considered for a forthcoming large liner, and seen in *Puritan* and later boats.

First, the compound engine, wherein steam is used twice between boiler and exhaust. The compound engines required large amounts of steam, which meant larger boilers. These had to be located fore and aft of the engine rather than side by side.

Second, the feathering paddle wheel buckets. The illustration below shows Mr. Peirce's wheel, with paddles that feather much like oars in the hands of an experienced crew.

Also shown is a drawing of the *City of Fall River*'s steam steering mechanism.

4. Steering Gear and Freight Deck.     2. Feathering Paddlewheel and Engine Connections.     3. Engine Room.

**NEW FREIGHT STEAMER CITY OF FALL RIVER.**

While electric lighting systems had been added to a few other boats before 1883, *Pilgrim* was the first large steamboat to be built with an electric lighting system as original equipment; 1000 bulbs lit the boat. Mr. Peirce courageously refused even to allow gas lighting aboard as a backup should the infant technology prove unreliable. Mr. Edison made the installation, and that was that.

Other electrical apparatus included the first automatic fire alarm system on a steamboat, with electric bells activated by thermostatic sensors; and an electric watchman station detection system. *Pilgrim* was also the first Sound steamer to have a specially trained lifesaving crew, the dormitory for which was on the top deck, near the lifeboats. An electric bell actuated from the pilothouse called this crew into action.

The next new boats of which Mr. Peirce was architect were three freighters, *City of Fall River* (1883), *City of Brockton* (1886), and *City of Taunton* (1892). And while the Providence and Stonington Line experimented with screw propulsion and oscillating steam engines (see Chapter 6), Mr. Peirce stayed a bit longer with the reliable if old-fashioned walking beam power plants.

Not that Mr. Peirce was old-fashioned. Born in 1829, he had begun his career by helping his father build sailing ships in Portsmouth NH, and had been ridiculed by his father for advocating the possibility of metal boats. Before the Civil War, he built railroads in the South; the war robbed him of his investment. He then worked on building U. S. Navy vessels at Portsmouth.

The 1869 Peace Jubilee at Boston (at which Jim Fisk got his nickname) involved building a large wooden structure for the concerts, to hold an audience of 50,000, a chorus of 10,000 and an orchestra of 1,000. When asked his opinion of the ampitheatre's design, Mr. Peirce said,"It'll fall down." The builders disregarded his advice and went ahead, for the changes Mr. Peirce recommended would have added to the cost.

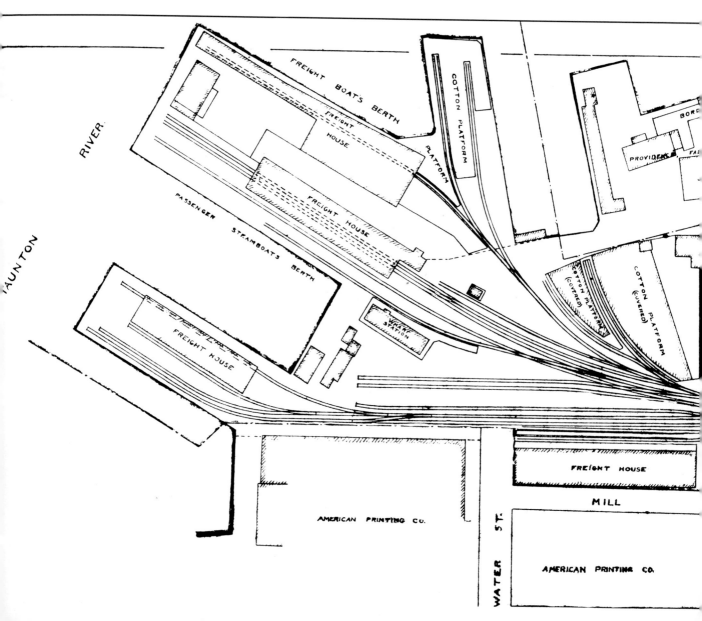

At the right, a diagram of the rail extension from Fall River to Newport RI, showing facilities as they existed in later years. There were, of course, railroad spurs to the steamboat shops as well as tracks to the piers.

The map below shows the area of the wharf at Fall River MA, including the railroad connection. The separate freight pier was used by the freight boats; the primary features were the large freight sheds. The volume of cotton transported to Fall River's mills is hinted at by the special "cotton platform." Fall River Iron Works was another early Borden family company.

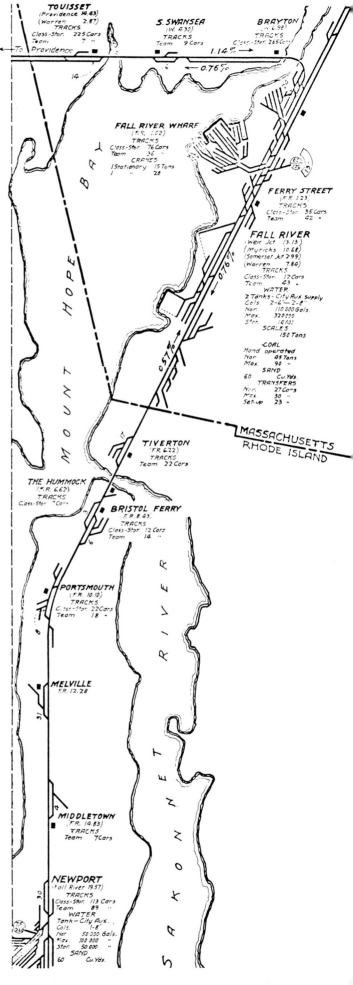

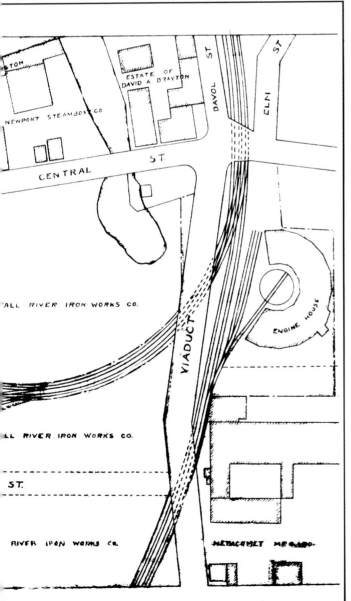

During construction, the building fell down. Whereupon Mr. Peirce was retained to build a proper building. From there, he went into his own shipbuilding firm. In 1878 he accepted the Old Colony Steamboat's offer to join them as Master Mechanic, from which he rapidly moved to General Supervisor of Steamers, which position he held until his death.

Captain Stephen Ayrault Gardner, who among other things had commanded a sailing ship in China trade and served as a Connecticut state senator, came from the Norwich Line to the Old Colony Steamboat Co. as Superintendent during that period. He later headed all of the NYNH&H steamboat operations, until his death in 1899. Even when faced with the success of the competition's *Richard Peck* in 1892, he and Mr. Peirce resisted the trend away from paddlewheel boats because the paddlers were more maneuverable, particularly in reverse. The shallow approach to Fall River was also a consideration. As one shipbuilder's representative was reported as saying, "The Fall River Line wants a four-story hotel with shallow draft, and you can't do that with a propeller."

But the Fall River Line after 1883 had a more pressing operating and marketing problem: business was improving rapidly as New England grew and industrialized. In 1886, the first schedule with two boats in the same direction each day was introduced; *Pilgrim* and *Providence* operated as a pair, with *Bristol* and *Old Colony* running opposite. But *Pilgrim* was considerably larger than *Old Colony*, which caused an imbalance in available space every other day. Management authorized Mr. Peirce to design and build another large boat.

George Peirce was more than ready to do so, and to build the largest steamer that had yet served on the Sound. This vessel would be considerably different from the wooden freight boats (which did not justify the greater cost of steel hulls). He had been working on two major improvements, the compound beam engine and the feathering paddle wheel.

The first rigid radial paddle wheels had what amounted to boards fastened across the spokes of two parallel wheels, in a fixed position as they entered and exited the water. But an experienced oarsman varies the angle of his oars by twisting

Another view of the facilities at Newport, with what appears to be the *City of New Bedford* at the wharf. The sign on the fence at right center says "Fall River Line to New York." The marriage of railroad with its roundhouse for locomotive service, and steamship facilities, is clearly shown.

At right the Official Timetables of the Old Colony system, featuring its primary link to New York in 1890. At this time, Old Colony was one of three large railroad systems in New England, and perhaps the most solid and profitable of the three. The OCRR controlled traffic south of Boston and throughout the industrialized sections of eastern Massachusetts. Its two steamboat lines to New York, from Fall River and New Bedford, gave it access to the west without total dependence on the New York and New Haven rails.

Below, *City of Fall River* salutes the Statue of Liberty while carrying many carloads of freight. While the palatial passenger steamers got the attention, it was the smaller freighters operating to Fall River and New Bedford that went a long way to making the Old Colony profitable.

# OLD COLONY RAILROAD SYSTEM

## Official Time Tables

FOR

## PASSENGER TRAINS

Corrected to JUNE 29, 1890.

BOSTON STATIONS:

KNEELAND STREET, - - - CENTRAL AND CAPE COD DIVISIONS
PARK SQUARE, - - - - PROVIDENCE DIVISION
KNEELAND STREET, - - - (B. & A. R.R.), NORTHERN DIVISION

KENDRICK, Gen'l Manager.     GEO. L. CONNOR, Gen'l Pass'r Agent.

Fire claimed one former and one active Fall River Line boat in 1887 and 1888. Loss by fire of wooden-hulled steamboats was nothing new, of course, beginning with *Lexington* in 1840. Stronger boilers and taller stacks reduced those hazards, but galleys were still a problem.

Above, the charred and twisted remains of *Empire State* after she burned at her Bristol RI dock in May 1887. The 40-year old boat had been sold by the Old Colony Steamboat Co. in 1878, and was in use as an excursion boat. The reports of her fire do not mention injuries.

them to offer less resistance when entering and leaving the water, and maximum push while in the water. This action is called "feathering."

George Peirce wanted to install a mechanical linkage that could do the same thing for the buckets on a paddlewheel. The more efficient wheel that resulted could be smaller and yet deliver the same thrust; a smaller wheel could revolve faster and provide more speed. But before committing a new passenger vessel to such an innovation, Mr. Peirce used the new *City of Fall River* as the test bed. She was equipped with the new feathering wheels; after tests and engineering refinements, the design was ready to be incorporated into a passenger steamer. There was, in Mr. Peirce's mind, more than mechanical improvement to be gained; gone would be the obvious and ornamented paddle-wheel enclosures; with a new feathering bucket sidewheel design, the wheel could be smaller, and could be tucked between rows of staterooms to smooth the lines of the ship. The smaller wheel also meant more staterooms.

---

**After the 1888 summer season, *Bristol* continued to operate for part of the winter. At 2:30 on the morning of Sunday, December 30, 1888, she arrived at Newport from New York; it was to be her last trip of the season.**

**Most of her passengers had gone ashore before a kettle of fat boiled over in her galley at about 6:30 AM. The alarm sounded, everybody scrambled off the boat in varying stages of undress, and the Newport fire department responded to fight the blaze along with *Bristol*'s crew. But the superstructure was dry and the wind brisk; the fire quickly became an inferno, engulfing the vessel. From the city it appeared that the sun was somehow rising in the west that morning.**

**By 8:30 AM, *Bristol* had burned to the waterline, The photo at the left shows the result. Another problem, no less serious, was that *Pilgrim* was in the slip to the south of *Bristol*, and the fire almost spread to the Iron Monarch's wooden superstructure. Had the wind not been blowing from the south, the Fall River Line could have lost two boats that morning. Perhaps three; *City of New Bedford* was in the slip to the north.**

**No lives were lost, and no one was seriously injured. The Old Colony Steamboat Company suffered a $500,000 loss (insured for $300,000), and the Newport papers called the blaze the "greatest fire in the history of the City of Newport."**

**Given the fact that Bristol burned to the waterline, you may be asked, "How did the paddleboxes survive?" The answer is, that those boxes had become so impregnated with salt over the years, that they resisted the flames even as all was collapsing around them.**

*Pilgrim*'s innovative running mate appeared in 1889, and used the second of the two "leftover" names; she was christened *Puritan*. The new boat had the first steel hull (as opposed to iron) on the Sound, measured 420 feet in length, and was registered at 4600 tons. Built at a cost of $1.25 million, she carried out the Old Colony's desire to operate the finest steamboats on the Sound.

Although *Puritan* had the last walking beam engine on the Fall River Line, her design was a

---

Below, the Fall River Line's executive letterhead in 1880 featured a miniature of a brochure's front cover. We can only speculate about the letter's ominous contents.

# THE STEAMER *PURITAN*

The new "Iron Monarch" of 1889 was the object of much attention within the shipbuilding and steamboat industry, as well as the general public.

Like *Pilgrim*, she had a double hull, this one of steel, fabricated by John Roach's Chester PA shipyard; and a walking beam engine built by the W. and A. Fletcher Co.

*Puritan* cost $1.25 million, and was designed to carry 800 passengers and a crew of 224; her passenger and crew sleeping accommodations were:

306 staterooms, 15 parlor bedrooms

629 berths in the 321 rooms

212 free berths in general cabins

123 free berths, immigrant quarters

964 berths total

The General Electric lighting system was used; one of GE's young men was to be Charles Peirce, George's son. *Puritan* turned out to be very much a family affair; at her launching, she was christened by Miss Rebecca Fales of Newport. And what was Miss Fales' connection with the new steamer? She was the fiancée of Charles Peirce.

*Puritan*'s first day on the job was June 18, 1889, after the start of the summer season. She proved herself immediately to be a fast and luxurious boat. On Christmas Eve 1890 she made the run from New York to Newport in 7 hours 54 minutes, breaking all records.

---

The East River ferry *Farragut* is coming from Brooklyn to Manhattan as *Puritan* heads for Fall River.

At right, a set of plans for each deck of *Puritan*, in descending order, along with a side elevation. The walking beam hides behind the cupola aft of the stacks on the Dome Deck. Note too that the paddlewheels, 35 feet in diameter, do not protrude up into the Gallery Deck, nor is there a great semicircular paddlebox enclosure on the side. George Peirce designed her to have graceful, uninterrupted lines; the paddlewheels hide behind false "windows" on the saloon deck.

Dome deck: A is the wheelhouse; B denotes staircases. C locates the Band quarters, D the quarters for the lifesaving crew.

Gallery deck: virtually all rooms, with rooms C through K for officers and officials.

Saloon deck: staterooms (P) clustered around the central room. The location of the walking beam engine is shown by the letters H, I, and J. The boilers are under the forward enclosure. The main lavatory facilities are located forward of the paddlewheels; women starboard (D and E), men port (K and L). Students of lavatory design will note a definite and blatant facility bias toward males; either it reflected the relative travel mix of the day (many more men traveled than females), or *Mrs.* Peirce was not consulted. Well, it was 1889, after all.

Around the quarterdeck (on the Main deck): $G_2$ is the Captain's office, $H_2$ the ticket office, $I_2$ is the barber shop, $J_2$ and $K_2$ clerks' rooms, $M_2$ the Chief Steward's room, $L_2$ the Stewardess' room. Forward on the Main deck were crew quarters, and the large open space surrounding the stacks (R) is the cargo area.

$U_2$ is the Ladies' cabin, with the private cabin aft. The Dining Room was below the quarterdeck and Ladies' Cabin, reached by stairs under the grand stairway (between $H_2$ and $I_2$) and staircase $N_2$ providing direct access for the ladies.

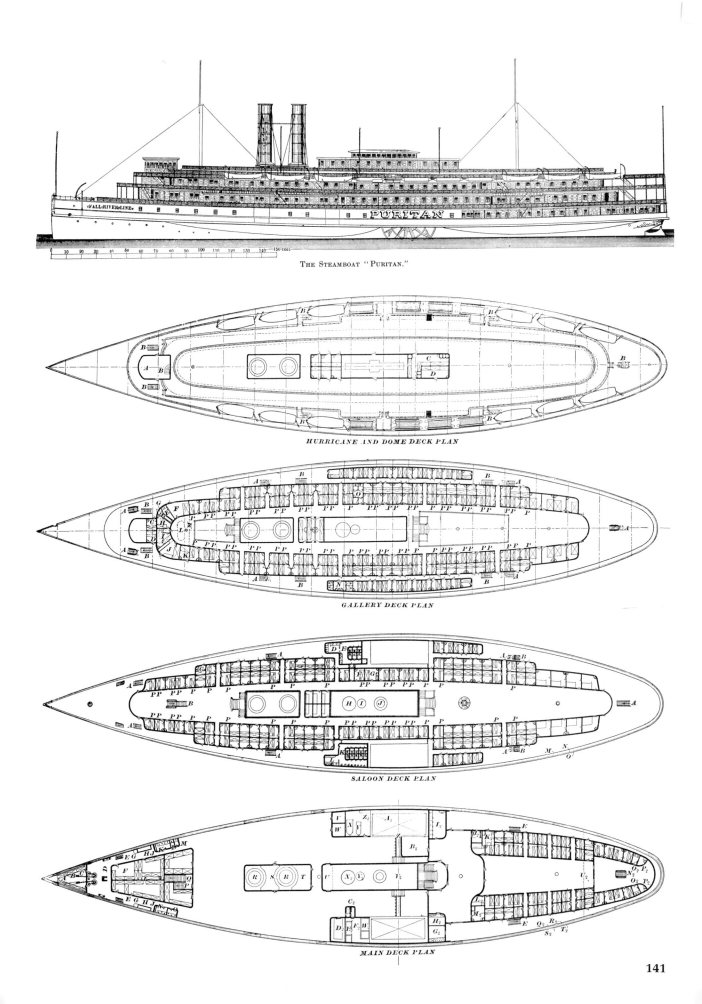

THE STEAMBOAT "PURITAN."

HURRICANE AND DOME DECK PLAN

GALLERY DECK PLAN

SALOON DECK PLAN

MAIN DECK PLAN

141

With the *City of Fall River* experimental compound engine successful, a larger version was installed in *Puritan*. In fact, *Puritan* was fitted with the largest walking beam engine ever put into a steamboat; a diagram appears at the left. There are two vertical cylinders on the left side of the engine, connected to the beam. The inner, smaller cylinder was the high-pressure cylinder, 75 inches in diameter; it had a 108-inch stroke. The outer cylinder, 110 inches in diameter, had a 168-inch stroke, and was connected at the outer corner of the walking beam. Because the inner cylinder was connected between the pivot of the walking beam and the edge, it described a smaller arc than the low-pressure cylinder's piston. That smaller described arc corresponded with the shorter stroke.

At right, a closeup of the massive rhombic walking beam. Below, one of the largest waterborne cranes in the area delicately lowers the 34-foot wide, 42-ton beam into position. Note the strain on the hoist apparatus, the extensive wooden bracing, and the deflection of the surface on which the crane is resting. That's how it was done in the 1880s.

*Puritan* required a crew of 224 to operate, including these two sets of gentlemen. Above, the engine crew, with Chief Engineer and First Assistant seated, center. Note the service marks on the Chief Engineer's sleeve; there are nine of them, each denoting five years of service.

Below, the officers assemble for their photograph; Commander Simmons is seated, fourth from left.

America's "best known lady" appears at right as *Puritan* rounds the Battery in New York harbor. (The Battery is so named because it is the site of a long-forgotten artillery battery defending Manhattan's southern tip.) This was a frequent scene until 1908, when *Puritan* was replaced by *Commonwealth*. *Puritan* and *Pilgrim* were both retired in 1912, scrapped in 1916.

departure from previous practices. The beam engine was a compound steam engine, with not one but two vertical cylinders connected to the beam. That Fletcher engine was not only the last, but also the largest, walking beam engine ever to be placed in a new Sound steamboat.

*Puritan* became well-known for her beauty, particularly for her smooth side lines without paddlewheel bulges. But for all her beauty, she was an expensive beast to operate when compared to her successors. Both *Pilgrim* and *Puritan,* with their walking beam engines, became obsolescent within a few years.

Meanwhile, *Bristol* burned at her dock on December 30, 1888, necessitating reinstatement of the almost-retired *Old Colony* until *Puritan* arrived. The fire also accelerated plans for construction of yet another new vessel. This one, to be named *Plymouth,* would be a smaller boat than *Puritan,* for winter service. Thus the smaller *Providence* (II) and *Plymouth* would operate all year, with the larger *Pilgrim* and *Puritan* coming on for the summer season.

*Plymouth* cost $900,000 and entered service in 1890. She was 352 feet long, and displaced 3771 tons. Although shorter than *Pilgrim,* she had an equivalent 247 staterooms and a passenger capacity of 1200, thanks to careful arrangement of staterooms in any available space on her decks. Staterooms, after all, meant revenue; the more the better. Her cargo capacity was the equivalent of 72 railroad carloads. With *Plymouth,* Mr. Peirce abandoned the walking beam engine in favor of a four-cylinder triple-expansion engine with inclined pistons. The W & A Fletcher Company, with their young associate Stevenson Taylor, carried out the design effort for the smaller boat.

We should point out that use of the word "small" to describe *Plymouth* is potentially misleading, as it would be, for example, to describe a "small" elephant. *Plymouth* was larger than *Pilgrim* and Mr. Fisk's *Providence* (II); larger than any other boat on the Sound at the time but for *Puritan.* And only one Sound boat larger than *Plymouth* would be built before the turn of the century: *Priscilla.* That's some "small" boat!

**Summer Edition, 1892.**

FALL RIVER LINE

FOR BOSTON THE NORTH AND EAST.

J. R. KENDRICK, GENERAL MANAGER.    GEO. L. CONNOR, GENERAL PASSENGER AGENT.

On the facing page, two views of the 1892 *City of Taunton*, at 283 feet in length the largest and last wood paddlewheel freighter built for the Sound. At top, her hull is virtually complete at Chelsea MA. Only three wooden-hulled steamboats larger than *City of Taunton* figure in our story: *Connecticut* (III), *Bristol* and *Providence.*

Larger steel freighters were, of course, built for the NYNH&H after 1900, but *City of Taunton* represents the last of her kind.

In 1892, it was still *Puritan*'s hour in the sun (or , more often, the fog), occupying the place of honor on the Fall River Line's timetable flyers. Clearly, this flyer was geared for the New York audience and the Boston trade. People did wave at the departing and passing boats, or at the people thereon.

The NYNH&H and its predecessors produced a variety of flyers and pamphlets designed to advertise their services; good early examples of advertising art.

## THE STEAMER *PLYMOUTH*

"There was times when you couldn't see one end of the boat from the other." Operating in fog required seamanship, along with equal parts of courage and prudence As a "year 'round" boat, *Plymouth* regularly faced another challenge: ice. Her steel double hull was rarely tested.

At right, *Plymouth*'s inclined engine, the successor to the walking beam. The new design replaced vertical cylinders and the rhombic link with inclined cylinders having direct linkages to the paddlewheel shaft. It was first tried on this, the smaller boat, before being put to a larger test in *Priscilla*. Note that the cranks are 90 degrees offset; This was standard practice on steam engines (including railroad locomotives), to ensure that at

least one pair of cylinders would always be in a position to exert its force against the cranks rather than being at the end of travel, a condition called "dead center".

The inclined engines proved to be considerably more efficient than the old walking beam engines, and were able to get from port to port on fewer tons of coal. Their increased efficiency and lower operating costs were sufficient to justify retirement of *Pilgrim* and *Puritan* after 29 and 23 years of service respectively. *Plymouth* and *Priscilla* were still going strong at ages 48 and 44 respectively in 1938.

As must happen in any coal burning vessel, ashes accumulate. On *Plymouth* and other steamers, those ashes were periodically flushed out at sea. That's the purpose of the stream of water in the photo on the opposite page; *Plymouth* is "shooting ashes." (Try that today without an environmental impact statement.)

*Plymouth* was the only major Fall River Line vessel to have one stack; the others had two. That made her easy to distinguish from the other boats, even from a distance.

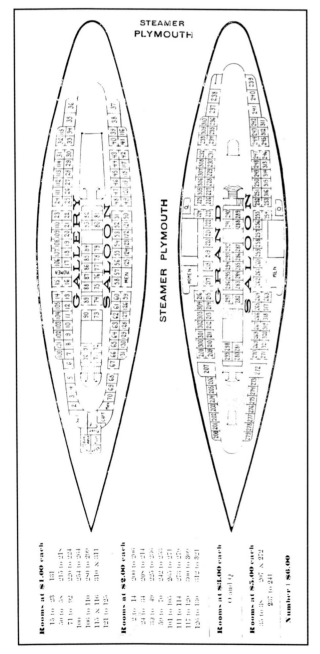

STEAMER PLYMOUTH

### The "Final Four"

*Plymouth* was the last of the Fall River Line boats to be launched under the Old Colony Railroad/Old Colony Steamship Company's independent operation. As we will see in subsequent chapters, more was yet to come as the Line, under control of the NYNH&H, responded to what it perceived to be the area's travel demand. The growth of New England industry and commerce is illustrated by this: in 1878 the Old Colony steamboats took in $352,000 in passenger revenue, and $288,000 in freight revenue. In 1886, the passenger revenue was $521,000 but the freight revenue had jumped to $606,000. For the record, during that same period stateroom revenue increased from $88,000 to $149,000; meal revenue from $55,000 to $83,000 and bar revenue from $15,000 to $22,000. While passenger revenue during those years rose by about 50 per cent, freight revenue more than doubled. There you see the reason to build the freight boats, and for the increased cargo capacity of *Plymouth*.

*Plymouth* was the first of the Fall River Line's "final four" passenger steamboats, the majestic liners that, more than any others, have established in the public mind and memory the splendor that sailed the Sound.

The "final four" comprised an outstanding quartet of steamers, two large and two smaller boats (in relative terms at least). They were:

*Plymouth*, launched 1890, small
*Priscilla*, launched 1893, large
*Providence* (III), launched 1905, small
*Commonwealth* (II), launched 1908, large (!)

The first two, *Plymouth* and *Priscilla*, were built under Old Colony Railroad management, before the NYNH&H became dominant. The second pair was launched by the NYNH&H, but their designers and managers were men who had come up through the Old Colony ranks.

Of course, neither Mr. Peirce or any of the other Old Colony managers had any idea that these would be the final Fall River boats. The travel demand of the era entirely justified boats of such large size; they often operated sold out.

Second of the "final four" was the most famous Sound steamer, *Priscilla* (which, according to legend, narrowly escaped being named "Mayflower," as had *Plymouth* before her). *Priscilla* was launched in 1893 and placed into service the following year. She carried up to 1500 passengers and 800 tons of freight, and cost $1.5 million. Priscilla's Italian Renaissance interior decoration made her the sentimental and aesthetic favorite of passengers and steamboat connoisseurs alike. While she was designed and built during the Old Colony management, by the time of her launch *Priscilla* belonged to the NYNH&H, which leased the Old Colony Railroad and its steamboat subsidiary in 1893.

On the eve of *Priscilla*'s debut, *Plymouth* spoiled the party. It was June 19, 1894, the day for *Priscilla*'s trial trip from Newport, with a boatload of dignitaries present by invitation.

And then that evening, as all preparations for the festive voyage were in place, word came that *Plymouth* had run hard aground on Rose Island in Narragansett Bay, tantalizingly close to Newport. Captain "Danger" Davis, the fog-eater, had somehow missed the channel this time, with 700 passengers on board.

No one was injured and no water was coming aboard, but the Captain's embarrassment could not have been more acute. Here were all of the dignitaries in Creation, including General Manager Kendrick, come to ride *Priscilla*, and the primary object on the hazy landscape as they went by was the stranded *Plymouth*, the result of Elijah Davis' miscalculation.

Passengers had been removed right away, and tugboats called. But *Plymouth* resisted the first attempts to pull her off; she was hard aground. Below, the first step in freeing *Plymouth* was removal of cargo to lighten the ship.

Following removal of cargo and supplies, flotation pontoons were emplaced under her hull with the aid of floating cranes, and *Plymouth* removed. For years afterward, the Fall River Line men referred to South Point Shoal on Rose Island as "Plymouth Rock," a nickname guaranteed to drive Elijah Davis wild.

*Plymouth* burned and was completely rebuilt in 1906-1907. One "spotting feature" that distinguishes old from new is the number of windows on the forward part of the main deck. Note in these older photos, between the words "FALL RIVER LINE" and the first cargo door, there are six windows. After rebuilding, *Plymouth* had seven.

PAR VALUE OF SHARES $100. EACH.

# Old Colony Steamboat Company.

Be it known that *Deborah S. Almond Trustee under the will of Benjamin Loundy of Medford Mass.* is the owner of — *Thirteen* — shares in the Capital Stock of the Old Colony Steamboat Company, subject to the provisions of the Charter and the By-Laws of the Company: the same being transferable by a conveyance in writing, duly recorded in the Books of the company

Dated at Boston, this *Fourth* day of *Feby* A.D. *1891.*

826

_____ Treasurer.          _____ President.

J. M. Whittemore & Co. Boston.

CANCELLED

At left, the classic pose of the skipper; in this case, Elijah Davis, who was given the nickname "Danger Davis" because of his uncanny ability to navigate through fog that stopped all other boats. Captain Davis was short; too short to see out of the wheelhouse's center window without standing on the special stool that had been made for him. His navigation skills, however, ensured his status as one of the giants of Sound steamboating.

Above, one of the stock certificates turned in and cancelled at the time the NYNH&H took over the Old Colony. It was a lease of the railroad, but the ownership shift was unmistakable.

Below, the svelte shape of things to come; *Priscilla*, the largest Sound steamer to be built in the nineteenth century and, some say, the most elegant steamer ever.

## Chapter Eight

# New Bedford and the Islands

Consistent with the traditions and preferences of New Englanders, New Bedford and the two Massachusetts islands of Nantucket and Martha's Vineyard are steeped in the seafaring spirit. New Bedford's harbor is synonymous with seafaring, whaling, and the Indomitable Sailor. As the whaling industry declined, textile manufacture grew. While New Bedford's textile industry never quite matched that of Fall River in size, it was nonetheless significant. The freight traffic pattern to New York City (cotton bales going east, cloth going west) was similar to that of Fall River, and it was the source of much steamboat freight revenue.

The islands of Nantucket and Martha's Vineyard also have a seafaring orientation and tradition. In sharp contrast to New Bedford, they are rather well-known summer resorts, not pockets of industry. We should pause at this point to emphasize the word "summer." The number of year-round islanders is far less than the total population during the warm-weather season. While current controversies in the islands concern the level of development and summer tourism, it can't be forgotten that winter on Martha's Vineyard or Nantucket involves ice, extreme cold, and stupefying storms. Whalers and sailboats manned by hardy souls in such an environment are the stuff of legend, and both legends and activity abounded in the often hostile sea beyond the protection of Long Island Sound.

Steamboat service between New Bedford and New York began in 1853, reflecting the growth in

---

**The joys of summer await these folks, on their way to board _Martha's Vineyard_ at Gay Head for an excursion. This beach landing scene is about as far removed from Pier 14 North River as you can get (which explains the islands' popularity as a resort), and yet it was all part of the same Old Colony/ NYNH&H steamboat system.**

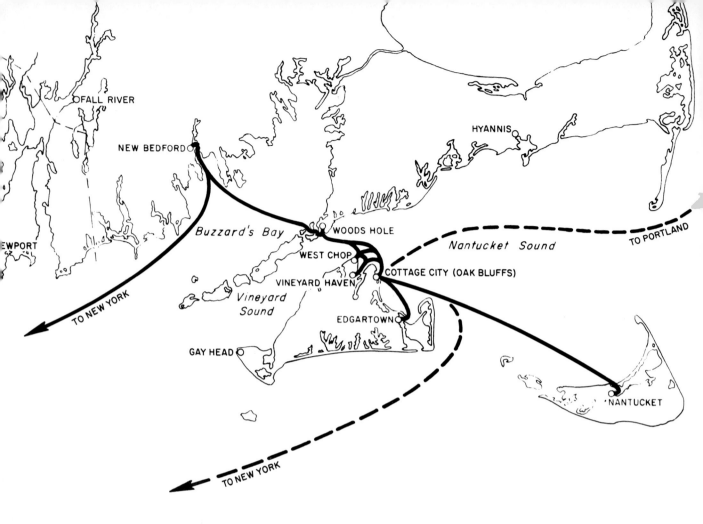

that area's economy from a pure whaling orientation toward textiles, shoes and related manufacturing. The boats connected with the Boston, Clinton & Fitchburg Railroad. The region's economy changed more radically as the whaling industry all but collapsed after Colonel Drake discovered a source of less expensive oil in Pennsylvania in 1859.

Both the railroad and the steamboat company experienced financial difficulties in the 1870s,

While not in Long Island Sound itself, the steamer services to the east were "part of the family" through ownership as well as customer perception. The primary island ports were Oak Bluffs (Cottage City) on Martha's Vineyard, and Nantucket City. The dashed line indicates the Maine Steamship Co. service between New York and Portland, with an intermediate stop at Cottage City.

with the result that in 1878 and 1879 both came under control of the Old Colony Railroad. The Old Colony Steamboat Co. took over the New Bedford–New York line. Almost immediately, the New Bedford–New York steamer service became a freight only operation; to simplify its operations, the Old Colony funneled its passenger traffic to the Fall River Line boats, with a rail connection between Fall River and New Bedford. As we have noted elsewhere, passenger convenience took second place to operating efficiency when railroad-trained managers of the era made the decisions.

## On Nantucket

The first steamboat was welcomed with indifference by the conservative sailboat-loving seafarers on Nantucket; *Eagle* of Norwich, now fitted with copper boilers after her accident at New London (see Chapter Five), was the first steamboat in these waters. She began service in May 1818 between Nantucket and the Thames River port. Three months later, suspicion and lack of business drove *Eagle* away. As a local newspaper described her, "The *Eagle* was an awkward little boat . . . and the quickest passage which this steamer is said to have made between New Bedford and Nantucket occupied eight hours and seven minutes."

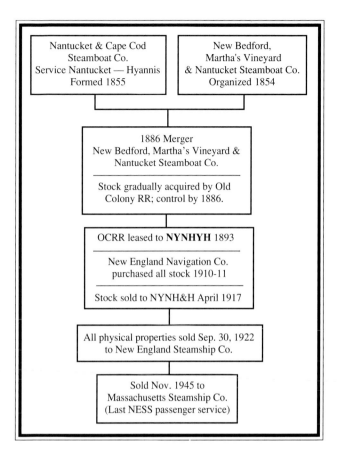

A similar lack of enthusiasm greeted Capt. Elihu Bunker when he brought the well-traveled *Connecticut* (I) for a prospecting trip in 1824. Nothing happened, and Capt. Bunker relocated to Providence, having only occasional contact with Nantucket thereafter.

If further evidence was needed to convince the islanders that steamboats were a joke, *Lafayette* or *Hamilton* provided it. The year was 1828, and the boat began Nantucket-New Bedford service. She was officially named *Lafayette*, and so named on her stern; but she carried the name *Hamilton* on her side paddle boxes. So underpowered was this craft that while she began such service, she often didn't complete it, unless conditions were very favorable. Strong tidal currents, for example, could render this schizophrenic steamer dead in the water. A contemporary account dismissed *Lafayette* as "not having power enough to get out of her own way." After a few months, her New Bedford-based owners moved her to Maine.

Jacob Barker put *Marco Bozzaris* into service between New Bedford and Nantucket in 1829, three trips a week. The boat's name derived from a Fitzgreene Halleck poem; the young poet Halleck was then a clerk in Barker's firm. In 1831, Barker experimented with a new type of fuel, coal; they abandoned its use as being "impractical." Capt.

Edward Barker, Jacob's nephew, commanded *Marco*, but she too was unprofitable and was sold away from the island in 1832. Jacob Barker and a group of Nantucket merchants put a new and larger steamer under Captain Barker in March 1833 (after the harbor ceased to be frozen over for the winter). Her name was *Telegraph*, operating three round trips weekly between Nantucket and New Bedford, with a stop at Vineyard Haven. Reportedly, *Telegraph*'s cabin boy often entertained passengers by playing his violin, a lonely forerunner to the Fall River Line's later orchestral concerts.

In 1842, the larger *Massachusetts* (II) joined the fleet. Despite the improved performance brought about by her size and modern design (including a hogback truss), the sail-driven sloops continued to capture the largest share of the shipping business. Towing, wrecking and salvage operations kept the Nantucket Steamboat Company in the black, there being no shortage of ships suddenly finding themselves on the nearby shoals.

*Monohansett*, built in 1862, went to war, serving two hitches in 1863 and 1865 as a dispatch boat for President Lincoln, and later as a troop carrier, both on the Potomac and James Rivers in Virginia. In the Matthew Brady photo above, she is seen in her military role. The charter brought the Company $500 per day from a grateful government.

Below, back in civilian life, *Monohansett* is docked while her passengers enjoy the island. The 38-star flag flying from her stern dates the photo as having been taken between 1877 and 1890.

At lower right, we're at the south side of the Nantucket wharf, circa 1870, as *Island Home* lays over in the morning, between runs. In September 1870, the Navy frigate *Guerriere*, carrying the remains of Admiral David Farragut ran ashore off Nantucket. *Island Home* was used to help refloat the frigate, as well as to carry the Admiral's remains to Hyannis and a connecting train for New York. *Island Home* thus became the last boat in which Admiral Farragut rode, although he was not available for subsequent comment.

## A Martha's Vineyard Company

The New Bedford and Martha's Vineyard Steamboat Company was formed in 1846 to operate *Naushon* (I) three times a week between Edgartown and New Bedford, with a stop at Woods Hole near Nobska Point on the mainland. That service went broke in a year. A tentacle extended from Connecticut in 1848 similarly withered; this was *Osceola*, operating to Nantucket from Hartford and New London. She was the first propeller-driven steamer to visit the islands, but her Connecticut owners soon gave up. The Nantucket Steamboat company was petitioned by Martha's Vineyard citizens for more intermediate stops there on the way to and from New Bedford and Nantucket. But the Nantucket Steamboat Company was reluctant to provide such stops, as they increased the travel time of Nantucket people who wanted an "express," not a multi-stop "local."

In 1854 the Nantucket company figured that running to Hyannis was better than running to New Bedford; it was a shorter water route, and there were land connections to Boston. The Martha's Vineyard-based New Bedford, Vineyard and Nantucket Steamboat Co. was almost immediately formed

and began to provide thrice-weekly New Bedford-Edgartown-Nantucket service. *George Law* began that service, operating for two months until the new *Eagle's Wing* was ready, Captain James Barker in command. *George Law* and *Eagle's Wing* were the first boats with walking beams to appear at Nantucket. With *Eagle's Wing*, Nantucket was at last looking at a real steamboat, with a dining room (a good dinner cost 50 cents) and capacity for 80 passengers.

As business for one boat line began looking up in 1854, a group of Fall River and Providence investors put *Metacomet* on a run from Edgartown to a railroad connection at Fairhaven (which is adjacent to New Bedford, on the Acushnet's opposite shore). *Metacomet* was commanded by Capt. Ben Simmons, whose later career with the Fall River Line we have already mentioned.

The older Nantucket company suffered a mishap when *Massachusetts* was damaged on a towing run. Adding some capital from Hyannis (and reflecting the interest by changing the company's name to the "Nantucket and Cape Cod Steamboat Co."), the company added the new *Island Home* to its roster in 1855. A combination of the new boat and departure of the popular James Barker as

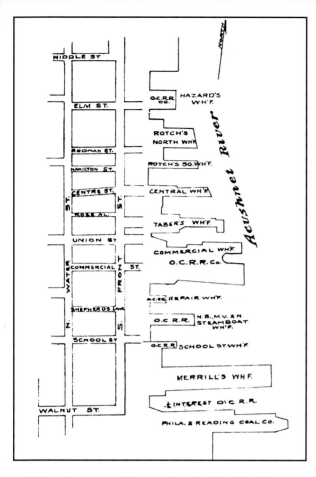

The wharves on the west bank of the Acushnet are diagrammed above as they existed in 1909. The Old Colony name still appeared, although all was now owned by New England Navigation. The repair wharf was mostly used for the Island steamers, as we shall see later in this chapter.

New Bedford had its own steamboat line to New York in the 1870s, operating steamers named *Acushnet*, *Albatross*, *Santee*, and *Wansutta*. Elijah Davis was one of the line's captains. The Old Colony bought the company's assets in 1879. The 1877 pass shown above was issued less than two years before purchase of the line's boats by the OCRR.

One of the vessels the New Bedford line operated was *City of Fitchburg*, shown below. In 1900 the Old Colony sold her to the Boston & Maine Steamship Co., for which line she ran between Boston and Portland ME. In 1902 she was renamed *Surprise*, and lived up to her name by showing up for a while as a Joy Line chartered vessel. She was stranded and damaged beyond repair off Fall River in 1907.

*River Queen* with her "turret" pilothouse appears in the two photos on the opposite page, awaiting her next trip. Freight for the islands was as important as passenger traffic.

captain of *Eagle's Wing* caused a patronage shift toward *Island Home*; *Eagle's Wing* stopped operating to Nantucket. That situation was an early illustration of the often-overlooked importance of people and human relationships, which often overshadow technology in accounting for the success of a transportation enterprise.

*Massachusetts* and *Telegraph* left the islands in 1858. *Island Home* held down the Nantucket-Hyannis schedule, operating out of Nantucket until 1896. *Metacomet* withdrew in 1857; she was sold and became the Navy gunboat *Pulaski*. *Eagle's Wing* burned in 1861 and the Vineyard company replaced her in 1862 with *Monohansett*. The new boat served until 1904, with a stint in Civil War service from 1863 to 1865.

*River Queen*, built in 1864, had one of the more fascinating histories for a New England steamboat. When new, she was assigned to General Grant as his personal dispatch boat. *River Queen's* main saloon was the site of the preliminary peace conference between President Lincoln and Confederate Vice-President Alexander Stephens. The President enjoyed using her, and did so frequently. In fact, Lincoln had been aboard her less than 48 hours before his assassination. The Martha's Vineyard company purchased *River Queen* in 1871; she was sold to the Nantucket company in 1873, running until 1881, when the *Queen* was moved to New York. Then, from 1891 until 1911, *River Queen* again operated on the Potomac, between Washington and Mount Vernon; she was thus operated in connection with three presidents in her lifetime.

The 1860s saw a boom in summer excursions to Martha's Vineyard, many occasioned by Methodist camp meetings at the large Wesleyan Grove meeting ground near Oak Bluffs. They called their outdoor tented auditorium the Methodist Tabernacle, and thousands of visitors, an estimated 50,000 per summer in the 1870s, came from all over the country to hear the best preaching the Methodists could muster. As many as fifteen excursion steamers a day landed at Oak Bluffs wharf in August, coming from such places as Providence, Boston, Bridgeport and even Hartford.

The Nantucket company extended *Island Home's* route to Martha's Vineyard in 1871. The next year, the Old Colony Railroad branch to Woods Hole (then known as Woods Holl) was completed; thereafter Woods Hole rather than Hyannis was her mainland port. The railroad connection at Woods Hole was a significant travel improvement, facilitating the passage of thousands of tourists to and from the Islands. Since the Vineyard company steamers also stopped at Woods Hole, transfers between the two lines meant the availability of service to New Bedford as well.

Not that New Bedford service was the goal; the small Old Colony Railroad terminal at Woods Hole was built with ferry services in mind; an extension of the two passenger terminal tracks ran out onto the steamer pier. The railroad began purchasing stock in the two island steamship companies at about that time. Some of the transactions are obscure because the full extent of the OCRR's interest wasn't fully known until years later. *Monohansett* was leased to the Old Colony Railroad to operate out of Woods Hole. The Vineyard company built *Martha's Vineyard* (I) in 1871; the two companies gradually began coordinating their services to and between the islands rather than competing. And by 1883, the last sailing packet was gone, leaving the field to the steamboats.

## A Brief Photo Tour of Martha's Vineyard

The visit of President Ulysses S. Grant and his wife and party in the summer of 1874 was a great occasion on Martha's Vineyard, and the folks went to great effort to make the First Couple feel welcome. Grant was neither the first nor the last political figure to enjoy the island's religious or recreational facilities. He arrived on *River Queen*, and departed for New Bedford on his own former *Monohansett*.

The horsecar's route sign reads "Steamboat Wharf and Camp Ground," on the Cottage Avenue line, and those were indeed the two most popular destinations in Cottage City.

Further examples of Martha's Vineyard hospitality are shown above. If he were looking for a quiet stay, the President would be disappointed. But his primary goal appears to have been to attend the Methodist camp meeting.

The cottages shown below indicate part of the reason for Martha's Vineyard's popularity as a place to enjoy and relax in the late nineteenth and early twentieth century. This was the case at least in the summertime; the year-round population of Cottage City was less than 1000 people in 1893. Yet in the summer, that population more than tripled.

How firm a foundation, ye saints of the Lord,
is laid for your faith in His excellent word!
What more can He say than to you He hath said,
to you who for refuge to Jesus have fled?
"The soul that on Jesus still leans for repose,
I will not, I will not, desert to its foes;
that soul, though all hell should endeavor to
shake, I'll never, no never, no never forsake."
— Methodist hymn

The Sea View Hotel in Oak Bluffs may be called an architect's nightmare today, but it was a land developer's dream when it opened in July 1872. It cost almost $140,000 and was, quite simply, the finest place to stay on the island, comparable with resorts anywhere. 125 rooms awaited the guests, with gas lighting, steam heat (for the fore and aft ends of the seasons) and speaking tubes connecting every room with the office.

The hotel overlooked the steamboat wharf and the railroad track. Its balconies provided rest for many cameras, for which we are grateful.

The photos above and below show the steamboat wharf as it existed before (top) and after (bottom) the Old Colony Railroad took over the steamboats and the Martha's Vineyard Railroad. Note the new signs on the platform shed roof in the later photo. Both pictures were taken from balconies of the Sea View Hotel. The wye tracks leading to the left were destroyed in the Sea View fire.

For many visitors, the beaches were the primary attraction, and the railroad carried bathers on a route parallel to the beach, in back of the row of bathhouses.

The parallel plank walk connected other structures, including a dining hall and observation tower, from which the lower photo was taken. The picture stands as mute testimony to Martha's Vineyard's popularity as a resort.

## The Martha's Vineyard Railroad

The idea of a railroad on Martha's Vineyard, between Oak Bluffs and Edgartown, had been a subject of conversation since the Civil War, but it was not until 1874 that the idea even came close to reality. The driving forces were two land and resort development companies, at Oak Bluffs and Katama. Each company built an impressive resort hotel; Sea View at Oak Bluffs, and Mattakeeset Lodge at Katama. There had been a short horsecar line built in Oak Bluffs in 1873, operating from town to and about the tents at Wesleyan Grove, but now there was to be a real steam-powered railroad, extending south of Edgartown to Katama thanks to the interest of the Oak Bluff and Katama Land Companies. Edgartown took part ownership and helped to finance the venture, and the Old Colony Railroad bought some of the new company's bonds.

The nine-mile, three-foot gauge railroad was built in less than three months; its narrow-gauge rolling stock consisted of one locomotive, passenger car, one excursion car and one box car. That first locomotive was a "dummy" engine, built with a silencer for its steam exhaust (hence the name, as akin to a "dumb" or silent person), and was made to look like a passenger car. Thus configured, it would be less likely to frighten horses as it travelled. But the dummy couldn't take the railroad's curves, and it was replaced with a more normal locomotive, rushed from the H. K. Porter works at Pittsburgh PA, and named *Active*. *Active*, which was essentially an 0-6-0 switcher-type locomotive (what else was available on such short notice?), arrived at the Old Colony dock at Woods Hole, and was promptly bumped into the water while being unloaded. Raised and refurbished by the OCRR, she was brought by *Island Home* to Martha's Vineyard on August 22, more than halfway through the 1874 summer season. Renamed *Edgartown*, she was to be the railroad's only locomotive.

In 1875, after a rocky start, the railroad was extended to South Beach, which attracted more passengers, and Edgartown was becoming the center of a bustling resort area. One additional passenger coach was added to the railroad's roster in 1876, and the following year the road made a tiny profit. As many as three thousand people traveled on the line's 30-lb rails during a summer weekend.

But the railroad was never truly successful financially, because it had been lightly constructed on that flimsiest of foundations, sand. The constant expense of keeping the roadbed in place was a drain on the company's wallet. The island's economy suffered in the 1880s; by 1891, Katama was approaching ghost town status. A further setback, in September 1892, was the destruction by a spectacular fire of the Sea View hotel at Cottage City (Oak Bluffs was known by that name between 1887 and 1907). That fire not only levelled the classic wooden structure, it destroyed the railroad's turning wye. Thereafter, *Edgartown* operated stern first toward her namesake village.

But by the time of the Sea View fire, the Martha's Vineyard Railroad had defaulted once too often on the group of bonds held by the Old Colony Railroad. In 1891 the OCRR took over management of the line. In 1896, two years after the NYNH&H took over the Old Colony, the Martha's Vineyard Railroad was abandoned at the end of the season. Part of the route was later used by an electric railway built in 1891 and abandoned in 1917.

The old locomotive *Active/Edgartown*, again renamed *South Beach*, had one more waterborne brush with glory before retiring to construction project work in Boston. The schooner on which *Active* was shipped to Boston became shrouded in fog; they rang the locomotive's bell constantly to alert other boats; it was the loudest bell aboard. And they narrowly avoided a collision with a steamer; crews later said that it was indeed the sound of *Active*'s bell that saved the day.

The Martha's Vineyard Railroad was originally constructed to connect the steamboat wharf with Mattakeeset Lodge at Katama, shown in the photo at the lower left. Mattakeeset, which opened in 1873, rivaled the Sea View's high quality in all points of comparison except location.

Above, a close-up of the line's only locomotive, *Edgartown*, nee *Active*. Three-foot gauge trains were not unheard of in Massachusetts; the Boston, Revere Beach and Lynn was a large one.

This "through" station is at Edgartown, and the railroad employees are showing off their train.

Above, mass transit meets the arriving steamboat passengers on Martha's Vineyard. The Trinity Park horsecar (two horsepower) is no "dinky;" it's the equivalent of horsecars found on the busy routes of large cities, and the weekend traffic justified the investment.

Below, *Island Home* and *Nantucket* share the Oak Bluffs (Cottage City) pier in the 1890s with the larger *Mount Hope*, apparently operating as an excursion boat from Providence. The popular excursions brought thousands to the islands on summer weekends.

Martha's Vineyard (I) was built in 1871 at Brooklyn for the old Martha's Vineyard company. She was considered the fastest boat in the island fleet. When Gay Head and Uncatena came on line, the company kept Martha's Vineyard while selling Island Home and Monohansett. Martha's Vineyard was sold in 1913 and, her name changed to Keyport, operated between New York and Keansburg NJ for three years before being sunk in a collision.

After the Sea View Hotel burned in 1892, the Oak Bluffs pier was rebuilt; here Gay Head is receiving passengers shortly before World War I. Gay Head was the first Old Colony-built island boat, built in 1891. She operated for the New Bedford Martha's Vineyard and Nantucket Steamboat Co. until 1923, when she was replaced by Islander (later Martha's Vineyard (II).)

Gay Head was sold to New York interests, renamed Pastime, and operated in New York harbor excursion service until 1926.

Spring cleaning at the repair dock in New Bedford saw *Gay Head* and *Nantucket* being spruced up for the summer season with, among other things, new coats of white paint. Ferry *Fairhaven* crosses the Acushnet in the background.

Many wealthy and/or famous people became regular visitors. As the dockside scene at left below shows, steamer trunks were not limited to ocean-going voyages. These people did not travel light!

Above, an 1885 panoramic view of Nantucket's harbor, complete with departing steamboat. The steamboat wharf is at the right edge of the picture.

The Knights Templar are marching ashore to music at Nantucket in the 1890s, having most likely come in on a charter vessel for a festive excursion. Look at the drum; is that the Sutton Commandery from New Bedford?

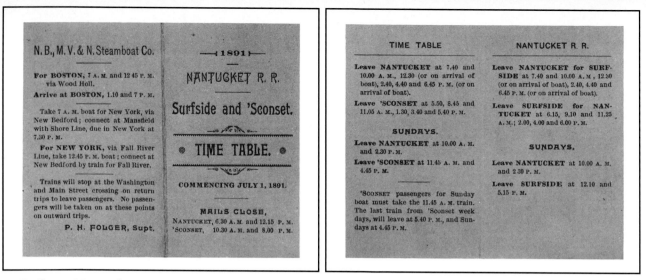

## Rails on Nantucket

Nantucket's narrow gauge railroad was con-
ceived and built a few years after the Martha's
Vineyard line, by Nantucket natives and interests,
led by Philip Folger. The line was built in 1880
from the steamboat wharf in the town of Nantucket
eastward to Surfside, where the Coffin family was
erecting a large hotel and founding a real estate development, and opened for traffic amid singing,
flags and celebration on July 4, 1881. The first
motive power was purchased secondhand from the
Boston, Revere Beach & Lynn; a 4-4-0 named *Dionis*, in honor of the matriarchal ancestor of the
island's Coffin clan. Descendant Charles Coffin
was one of the road's first managers.

The Nantucket railroad was a larger enterprise
than its sister to the west; the line was extended in
1884 to 'Sconset (more formally, Siasconset), which
sent traffic and revenues soaring. A second locomotive was purchased in 1885, an 0-4-4T Mason
Bogie engine named *Sconset*. But in the next few
years the weather and the economy wreaked their
joint hardships on Nantucket too, and the Coffins'
Surfside development went under in 1887. A boom
at 'Sconset mitigated the railroad's suffering, allowing local interests to retain ownership of the
line until 1906. The Old Colony Railroad/NYNH&H
was not a creditor, so the line kept running; there
were no orders from New Haven to shut it down.
The Surfside properties were taken over and refurbished by New York capital, lasting until 1898. The
big hotel never quite matched her earlier glories.

But the Nantucket Railroad was decidedly less
than first class transportation, due to the action of
repeated storms in the 1890s. There were frequent
derailments and washouts, causing people to travel
by wagon or hack rather than relying on the train.
In 1895, the railroad (now known as the Nantucket
Central Railroad after a reorganization) was relocated away from Surfside, rebuilt on a more direct
route to Siasconset (see map). A severe storm in
1898 wrecked many buildings on Nantucket, including the Surfside Hotel. It also washed out the
railroad right of way which, like the line on Martha's
Vineyard, was built on the sand that constituted
the island. The railroad's remains were sold for
$10,500 to the next round of optimistic investors.
But the track was rebuilt more easily than the
hotels, and did indeed operate, profitably, the
following summer.

1907 saw the railroad's sale to New York interests, and the steam train replaced by a gasoline-
powered railcar known as "The Bug." The steam
trains were brought back in 1910, with the line's
third engine, another veteran of the Revere Beach
line. Two new passenger cars also arrived. But by
1917, as on Martha's Vineyard, the automobile
and, more particularly, the "jitney" car, were more
attractive means of getting around the island. Both
of the island railroads were sacrificed to the scrap
metal drives of World War I.

The Nantucket Railroad's first incarnation involved two locomotives; the first, *Dionis*, is shown above. The second, *Sconset*, the Mason Bogie engine, appears at right.

Use of autos on the island was discouraged in favor of horsedrawn carriages for some years after the turn of the century, giving rise to the lineup scene meeting the train at the lower left.

Early in the 1900s, Siasconset became a haven for actors. It was said in those days that the Lambs' Club of New York could have mounted a quorum for a meeting at 'Sconset during the summer season. The celebrity passengers had of course begun their trips at a North River pier, going by steamboat to Fall River (and a connecting train) or New Bedford, from which place could be caught an island steamboat. The last leg of the trip, by rail, terminated at 'Sconset station, shown below.

The Nantucket train en route to 'Sconset near the shore, with two of the passenger cars in the fleet. More than any other, the photo above shows the sandy, windswept conditions in which the island railroads operated; track maintenance was an almost daily adventure.

The top right photo shows the train at the wharf near the end of its career. *Dionis* is about to depart with three cars, including the open car at the end of the train. While the open car, an idea copied from streetcar lines, was a delightful ride most of the time, the side canvas was used in windstorms.

## ODE TO "THE BUG"

Oh, that funny little Bug.
Hear his coughing chug-a-chug!
See him swing his little tail
As he canters o'er the rail
    From Nantucket to his
        bughouse by the sea!
He'a a nightmare, he's a dream.
And his appetite is keen,
    for he feeds on gasoline
And his like is yet
        unknown to historee.

Every now and then he tries to
Skid along the rotten ties to
Shorten up the journey
      from Nantucket,
And his single eye gleams red
When he rounds
      Tom Never's Head
And he sees his little shed —
He is lucky if he doesn't
    kick the bucket —
But he does the best he can
Over seven miles of sand
Though they tell me that he
    sometimes leaves his tail!

Every day this fiery dragon
With his tipsy little wagon
Like a sailor with a jag on
Comes careening o'er the
      crooked iron rail.
And though rocky as to gait
And occasionally late,
He is sure to keep his date,
And he never yet forgot
      to bring the mail!
          — J. L. Wood

The folks who purchased the Nantucket Railroad in 1907 came to believe that steam locomotives and passenger cars, however quaint, were inefficient; a more modern transportation mode was called for. Their gasoline-powered contribution to modern railroading is shown below, left. The train derisively became known as "The Bug and the Birdcage," inspiring literary works such as the one on this page.

The Bug and Birdcage operated for one or two years, depending on whom you believe, and for 1909 the rickety combo was replaced by the more typical gas motor car shown below. Still, the motors were no substitute for steam trains in handling weekend passenger demand. Something new was called for. . .

And something new indeed arrived in 1910; a steam train, shown above being unloaded (whoops; easy there!) at Nantucket. The 2-4-4 tank locomotive, combine and coach, freshly painted, pause for their portrait, below. Despite its number, the engine was the third locomotive on Nantucket. The wooden cars were of a type that would have been equally at home on the Denver and Rio Grande Western. June 7, 1910 saw the first trip, as the Nantucket folks delighted in their new train.

New train or no, the basic problem could not be solved: a railroad's heavy capital investment could not be justified with a two or three-month operating season on Nantucket. In 1917, the railroad went to war, in the form of rails, equipment and scrap.

Above right, the Nantucket waterfront as it looked just before World War I, complete with one-car train, on its way to 'Sconset. The smokestacks tell us that *Sankaty* is at the wharf (*Sankaty* was the only island steamer with two stacks), while a group of fishing schooners occupies much of the harbor.

At right below, the train returns from Siasconset, crossing the cobblestone street near the wharf and the center of town. Even on Nantucket, grade crossings were unavoidable. This one was at the station (Note the "R.R. Waiting Room" sign on the building by the combine).

*Uncatena*, built in 1902 and named for one of the smaller Elizabeth Islands, was the first steel-hulled boat built for Nantucket/Martha's Vineyard service, and the first to be equipped with electric lights. She was commanded by Captain Francis Marshall for most of her life.

*Uncatena* gives us the opportunity to present a construction photo in the shipyard (above), the breaking of a bottle of champagne on her bow prior to her launching (upper right), and the launching itself (lower right). The last sidewheeler built for island operation,

## Old Colony Steamboats

By 1886, the Old Colony Railroad had acquired sufficient ownership to exercise working control of the island steamboat companies. The railroad at once merged the two companies, and put the new *Nantucket* on the line, which bumped *Martha's Vineyard* to spare boat status. The last and largest nineteenth century boat was *Gay Head*, new in 1891. Her design bore at least one trademark of her mainland owners. *Gay Head*'s paddle wheel covering was apparently influenced by George Peirce's 1889 *Puritan*; it was "flush" wood paneling rather than the older ornamented semicircle design.

The last sidewheeler to be built for island service was *Uncatena*; she was also the first steel-hulled vessel, and the first one with electric lights, to serve those routes. While cost may have been a factor, we must pause to marvel at the fact that all of the boats we have discussed in this chapter until now had wooden hulls; remember that they had to break through ice in winter, and that they were out on the open ocean for most of their trips, not in the more protected Sound. The thrice-weekly schedule continued to be the service level even after the turn of the century.

Uncatena was called the "mother duck" by Nantucket regulars because of her perceived waddle in the water compared to the more modern *Islander* and *Nobska*. She operated in island service until 1929, was sold in 1930, and was renamed *Pemberton* by her new owners, the Nantasket-Boston line.

Coincidentally, she was scrapped in July 1937, the same month that Fall River Line service stopped.

## THE FAIRHAVEN FERRY

The Fourth of July, 1833 was more festive than usual in New Bedford and Fairhaven MA; on that date, the steam ferryboat *Acushnet* began operating on a regular schedule from the foot of Commercial Street in New Bedford to the foot of Center Street in Fairhaven. The ferryboat fare was 6-1/4 cents. In June 1835, *Acushnet* was replaced by *Fairhaven* (I), which became known as "The Crab" (top left) because of the underpowered craft's sideways motion when fighting the river's currents.

Opening of the Fairhaven Branch Railroad in 1854 brought with it a new ferry, named *Union* (top right and below). Her first run was on September 30, 1854. The landing points were changed at this time; *Union* began operating from a new ferry house at the foot of School St. in New Bedford.

*Union* burned in September 1858, and the company used *Fairhaven* (I) and chartered the Brooklyn NY ferry *Agnes* to fill in until *Union* was rebuilt. *Agnes* departed for Civil War service soon thereafter.

*Union*'s last run, coincidentally, was on September 30, 1873, as service was terminated for "financial reasons." Yes, a horsecar line had been established on the bridge, and tolls removed, so

fewer people were riding the ferry. But there was also a whiff of railroad manipulation in the air. The Fairhaven Branch had gone into the Old Colony system, while the line from New Bedford west and north was part of the competing Boston Clinton & Fitchburg system, which also controlled the ferry. Closing the ferry meant that traffic would be denied to the Old Colony. *Union* was sold in 1875 to the Boston, Revere Beach & Lynn Railroad.

By 1883 the question was moot, as the Old Colony in that year took control of the ex-BC&F lines. Citizens continued to clamor for renewal of ferry service, and in 1895, a court compelled the Old Colony (under NYNH&H control) to restore ferry service. *Fairhaven* (II) began that service in February 1896, accompanied by celebration and band concerts.

But the music overall was discordant; the railroad wanted to discontinue the ferry, and was accused of going out of its way to make the service unattractive. When *Fairhaven* (II) left the area in 1920, *Yvonne* replaced her. *Yvonne* was a loud, uncomfortable, small, smelly motor launch; in a few months *Winifred* replaced her on the route until the ferry stopped running on March 30, 1929.

Ferry service resumed in February 1896 with the new *Fairhaven* (II), and continued until 1920 when she failed her annual inspection. The railroad was unwilling to make the repairs, and laid her up.

*Below, Fairhaven* (II)'s crew poses on the gangway about 1900. *Fairhaven* (II) was sold to the City of New London and renamed *Mohican* for use as a Thames River ferry.

# Chapter Nine

# The "Consolidated"

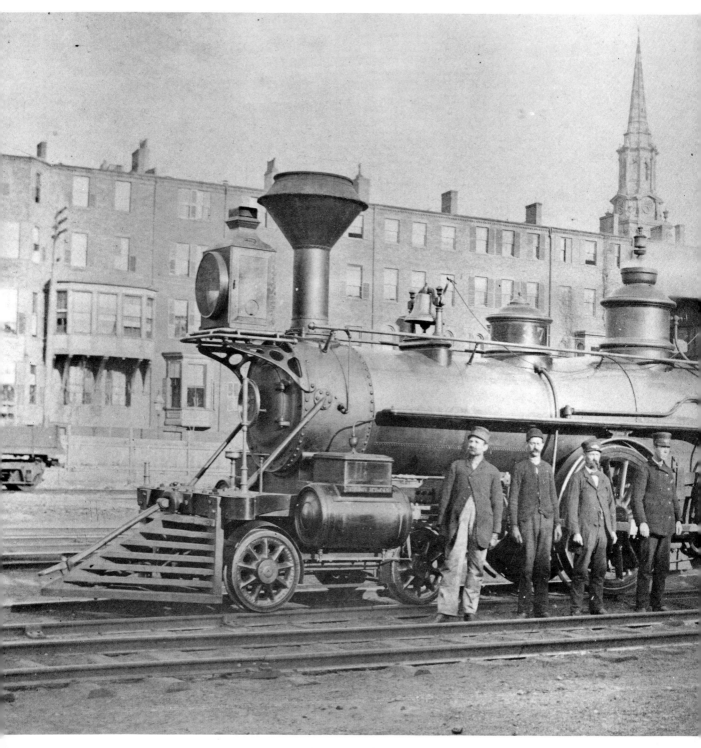

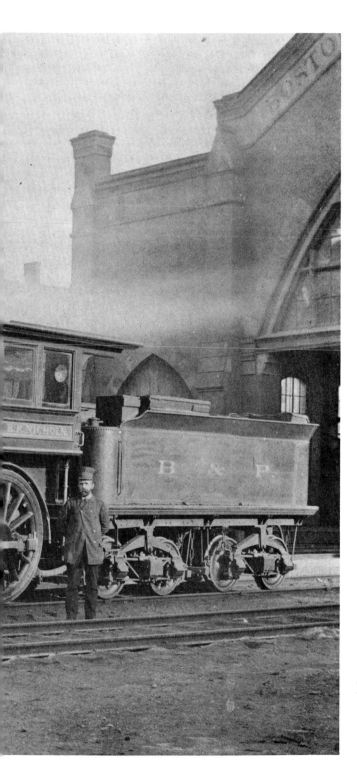

The American economy boomed in the period after the Civil War. New England was experiencing population and economic growth, and the long-distance steamboat lines on Long Island Sound were competing heavily for the freight and passenger trade to and from New York. This competition took the form of cutthroat rate wars followed by an agreement ending the war, followed by periods of uneasy truce and uniformly high rates; the more or less normal cyclic pattern of steamboat economics.

Most of the freight on the steamboats was related to the textile and manufacturing industries that flourished in New England in the Nineteenth century. Fall River and Worcester, for instance, were among the top cities for textile production. That *Atlantic* was crammed with cotton bales on the night of her fatal fire was nothing unusual; cotton in bales was the most significant eastbound commodity. Finished textile goods were carried to New York on the westbound trips. Similarly, large quantities of metals, hardware and other manufactures moved from Bridgeport and New Haven.

The steamboats got this business not so much because of low rates, but because of convenience. A large part of that convenience centered around the location of the steamboat companies' New York piers. Manhattan Island was and is very poorly served by the railroads. The only direct freight access was the New York Central's west side freight line from the north. Most railroad freight consigned to New York was carried across the Hudson or East Rivers for part of its journey on lighters or barges; each railroad operated its own fleet of tugs and barges, and maintained riverside freight terminals in Manhattan, The Bronx or Brooklyn and Queens. By contrast, the steamboat companies delivered the goods without such transshipment delays and costs, at Manhattan piers convenient to the industrial area. The railroads could not do

The Boston & Providence Railroad was the first railroad to reach a Sound steamboat connection, in 1835. The line's managers concentrated on railroading between its namesake cities, rather than on route speculation. As this photo shows, well-maintained equipment and a sense of purpose combine to instill pride in an operation. Here the proud crew shows off its best.

The New York, New Haven and Hartford Railroad, as consolidated, is shown here, as a means of providing an overall perspective. There are, however, some fascinating details. The original line of the surviving company ran between New York and New Haven, and grew by merger, lease and acquisition. The Morgan-imposed northern "boundary," in the form of the Boston & Albany Railroad, remains virtually intact.

## THE NEW YORK, NEW HAVEN AND HARTFORD RAILROAD CO.,

### OPERATED AND CONTROLLED LINES

*Figures on Each Line Indicate Number of Table Showing Service*

Virtually every railroad track east of Providence and south of Boston was part of the Old Colony system. The Old Colony lease proved to be the keystone to the NYNH&H monopoly, inasmuch as it completed the link to Boston as well as bringing in two strong steamboat lines. The final links were the New York and New England and Central New England lines, the latter bringing with them the Hudson River crossing at Poughkeepsie.

quite as well, just as they were outclassed in later years by the convenience of truck shipment.

The competition for increasing business after the end of the Civil War set off a rate reduction war on the Sound in 1867. For a while, the New York-Boston fare dropped from $5.00 to as low as $1.00, which hurt all of the operators. As noted in Chapter Seven, the relative opulence of Jim Fisk's Bristol Line boats helped set them above and apart from the normal run of steamers; the flashy "Admiral" had indeed established the Narragansett company as a power on the Sound. After Fisk's death, that power shifted to the Old Colony Railroad.

After the "Truce of 1869," passenger fares were raised to $5.00, and the revenue division was set at two-thirds to the steamboat company, one-third to the railroads. Ruinous competition had been averted, for the time being. The companies could afford to buy and equip newer, larger, boats, and they did so.

By 1880, a high service level and amenity package was necessary to attract passengers in sufficient numbers. The railway sleeping car was, it seemed, preferable to ordinary small and spartan steamers; but Mr. Pullman's cars were no match for the *Bristol* and *Providence*, and their sybaritic successors on the Fall River Line.

Another rate war erupted in the late 1870s, brought on in part by completion of all-rail routes for freight and in part by dissatisfaction with the Old Colony's stronger position under the terms of the 1869 agreement. At the height of combat in 1879 and 1880, six different entities were operating boat-rail service between New York and Boston, with the "normal" $5.00 passenger fare discounted all the way to $1.00 on a regular basis, and occasional discounts to 50 cents! As you might expect, the war was settled by what became known as the Sound Lines Agreement of 1881, under which the steamboat rates were restored, i.e., raised, to levels just below the railroad fares to comparable points.

The rate-cutting process often meant that fares to intermediate points, where there was no competition, were often higher despite the shorter distances. For example, the Old Colony rail fare between Boston and Newport RI was $1.60 for the 68-mile journey at the same time that the Old Colony was charging a $1.00 fare for the 230-mile boat-rail run from Boston to New York. So it was that a sharp Harvard student in 1880 sought to beat the system by buying a ticket to New York, even though his destination was Newport. But the OCRR people wouldn't let him leave the dock at Newport without paying the sixty cents. He sued the railroad and lost the case, the court holding that the student accepted the terms of the company's fare structure when he boarded the train, and the terms were as stated. In those days, railroads (and other types of business) had an unquestioned right to charge whatever they thought appropriate for services.

---

**Table 9-1**

**Steamboats and Ports, circa 1867-1869**

Between New York and:
Bridgeport: *James B. Schuyler, Bridgeport*
    (*Stamford*)
New Haven: *Elm City, Continental*
Hartford: *State of New York, Granite State,*
    *City of Hartford*
New London: *City of Boston, City of New York,*
Norwich: *City of Lawrence, City of New London*
Stonington: *Stonington, Narragansett*
Providence: *Electra, Galatea, Oceanus*
Bristol: *Bristol, Providence*
Newport: *Old Colony, Newport*

    (relief boats in parentheses)

**Table 9-2**

**Steamboats and Ports circa 1895**

Between New York and:
Bridgeport: *Nutmeg State, Rosedale, Josephine*
New Haven: *Richard Peck, C. H. Northam,*
    (*Elm City, Continental*)
Hartford: *Hartford, Middletown*
New London: *City of Lowell, City of Worcester*
    (*City of Lawrence*)
Stonington: *Maine, New Hampshire* (*Rhode Island*)
Providence: *Massachusetts, Connecticut**
    (*Rhode Island*)
Fall River: *Priscilla, Puritan, Plymouth, Pilgrim*
    (*Providence*)

           * Assuming she was running.

**The steamboat assignments shown in these tables do not even attempt to depict the shuffling of boats that went on in response to traffic and mechanical conditions. They are, however, the general assignments of boats to ports.**

**The tables do, however, reveal the marked change that took place on the Sound between 1868 and 1895. The line boats have become spares or have disappeared. And some of the 1895 boats were still running in 1938.**

Old Colony RR engine No. 232 was typical of the Boat Train engines used in the 1800s. Built as a compound engine (just as in the steamboats, the steam was used twice), she was later converted to a simple engine and renumbered 832 by the NYNH&H.

The name "Old Colony," for the benefit of those not familiar with the area, derives from the local name for the first settlement of Pilgrims at Plymouth MA. It does not refer to Massachusetts in general. Among the railroads acquired by the Old Colony in its expansion program was the Granite Railway, about two miles long, between Milton and Quincy MA. Its significance is that it was America's first railroad, albeit horse-powered. OCRR (and later NYNH&H) officials took great pride in having the nation's eldest rail line in their past, but that pride was undeserved. The OCRR didn't buy it until 1870.

## The Old Colony Expands

The "Sound Lines Agreement" of 1881 settled the rate war of the late '70s by setting fares and rates at profitable levels. By that time, the most powerful steamboat interest on the Sound was the Boston-based Old Colony Railroad.

The Old Colony had embarked on a program of acquiring its extensions in the 1870s. It leased railroads and bought the steamboat lines with which it connected, notably the Fall River, New Bedford, and Island steamers. For example, it was in Boston that decisions were made to close down direct passenger steamboat service between New Bedford and New York, in favor of the more cost-effective (for the railroad) Fall River Line and the OCRR rail connecting trains. It is not likely that an independent steamboat company would have set up its routes in that way. The OCRR also consolidated the Martha's Vineyard and Nantucket routes toward a mainland rail/boat terminal at Woods Hole MA (known as Woods Holl in those days). That orderliness brought about improved profit for the Old Colony, however much it might have increased the travel time for some passengers.

# THE STEAMER PRISCILLA

Launched in 1893 and in service for the 1894 season, *Priscilla* fast became the sentimental favorite of travelers and steamboat fans, particularly those who honeymooned trips aboard her (and their descendants).

At the time of her launch, she was the largest steamboat afloat, some 20 feet longer than *Puritan*. Only one of her later sisters, the 1908 *Commonwealth*, exceeded her size. Her decor was considered breathtaking (see Chapter 13), and *Priscilla* became the favored travel mode for anybody who was anybody.

Only two major accidents marred her 43-year career. In July 1902, the summer that the Marine District wanted to forget, the Merchants & Miners ship *Powhatan*, bound from Baltimore to Providence with 130 passengers, collided with *Priscilla* on a foggy night, ripping a fearsome hole in the lady's bow. More than 1000 passengers were on board; they never made it to New York, being trapped on board the disabled steamer between midnight and dawn. Not one passenger was injured; they were towed back to Newport by *Puritan* the next morning. There was one fatality: a deckhand who was in his bunk in the forward compartment at the point of impact. An example of fog's power to distort signals is this: the accident happened off Newport, and *Priscilla*'s whistle was blown all night long as a distress signal. Nobody on shore heard the signal.

The second violent encounter occurred in June 1926, when *Priscilla*, headed for Fall River in a fog at reduced speed, suddenly bashed a government wharf and grounded at Great Gull Island at the south edge of The Race. 560 passengers were aboard for that trip; no passenger or crewmember was injured. Plainly and simply, Capt. Fred Hamlin was off course; a changing tide had moved the boat south of the Race channel. The Government inspectors suspended Capt. Hamlin's pilot's licence for fifteen days; whether that action was justified was a topic of conversation for years afterward.

Below, the interior view of *Priscilla*'s wheelhouse shows three steering wheels, but only the forward wheel was in everyday use with the steam steering gear. The aft two wheels were to be connected and used only in case of a failure of the power steering mechanism. Note the block on the floor rendering them immobile during normal operation. Pilot Brayley is at left, Quartermaster Rector is at the wheel, and Captain Abe Simmons is at the customary middle window station.

The opulence that characterized *Priscilla* extended even to the engine room, shown at the lower right; note the ornate chandeliers and wood paneling. The crankshaft is in the foreground, with the cylinders below the platform on which the controls were mounted.

Possible inconvenience to customers was the farthest thing from the OCRR managers' minds. Passenger travel on the steamboats was booming; most boats sailed at close to capacity in the summer, and the summer season was lengthened; travel was heavy from March to November. While fares had been lowered during rate wars, there is nothing to indicate that food or beverage prices were reduced, so total revenues were not inadequate. It is helpful to note that, even at the height of the rate war, the Old Colony Steamboat Co. could still set money aside for a large new boat, *Pilgrim*.

But the railroads' through freight and passenger trains were hurting during the steamboat war, carrying twenty per cent of normal loads. Nearly everybody was traveling aboard the low-fare boats. The greatest sufferer was the New York, New Haven & Hartford Railroad. Here, around 1881, in spite of another rate-setting agreement, we can see the early seeds of the NYNH&H Railroad's drive to monopolize transportation facilities in New England. The motivation was not so much greed as it was fear, and the NYNH&H management's desire to insulate itself and the stockholders from the consequences of full steamboats and empty trains.

### "The Consolidated"

The New York and New Haven Railroad (cf. Chapter Two) provided the western link in what became southern New England's transportation monopoly. Through a series of leases and acquisi-

tions, the New York and New Haven extended its services; in 1870 a joint operating agreement between the New York and New Haven and the Hartford and New Haven, along with the lease of the Shore Line Railway (cf. Chapter Four) created the New York, New Haven and Hartford Railroad system, from New York, with two major lines from New Haven through Hartford to Springfield MA, and along the shore to New London. Since the Hartford and New Haven owned a New Haven-New York steamboat line and Belle Dock, the NYNH&H was also in the steamboat business.

The companies were consolidated in 1872, which gave rise to the NYNH&H's nickname of that era: "The Consolidated." Considering the later growth and acquisition spree that was to be conducted by the NYNH&H, it was a far-seeing description indeed. The New York, New Haven and Hartford Railroad named as its first President William D. Bishop of Bridgeport, a son of Alfred Bishop and

---

The New York, New Haven and Hartford and the New York and New England railroads jointly operated the famous "White Train" between New York and Boston, via Willimantic, not the shore route. It was a ghostly apparition that attracted much favorable attention, in competition with the steamboat services. For all the White Train's notoriety, it lasted only four years (1891-1895). When the trains got electric lights, steamboat patronage declined somewhat, and rail traffic increased.

consequently brother to Ferris, whom we met in Chapters Two and Three.

The NYNH&H management spent the next few years beating off or buying out groups seeking to build railroads parallel to the Consolidated lines, and in leasing or acquiring other potential links in a New York-Boston chain. The use of the lease as a control device was an interesting headache remedy: for, say, 8 per cent on the invested capital per year, the Consolidated would lease the interloper for 99, 499, or 999 years. Because the NYNH&H group saw their own salvation in eliminating competition and ruinous rate-cutting, it became a profitable activity for a while to launch parallel railroads and lease or sell them, built or not, to the Consolidated, which could easily afford the lease or purchase payments because their rates were not being undercut by competitors.

Two major segments of the NYNH&H system were added in 1892. The New York Providence and Boston was leased. The NYP&B had built a drawbridge across the Thames River between New London and Groton in 1889, thus closing the last physical gap in the Shore rail line between New York and Boston (see Chapter Five). But the Consolidated still did not control a complete New York-Boston rail line. Despite its name, the NYP&B extended eastward only to Providence; the last 45 miles to Boston were under Old Colony Railroad control.

The other major 1892 addition was the Housatonic Railroad, operating northward from South Norwalk and Bridgeport through the western part of Connecticut to Pittsfield MA.

So, in 1892, three railroad systems had been forged from the more than 200 incorporated railroad companies in the area relevant to our discussion. The NYNH&H system (with owned steamboat services serving Providence and Stonington and independent steamboat service connections at Bridgeport, New Haven, and Hartford) owned about 150 miles of railroad and leased another 503. The Old Colony system (steamboats to Fall River and New Bedford) contained just over 450 rail miles, and a third group, the New York and New England Railroad (New London steamboats), was a 500-mile system. Before considering further consolidation, let us meet the man under whose leadership that activity took place.

## The Boss and the Would-Be Monopoly

John Pierpont Morgan was born in Hartford CT. He entered the investment banking business with a considerable advantage: he joined his father's firm, which had strong ties to European sources of capital. His grandfather had been a backer of the original Hartford and New Haven Railroad.

Pierpont Morgan's first railroad-related battle, in 1869, saw him beat out Jay Gould for control of a small railroad in New York state. Ten years later, William Vanderbilt asked Mr. Morgan to sell a large block of New York Central stock. The deal put the financier on the Central's Board of Directors. Activities with other railroads followed, with only one of them being a directorship in the New York Providence & Boston, beginning in 1887.

Mr. Morgan gradually became more powerful as a regulator of railroads than the Interstate Commerce Commission (formed in 1887). Most of the Morgan-imposed solutions involved reduction or elimination of competition, and working arrangements or mergers. This was to be the blueprint for his beloved New England.

Those who disagreed with J. P. Morgan soon had reason to suppose that the man had no sentiment. Yet, one wonders whether the New York, New Haven and Hartford Railroad's Quixotic quest for a New England transportation monopoly would have been allowed to get as far out of hand if Mr. Morgan hadn't been a local boy, from Hartford. Here is one indication of his mind-set: whereas most people called the railroad "The New Haven" or "The Consolidated," Morgan always referred to it as "The Hartford."

With the NYP&B lease in 1892, J. P. Morgan joined "The Hartford's" Board, bringing a combination of a forceful personality, a proven record of resounding financial successes, and desire for non-competitive stability that, if possible, exceeded the feeling already present in the breasts of the NYNH&H directors. His influence immediately began to be felt. Charles Mellen was later to say that the activities of the Consolidated Board of Directors without J. P. Morgan would have been "as lacking in interest as a herd of cows deprived of a bull." Membership on the NYNH&H directorate was an outstanding status symbol, and no member wished to risk

---

On the next pages, you will find the timetables for one of the more remarkable railroad services ever operated in America. The need grew out of the 1876 American Centennial; Grand Central Station existed in New York City, but Penn Station and the Hell Gate Bridge did not. To reach Pennsylvania Railroad tracks for the Centennial Exposition site at Philadelphia, a journey by water to Jersey City was required. Well; why not ferry the cars from a New England train down the East River and to the PRR?

Thus was born the Boston-Philadelphia Express, getting you there "with no change of cars." Two successive ferry steamers named *Maryland* carried the cars between Jersey City and the NYNH&H's Harlem River facility. NYNH&H and NY&NE rails took the train to Boston.

Opening of Pennsylvania Station in New York in November 1910, however, meant only a short taxi hop to Grand Central Terminal. The *Maryland* service ended in 1912, after the *Titanic* disaster caused doubts in the NYNH&H's president's mind.

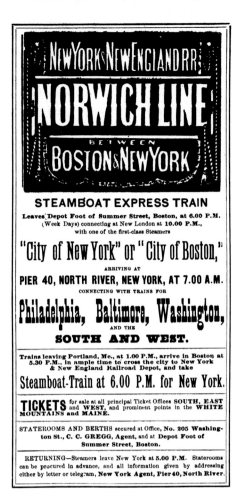

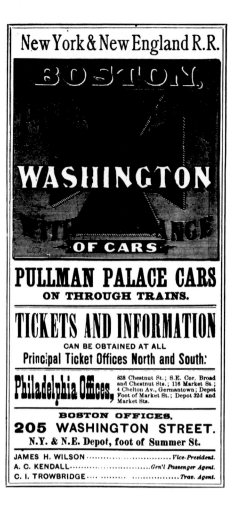

# New York & New England R.R.
## AND CONNECTING LINES.

### WESTWARD.

| | | EXPRESS. | EXPRESS. |
|---|---|---|---|
| Boston (via N.Y. & N.E.R.R.) | lve | *6.00 p.m. | ........ |
| Worcester " | " | *7.30 " | ........ |
| Providence (via P. & W. R.R.) | " | ........ | ........ |
| Putnam | " | 8.20 " | ........ |
| Willimantic | " | 9.15 p.m. | ........ |
| Hartford | " | 10.30 " | ........ |
| New Haven | " | 11.40 " | ........ |
| Jersey City (via Transfer Steamer Maryland) | arr | 4.35 a.m. | ........ |
| Jersey City | lve | 4.35 a.m. | ........ |
| Newark | " | ........ | ........ |
| Elizabeth | " | ........ | ........ |
| Trenton | " | ........ | ........ |
| Philadelphia | " | 9.00 a.m. | ........ |
| Lancaster | " | 11 05 " | ........ |
| Harrisburg | " | 12 10 p.m. | ........ |
| Altoona | " | 4.00 " | ........ |
| Pittsburg | arr | 7.30 " | ........ |
| Pittsburg (via C. & P. R.R.) | lve | ........ | ........ |
| Wheeling | arr | ........ | ........ |
| Cleveland | " | ........ | ........ |
| Pittsburg (via P., Ft. W. & C. Ry.) | lve | ¶7.30 p.m. | ........ |
| Alliance | arr | 10.10 " | ........ |
| Orrville | " | ........ | ........ |
| Mansfield | " | ........ | ........ |
| Crestline | " | 1.30 a.m. | ........ |
| Forest | " | ........ | ........ |
| Lima | " | 3.27 " | ........ |
| Fort Wayne | " | 5.00 " | ........ |
| Plymouth | " | 6.25 " | ........ |
| Chicago | " | 9.00 " | ........ |
| Pittsburg | lve | ¶11.45 p.m. | ........ |
| Mansfield (via North Western Ohio R'y.) | " | 6 45 a.m. | ........ |
| Toledo | arr | 10.40 " | ........ |
| Pittsburg (via Pan-Handle Route) | lve | ‖7.32 p.m. | ........ |
| Steubenville | arr | 8.00 a.m. | ........ |
| Newark | " | 1.15 " | ........ |
| Columbus | " | 2.30 " | ........ |
| Xenia | arr | ‖9.35 a.m. | ........ |
| Dayton | " | ........ | ........ |
| Cincinnati | " | 6.55 " | ........ |
| Urbana | arr | ‖8.07 a.m. | ........ |
| Piqua | " | 8.58 " | ........ |
| Bradford Junction | " | 9.22 " | ........ |
| Logansport | " | *2.30 p.m. | ........ |
| State Line | " | 10.20 " | ........ |
| Chicago | " | 8.30 " | ........ |
| Richmond | " | ‖10.33 a.m. | ........ |
| Cambridge City | " | 11.04 " | ........ |
| Indianapolis | " | 12.55 p.m. | ........ |
| Cincinnati (via L.C. & L. R.R.) | lve | *3.10 p.m. | ........ |
| Louisville | arr | 7.45 " | ........ |
| Indianapolis (via J.M. & I. R.R.) | lve | *6.25 p.m. | ........ |
| Louisville | arr | 11.00 " | ........ |
| Indianapolis (via Vandalia Line) | lve | *1.00 p.m. | ........ |
| Vincennes (via E. & T. H. R.R.) | arr | 5.37 " | ........ |
| Evansville | " | 7 40 " | ........ |
| Indianapolis (via I. & V. R.R.) | lve | ........ | ........ |
| Vincennes | " | ........ | ........ |
| Indianapolis (via Vandalia Line) | lve | ‖1 00 p.m. | ........ |
| Terre Haute | " | 3.05 " | ........ |
| Effingham | " | 5.40 " | ........ |
| Vandalia | " | 6.33 " | ........ |
| St. Louis | " | 9 00 " | ........ |

‖ Daily.    * Sundays excepted.    ¶ Saturdays excepted.

# New York & New England R.R.
## AND CONNECTING LINES.

### EASTWARD.

| | | EXPRESS. | EXPRESS. |
|---|---|---|---|
| St. Louis (via Vandalia Line) | lve | ‖8.00 a.m | ........ |
| Vandalia " | " | 11.00 " | ........ |
| Effingham " | " | 12.00 m. | ........ |
| Terre Haute " | " | 2.45 p.m. | ........ |
| Indianapolis " | arr | 5.35 " | ........ |
| Vincennes (via I. & V. R.R.) | lve | *12.35 p.m. | ........ |
| Indianapolis " | arr | 5.35 " | ........ |
| Evansville (via E. & T. H. R.R.) | lve | *8.50 a.m. | ........ |
| Vincennes " | " | 11.35 noon | ........ |
| Indianapolis (via Vandalia Line) | arr | 5.35 p.m. | ........ |
| Louisville (via J. M. & I. R.R.) | lve | *7.30 a.m. | ........ |
| Indianapolis " | arr | 12.00 m. | ........ |
| Louisville (via L. C. & L. R.R.) | lve | ‖3.25 p.m. | ........ |
| Cincinnati " | arr | 8.00 " | ........ |
| Indianapolis (via Pan-Handle Route) | lve | ‖6.45 p.m. | ........ |
| Cambridge City " | " | 7.58 " | ........ |
| Richmond " | " | 8.40 " | ........ |
| Chicago " | " | *8.40 a.m. | ........ |
| State Line " | " | 6.30 " | ........ |
| Logansport " | " | 1.40 p.m. | ........ |
| Bradford Junction " | " | ‖3.30 " | ........ |
| Piqua " | " | 10.20 " | ........ |
| Urbana " | " | 11.14 " | ........ |
| Cincinnati " | lve | ‖8.30 p.m. | ........ |
| Dayton " | " | ........ | ........ |
| Xenia " | arr | 10.50 " | ........ |
| Columbus " | " | ‖1.00 a.m | ........ |
| Newark " | " | 2.00 " | ........ |
| Steubenville " | " | 6 00 " | ........ |
| Pittsburg " | arr | 7.50 " | ........ |
| Toledo (via M.C. & L.M Ry | lve | ........ | ........ |
| Mansfield " | " | ........ | ........ |
| Pittsburg " | " | ........ | ........ |
| Chicago (via P., Ft. W. & C. Ry) | lve | ‖3.50 p.m | ........ |
| Plymouth " | " | ........ | ........ |
| Fort Wayne " | " | 8.10 " | ........ |
| Lima " | " | 9.40 " | ........ |
| Forest " | " | ........ | ........ |
| Crestline " | " | 11.55 " | ........ |
| Mansfield " | " | 12.25 a.m | ........ |
| Orrville " | " | 2.30 " | ........ |
| Alliance " | " | 4.10 " | ........ |
| Pittsburg " | arr | 7.30 a.m. | ........ |
| Cleveland (via C. & P. R.R.) | lve | ........ | ........ |
| Wheeling " | " | ........ | ........ |
| Pittsburg " | arr | ........ | ........ |
| Pittsburg " | lve | ‖8.45 a m | ........ |
| Altoona " | " | 12.10 p.m | ........ |
| Harrisburg " | arr | 3.45 " | ........ |
| Lancaster " | " | 4.45 " | ........ |
| Philadelphia " | " | 7.30 " | ........ |
| Trenton " | " | 7.48 " | ........ |
| Elizabeth " | " | ........ | ........ |
| Newark " | " | 9.00 " | ........ |
| Jersey City " | " | 9.18 p.m. | ........ |
| Jersey City (via Transfer Steamer Maryland) | lve | *10.35 p.m. | ........ |
| New Haven " | " | 2 20 a.m. | ........ |
| Hartford " | " | 3 45 " | ........ |
| Willimantic " | " | 5.00 " | ........ |
| Putnam " | " | 5.50 " | ........ |
| Providence " | " | ........ | ........ |
| Blackstone " | " | ........ | ........ |
| Worcester (via N. & W. Div) | " | 6 43 " | ........ |
| Boston (via N.Y. & N.E.R.R.) | " | 7.30 " | ........ |
| | " | 8.00 " | ........ |

‖ Daily.    * Sundays excepted.    ¶ Saturdays excepted.

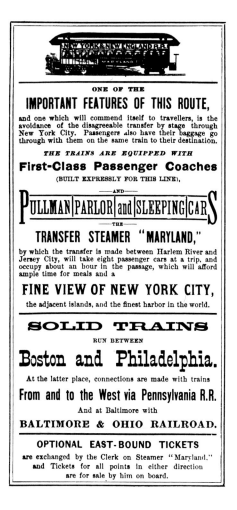
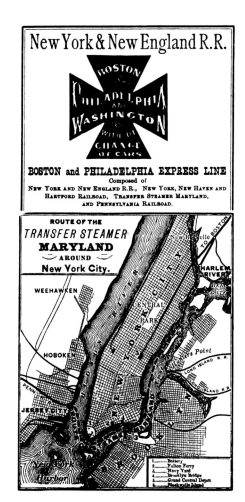

## THE STEAMERS *MARYLAND* (I AND II)

*Maryland* (I) was built in 1853 by Harlan & Hollingsworth for a Pennsylvania Railroad predecessor to cross the Susquehanna River near Havre-de-Grace MD. When purchased by the NY&NE in 1875, she was extensively rebuilt for carferry service in New York harbor. The first Centennial Trains, two a day each way, ran between Boston and Philadelphia in May 1876.

After the Exposition closed, the day train was cancelled and *Maryland* (I) shuttled freight cars during the day in addition to the night train,

renamed the *Federal Express*. A fire on one of the Pullman cars in December 1888 spread to the ferry; all was a total loss, although the people escaped.

A second *Maryland* was built, with iron hull, a bit smaller than *Maryland* (I). She began service in February 1890. A day train, the *Colonial Express*, was added to the schedule by the NYNH&H in 1892; we see it at right, approaching Jersey City.

As we noted, the handling of passenger trains by carferry was discontinued in 1912. The night train was rerouted via the Poughkeepsie Bridge until the Hell Gate Bridge opened in 1916.

his standing by raising objections to the Plan of the Moment. Mr. Morgan's method of ending discussion was simple: he would pound the table and call for a vote, saying "Let's see where these gentleman stand." Where they stood was mostly out of Mr. Morgan's way.

The NYNH&H set out to attain three goals in 1892: (1) to complete the destruction of the New York and New England system; (2) to place a rail line between New York and Boston under its direct ownership and control; (3) to control the rail-water Sound routes.

## The New York and New England

For the NYNH&H and for J. P. Morgan, attainment of goal (1) was paramount. The New York and New England was a dedicated if disadvantaged competitor, running southwest out of Boston through central Connecticut to Fishkill, on the Hudson River. The NY&NE's disadvantages arose out of two circumstances: the Boston and Albany had a better westward connection to the north, and the NY&NE did not have its own rail entrance into New York City. In earlier years, a connection with the

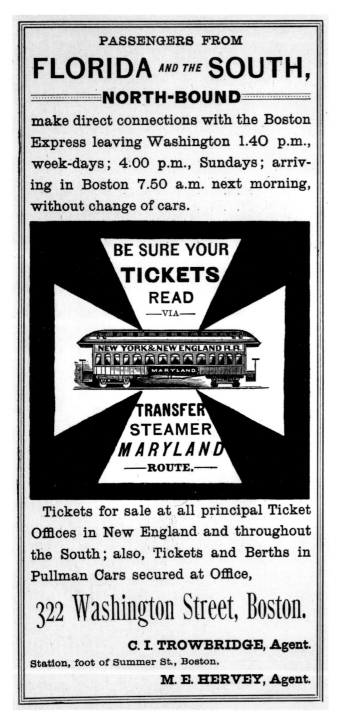

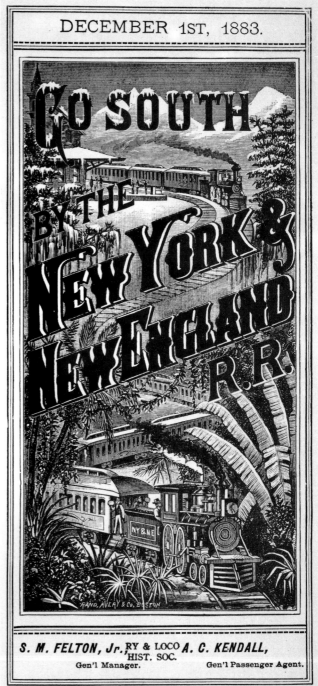

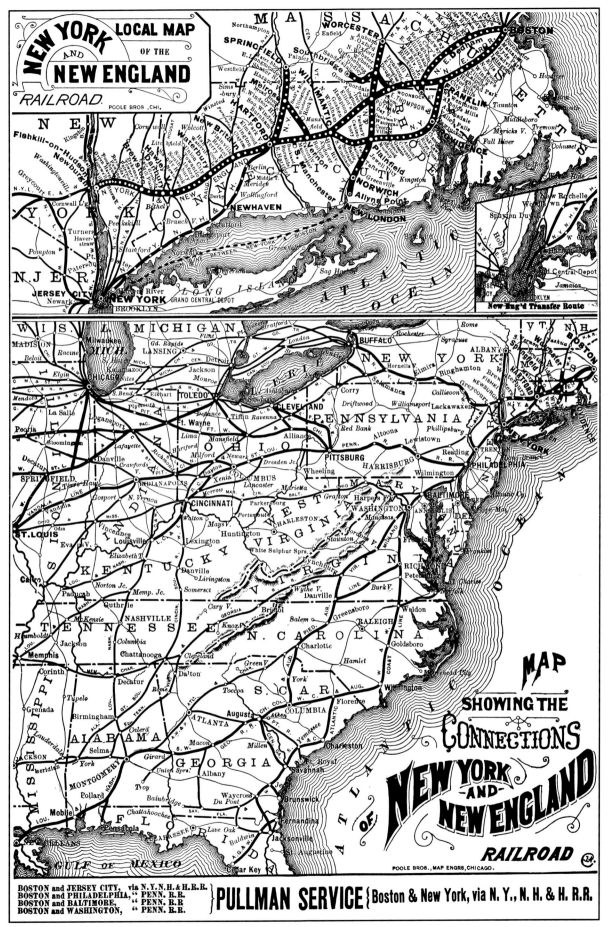

BOSTON and JERSEY CITY, via N.Y.N.H.&H.R.R.
BOSTON and PHILADELPHIA, " PENN. R.R.
BOSTON and BALTIMORE, " PENN. R.R.
BOSTON and WASHINGTON, " PENN. R.R.

**PULLMAN SERVICE** { Boston & New York, via N. Y., N. H. & H. R.R.

This later NY&NE timetable (February 1884) gives us a good overview of the line's well thought out operations. If you are traveling between Boston and Philadelphia, the NY&NE and its transfer steamer *Maryland* will allow you to "Avoid Vexatious Transfer" through New York City and across the Hudson (likely to be the object of much present-day envy). The cover engraving features *Maryland* (I) rounding the Battery on her way to Jersey City. This involves a bit of artist's license, as the trip in that direction was made in the wee dark hours of the morning.

If you prefer, the Norwich Line (next page) will take you on the *City of Worcester* or *City of New York* to New London, and to connecting trains. Or (overleaf), the heavy steel rails of the popular line via Fishkill Landing will whisk you eastward from the Hudson, "through magnificent scenery."

But the real sleeper here is the Boston Night Train (overleaf), departing Grand Central Terminal at 11:35 PM, almost six hours later than the Sound steamboats. No sea air, no orchestra; but long after the steamers sailed into memory, the NYNH&H's *Owl* did that job.

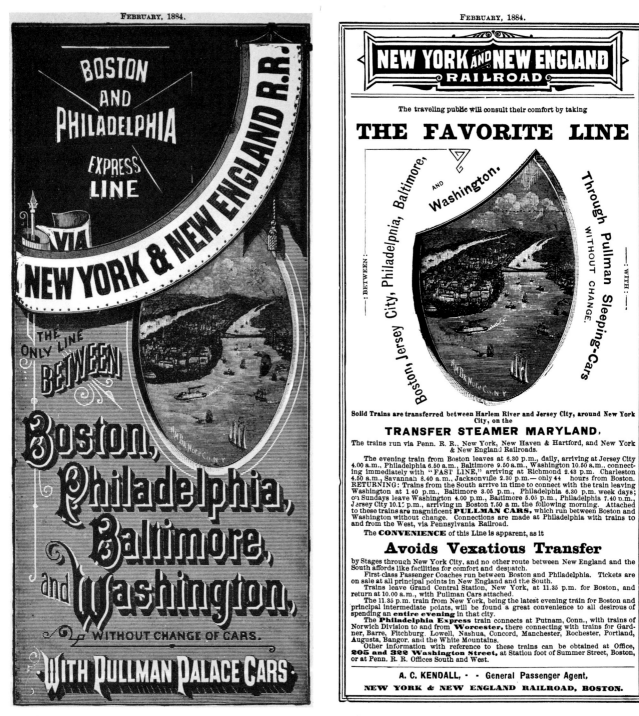

Hartford and New Haven at Hartford allowed a rail connection to New York, but that connection came under control of the Consolidated. The NY&NE could and did move freight on barges down the Hudson from Fishkill, but most freight, from eastern Massachusetts, went via steamer through Norwich and Allyn's Point. The New York and New England's difficulty on the New York end was somewhat balanced by the Consolidated's lack of a rail entry into Boston; these were controlled by the Old Colony, the Boston and Albany, and the NY&NE.

The NY&NE system grew out of a group of smaller railroads that merged into the Boston, Hartford and Erie Railroad in 1864. This was a Massachusetts company, controlled from Boston, and it received some help from that State's legislature in building its extensions. Connecticut's legislators regarded the BH&E with jaundiced eyes, and for good reason.

Unfortunately for the region, the Boston Hartford & Erie was looted by a succession of buccaneers almost from the start. Jim Fisk, Dan'l Drew and Jay

---

---

Gould all had their hands in the action. Some of the construction was done by the same interests that had built the Union Pacific, a national scandal that involved literally dozens of U. S. Congressman, Senators and other officials.

So the BH&E was never financially strong, and went bankrupt in 1870. One of the receivers appointed was Charles Peter Clark, who had considerable experience in the China trade. The BH&E was destitute; upon taking over, the receivers found only $10 in the railroad's checking account.

The company emerged from receivership as the New York and New England Railroad, with more or less direct financial links to the Erie Railroad across the Hudson. The physical link started as a train ferry connection in 1881 between Fishkill and Newburgh. Another element of the NY&NE system important to us was the Norwich and Worcester Railroad, which also owned the Norwich/Allyn's Point steamboat service to New York. That lease of the Norwich & Worcester was held to have been the one smart move that the BH&E people had made.

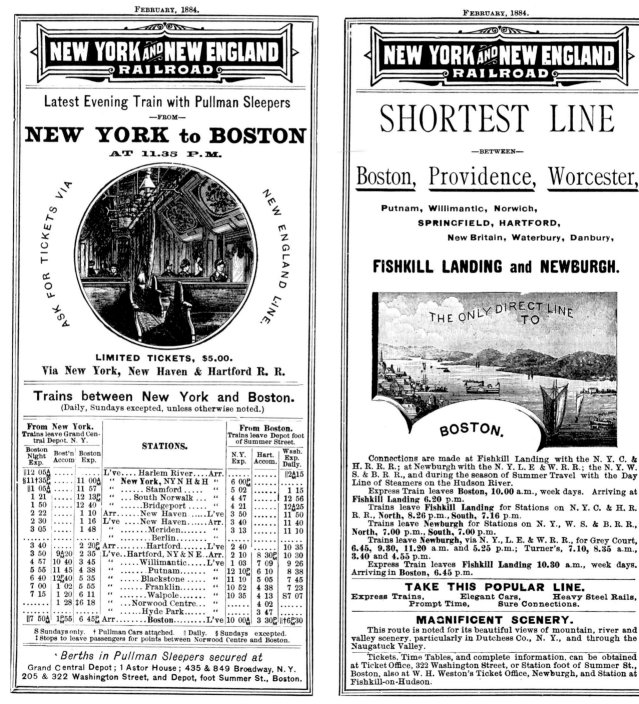

Fishkill NY (now called Beacon) became a gateway to New England in 1881, as the New York & New England built the rail line to the shore. The railroad bought the sidewheel ferry *William T. Hart*, (named for the President of the Boston Hartford & Erie and first President of the NY&NE) for the river crossing work to the Erie Railroad at Newburgh on the Hudson's west shore.

When the New York transfer ferry *Maryland* (I) burned in 1888, the trains that used it were diverted to the Hudson River crossing until *Maryland* (II) was placed into service in 1889.

The NYNH&H discontinued the Fishkill-Newburgh trans-Hudson ferry in 1907, after acquiring and strengthening the Poughkeepsie bridge.

By 1887, the Erie connection was disquieting to the Consolidated; Jay Gould still sat on the NY&NE board, along with other New Yorkers. And now the Central New England was building a bridge across the Hudson at Poughkeepsie. Mr. Gould also tried to create a New York connection, using a line named the New York and Northern, in New York's Bronx, Westchester and Putnam counties.

That made the NY&NE situation a battle in a larger war between the Erie interests and the Morgan/New York Central/NYNH&H interests. The Consolidated responded to this invasion in a mood to take no prisoners. First, they hired Charles Peter Clark, Receiver and President of the NY&NE, as President of the NYNH&H system, in 1887. In addition to being an effective railroad executive, Mr. Clark knew the NY&NE's strengths and weaknesses; he proceeded to strangle his old system.

In 1892, Charles Mellen (whom we met briefly in Chapter Two) returned to New England after a stint with the Union Pacific Railroad, to become General Manager of the NY&NE. His performance there in only a few months was sufficient to cause Charles Clark to hire Mr. Mellen away from the NY&NE, making him Second Vice President (Traffic) of the NYNH&H. So impressed was J. P. Morgan with Mr. Mellen's competence and audacity that in 1893 the financier arranged for Mr. Mellen to become President of another Morgan-controlled property, the Northern Pacific Railroad, which was in need of help. During his Northern Pacific period, Charles Mellen improved revenues, improved the railroad, and acquired the friendship of a New Yorker who owned a North Dakota ranch. The part-time rancher was Theodore Roosevelt.

But in 1892, Messrs. Clark and Mellen wrought havoc on the NY&NE. The details of that struggle, while colorful, are beyond the scope of this volume. Suffice to say that the NYNH&H gradually withdrew all connecting traffic and tariff arrangements with the NY&NE. No through tariffs at Hartford. No through traffic from the Pennsylvania Railroad from New York. (The PRR had no love for the Erie management either.) The New York and Harlem (New York Central) blocked the New York City rail entry plan. But the NY&NE was nothing if

---

Portrait of a busy freight terminal, Fishkill Landing on the Hudson River. Freight cars bearing the insignia of once-familiar railroads occupy the riverfront terminal. Most prominent, of course, is the Maltese cross of the New York and New England.

The *William T. Hart* is on its way with another group of cars. This western gateway service, started in 1881, would not have been possible before June 22, 1880, the day that marathon labor turned the Erie Railroad from a 6-foot gauge line to the compatible standard 4' 8-1/2" gauge.

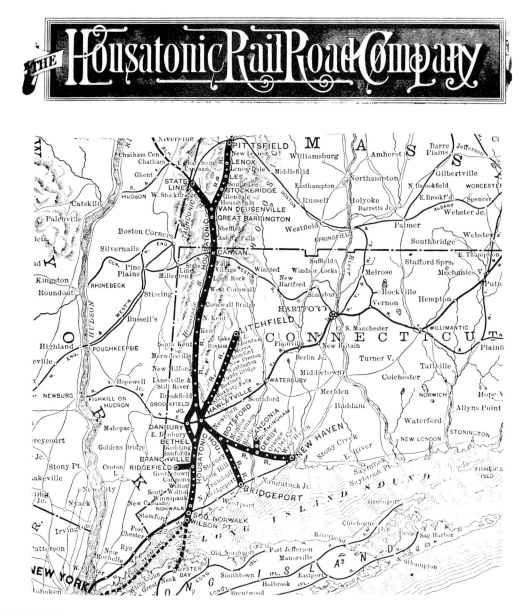

CAPE CHARLES

## FROM WILSON'S POINT TO OYSTER BAY BY RAIL

The map at the left shows the routing of the *Long Island and Eastern States Express*, an overnight passenger train between New York and Boston. It has been described as the most creative routing of any train in New England. Necessity mothered this invention in 1891 after the NY&NE was deprived of its direct rail connection to New York City.

The New England Terminal Co. (not to be confused with the New England *Transfer* Co.), had been set up in 1890 by the Housatonic Railroad with help from the NY&NE. The Terminal Company ferried cars between Wilson Point at South Norwalk CT and freight facilities at Pier 45 East River, using the carferry *Express* as the prime mover. The routing offered an alternative to the NYNH&H to move freight to New York City; it was not well received in the Yellow Building.

The Oyster Bay service was handled by a former Chesapeake Bay carferry named *Cape Charles*, purchased in 1891. She is shown at the lower left in the livery of her original owner, the New York, Philadelphia and Norfolk Railroad (PRR). The *Long Island and Eastern States Express* and a few freight trains operated from Long Island City on the Long Island Rail Road to Oyster Bay NY, where the *Cape Charles* took over, moving the cars across the Sound to Wilson Point at South Norwalk CT, connecting with the Housatonic Railroad. Housatonic and NY&NE rails completed the route to Boston.

Service started in September 1891 and ended abruptly less than a year later in July 1892, when the NYNH&H acquired control of the Housatonic Railroad as part of their plan to rid the world of the NY&NE. At top right, we're on board *Cape Charles* as LIRR and NY&NE officials watch their business car come aboard for the inspection trip that preceded service introduction. Below, a view from the float bridge toward *Cape Charles* as construction work crews put the finishing touches on the bridge and approaches. *Cape Charles* was sold by the NYNH&H to a Louisiana company in 1896.

not creative. A working arrangement with the Housatonic Railroad in 1888 allowed the NY&NE to offer a long car-float service from Wilson's Point to Manhattan's East River piers.

In 1892, the Consolidated (with commissionable help from the Morgan banking firm) gained control of the Housatonic railroad and removed the Wilson's Point connection. The severely wounded NY&NE's last hope was the New York and Northern, and in 1892, J. P. Morgan reportedly orchestrated the death blow. It was done simply enough; the New York Central leased the New York and Harlem. Mr. Morgan personally acquired controlling interest in the New York and Northern, reorganized it as the New York and Putnam, and leased it to the New York Central.

## The Central New England

Beginning with the Connecticut Western Railroad in 1871, a group of railroads were formed and built to operate between Springfield and Hartford on the east and two Hudson River points on the west. These were Poughkeepsie and Rhinecliff. By 1889, these lines had been brought together under the control of the Philadelphia and Reading interests. This small combine was known as the Central New England & Western. The "western" part was the Poughkeepsie Bridge across the Hudson River, financed by Philadelphia interests primarily to facilitate the movement of coal to New England.

A. A. McLeod became President of the Philadel-

---

### NEW YORK AND NEW ENGLAND RAILROAD

#### BOSTON & THE EAST to all Points West
— VIA —
NEW YORK & NEW ENGLAND R.R., New York, Lake Erie & Western R.R.
Buffalo, Niagara Falls, Chatauqua Lake & Chicago & Gr. Tr. Ry.

| DAILY, except Sunday. | SCHEDULE. | DAILY, except Sunday. | |
|---|---|---|---|
| 8 30 A.M. | Lv. BOSTON....... N.Y.&N.E. Ar. | | 6 10 P.M. |
| 9 25 " | " Franklin........ " " | | 5 19 " |
| 9 48 " | " Blackstone... ... " " | | 5 00 " |
| 9 35 " | " Worcester.......... " " | | 5 33 " |
| 10 45 " | " Putnam............. " " | | 4 05 " |
| 9 10 " | " Providence........ " " | | 5 50 " |
| 11 35 " | " Willimantic....... " " | | 3 25 " |
| 9 20 " | " Rockville......... " " | | 3 02 " |
| 7 40 " | " Springfield........ " " | | 7 35 " |
| 12 50 P.M. | " Hartford.......... " " | 9 30 P.M. | 2 10 " |
| 1 10 " | " New Britain,...... " " | 9 08 " | 1 52 " |
| 1 20 " | " Plainville........ " " | 9 00 " | 1 43 " |
| 1 32 " | " Bristol........... " " | 8 50 " | 1 32 " |
| 12 40 " | " Meriden........... " " | | 2 17 " |
| 2 10 " | " Waterbury......... " " | 8 15 P.M. | 1 00 " |
| 3 00 " | " Hawleyville....... " " | 7 15 " | 12 02 " |
| 3 15 " | " Danbury........... " " | 7 00 " | 11 50 A.M. |
| 3 35 " | " Brewsters......... " " | 6 35 " | 11 30 " |
| 4 55 " | " FISHKILL ON HUDSON " | 5 10 " | 10 00 " |
| 6 30 " | " Newburgh.......... Erie R. | 4 15 " | 9 31 " |
| 8 04 " | " Turner's.......... " " | 3 27 " | 7 40 " |
| | " Greycourt......... " " | | |
| 12 56 A.M. | Ar. Binghampton.... " " | 10 27 A.M. | 11 41 P.M. |
| 2 25 " | " Elmira............ " " | | 9 57 " |
| 2 56 " | " Corning........... " " | | 9 20 " |
| 4 07 " | " Hornellsville..... " " | | 8 05 " |
| 7 00 " | " Buffalo........... " " | 4 30 A.M. | 8 30 A.M. |
| 7 28 " | " Niagara Falls..... " " | | 7 43 " |
| 7 35 " | " Suspension Bridge....... " " | 3 22 A.M. | 7 35 " |
| 7 35 " | Lv. Suspension Bridge....Gr.Tr.R. | 3 22 " | 7 15 A.M. |
| 9 10 " | " Hamilton.......... " " | 1 52 " | 5 45 " |
| 12 57 P.M. | " P't Huron(C'trl.Time)C.&G.T.R. | 8 50 P.M. | 1 55 " |
| | " Battle Creek...... " " | | 8 20 P.M. |
| 9 30 " | Ar.Chicago........ " | 11 25 A.M. | 3 00 " |
| | Lv. Salamanca (C'trl Time) Erie R. | 4 50 " | 5 20 P.M. |
| | " Jamestown......... " " | 2 50 " | 3 15 " |
| | Ar.Lakew'd(ChautauquaL.). | | 3 00 " |
| | " Corry............. " " | 2 07 " | 2 20 " |
| | " Meadville......... " " | 12 55 " | 1 00 " |
| | " Oil City.......... " " | 8 20 " | 3 20 " |
| | " Leavittsburg...... " " | 10 40 P.M. | 9 55 A.M. |
| | Lv.Leavittsburg.......... " " | 10 35 " | 9 45 " |
| | Ar.Cleveland............ " " | 6 00 " | 8 15 " |
| | " Mansfield......... " " | 7 28 " | 6 00 " |
| | " Galion............ " " | 6 52 " | 5 17 " |
| | " Marion............ " " | 6 20 " | 4 20 " |
| | " Lima.............. " " | 4 40 " | 2 50 " |
| | " Huntington........ " " | 2 30 " | 12 35 " |
| | " Chicago........... " " | 10 00 A.M. | 7 45 P.M. |
| | " Urbana............ " " | 4 28 P.M. | 12 46 A.M. |
| | " Springfield....... " " | 4 05 " | 2 24 " |
| | " Dayton............ " " | 3 25 " | 1 40 " |
| | " Cincinnati........ " " | 1 20 " | 11 30 P.M. |
| | " Louisville........ L.&N.R.R. | | |
| | " Louisville ....... O.&Miss.R. | | |
| | " St. Louis......... | | |

THROUGH Pullman Sleeping Cars and Coaches from Turners' via N.Y.,L.E.& W.R.R.&C.&G.T.R. Passengers transferred between Fishkill on Hudson and Newburgh by Weston's Carriage Transfer. Space reserved in Pullman sleepers in advance upon application to agents of N.Y.&N.E.R.R.

---

### NEW YORK AND NEW ENGLAND RAILROAD

#### "Washington Night Express Train."
PULLMAN SLEEPING CARS, WITHOUT CHANGE

BETWEEN

**BOSTON, PHILADELPHIA, BALTIMORE, AND WASHINGTON,**

CONNECTIONS FOR

## Chicago and the West,

— VIA —

New York and New England R. R.,

"POUGHKEEPSIE BRIDGE," READING R. R. SYSTEM,

AND

### Baltimore and Ohio R. R.

| SOUTHBOUND. | Washington Night Express Daily. | NORTHBOUND. | Washington Night Express Daily. |
|---|---|---|---|
| Lv. Boston, N.Y. & N.E. Summer Street Depot. | *7 00 P.M. | Lv. Chicago, via Bellaire ..... | 9 50 P.M. |
| Franklin...... | 7 42 " | Pittsburg ..... | 9 20 " |
| Putnam...... | 8 36 " | Washington, B. & O. R. R..... | *2 40 " |
| Willimantic .. | 9 20 " | Baltimore...... | 3 40 " |
| Hartford...... | 10 25 " | Phil'hia, P.&R.. | 7 00 " |
| Winsted...... | | Maybrook..... | 12 03 A.M. |
| Poughkeepsie. | 2 00 A.M. | Ar. Poughkeepsie. | 12 54 " |
| Maybrook. | | Winsted...... | |
| Ar. Philadelphia.. | 7 50 " | Lv. Hartford ...... | 4 25 " |
| Baltimore.... | 10 30 " | Vernon........ | 4 47 " |
| Washington .. | *11 20 " | Willimantic... | 5 20 " |
| Pittsburg..... | 8 35 P.M. | Putnam........ | 6 04 " |
| Chicago...... | 11 55 A.M. | Franklin....... | 6 58 " |
| | | Ar. Boston, Sumner Street Depot. | *7 45 " |

* Daily, Sundays included.

The Poughkeepsie Bridge was considered a remarkable structure when it opened in 1887; 4618 feet long (3095 feet in truss spans across the river, and 1523 feet of approaching trestlework), with double tracks 212 feet above the river. It will probably surprise no reader of this volume to learn that the first revenue train across the new bridge was P. T. Barnum's circus train, which just happened to be where the maximum publicity could be obtained.

But the Philadelphians who financed and built the Poughkeepsie Bridge saw it as a means of improving the flow of commodities, primarily coal, from Pennsylvania to New England.

One passenger train service made possible by the bridge began in 1893 as the Isabella Express, to the magnificent Columbian Exposition in Chicago. (As with so many public projects, this fair to commemorate the 400th anniversary of Columbus' activities in 1492 got started a bit late.)

In later years, the bridge became a primary transfer point for freight, bypassing the congestion and carferries of New York City. The NYNH&H acquired it along with the Central New England Railroad in 1904. After 1968, the bridge fell into disrepair and disuse; traffic was diverted north almost to Albany.

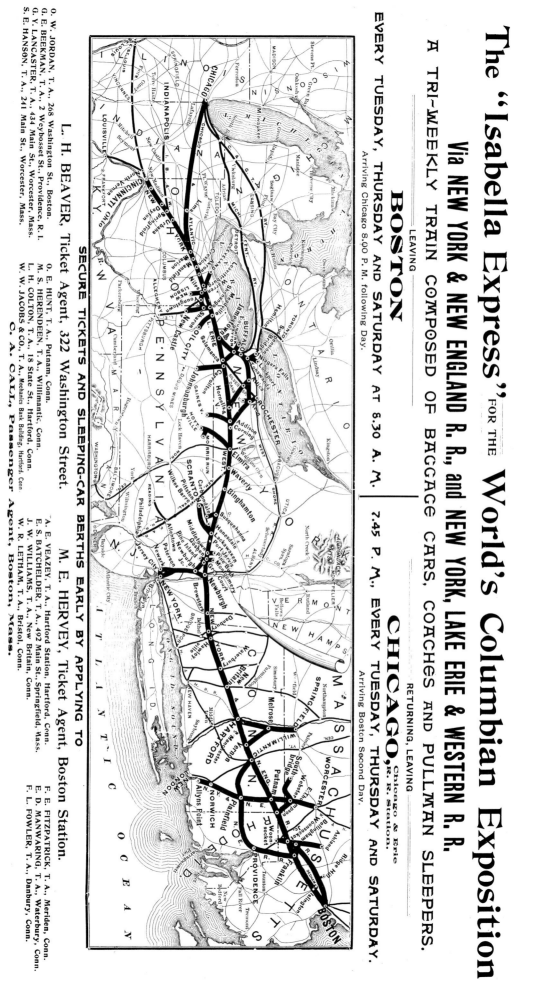

phia and Reading lines (which controlled the Central New England & Western, now known as the Philadelphia Reading and Northeastern) in 1893. Mr. McLeod set his sights on larger targets; he gained control of the Boston and Maine and New York & New England railroads, to form the New England extension of his coal routes. We can speculate on the extent of damage done to the ceiling above J. P. Morgan's desk when news of this competitive intrusion reached 23 Wall St. Mr. Morgan was offended because he had reorganized the anthracite industry a few years before, and now Mr. McLeod was trying to upset the Morgan-imposed balance. This obviously could not be permitted.

Needless to say, Mr. McLeod got nowhere against the NYNH&H's and Mr. Morgan's assault tactics, and the NY&NE went into bankruptcy in 1893. In fact, the Philadelphia and Reading itself was forced into bankruptcy, losing control of the Boston and Maine in the process as well. The word at the time (denied by all concerned) was that J. P. Morgan was taking no prisoners in New England; upstarts would be dealt with severely. Two years later, the NY&NE was reorganized as the New England Railway, with the Consolidated in control. This activity too was carried out through Mr. Morgan's reported efforts. An 1898 lease of the New England Railway to the NYNH&H obliterated the NY&NE from the map.

The Central New England continued its operations between Poughkeepsie, Springfield and Hartford. It is likely that the CNE was allowed to live for a time in the interstice between the Boston and Albany and the NYNH&H because of the mitigating involvement of the Chapin family, specifically Chester W. Chapin Jr., and his ties with the Boston and Albany. NYNH&H acquisition of the Central New England did not come about until 1904; it was the first sizeable acquisition made under Charles Mellen's presidency.

## A Little Visit with Mr. Morgan

With Alexander McLeod and his dreams of empire squashed, Mr. Morgan summoned the leading lights of the Boston and Maine and NYNH&H railroads to a meeting at his home in New York. The date was March 6, 1893. The resulting solution which was imposed upon both railroads essentially restricted their expansion plans, and rationalized the New England rail network. In brief, The New Haven was to operate south of the Boston and Albany main line, and the Boston and Maine north of the B&A. Neat, simple, and, to Mr. Morgan's mind, equitable.

But note that this agreement was made three years after passage of the Sherman Anti-trust Act, and was illegal by the terms of that law. Of course, there was little danger that the Sherman Act would actually be enforced.

## The Old Colony Lease

Goals (2) and (3) of the NYNH&H as stated above were neatly achieved in the months following the gathering at Mr. Morgan's. The Old Colony Railroad hit a stumbling block as a result of large accident claims, and became financially vulnerable, i.e., available for takeover. The Reading's McLeod attempted to acquire control, but his financing sources dried up when it became known that the Morgan banking firm was also putting together a package and might be displeased with anyone who helped Mr. McLeod. J. P. Morgan & Co. arranged for the lease of the Old Colony Railroad and its steamboat lines, collecting a suitable fee for its assistance. The New Haven set up a Marine District as its steamboat operating arm.

Capt. Stephen Gardner of the Old Colony was named to head the Marine District steamboat operations. While J. W. Miller, formerly of the Providence & Stonington lines was named chief operating officer of the steamboat services after Capt. Gardner's death in 1899, Old Colony steamboatmen made up the bulk of the company's executive ranks. In a practical sense, the NYNH&H steamboat operation was the former Old Colony Steamboat Company with a new name on the door, and the former NYNH&H-related operations folded in. The company's reports now went to railroad headquarters at New Haven instead of Boston.

While the ownership of the Old Colony's Sound steamboat lines subsequently progressed through a bewildering series of corporate entities, the management group and organization that had operated the Old Colony Steamboat Company was the nucleus that, with individual successors in the ranks over the years, formed the team that guided the NYNH&H Sound steamer services until their 1937 demise.

But the flow of control to New Haven rather than Boston caused a latent political problem: a Connecticut railroad had swallowed two Massachusetts railroads, a fact that did not sit well in Boston. It was a condition that was to prove troublesome later on for the Consolidated.

---

In 1897, the Marine District resumed summer passenger service to Providence using *Massachusetts* and *Rhode Island*. (The NYNH&H had given up on *Connecticut* for regular service about 1896.) *Priscilla* and *Puritan* covered the Fall River run. This July 1898 timetable shows that *Plymouth* replaced *Massachusetts*, and that the old Providence & Stonington Steamship Company insignia was used; corporate image unification was a few years in the future. This service did not provide employment for two more orchestras, as the tradeoff was elimination of the four-boat summer service to Fall River.

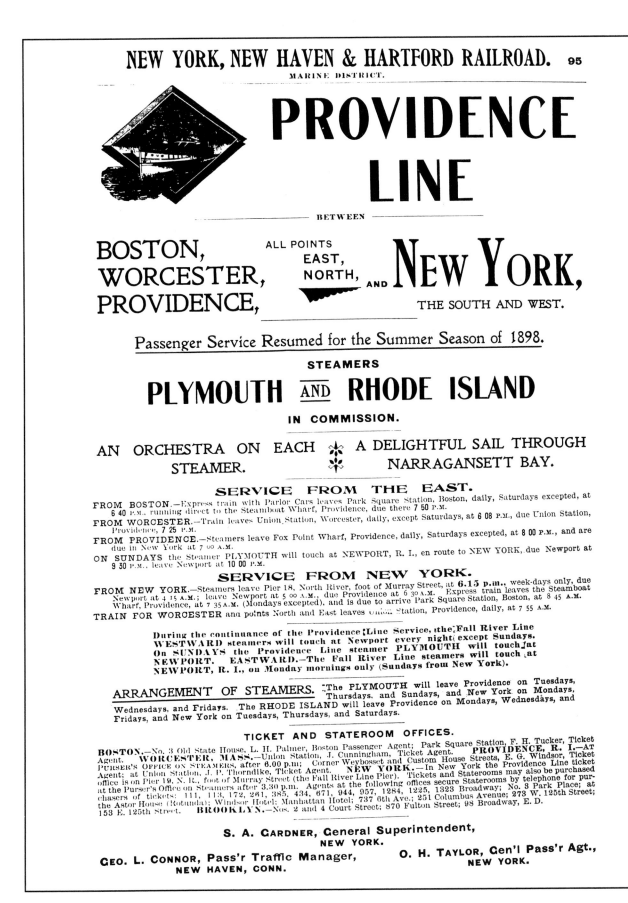

# Chapter Ten

# Let There Be Sounds of Joy

For anyone to challenge the mighty NYNH&H financial juggernaut as it was leasing, acquiring, and consolidating the rail and steamship facilities between New York and Boston, would quite possibly have been grounds for questioning the challenger's sanity. By 1899, there was no doubt where the power was on the Sound, and it centered in the NYNH&H's Yellow Building in New Haven, with a fiscal hawser running to 23 Wall Street, New York, the headquarters of J. P. Morgan & Co. The steamboat companies controlled by the Consolidated were still separate on paper, but the railroad's Marine District, formed around the Old Colony Steamboat Co. operational nucleus with Capt. J. W. Miller in charge, was unifying the services and operations into one system.

Given that knowledge, who would be intrepid (or foolish) enough to start a Long Island Sound steamship line in 1899? Anyone with any experience in the area knew that such a proposition could not succeed. First, financing. Remember what happened to A. A. McLeod of the Reading Railroad? No bank or financial source would touch him after The Boss broadcast the merest hints of displeasure. Second, dock space. The NYNH&H owned or controlled most of it, and their allies most of the rest. Boats? The NYNH&H had no steamboats for sale secondhand except to friendly buyers who would guarantee their non-appearance within miles of Hell Gate or The Race. Traffic? Expect a cutthroat

At Fox Point wharf in Providence . . . *Rhode Island*, an older boat operating on the New Line; and *Pilgrim* on the Providence Line. Their common owner's enemy was the upstart Joy Line.

rate war for passenger and freight business. Even fuel might be hard to come by. And people: could it be true that a man who worked for a NYNH&H competitor forfeited whatever chance he might have to hook on with the NYNH&H at a later date?

Only a well-financed and well-connected entity, or a group of complete newcomers, would reasonably be expected to start such steamboat lines. And in fact, two entities, one of each type, were making just such plans, simultaneously and unknown to each other as well as to the Consolidated. The well-heeled one was led by Chester W. Chapin Jr., whom we met, along with his father, in Chapter Two. The other company was one formed by three young men recently arrived from Out West, and therefore not aware that what they were doing bordered on folly at best and commercial suicide at worst.

## Genesis of the Joy Line

Suddenly, dockside gossip had it that somebody nobody had ever heard of bought the old *City of Bridgeport* from the (independent) Bridgeport Steamboat Co. The new outfit was called the Joy Steamship Company; incorporated 1899 in New Jersey, capital $100,000.

The three young founders were Charles Dimon, Frank Dunbaugh, and J. Allan Joy. Of the three, only Mr. Dimon had any steamboat experience, and that had been on San Francisco Bay and Puget Sound. Messrs. Dunbaugh and Joy were cousins, from Colorado. They had met Mr. Dimon in Chicago; he was seeking help in solving part of Alaska's meat shortage, at a profit. The trio bought a flock of sheep, transported them to Seattle (via Mellen's Northern Pacific?) and loaded them on a barge for Alaska. While the animals' condition on arrival was likely less than prime, prospectors, specula-

---

*Rosalie* was the Joy Line's first vessel, a proud if secondhand product. Built in Port Jefferson, NY as *City of Bridgeport*, she hauled many tons of metal goods and hardware to market in her extra-strong wooden hull.

Freight was the mainstay of the Joy Line. At right we see *Martinique*, front, and *Old Dominion*, rear, being loaded in New York. *Martinique* will soon be off for Providence, and *Old Dominion* will take the outside route around Cape Cod to Boston.

tors, and other Alaskans feasted on expensive and well-traveled lamb and mutton.

And the three entrepreneurs wondered what to do with their profits. Somebody apparently suggested Long Island Sound steamboating, so the boys headed for New York. They were to find that such a venture looked considerably simpler from Chicago than it did from Pier 1 North River.

As we have seen, the market was there; the growth and industrialization of New England in the 1890s caused greatly increased traffic levels, particularly freight traffic. While the Joy Line could not hope to match the opulence of the Fall River Line boats, the periodic fare wars had revealed a passenger market segment waiting to ride at lower fares. That fact had been proven with each previous rate war; lower fares brought steamboat travel within the reach of many more people, and many more people traveled.

But freight cares nothing for the elegance of its surroundings, and it is here that the Joy Line sought the bulk of its business. The former *City of Bridgeport*, now renamed *Rosalie* (in honor of Mr. Dimon's wife) reflected this; she was definitely a freight boat with some passenger accommodations, rather than a passenger boat that carried freight.

*Rosalie* began Joy Line service between New York and Providence in March 1899. Under the command of Captain David Wilcox, like the *Rosalie* late of the Bridgeport Line, she left New York at 5 PM and pushed through a howling storm to land in Providence about noon the next day. Her welcome by the merchants of Providence was enthusiastic; here was a lower-rate freight service to New York, in opposition to the railroad monopoly. Two round trips each week were well-patronized, and the future of a New York-Providence run looked bright. For two months.

### The Narragansett Bay Line

In May 1899, Chester W. Chapin Jr. began his Narragansett Bay Line service between New York, New Haven and Providence, as we noted in Chapter Two. Here was a much more significant competitor to the Consolidated's Providence Line. *Richard Peck* inaugurated Bay Line service on June

12, with the second boat being the Montauk (Long Island) Line's *Shinnecock*, on charter. Bay Line boats charged a passenger fare of $2.50 between New York and Providence, as opposed to the Providence Line's $3.00.

The *Shinnecock* and *Lincoln* (from the Kennebec Line) were operated under short-term charters because the New Haven Line had no boats of its own available until July, when *C. H. Northam* returned to service after repairs necessitated by her collision with *Richard Peck* in June. The Bay Line's stop at New Haven meant that the running times between Providence and New York were longer than those of the NYNH&H Providence Line, but because it was an overnight service, the stop caused little inconvenience. Passengers and freight moved in significant numbers and quantity to the new service, in part to avoid the railroad monopoly.

With *Richard Peck* and *C. H. Northam* in daily service, Mr. Chapin's effort quickly eclipsed the little Joy Line in the Providence business community's collective consciousness. The Narragansett Bay Line was an immediate success, and was expected to become even more successful after arrival of its new boat, the *Chester W. Chapin*, scheduled for December 1899. The Joy Line was still carrying satisfactory amounts of freight on *Rosalie*, but the growth potential was now limited.

## "Let's Try Boston"

Because much of their expected freight business was going to this unexpected new competition, the Joy Line owners reassessed their plans to add a second boat to the Providence service. Mr. Dimon had purchased a second vessel, a burned-out Chesapeake Bay hulk named *Cape Charles*, (not the carferry) which was rebuilt as a freighter and renamed *Allan Joy*.

Instead, the Joy Line announced that the *Allan Joy* would begin operation between New York and Boston, on the "outside" route through the Sound and around Cape Cod. In so doing, the Joy Line squared off against another formidable competitor, the Metropolitan Steamship Co., owned by the Whitney family of Boston and friendly to the NYNH&H interests.

In spite of predictions of doom, the Joy Line Boston service found a similar community of merchants and businessmen eager to support a lower-cost transportation alternative to New York, and to keep the monopoly honest. *Allan Joy* began operating in June 1899, and soon was doing a good business. But *Allan Joy* was not really an ocean-going steamer; the winter months would present her with formidable problems. The Joy Line purchased another boat for the Boston service, and sold *Allan Joy* to the Bridgeport Line (from which *Rosalie* had been purchased) in December 1899.

The Bridgeport Line rebuilt the *Allan Joy* with more passenger staterooms.

The Joy Line's "new" boat was the ocean-going sidewheeler *Old Dominion*, built in 1872 to run between New York and Richmond VA. *Old Dominion* may have been relatively old, and relatively slow (10 to 12 knots as opposed to *Richard Peck*'s 20 to 22); but she met the Joy Line's primary criterion in steamship acquisition: she was "affordable;" i.e., inexpensive. As an ocean-going vessel, *Old Dominion* also had the capability (like her larger Metropolitan Line competitors) of sailing to Boston via the Atlantic rather than the Sound, on nights when the Sound was fogged in.

*Old Dominion* made her first New York-Boston run December 30, 1899, and proved to be steady and dependable, if slow. But she sometimes did not have the power to buck Hell Gate currents without the assistance of a tug. When all went well, her New York-Boston travel time was about 24 hours, which meant a twice-a-week service departing Boston on Mondays and Thursdays, New York on Wednesdays and Saturdays.

In March 1900, *Rosalie* made her last Providence trip, not because of lack of business, but because the Joy Line was able to charter her to the Old Dominion Line for more money than she could earn in Providence service. The next day, fire put *Old Dominion* out of commission for three weeks, which meant no Joy Line service to Providence or Boston, and freight piling up on the Joy Line docks. Messrs. Dimon, Dunbaugh and Joy were clearly down for the count, when a shocking event turned the situation completely around.

## Back to Providence

That event was the sale by Chester W. Chapin, Jr. of the New Haven steamboat line, including the Narragansett Bay Line, to the NYNH&H. The NYNH&H moved *Plymouth* and *Pilgrim* to Providence Line service, cutting the *Peck* and *Chapin* back to a New York-New Haven route. The Bay Line was eradicated.

The shock, anger and anguish expressed by Providence merchants at Mr. Chapin's desertion of their anti-monopoly interests was quickly transmuted into renewed ardor toward the Joy Line. With Captain Wilcox in command, *Seaboard*, newly purchased from a Florida company, reestablished three-a-week Joy Line Providence-New York freight service May 14, 1900. *Seaboard* proved to be both larger and faster than *Rosalie*; she was welcomed by the Providence folk with cheers and (more importantly) bills of lading.

## Passengers and Excursions

When *Old Dominion* went back into service to Boston a week later, she began carrying passengers;

passengers who were not in any great hurry to get to Boston. Surprisingly, there were more than a few people who preferred the leisurely all-water trip and the $3.00 fare. (The boat-rail Fall River Line fare was $4.00 at the time.)

Passengers? The Joy Line had started as a freight carrier. Only a handful of passengers was occasionally carried, and only the freight service was advertised. But the Bay Line had carried passengers, and the Joy Line sought to take up where Mr. Chapin had left off. No, they had nothing comparable to *Richard Peck*, but they did charter the 50-stateroom *Martinique* (which, as *Lincoln*, had run on the Bay Line a year earlier) alternating with *Seaboard*. Starting in June, the Joy Line had a modest daily New York-Providence passenger and freight service. The passenger fare was $1.75, and a gratifying number of people was paying it.

*Martinique* also gave the sweltering citizens of Providence something that had not been happening there: Sunday steamboat excursions. While boats from other ports had been operating Sunday excursions in the 1890s, Providence Line boats had not done so. The Joy Line filled what became a profitable niche with a series of $1.00 Sunday all-day outings from Providence to Martha's Vineyard that became very popular. Too popular, in fact.

**The Hammer Falls**

News of the reborn Joy Line's success in Providence, particularly with its excursions, was not well received in the Yellow Building. By July, the NYNH&H response was ready, and it did not include conciliatory meetings aboard yachts. In July, the NYNH&H announced the "New Line" serving Providence, using the steamer *Massachusetts*. By the most amazing of coincidences, the New Line began to offer a $1.00 fare service between New York and Providence, and a Sunday excursion to Martha's Vineyard.

Three circumstances combined to keep the Joy Line in business in spite of this onslaught. First, Providence shippers knew full well that the railroad's motives were not benevolent, and they continued to support the Joy Line. Second, the lower fares of both the Joy Line and the New Line attracted enough new passenger business to fill both *Martinique* and *Massachusetts*. Third, the Joy Line was in the unusual position of operating the "better" service, with smaller crowds and more courteous personnel. Service amenities on the New Line approached steerage conditions, making the Joy Line preferable despite its slightly higher fare.

The net result was that the railroad was hemorrhaging. The New Line was operating at a planned loss, while the large, expensive full-fare Providence Line boats (usually *Pilgrim* and *Plymouth*) were operating with an unplanned loss, at less than half of capacity. The railroad was thus losing

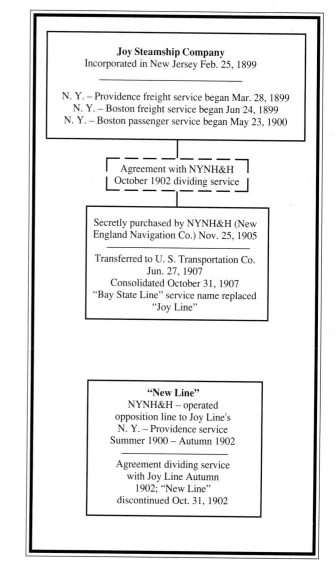

**Joy Steamship Company**
Incorporated in New Jersey Feb. 25, 1899

N. Y. – Providence freight service began Mar. 28, 1899
N. Y. – Boston freight service began Jun 24, 1899
N. Y. – Boston passenger service began May 23, 1900

Agreement with NYNH&H
October 1902 dividing service

Secretly purchased by NYNH&H (New England Navigation Co.) Nov. 25, 1905

Transferred to U. S. Transportation Co.
Jun. 27, 1907
Consolidated October 31, 1907
"Bay State Line" service name replaced "Joy Line"

**"New Line"**
NYNH&H – operated opposition line to Joy Line's
N. Y. – Providence service
Summer 1900 – Autumn 1902

Agreement dividing service with Joy Line Autumn 1902; "New Line" discontinued Oct. 31, 1902

money at both ends of the scale. To the chagrin of the Yellow Building denizens, the more frugal Joy Line was making a profit, which delighted its Providence supporters and its three maverick owners.

At summer's end, *Martinique*'s charter expired, and she returned to Florida. The Joy Line chartered the Montauk Line's *Shinnecock* for the winter, as she had just finished her summer service to Long Island. But winter traffic volumes (after the heavy September clothing shipments to New York) were not great enough to offset the NYNH&H competition. That competition intensified in 1901 and 1902, because of the animosity toward the Joy Line owners shown by the NYNH&H's new President, John Hall.

The NYNH&H took virtually all of the passenger business by changing the assignment of the superior *Chester W. Chapin* to the New Line for the winter. The *Shinnecock*, *Seaboard*, and newly-acquired *Tremont* carried the freight that enabled the Joy Line to survive the winter which was a hard one.

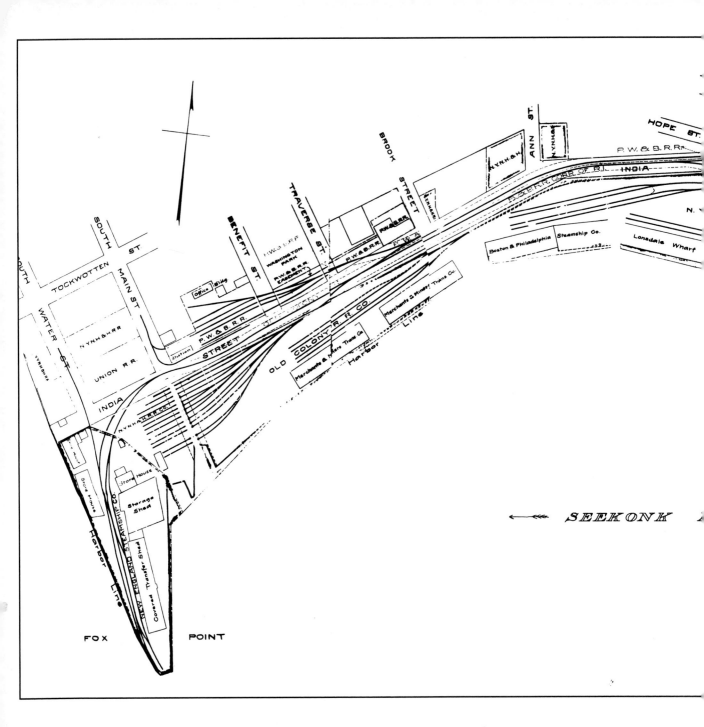

On one trip, *Seaboard* became icebound off Whitestone on her way to New York; after some time, her two dozen passengers merely stepped off onto the ice and walked to the Long Island Rail Road station to catch a train.

The Joy Line's early 1901 service saw *Old Dominion* and *Seaboard* alternating to Boston, while *Tremont* and *Shinnecock* operated to Providence. The New Line quickly followed the Joy Line's lead in offering daily service to Providence, using the newly-repaired *Connecticut* and the *Rhode Island* at a 50 cent fare. The Joy Line stayed with its "higher-class" service and its $1.00 fare. *Penobscot*, from Maine, was chartered to replace *Shinnecock* when the latter returned to her Long Island

summer service. There were no summer Joy Line excursions, because neither *Tremont* nor *Penobscot* was fast enough to make it to Martha's Vineyard and back in one day.

The summer started out looking bright, but accidents to *Old Dominion* (grounding near Rye, NY) and *Tremont* (collision with the yacht *Wild Duck*) put the Joy Line back to the brink of bankruptcy, because of lack of boats to handle the business. Further, the NYNH&H was working behind the scenes to block renewal of the *Penobscot* charter, and chartering of *Shinnecock* and other boats. While direct intervention would have been illegal (the Sherman Anti-trust Act), quiet conversations in elegant recreational settings between, say, Wil-

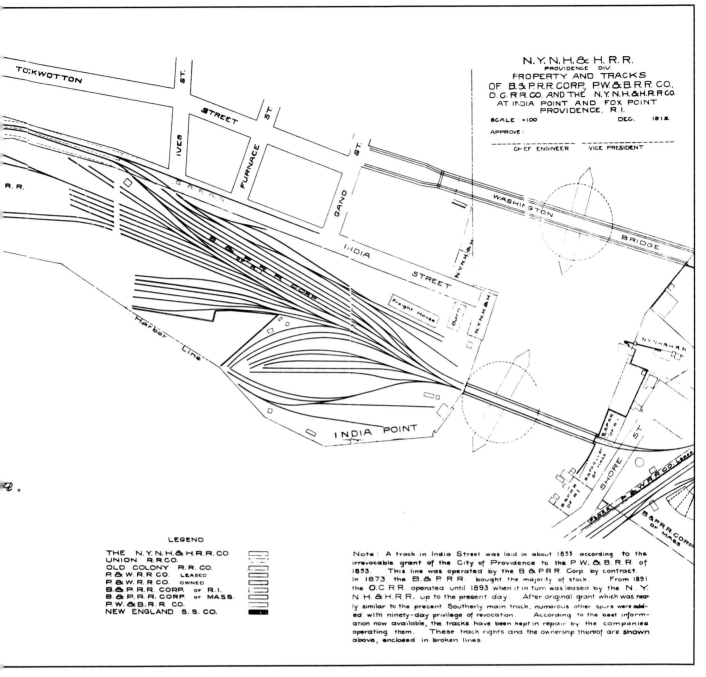

LEGEND

THE N.Y.N.H.&H.R.R.CO
UNION R.R.CO.
OLD COLONY R.R.CO.
P.&W.R.R.CO.  LEASED
P.&W.R.R.CO.  OWNED
B.&P.R.R. CORP. or R.I.
B.&P.R.R. CORP. or MASS.
P.W.&B.R.R. CO.
NEW ENGLAND S.S. CO.

Note: A track in India Street was laid in about 1855 according to the irrevocable grant of the City of Providence to the P.W.&B.R.R of 1853. This line was operated by the B.&P.R.R Corp. by contract. In 1873 the B.&P.R.R. bought the majority of stock. From 1891 the O.C.R.R. operated until 1893 when it in turn was leased by the N.Y. N.H.&H.R.R. up to the present day. After original grant which was nearly similar to the present Southerly main track, numerous other spurs were added with ninety-day privilege of revocation. According to the best information now available, the tracks have been kept in repair by the companies operating them. These track rights and the ownership thereof are shown above, enclosed in broken lines.

liam Rockefeller (a NYNH&H director) and Henry Flagler (a partner of Mr. Rockefeller's father) got the message across: do not sell or charter any steamboats to the Joy Line. Finally, Mr. Dimon found *Virginia* on Chesapeake Bay, and the NYNH&H somehow "allowed" the charter. In spite of all these hardships, the Joy Line reportedly showed a small profit in 1901.

The NYNH&H also contacted the Joy Line's freight customers, alternating pressure and inducement. The former was sometimes successful, the latter more likely refused. The shippers knew that if the Joy Line ceased operations, their shipping costs would shortly be increased. Save now, pay (through the nose) later.

The map on these pages shows the wharf facilities at Providence as of 1912. At the left is the old Providence & Stonington pier at Fox Point, locale of the photograph on pages 214-215. Three railroads are shown as property owners, all under NYNH&H control: Old Colony, Boston & Providence and NYNH&H itself. India Point was the Boston & Providence terminal. The Merchants and Miners line used the former Old Colony Railroad freight piers. Far more of the Providence facilities were devoted to freight service than passenger, particularly yard tracks and sidings devoted to boat-rail transfer.

*Allan Joy*, above, is shown here with a Bridgeport Line label, but she was a Joy Line Providence boat at the time we cover in this chapter. After cessation of Bridgeport service in 1920, *Naugatuck* (which she had become) frequently operated between Block Island and Providence until her retirement in the early 1950s.

The sleek *Chester W. Chapin*, below, was the New Haven Line's newest entry into the Providence battle, while the old reliable *C. H. Northam* filled in on the longer run when needed. For the short period before Mr. Chapin (Jr.) sold out, the "NEW HAVEN AND PROVIDENCE LINE" legend appeared on their bows.

During the short independent operation of the Narragansett Bay Line under Chester W. Chapin, the line used the Lonsdale Wharf (see preceding page), arrangements for which were made under the NYNH&H's very nose. The Joy Line was out of the picture, or at least off the map, to the left.

# THE FALL RIVER LINE

### Forms a GRAND HIGHWAY between

# NEW YORK AND BOSTON

## Via NEWPORT and FALL RIVER,

And is A NATURAL ROUTE between New York and Newport, Fall River, Boston, Taunton, New Bedford, Middleboro, Warren, Bristol, and Providence, R.I., Bridgewater, Brockton, Braintree, South Framingham, Lowell, and the very many important manufacturing and business communities of Eastern New England.

It is also the natural and most satisfactory route between New York and Lawrence, Lynn, Portland, Bangor, St. John, N.B., Halifax, N.S., and all other eastern points.

**THE FALL RIVER LINE is patronized** by hosts of people from all over the world, and during the season of pleasure travel forms a most delightful pleasure route between New York and Cottage City, Nantucket, the South Shore of Massachusetts, Cape Cod, Cape Ann, the White Mountains, Bar Harbor, and the very many delightful Seashore, Inland, and Mountain Resorts in New England, New Brunswick, Nova Scotia, Cape Breton and Prince Edward Islands.

### STEAMERS

### PRISCILLA and PURITAN

#### IN COMMISSION.

The Steamboats of this line are unsurpassed by any other transportation establishment in existence.

Each Steamer has its own Orchestra, and Music is an all-the-year-round feature of the Fall River Line.

Steamers leave New York from Pier 19, North River, foot of Warren St.

The **PROVIDENCE LINE** will be operated for passenger service for the Summer Season of 1899 from Monday, June 19th, until Saturday, September 30th, inclusive, with the steamers PLYMOUTH and PILGRIM in commission. Schedule will be about the same as during the summer of 1898, viz.: From New York daily, except Sundays; from the East daily, except Saturdays.

During the continuance of the Providence Line service, the Fall River Line Steamers will touch at Newport Monday mornings only on their eastward trips, and on every night of the week, except Sunday, on westward trips. On Sundays the Providence Line steamer will touch at Newport, leaving there at 9 00 p m. for New York.

## CONDENSED TIME-TABLE.

### FROM NEW YORK.

| | Ms | | | |
|---|---|---|---|---|
| Lve. Jersey City P.R.R.Sta., via Annex | | *5 00 P.M. | | |
| Lve. New York, Steamer..... | | *5 30 P.M. | | |
| Due. Newport.... ......... | 163 | *3 00 A.M. | | |
| Lve. Newport... ..... .... | | *3 45 A.M. | | |
| Due. Fall River... ..... ..| 181 | *5 00 A.M. | | |
| Lve. Fall River (*Wharf*)........ | | †5 48 A.M. | *6 40 A.M. | †7 52 A.M. |
| Due. Boston (*Park Square Sta.*) | 230 | 7 15 A.M. | 8 00 A.M. | †9 15 A.M. |
| Lve. Fall River (*Wharf*)........ | | †5 48 A.M. | *6 42 A.M. | |
| Due. Taunton................ | 196 | 6 14 " | 7 15 A.M. | |
| " Mansfield............... | | †6 35 " | 7 35 A.M. | |
| " South Framingham...... | 229 | 7 30 " | | |
| " Lowell.................. | 257 | 8 35 " | | |
| " Fitchburg............... | 266 | 9 00 A.M. | | |
| Lve. Fall River (*Wharf*)...... | | †7 15 A.M. | §7 30 A.M. | |
| Due. New Bedford ............ | 204 | 8 23 A.M. | 8 23 A.M. | |
| Lve. New Bedford (*Steamer*)... | | †2 25 P.M. | ‡2 25 P.M. | |
| " Woods Hole.............. | | 3 45 " | 3 45 " | |
| Due. West Chop...... .. | | .... | ... | |
| " Cottage City.......... | | 4 30 " | 5 00 " | |
| " Vineyard Haven....... | | .... | 4 30 " | |
| " Edgartown............. | | | 5 45 " | |
| " Nantucket............. | | 6 45 P.M. | | |
| Lve. Fall River (*Wharf*)...... | | †7 15 A.M. | §7 30 A.M. | |
| Due. Plymouth............... | 213 | 8 35 A.M. | 10 37 A.M. | |
| Lve. Fall River (*Wharf*)...... | | †7 15 A.M. | §7 30 A.M. | |
| Due. Brockton............... | 215 | 8 30 " | 9 02 " | |
| " South Braintree......... | 224 | 8 53 " | 9 23 " | |
| " Braintree.. ........ | | 8 58 " | 9 28 " | |
| Due. Boston (*Terminal*)... .. | 235 | 9 17 A.M. | 9 51 A.M. | |
| Lve. Fall River (*Wharf*)...... | | †7 15 A.M. | §7 30 A.M. | |
| Due. Middleboro ............. | 197 | 7 56 " | 8 14 A.M. | |
| Lve Middleboro............... | | †9 10 " | 9 10 A.M. | |
| Due. Marion................ | 213 | †9 44 " | | |
| " Mattapoisett........... | 218 | *9 53 " | | |
| " Woods Hole........... | 237 | †10 40 " | | |
| " Hyannis ............ | 241 | †10 57 " | 10 57 A.M. | |
| " Chatham ........... | 254 | †11 45 A.M. | | |
| Due. Provincetown............. | 282 | †12 25 NO'N | | |
| Lve. Fall River............... | | †6 38 A.M. | †7 37 A.M. | §7 38 A.M. |
| Due. Warren................ | 190 | 7 02 " | 8 02 " | 8 02 " |
| " Bristol...... ...... | 194 | 7 10 " | 8 10 " | 8 10 " |
| One. Providence (*Fox Point*).. | 200 | 7 30 A.M. | 8 30 A.M. | 8 30 A.M. |

### TO NEW YORK.

| | | | |
|---|---|---|---|
| Lve. Boston (*Park Sq. Sta.*) | *6 00 P.M. | | |
| Due. Fall River (*Wharf*)... | 7 20 P.M. | | |
| Lve. Fitchburg ............ | †5 00 P.M. | | |
| " Lowell .. | 5 25 " | | |
| " South Framingham | 6 30 " | | |
| " Mansfield............ | 7 25 " | | |
| " Taunton........... | 7 46 " | *6 45 P.M. | |
| Due. Fall River (*Wharf*)... | □ | 7 18 P.M | |
| Lve. Nantucket (*Steamer*) | | †7 00 A.M. | |
| " Edgartown........ | †6 15 A.M. | | |
| " Cottage City....... | 7 00 " | 9 20 " | |
| " Vineyard Haven.... | 7 25 " | | |
| " West Chop........ | | | |
| Due. Woods Hole........ | 8 10 " | 10 00 " | |
| " New Bedford........ | 9 45 A.M. | 11 25 A.M. | |
| Lve. New Bedford........ | *5 37 P.M. | | |
| Due. Fall River (*Wharf*)... | 6 45 P.M. | | |
| Lve. Provincetown ....... | †2 35 P.M. | | |
| " Chatham........... | 3 15 " | | |
| " Hyannis .......... | 4 03 " | | |
| " Woods Hole....... | 4 20 " | | |
| " Mattapoisett....... | 5 07 " | | |
| " Marion............ | 5 16 " | | |
| Due. Middleboro........ | 5 53 " | | |
| Lve. Middleboro........ | *6 04 " | | |
| Due. Fall River (*Wharf*)... | 6 45 P.M. | | |
| Lve. Plymouth........... | *5 25 P.M. | §3 53 P.M. | |
| Due. Fall River........ | 6 45 P.M. | 6 45 P.M. | |
| Lve. Boston (*Terminal*)... | '4 43 P.M. | §4 43 P.M. | |
| " Braintree.......... | 5 04 " | 5 04 " | |
| " South Braintree... | 5 11 " | 5 09 " | |
| " Brockton.......... | 5 32 " | 5 30 " | |
| Due. Fall River........ | 6 45 P.M. | 6 45 P.M | |
| Lve. Providence......... | *6 30 P.M. | | |
| " Bristol........... | 6 50 " | | |
| " Warren........... | 7 00 " | | |
| Due. Fall River (*Wharf*)... | | | |
| Lve. Fall River, Steamer | *7 40 P.M. | | |
| " Newport, Steamer... | 9 15 P.M. | | |
| Due. New York........ | 7 00 A.M. | | |
| Due. Jersey City... ....... | Annex boat leaves Pier 19, North River, for Penna. R.R., Jersey City, at 7 00 a.m., or on arrival of steamer. | | |
| *Penna. R.R. Sta., via Annex* | | | |

*Daily; † daily, except Sunday; § Sunday only; ¶ daily, except Monday; □ due Newport only; 8 50 p.m., connecting there with steamer.

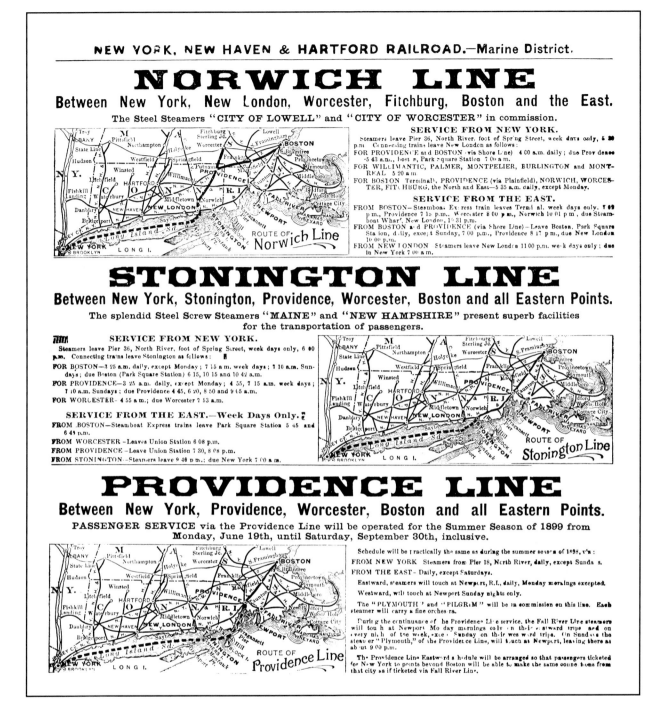

Here are two facing pages from an 1899 *Official Guide*, showing the Marine Division routes in a "family" setting for the summer. Careful study will reward the reader with the details of the schedules of boats and connecting trains, including such delights as an opportunity to spend a day in New Bedford between the arrival of the steamboat from Nantucket at 9:45 AM and the departure of the train for Fall River at 5:37 PM. Connections could have been better, and were better in later years.

If you compare this timetable with the Old Colony timetable extract on Page 118, you will notice that railroad routes have mysteriously appeared in the state of Connecticut. The cartographer's paycheck now came from the railroad, after all, and thus the interconnecting network could be shown.

With the exception of Old Colony's *Plymouth* and *Pilgrim* operating on the former P&S Providence Line, the vessel assignments reflect the former operating companies on the routes.

Note too, perhaps partially because of the Old Colony management, partially because of the immense popularity of the trade name, that "Fall River Line" is beginning to be used as the generic name for the NYNH&H Sound boats regardless of their actual destination.

A local contractor had been carrying freight from Providence to Fall River for the Joy Line; he stopped operating the service when the NYNH&H paid him more to stay home than he could earn by running for the Joy Line. When the Joy Line sought to establish its own lighterage service, the City Councils in Fall River and Newport refused dock space. The Joy Line was forced to establish its own drayage/delivery service. In New York, the Pennsylvania Railroad (the NYNH&H's largest interchange partner) was apparently persuaded not only to refuse charters of its Long Island Rail Road vessels, but also to refuse to carry any freight that had come to New York on Joy Line boats.

A 1902 Joy Line plan to run a steamship line between New York and Philadelphia (because of the Pennsylvania Railroad's intractability) was shelved because of the famous coal miners' strike of that year. The resulting shortage increased the price of such coal as was available, reducing the Joy Line's already paper-thin profit margins to a point where expansion became impossible. Still, Charles Dimon found another "affordable" boat, *City of Key West*, the least desirable boat on the Flagler fleet list in Miami. *City of Key West* had been built in 1865 as the *City of Richmond*, for service in Virginia, but most of her life was spent in Maine waters. She had only been in Florida since 1897. Now she would be the spare boat in the Joy Line's Providence service, which in itself represented an improvement: to the Joy Line, "spare boat" was a new and wonderful operating concept. Also purchased in 1902 was the former International Line (Boston-St. Johns) *Cumberland*, which had been declared a total loss after a collision on the same day as *Priscilla*'s unfortunate mating with *Powhatan*. To the Joy Line, a "total loss" represented a "fixer-upper," and they proceeded to do so. The rebuilt *Cumberland* became *Larchmont*, joining *Tremont* for seven-night a week service between New York and Providence.

But 1902 was to be the NYNH&H Marine District's turn to have a poor operating year, as they shuffled a diminishing number of steamers from route to route. The *Massachusetts*, *Connecticut*, *Rhode Island* and *Chester W. Chapin* were either ill or being overhauled that spring. On May 6, *Mohawk* burned to the water line. Two days later, *Pilgrim*'s engine shattered itself. *City of Brockton*'s engine blew in June. *Massachusetts*' massive walking beam broke in July; a fatal injury as it turned out. Less than a week later, *Priscilla* was injured in a collision with the Merchants and Miners Line freighter *Powhatan*. *Richard Peck*'s engine began coughing expensively shortly thereafter. On August 10, the brittle *Connecticut* reverted to type with engine trouble; within 12 hours the *Rhode Island* was damaged running over a sand bar. The railroad was having a tough time of it.

One casualty of the steamer breakdowns was suspension of service between New York and Stonington for a few weeks, to concentrate the NYNH&H's available boats on more popular runs. So, by Fall 1902, both the Joy Line and the NYNH&H were having troubles on the Sound, despite good business for both. On October 1, the New Line was discontinued; the railroad gave the reason as the coal strike. This action meant that the Joy Line had the only low-fare line to Providence.

That was true, but there were certain circumstances not known to the public. A secret agreement had been negotiated between the railroad and the Joy Line. The NYNH&H withdrew the New Line, while the Joy Line agreed to limit the range of destinations for its freight and to raise its fares and rates. The NYNH&H's Providence Line continued, charging higher fares and freight rates than the Joy Line, which continued under its own management. Technically, the Joy Line was independent, but the secret agreement was later construed as railroad "control" during an investigation.

*Shinnecock* figures in our story as a visitor, having been chartered a few times by the Joy Line from her owner, the Montauk Steamboat Co., a Long Island Rail Road affiliate. Built in 1896, she was newer than *Priscilla*.

*Seaboard* was an older boat, built in 1874, and bought by the Joy Line from the Old Bay Line. She was not exactly on her last legs when the Joy Line ended in 1907; *Seaboard* lasted until 1931 on the Merchants' Line to Bridgeport (H&NYTCo) and was then dieselized for tanker service.

---

### Control of the Hartford Line

The agreement between the NYNH&H and the Joy Line was only one of those entered into by the railroad. Another, which came to light in 1915 during a trial of NYNH&H directors, was between the NYNH&H and the Hartford and New York Transportation Company (cf. Chapter 4).

In testimony at the 1915 trial of NYNH&H directors, Charles Goodrich testified that an agreement had been entered into in 1901, the intent of which was to allocate revenues, business and profits in the Connecticut River valley in a manner similar to the better-known 1902 agreement between the NYNH&H and the Joy Line.

In fact, there is reason to believe that the railroad and Mr. Goodrich's New York and Hartford Transportation Co. had reached an understanding before 1901. It was alleged that the NYNH&H had helped Mr. Goodrich to add the steamer service to his tug operations back in 1884. In 1899, the Hartford line was able to charter *City of Lawrence* when *Hartford* (I) was purchased by the Army; at about that same

time, the Joy Line found itself blocked at every turn in its attempts to charter a vessel.

The NYNH&H indeed carried freight between New York and Hartford; and in the winter when the Connecticut River was frozen, the railroad carried freight on behalf of the steamboat company. It seems clear that some understanding about division of business was reached between the NYNH&H and the Hartford Line in the 1880s or 1890s, whether written or unwritten. In fact, it is not unlikely that such an arrangement existed as early as 1884, when Mr. Goodrich's Hartford and New York Transportation Company first added the steamers to their tug operations. In that 1915 trial, Mr. Goodrich was of no help to the government in their attempt to prove that the railroad had been oppressive in their tactics; he claimed to have had only a beneficial relationship with the NYNH&H throughout.

The 1901 agreement provided, among other things, that the Hartford Line's season would end when it had earned $184,000 in profit for the year, likely sometime in October. Presumably at that point, the railroad alone would carry the freight and passengers until the next spring. Such provisions would give the railroad effective control over Hartford Line operations in 1901, not 1905.

### Changes in 1903

For the NYNH&H Marine District, the 1903 season was marred by the collision between *Plymouth* and *City of Taunton* just before midnight on March 19. *City of Taunton*, proceeding to New York on a foggy night, rammed *Plymouth* on the starboard side of her bow. *Plymouth* was bound for Fall River with about 500 persons on board.

The accident resulted in the only passenger fatality on a Fall River Line boat. Five crewmembers also perished, as the *City of Taunton* penetrated and flooded *Plymouth's* forward sleeping area, occupied by the crew.

As 1903 began, the Joy Line was running *Old Dominion* and *Seaboard* from New York to Boston while *Tremont* and *Larchmont* operated to Providence. Both of the Boston boats were out of commission for a while in January; *Old Dominion* collided with a schooner, while *Seaboard* ran aground, both in the fog. *Surprise* was quickly chartered to fill in until May; a new experience for the Joy Line, not having doors mysteriously closed.

George Olweiler took command of *Tremont* in 1903; he remained with the Joy Line and the later Dunbaugh-owned Colonial Line until his retirement in 1938. Among his duties were a few Hudson River Sunday excursions, while *Larchmont* reinstituted Sunday excursions from Providence. *Tremont* broke a steam pipe during a late August storm and sought shelter in Long Island's Huntington harbor. She returned to service after repairs.

The Metropolitan Line, meanwhile, had arranged with the Savannah Line to run a low-rate twice a week service to undercut the Joy Line between Boston and New York. The Metropolitan was decidedly not a party to any agreements with the Joy Line, secret or otherwise. By the end of 1903, it became apparent that the Savannah service was drawing more blood from the Metropolitan than from the Joy Line, so the opposition boats were withdrawn.

The end of 1903 also saw the NYNH&H shifting its steamers and its priorities. Superindendent of Steamers George Peirce, designer of the widely acclaimed Old Colony/Fall River boats, had passed away in 1902, immediately after finishing the plans for a new boat to be named *Providence*. Mr. Peirce was succeeded by J. Howland Gardner, an MIT marine engineering graduate who quite literally grew up with the Fall River Line; he was former Vice President Stephen Gardner's son. Howland Gardner's appraisal of the steamboat operations resulted in accelerated retirement for walking-beam and wooden-hulled boats. *Pilgrim* and *Connecticut*, in particular, were evaluated as the line's most expensive vessels per hour of availability. Some reassignments and streamlining of service were in order. *Connecticut*, *Rhode Island*, *Massachusetts* and *City of Worcester* were retired, but

---

Two members of the Joy Line's "Fixer-upper fleet" were *Larchmont* and *Tremont*, wooden-hulled boats that had sailed northeast out of Boston before coming to the Sound. *Tremont* was the older, built in 1883. *Larchmont* was built two years later. Both boats came to tragic ends; *Tremont* in a 1904 fire at her dock, and *Larchmont* in a 1907 collision that left only 17 of the 128 people on board alive.

The serious *Larchmont* disaster indeed raised many questions about the Joy Line's operations, training, and personnel qualifications, and may have contributed to the NYNH&H's decision to eliminate the line as a separate entity later that year.

| Table 10-1 |
| --- |
| **Steamboats and Ports, 1903** |

Passenger, between New York and:
Bridgeport: *Allan Joy* and *William G. Payne*
New Haven: *Richard Peck* and *New Hampshire*
New London: *Chester W. Chapin* and *City of Lowell*
Providence Line: *Plymouth*, *Pilgrim*
Fall River: *Priscilla*, *Puritan*
Relief boat: *Maine*

Freight between New York and :
Providence: *Nashua, City of Fall River*
Fall River: *City of Taunton, City of Brockton*
New Haven: *Eleanor F. Peck*
New Bedford: *Pequot*
New London:
   (Central Vermont) *Mohawk, Mohegan*
Stonington: *City of Lawrence*

only the *Massachusetts* was actually scrapped in 1903; the others were moved to the idle docks at Stonington for storage. *Pilgrim* was to be replaced by the forthcoming *Providence* (III). Looking ahead, the larger *Puritan* was the next candidate for replacement, which would not come until 1908.

Storage space at Stonington was available because Stonington-New York passenger service was eliminated in December 1903; some involuntary market research had been done the previous year

---

The aftermath of *Plymouth*'s collision with *City of Taunton* on a foggy night in March 1903. Five crewmembers were killed, along with the only passenger ever lost on a Fall River steamer (not counting the few inevitable suicides, one of which is fictionalized in the novel "Butterfield 8").

Both vessels made for New London, *Plymouth* under her own power (and Elijah Davis' will), *City of Taunton* under tow by *Nashua*. They were rebuilt and returned to service.

by stopping Stonington service during a shortage of boats. The result showed only small losses from shutting down Stonington passenger service; smaller freighters could adequately serve Stonington. The New Line to Providence was also no longer operating. Mr. Gardner's operating lineup at the end of 1903 is shown in Table 10-1.

The Joy Line purchased the former Morgan Line steamer *Aransas*, and placed her on the Boston run with *Old Dominion*. Joy Line assignments were

    Boston: *Old Dominion*, *Aransas*

    Providence: *Tremont*, *Larchmont*

    Relief boats: *Seaboard* (Boston),

           *City of Key West* (Providence) and

           *Rosalie* (when and where needed).

*Rosalie* was used for extra trips, to augment the regular boats. Business was indeed that good at times. And to show how far the Joy Line had come, *Seaboard* was chartered to the Clyde Line for a time early in 1904. The Joy Line was actually on the owning end of a charter instead of the begging end.

## President Hall Retires

The most significant change in 1903 was the retirement of NYNH&H president John M. Hall and the appointment of his successor. Mr. Hall, an attorney and former judge, had been in office since Charles P. Clark's resignation in 1900. As the NYNH&H Board of Directors discussed who would succeed Judge Hall, it appears from the surviving records that J. P. Morgan favored a president with a more extensive railroad background; his candidate was Charles Sanger Mellen, formerly of the NY&NE and NYNH&H, and more recently the Morgan-installed President of the Northern Pacific. There was the customary amount of opposition to Mr. Morgan's wishes; Mr. Mellen took over in January 1904. It should be noted here that while Mr. Mellen has been regarded as a main figure in the NYNH&H's drive toward monopoly, the general policies, desires and attitudes of the NYNH&H were firmly in place before Mr. Mellen's arrival in the President's office.

# Chapter Eleven

# Mr. Mellen Takes Over

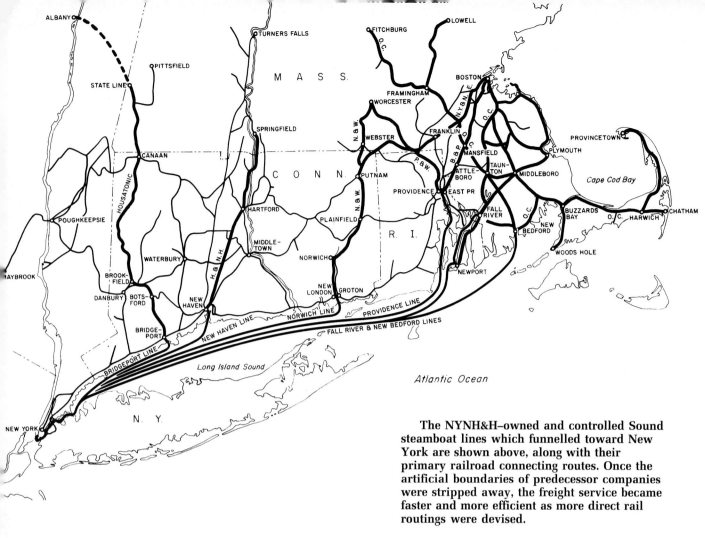

The NYNH&H–owned and controlled Sound steamboat lines which funnelled toward New York are shown above, along with their primary railroad connecting routes. Once the artificial boundaries of predecessor companies were stripped away, the freight service became faster and more efficient as more direct rail routings were devised.

January 1, 1904 marked the beginning of a turbulent era for transportation in New England, as Charles Sanger Mellen became President of the NYNH&H. Mr. Mellen, it will be remembered, was a native New Englander with a sharp tongue and an audacious manner; his performance out west had pleased J. P. Morgan. The telephone call from Morgan to Mellen allegedly lasted all of 30 seconds, and was in the nature of a transfer order, not an offer of a higher position in the normal sense.

Mr. Mellen came home to the winters of 1903-1904 and 1904-1905, two of the coldest recorded in New England. Storms raised more havoc than usual with the railroad, and with the Sound steam-

On the preceding two pages, the freighter *City of Brockton* from the Old Colony Steamboat Co. chases *Nashua* from the Providence and Stonington Line around the Battery. The NYNH&H rail-boat freight service was overhauled and streamlined under Charles Mellen's tenure, as the predecessor lines were unified into one system.

boat fleet and its schedules. Fog, snow and high winds took turns impeding navigation, while ice floes damaged hulls and sidewheels. Delays and cancelled sailings disrupted commerce.

The winter of 1904-1905 had as its major problem ice blockages in the western end of Long Island Sound. The freighters *Pequot* and *City of Fall River* were injured, as was the Joy Line's *Aransas*. For a time, the major boats ran between New York and Narragansett Bay on the outside route because of the ice in the Sound.

The Joy Line's *Tremont* burned at her dock in New York early in the morning of Monday February 8, 1904; the fire started in the galley during breakfast preparations. It was this fire that generated the "ferocious lion" legend. Newspaper stories had the firemen and crew threatened by lions during the blaze, and indeed there were two lions aboard *Tremont* that day; the animals were part of a circus act. Their owner had shipped them from Providence. But the lions were never encountered by firemen, having likely perished early in the blaze from smoke inhalation. *Tremont* was lost, burned beyond even the Joy Line's "fixer-upper" level of salvageability. One life was lost among the almost 50 crew members sleeping on board, largely thanks to the efforts of First Pilot George McVay, who ran through the smoke pounding on doors. Mr. McVay's courage was to be more severely tested three years later.

To replace *Tremont*, the Joy Line bought *State of Maine* from the Maine Steamship Co., renaming her *Edgemont*; the "mont" suffix had captured someone's fancy. What was interesting was the fact that Mr. Dimon encountered no problems whatsoever in getting a reasonable steamboat in relatively short time. There was, of course, no NYNH&H opposition to the purchase, and that made all the difference.

Fog and storms had caused many mishaps, and these were often made worse by the isolation in which they occurred. In case after case, one or more crew members had to row to shore to find a tele-

---

Charles Sanger Mellen, right, is about to board a carriage on his way to yet another meeting. With him is the NYNH&H lobbyist, Timothy Byrnes. Mr. Byrnes' services were invaluable in persuading the Massachusetts legislature, among others, that the NYNH&H's goals were worth supporting.

phone, or just wait for what could be a few hours for a passing boat to become aware of the difficulty and bring help. A new era in communications came to the Sound steamers in March 1904, as the new Marconi wireless was tested on board *Plymouth*, and was pronounced a success. Over the next year, wireless installers were at work on other NYNH&H boats, with priority given to the Fall River passenger liners. Some contemporary accounts called this the first fleet installation of wireless in the nation.

Two 1904 mishaps to vessels of other steamboat lines that could not help but affect the consideration of alternatives and improvements were the *General Slocum* disaster on June 15, in which more than a thousand people lost their lives on a Lutheran church summer picnic cruise in New York's East River near Hell Gate. A few months later, on December 16, *Glen Island* of the Starin Line burned (in the western Sound, off Throggs Neck NY). Seven crew members and two passengers were lost in the flames. In response to public shock and concern over fires aboard steamboats, the NYNH&H announced a program to install sprinkler systems in the major passenger boats. The implementation lagged a bit; *Plymouth* was the first boat so equipped, in 1907, as part of her rebuilding following a fire.

Derricks lifting Steamboat "TREMONT"

Feb. 22-1904.

## Reorganization

As any new chief executive would do, Charles Mellen ordered a complete review of the NYNH&H's operations and organization. Stevenson Taylor was hired to perform a full audit and appraisal of the steamboat operations and properties on land and afloat. Mr. Taylor had been serving as a vice-president of the Fletcher shipyard in Hoboken.

It was Mr. Mellen's desire to simplify the NYNH&H's organizational patchwork; although operated as one overall unit under the Marine District, the steamboat companies were still separate entities because their affiliated railroads had been leased and purchased as separate entities. A single ownership would match the Marine District's unified operation, and would avoid the possibly illegal anti-trust issues surrounding corporate subsidiaries, interlocking directorates, and rights of bondholders.

The full reorganization thus set in motion was not completed until late in 1905. But one early change was a complete realignment of the "other" boat trains, the network of freight trains that operated to all of the steamer ports. In truth, it was neither the steamers nor the railroad alone that gave New England its unequalled level of freight service; it was the combination of the two modes, working together. Thus, almost three quarters of the freight carried on the Sound steamers also traveled on connecting NYNH&H trains.

Yet, the route and schedule configuration of the boat trains found by Charles Mellen was little changed from the system that had prevailed under the former multiple ownerships of railroads and steamboat lines. Trains ran from a given town to two or three port cities, not always the closest ones, because "it had always been that way." Mr. Mellen ordered "it" analyzed and fixed without delay.

The whole system was rationalized in 1904. The "loser" was Stonington, which had become operationally redundant. The freight service was discontinued May 28, 1904, with most freight routed on to New London. Interestingly, the "winner" in the freight realignment was New Bedford, which became the port of choice for freight from Lowell, Fitchburg and the Boston and Maine connections.

The new freight pattern was a great success for Mr. Mellen. It reduced costs and improved service to shippers. One customer-oriented touch was based on the fact that New Bedford and New London lines berthed in New York at Pier 40 North River, while the Fall River and Providence lines tied up at Pier 18. (The move to Pier 14 was made in 1912.) It made no difference to a shipper which line in the pair was used, as long as his shipment wound up at the proper pier. Thus a new contingency plan calling for rerouting a boat train to Port B on short notice if Port A was clogged that day. That freight

The Joy Line had a small advertising budget, but managed to turn out some credible examples of the era's advertising art.

When *Tremont* burned, the results would have disheartened any steamboat manager. Her remains are shown in the top photo at left. About two weeks were consumed in dismantling her superstructure prior to removal from the pier.

Merrit and Chapman were justifiably proud of their efforts in removing *Tremont's* carcass; they distributed to prospective clients many copies of this photo showing the crane barges *Reliance* and *Century* supporting *Tremont's* hull while a trio of tugs moves the group toward the scrapyard. (The third tug is the one from which the photo was taken.)

rerouting program was itself the most persuasive argument in favor of the efficient, unified transportation system that Mr. Mellen was trying to create.

## Appraisal and Values

In November 1904, Stevenson Taylor completed his appraisal of the steamship properties. The first consolidation moves followed almost immediately, with the NYNH&H setting up a single subsidiary company to own the steamboat properties. This subsidiary had been incorporated as the Colonial Commercial Company; the NYNH&H purchased Colonial Commercial as a "shell" and changed its name to the New England Navigation Co. The charter was valuable because it contained an unusually broad range of powers, including the ability to act as a holding company; that is, to own stock in other corporations. The NYNH&H itself, chartered as a railroad, could not act in this manner without obtaining legislative approvals, a process which hampered the management's freedom of operation. The NYNH&H, controlled by J. P. Morgan and his designated president, had a valuable tool in the New England Navigation Company with its holding company charter. Between 1904 and 1913, the Navigation Company and other subsidiary corporations were used in the NYNH&H's continuing drive to create a transportation monopoly in New England. That drive was to fail, and was to cripple the NYNH&H financially.

But the first steps were innocent enough. On December 10, 1904 the properties of the Bridgeport, New Haven, New London (Norwich), Block Island and Providence lines were transferred to the New England Navigation Company. The Old Colony Steamboat Co. remained a separate corporate entity until its stockholders had a chance to vote on the transfer. In July 1905 it was brought under the Navigation Co. banner.

The values assigned to these properties as they were transferred between corporations were set by the management. Thus the management could assign a high value to a property transferred from Company A to Company B. This would have the effect of showing a profit on the sale in the books of selling Company A, and a high cost basis which would make buying Company B appear to have greater assets. If the same property were to be transferred again to Company C at a still higher "price," the illusion of increasing value could be made to appear. Of course, in reality the value was unchanged, but the books were "pumped up" by successive transfers to make the corporations' securities appear to be more valuable. Such tactics are illegal in today's securities markets, which require that assets be valued in financial reports "at cost or market value, whichever is lower". But there was no Securities and Exchange Commission to act as watchdog until the 1930s.

The publicity caused by Congressional investigations and trials between 1913 and 1916 may mislead one into believing that the quest for monopoly was a feature only of the Mellen years. But the monopoly drive had been going on since 1892 with railroads and steamboat lines. Mr. Mellen carried out the Morgan desire to include trolley lines, and truck and bus lines; virtually any com-

At right, it's around the turn of the century, and we're looking west along Park Place past City Hall in New York, toward the North River piers from which departed the Fall River line and related vessels. The Ninth Avenue Elevated tracks changed avenues at this point.

The lower left photo is of Newport RI at about the same time, showing the station, small freight yard and pond, later filled in. The steepled batten-board building in the right foreground is believed to be the building in which George Peirce had his office. In this decidedly unassuming structure, some of the most opulent steamboats in the world were designed.

pany that carried people or goods in New England was a candidate for purchase by the NYNH&H. Indeed, Mr. Mellen was called "New England's largest antique dealer," because of the large number of old steamboats and trolley cars he purchased in those years, many at premium prices.

## A Few Legal Precautions

But as the NYNH&H acquisition program continued, there seem to have been some niggling doubts in the Yellow Building as to whether all of these purchases, however much they would benefit the NYNH&H (and therefore would, of course, automatically benefit New England), were totally in keeping with the NYNH&H's corporate charter and the various laws governing business activities. The Sherman Anti-trust Act of 1890, for instance, prohibited "combinations in restraint of trade," but the only major prosecution under this Act had been of a labor union. Enforcement was, to say the least, weak under Presidents Cleveland and McKinley.

The possibility of future legal unpleasantness by those who failed to see the benefits to New England of a NYNH&H monopoly, along with some perfectly normal freewheeling financial practices of the day, led the NYNH&H legal and financial talent, including the considerable expertise of the banking firm of J. P. Morgan and Co., to construct a corporate edifice involving more than 300 subsidiary companies. These were designed in part to shield from prying and uneducated eyes the true nature and extent of transactions made to carry out Mr. Morgan's general plan for the New England transportation monopoly. Properties and entire companies were transferred back and forth between these subsidiaries until even Mr. Mellen often became confused about who owned what. And with each transfer, the corporate books took on more of an aura of fiction.

One pertinent example will suffice; perhaps it will suffuse. The NYNH&H steamboat properties had been consolidated into the New England Navigation Company in 1904 and 1905. In April 1907, the Consolidated Railway Co. bought the properties for $20 million (the amount of a just-rejected offer to purchase the lines, not necessarily their appraised value), but not for cash. New England Navigation, a NYNH&H subsidiary, got 200,000 shares of Consolidated stock at $100 per share. Yet, the Consolidated books now showed the steamboat assets, an apparent $20 million that wasn't there before. New England Navigation's books showed a gain on the sale; apparent income that wasn't there, but which made the parent NYNH&H's income statement look better to investors.

**METROPOLITAN STEAMSHIP CO.**

In May, the NYNH&H and Consolidated were merged, emerging with the NYNH&H name. The Navigation Company now owned 200,000 shares of its parent company's stock, which it apparently used to buy a welter of trolley lines and other enterprises that might have been publicly embarrassing for the NYNH&H to do in its own name. Indeed, in 1907, New England Navigation was listed as the entity owning the most shares of NYNH&H stock. The railroad's largest "investor" was one of its subsidiaries!

In June 1907, the NYNH&H contracted with the New England Steamship Co. (NESS), a newly-formed subsidiary, to operate the NYNH&H vessels. In September, the NYNH&H sold the steamboat properties to NESS for $11 million in NESS bonds and a note for almost $400,000. Again, no cash changed hands. Net book reduction in NYNH&H assets from this transaction: about $8.6 million. But there were now the NESS bonds to sell, with commissions to the investment banking company doing the selling. Wonder who that was?

Six months later, NESS sold the same property (for which it had paid $11.4 million) to the Navigation Company for $250,000 and assumption of debts, including the bonds and note. Net gain to NESS: $250,000. Net price to New England Navigation: $11,650,000.

The next transaction in that particular chain took place four years later: the June 1912 sale of the steamboat property by New England Navigation to NESS for $9 million in bonds and $5,750,000 in cash, a total of $14,750,000. But the cash had been obtained by NESS through sale of its stock to the Navigation Company; it was still a wash.

This shuffling of assets yielded two results: the pumping up of asset values on one or another set of books, depending on which one needed help to appear attractive to potential investors; and the funneling of resources, without undue publicity or traceability, to where they were needed. As noted, this is but a small sample of the thousands of transactions that characterized the NYNH&H's way of doing business in what came to be called the "Morgan manner."

The Interstate Commerce Commission conducted hearings into the activities of the NYNH&H in 1912; these will be covered at greater length in Chapter 14. To set the scene, though, here is a quote from their report:

"The Hartford & New York Transportation Co. cost the New Haven $2,538,916.78; the Eastern Steamship Corporation cost $4,200,000; the Merchants and Miners Transportation Co. cost $5,774,500; the New Bedford, Martha's Vineyard & Nantucket Steamboat Company cost $141,700; the New England Steamship Co. cost $12,100,000; the Maine Steamship Co. cost $17,300 or a total of $24,772,416.78.

"The testimony shows that the physical valuation of the properties acquired as a result of these outlays approximates something like $10,000,000. The New Haven advises that it has recently disposed of its holdings in the Merchants & Miners' Transportation Company at a loss of $3,594,500.

"These steamship lines were not acquired by the New Haven openly, but covertly and by devious methods. Dummy companies, and dummy officers and directors were used in financial maneuvering that resulted in the New Haven controlling these steamships."

**The Hated Competitor**

The program was only momentarily disrupted by a competitor's announcement. With the aid of a group of banks he controlled, Charles W. Morse continued to acquire shipping lines and announce expansion far beyond the state of Maine. The Metropolitan Line was to have two new very fast first-class steamboats operating between New York and Boston, all the way by water, using the 330-mile route around Cape Cod. The two boats were to be turbine-powered, among the first such vessels in America. They were to be named for the schools being attended by Mr. Morse's two sons, one of whom was at Yale, the other at Harvard.

Charles Wyman Morse, a native of Bath ME, had showed a talent for business and financial accumulation even while in college; he was reported to have earned more than a half million dollars while still an undergraduate. He emerged upon the Wall Street scene as a major influence at age 41, in 1897, when he merged 21 small New York ice companies into the Consolidated Ice Company, with the aid of New York Mayor Robert Van Wyck.

In those days before mechanical refrigeration, homes and businesses bought ice in blocks; it was a necessity for even the poorest families. Much of the ice used in New York came from frozen-over Maine rivers, cut into large blocks and transported to the city on the ice company's fleet of sailing ships. If you needed ice in New York (and everybody did), the Consolidated Ice Company was the only place to get it.

The "Ice Trust" earned itself and Mr. Morse considerable public enmity when, during the hottest part of 1900's summer, the price of ice was suddenly raised from 30 cents to 60 cents for a hundred-pound block. The public uproar caused the price to be rolled back, but the damage had been done. Because of his role in the Ice Trust, relatively minor though it was, Mayor Van Wyck lost first his popularity and then the 1901 election. The Ice Trust's leader, Charles Wyman Morse, was pictured as a

---

Above left, a brochure cover for Metropolitan Steamship suggests the total seaworthiness of *H. E. Dimock*.

Below, the 1904 freighter *Boston* (II) in her original coat of white paint and proud "Fall River Line" designation, which the NYNH&H maintained as a valued trademark. The freighters later were painted dull black by a less enlightened management.

prime walking example of the unsavory robber baron, cited by reformers as a cancer to be eliminated from society.

Meanwhile, Mr. Morse sought to control more than ice; he wanted to own all of the coastwise steamships on the east coast. Mr. Morse purchased the Hudson Navigation Co. with its New York to Albany boats, and in 1905 he bought out H. M. Whitney's interest in the Metropolitan Line, merging the properties under the name of Consolidated Steamship Co., with Calvin Austin as President.

Then, with the overly liberal aid of financial resources from a group of banks Mr. Morse controlled, he continued to acquire shipping lines and announce expansion. And now the Metropolitan Line announced its intention to have two new very fast first-class steamboats operating between New York and Boston, all the way by water, using the 330-mile route around Cape Cod.

## NYNH&H Counterpunches

Mr. Mellen responded to the Morse threat by ordering four more vessels in 1905. Three new turbine-powered freight boats were ordered for a new all-water service to operate as the Boston Merchants' Line. These were to be named *Bunker Hill*, *Massachusetts* and *Old Colony*. And MIT graduate J. Howland Gardner, successor to George Peirce, was also instructed to design and build a new large Fall River passenger liner to replace *Puritan*. Mr. Mellen wanted a boat that would unquestionably be the finest on the Sound. That boat would be named *Commonwealth*.

Three other projects were undertaken as the result of a series of proposals made by Mr. Mellen to members of the NYNH&H Board of Directors in September 1905. First, the formal integration of the

# THE STEAMER *PROVIDENCE* (III)

*Providence* (III), George Peirce's last design, was placed in service in March, 1905. Her capacity was close to that of *Priscilla* despite being almost 47 feet shorter. *Providence* offered 404 staterooms, 1202 berths, and ten bridal chambers(!). She cost $1.3 million to build, and contained 1.5 million board feet of wood, 700,000 rivets, 35,000 nails and 100,000 sheets of gold leaf.

Her interior was of French Renaissance design, heavy on old ivory paint with black and mahogany trim. But the innovation that attracted the most attention at the time was functional: *Providence* was the first Sound liner built with a complete telephone system aboard.

*Providence* was christened in Quincy MA in July 1904, with Miss Martha Willson, a cousin of Providence's mayor, doing the honors. The photo below shows the christening party and the special train that took the group to the shipyard.

Unlike other large steel-hulled Old Colony vessels, Providence was not built at Chester PA, but at the Fore River yards in Quincy MA. Some internal memos suggest that the NYNH&H made that decision on grounds of regional or financial interest.

Less than four months after entering service she suffered a broken shaft, and was towed to New London by *City of Taunton*. A second broken shaft occurred a year later in 1906, but no serious failures were reported after that.

The Brooklyn ferry *Baltic* collided with *Providence* in the East River on a foggy December evening in 1907. One ferry passenger perished.

In March 1908, a small fire was discovered aboard, and the crew's fire and lifesaving training paid off. Passengers were transferred to the nearby *Richard Peck*, and the fire extinguished. A similar incident did not occur until March 1933, when once again *Richard Peck* received the passengers, 600 this time, in less than 20 minutes. Captain Appleby said of the later occurrence, however, that the wireless on board in 1933 had made the job much easier; instead of frantic whistle and light signals, a simple call brought help within a few minutes.

Two incidents in December 1928 marred her record. On December 1, heavy seas off Point Judith stove in her port bow, whereupon *Providence* proceeded to New York for repairs. On the way to the repair yard, she collided with a carfloat, damaging a paddle wheel. *City of Lowell* replaced her during the subsequent repairs. It apparently was *Lowell*'s last outing before being rebuilt with one stack.

In the photo at right, taken from a naval vessel, *Providence* is seen leading a procession of gaily decorated steamships down the Hudson River past Morningside Heights. The event is likely the Hudson-Fulton celebration of 1907. Note Grant's Tomb just aft of *Providence*'s stern.

Old Colony lines into the New England Navigation Company was completed in terms of formal ownership as well as in operational fact.

Second, the NYNH&H formally purchased the Hartford and New York Transportation Co. (H&NYTCo), keeping it as a separate subsidiary. We have noted elsewhere that evidence points to the NYNH&H as having had a hand in the H&NYTCo. from its inception; now it was formally brought into the fold. Third, the NYNH&H bought the Joy Line outright from Messrs. Dimon, Dunbaugh and Joy, and assigned its operations to the H&NYTCo. The fact of the Joy Line purchase was not made public at that time.

We should note that another action proposed by Mr. Mellen was not approved by the NYNH&H Directors; it would have had New England Naviga-tion starting up more steamer freight services between New York and Stamford, Norwalk and other smaller ports, to force out any smaller companies operating those routes. The rejected proposal provides some insight into the President's philosophy, which was not far removed from that of his sponsor. Like Mr. Morgan, Mr. Mellen appeared ready to overwhelm and defeat any "competition," anywhere, no matter how small.

### The Enterprise Line is Squashed

The NYNH&H's new steamer *Providence* came on line in June 1905 as the second "smaller" boat. She was the last boat designed by Old Colony veteran George Peirce; he had passed away in 1902 shortly after completing the plans and documents for her construction. *Providence* had been ordered

as a "smaller" boat to replace the expensive *Pilgrim* as *Plymouth*'s partner on the Providence summer service and Fall River winter service. Also delivered to the Fall River Line in 1905 was a new freighter, *Boston*, joining the older *Cities* of *Taunton*, *Fall River* and *Brockton*.

In that same month, a new steamboat company, the Enterprise Transportation Co., began operating competitive overnight service between New York and Fall River. Enterprise Transportation was ostensibly the project of one David Whitcomb, a businessman from Worcester. Known as the "New Line," the low-fare operation featured the former Maine Central steamer *Frank Jones* carrying freight

Here we present three Joy Line boats and one NESS vessel that had every reason to be unsung.

The Joy Line bought *Aransas*, upper left, from the Morgan Line (Charles, not J. P.) in 1904. She sank in 1905, off Cape Cod.

*Martinique*, upper right, built as *Lincoln*, was chartered by the Joy Line in 1900, until NYNH&H power made her unavailable. As *Kentucky*, she later operated on the Joy Line between 1906 and 1910.

*Fairfield* had been *Richard Borden*, built in 1874. In 1906 she was sold to the Joy Line and renamed. She was scrapped in 1908.

At the lower left, a view of one of NESS's local workhorses that never appeared on a travel folder, *John M. Worth* as she ran in Boston Harbor.

and passengers three trips per week, and another former Maine coastal steamer, *Surprise,* filling in for cargo only on the alternate three nights.

The New Line came as a shock to the NYNH&H executives, because it was the first time that an independent competitor had attacked the railroad-owned lines on the New York-to-Fall River battle-ground. Elsewhere yes, but never Fall River. A more shocking event followed: after an apparent backbone transfusion, the Fall River City Council broke its long-standing tradition and allowed the interloper some wharf space.

But the Enterprise Line did not hurt the sumptuous Fall River service; with its $1.00 fare it actually took most of its passengers away from the $2.00 fare Joy Line boats operating to Providence. The New Line's advertising and sales activities took direct aim at the Joy Line as if the New Line people knew every Joy Line weakness. And indeed they did, for the Enterprise Company had hired as its New York agent one George Brady, who had been dismissed from the Joy Line by Mr. Dunbaugh a year before. Mr. Brady enjoyed harpooning his former employer; actually, he was attacking his two former employers, for he had been let go by the NYNH&H before signing on with the Joy Line.

Whereas the NYNH&H had in the past reached quiet accommodation with the H&NYTCo's predecessor firm and with the Joy Line, Mr. Mellen drew the line here. He suspected, but could not prove, that Charles Morse was somewhere in the shadows behind David Whitcomb. No matter; the Enterprise Line or New Line, whatever, would soon taste the master's lash!

The Joy Line fare was dropped to $1.50. The railroad refused to sell or honor through rail tickets between Fall River and Boston for the New Line. Further, the railroad refused admittance to the Boat Train platform to anyone who had not arrived on a Fall River Line boat. "New Line passengers? Let 'em go up to the regular depot and wait for a regular train." The New Line filed suit, and a court that the NYNH&H did not control soon put a stop to that practice, but it was fun while it lasted.

New Line freight operations fared no better, as their customers faced a combination of harassment and inducement. It was all a vaguely familiar scenario to the Joy Line people, although five years earlier they had been on the receiving end of similar treatment. Now they were fighting side by side with troops of the New England Navigation Company (their new secret owner) to repel Whitcomb the interloper. Still, the Enterprise Company survived the summer season.

For part of the winter, when *Priscilla* and *Puritan* were replaced by the smaller *Providence* and *Plymouth* on the Fall River run, Fall River Line fares were cut to the unheard of sum of $1.50. The NYNH&H planned to take no prisoners. Cutting the Fall River Line fare, however, was clearly not a long-term solution.

So for the 1906 season, the Joy Line managers were instructed by secret sealed orders from the Yellow Building to begin a new $1.00 fare Fall River to New York service, and did so using the steamers *Kentucky* (nee *Martinique*) and *Tennessee.* While they were at it, the Joy Line also was told to start a line to Bridgeport to counteract some local businessmen there. These upstarts had begun to operate something called the Merchants' Line, using chartered boats; first *Conoho* from Narragansett Bay, and later *Meteor* (I) from the Long Island Rail Road. The Joy Line bought and rebuilt the trans-Narragansett Bay ferryboat *Richard Borden* for their competitive service, renaming her *Fairfield.* Remember, at that time the public still did not know that the Joy Line was owned by the NYNH&H, any more than the railroad knew that the Enterprise Line was backed by Charles Morse. More important, the Merchants Line people didn't know that the Joy Line was owned by the railroad, and when their cash ran out they arranged with the Joy Line to take over their business, as a means, they thought, of keeping it out of the Consolidated's hands. The Joy Line was only too happy to "help out," in a spirit of brotherhood; they even took over the Merchants Line name. That second service operated, using *Seaboard,* until 1931.

Back in Fall River, the Enterprise Line was having a rough time of it, but was surviving. In fact, the new announcement was that the Enterprise Line would begin running to Providence as well as Fall River. Providence dock space was at a premium, but the Clyde Line wharf was made available. The Clyde Line was owned by Charles Morse. If Mr. Morse had not been involved before, it was pretty clear (but still stoutly denied) that he was somehow involved now.

The Enterprise Line battle continued until late 1907, until it was terminated by events which will be covered in the next chapter.

---

**At the upper right,** *City of Fall River* and *Plymouth* **rest at Newport. The photo was taken from another steamboat, name unknown.**

**Below right,** *City of Brockton* **occupies another Newport slip, in the period before drab paint became the rule.**

# Chapter Twelve

# The High-Water Mark

Charles Wyman Morse approached Charles Sanger Mellen in January 1907 and offered to pay $20 million for the NYNH&H steamboat properties. Mr. Mellen thought the idea had merit, but he took the precaution of checking with his old friend from North Dakota, now living on Pennsylvania Avenue in Washington. President Theodore Roosevelt opposed such a sale to Charles Morse, as it might create an undesirable concentration of transportation resources in the hands of a known (but as yet unconvicted) villain. The NYNH&H Board agreed with Teddy, and Mr. Morse's offer was refused.

Let us pause and reflect on this: Mr. Mellen was told that retention of the Sound steamboat lines by the NYNH&H was less likely to bring about an undesirable concentration of power than having the boats fall into the hands of the nationally unloved Charles Wyman Morse. Thus was the NYNH&H cast as the protector of new England against ruthless monopoly power. Far from being merely ironic, the fact that such an opinion had been conveyed to Mr. Mellen, and through him to Mr. Morgan, helps to explain the self-assured state of mind that guided the NYNH&H's bewildering binge of acquisitions in those years.

His faith in coastal steamships matched only by his ambition, Mr. Morse and his Consolidated Steamship Company had already acquired the Clyde Line (Boston and Providence-Jacksonville FL) in February 1906, to add to his Maine interests. This

---

*Pilgrim* heads downriver, while *Maryland* (II) brings a passenger train upriver through a forest of masts. More mundane vessels hog the foreground, including tugs and lighters. The photo was most likely taken in the 1890s, when the second *Maryland* was relatively new and *Pilgrim* was still a familiar sight on the East River.

Sometime between 1905 and 1913, the camera captured a four-stacked example of transAtlantic royalty as it glided upriver surrounded by attendant tugs, ferries and other vessels. (Could it be the ill-fated *Lusitania*?) In the foreground, the Fall River Line's *Providence* (III) and *Puritan* remained in their berths, calmly awaiting their 5 o'clock departure. At the other end of the line in Fall River, *Priscilla* and *Plymouth* were being readied for their runs in the opposite direction.

was followed in the next few months by the Mallory Line (Galveston TX-Boston, a primary conveyor of cotton), the Ward Line (New York-Havana) and the New York and Porto Rico Steamship Co. Mr. Morse may not have acquired all of the Atlantic and Gulf coast shipping lines, but he had more of them than anyone else.

The NYNH&H, for its part, got into coastwise shipping by acquiring the Boston-Philadelphia Winsor Line, and the Merchants and Miners' Transportation Co. which operated between a number of coastal ports, notably to Jacksonville FL. Mr. Mellen later said that the NYNH&H made this and other steamship moves as defensive rather than aggressive measures.

Of course, Mr. Morse was not the only party to be "defended" against. From the back office of 23 Wall Street, the acquisition made even more sense.

J. P. Morgan & Co. had assembled the Southern Railway System out of a clutter of small rail carriers in the old Confederacy a number of years before; it made good sense to link directly the Southern and the New Haven. As the Pennsylvania Railroad was becoming the NYNH&H's largest rail interchange partner as well as the connecting land link in the cotton conveyor, having coastwise steamship resources that could bypass the Pennsylvania put the NYNH&H and the Southern in a stronger position when the discussion turned to a mutually equitable division of through freight revenues between the three railroads.

### United States Transportation Co.

Another project in response to what Charles Mellen felt sure was more Morse mischief was started in 1906, but was not ready until 1907. The independent but faithful Stevenson Taylor started a steamboat company, the United States Transportation Company, in October 1906. The public was assured that, despite the long-standing relationship between Messrs. Taylor and Mellen, Mr. Taylor was acting entirely on his own, with no connection to the NYNH&H. This posture was maintained even after the New England Navigation Co. sold the idle steamers *Connecticut* and *Rhode Island* to the new company, which then spent $191,000 on *Connecticut* and $86,000 on *Rhode Island* to get them ready for service.

We now know, of course, that the NYNH&H was the real party at interest; a letter, dated September 12, 1906, from Mr. Mellen to Mr. Taylor later came to light, containing this phrase: ". . . to express the matter plainly, whatever you are doing regarding this lease [for wharf space at Fall River] you are in reality operating for our account, and as such you should be held harmless, in which position it is my intention by this letter to secure you."

*Rhode Island* and *Connecticut* were ready in June 1907, when they went into service between New York and Fall River, under the trade name "Neptune Line." At the same time, the Joy Line deferentially gave up its Fall River route, and the odor of Yellow Building rodent could be smelled all across Narragansett Bay. Not only was it more or less obvious that the United States Transportation Co. was an appendage of the NYNH&H, but now there was real reason to suspect that the Joy Line was not as independent as it had hitherto appeared to be. Of course, there were those who said that had Mr. Mellen really been trying to help Mr. Taylor, he wouldn't have sold him the cantankerous *Connecticut*. That boat broke down again after only a few months in service. This time, she was retired; two years later she was scrapped.

The United States Transportation Company operated its two dowager steamers on the Neptune Line to Fall River in direct and brutal competition with the Enterprise Line through the 1907 season, which was the last season for both lines.

At about the same time, the Joy Line sold its New York-Boston outside freight line to the Metropolitan Line, i.e., Charles Morse. It was the only recorded instance of the NYNH&H selling any part of its services without a preceding court order or ICC directive.

## Maine Steamship Co.

United States Transportation also bought the Maine Steamship Company late in 1906. This was a New York to Portland ME operation that had been operating since 1868. In those days, the 30-hour steamship voyage between the two cities was faster than the rail freight and passenger service which, at minimum, required passengers to transfer at Boston. Freight was often not seen for several days en route by rail. The Maine Steamship Company's prosperity becomes easier to understand when it is realized that, in addition to being Maine's principal city, Portland was also the most convenient winter port for access by rail to Montreal, and many tons of freight went through Portland between Montreal and New York. (If this sounds like the "convenient" route to Albany via Bridgeport described in Chapter Three, it was indeed similar.)

The Maine Steamship Company was only one of a number of companies serving that rocky coast.

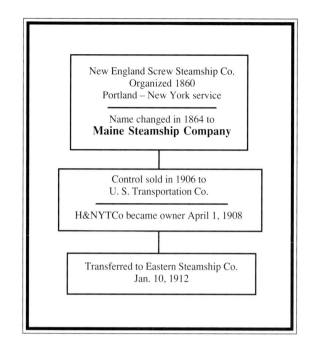

| |
|---|
| New England Screw Steamship Co. Organized 1860 Portland – New York service |
| Name changed in 1864 to **Maine Steamship Company** |
| Control sold in 1906 to U. S. Transportation Co. |
| H&NYTCo became owner April 1, 1908 |
| Transferred to Eastern Steamship Co. Jan. 10, 1912 |

An engraving of *the* wooden-hulled *Cottage City* adorns the January 1899 Maine Steamship ad below, despite the note that *Horatio Hall* and *Cottage City*'s twin sister *Manhattan* are in fact providing the three-a-week service between New York and Portland ME. *Cottage City* had been sold to Seattle interests in 1898.

## MAINE STEAMSHIP CO.

### 3 Trips per Week.

## PORTLAND and NEW YORK Direct Line.

Scenic Route along the New England Coast and Long Island Sound.

The new, elegant, and swift steamships **Horatio Hall**, 3,800 tons, and **Manhattan**, 2,000 tons, alternately leave Franklin Wharf, Portland, for New York, every Tuesday, Thursday, and Saturday, at 6.00 p.m. Leave Pier 38, East River, New York, for Portland, every Tuesday, Thursday, and Saturday, at 5.00 p.m.

**Commencing Nov. 1st, 1898, Fare, one way, $3.00.**

(Staterooms and Meals Extra.)

H. HALL, Gen. Fgt. Agent, New York, N.Y.

THOS. M. BARTLETT, Agent, Portland, Me.

J. F. LISCOMB, Gen. Pass'r Agt., Portland, Me.

VALVE MOTION AND GENERAL CONNECTIONS OF THE ENGINES OF THE CONNECTICUT.

COMPOUND OSCILLATING ENGINES OF THE STEAMER CONNECTICUT.

# The Oscillating Engine on the Steamer *Connecticut*

The steamer *Connecticut*, the largest wooden-hulled vessel in Sound service, was generally considered to be a well-designed, well-appointed vessel, cursed from birth in 1889 by an engine that functioned only intermittently. Had she been an automobile, her engine would definitely have put her in the "lemon" category.

She had the only oscillating steam engine installed on a Sound passenger boat; frequent breakdowns made her unreliable. The freighter *Nashua* had the only other oscillating engine in the fleet; it was of smaller size. Between 1895 and 1901, several major attempts were made to get *Connecticut*'s engine operating; the most extensive was in 1900, when she was towed to Fletcher's yard in Hoboken for diagnosis and repair. Nine months later, in January 1901, she came out of the shops, in working order. Another major breakdown occurred in 1902. She was patched again, but laid up in 1903 at Stonington, emerging only for some service with the Enterprise Transportation Co. in 1908.

Every published report on *Connecticut* has said that she had a cantankerous oscillating engine, and no more. In search of a more detailed reason for such problems, we asked Kenneth L. Douglas, a mechanical engineer who has served as Chief Engineer of a destroyer in the U. S. Navy, two questions: 1) What was an "oscillating engine", anyway?; and 2) What was there about the *Connecticut*'s engine that would bring about such problems, particularly inasmuch as the oscillating steam engine had been successful on *Nashua* and some European vessels? He provided this reply:

The engines on all Sound steamers other than *Connecticut* and *Nashua* were designed with fixed cylinders; that is, while the piston moved back and forth (or up and down), the cylinder remained stationary while the engine was in operation. Thrust was transmitted to the rotating crankshaft by means of a main rod with a pivot, or crosshead. Such an arrangement is used in automobile engines and on railroad steam locomotives.

In the oscillating main engine arrangement on *Connecticut*, the cylinders were mounted on trunnions which allowed the complete cylinder to rotate through an arc of about 30 degrees as the paddle shaft rotated. This made it possible to connect the piston rod directly to the paddle crank without a crosshead. With the cylinder rocking back and forth about the trunnions, there was only one practical place for the steam inlet and exhaust pipe connections to the cylinder: through the trunnions.

The trunnion assembly thus was required to perform three functions. First, it provided the pivot points for the cylinder. Second, it formed a steam connection to the cylinder, which required a seal to prevent steam leaks. Finally, the trunnions had to withstand the reaction load from the piston rod pushing on the paddle crank. Performing all of these functions required different design features and not all of them were mutually compatible. Flexibility and rigidity are not easy to obtain simultaneously. Both the oscillating motion and the heavy loading on the trunnion could have created problems in sealing the steam connection.

Another possible problem was the side load on the gland seal where the piston rod entered the cylinder. On conventional reciprocating steam engines, there is little side load on the gland because the piston rod is supported on its outer end by the crosshead. On an oscillating engine, there is no crosshead and the piston rod is pushed or "flapped" from side to side by the paddle shaft crank. This load is transmitted to the cylinder through the piston rod gland, causing gaps through which steam could leak. Friction and wear made this condition worse in a shorter time than if the piston were not subject to sideways forces.

It is therefore not unlikely that the difficulty with the oscillating engine was maintaining the steam seal both at the cylinder mounting trunnions and at the piston rod gland. The number and length of breakdowns in *Connecticut*'s early years suggests frequent repair of leaking seals rather than replacement of broken large metal parts.

These problems exist with oscillating steam engines of any size. They are more serious in larger engines than smaller engines, more serious in high-pressure engines than in low-pressure engines. The likely reason for *Connecticut*'s difficulties is simply that the oscillating steam engine design was pushed to a size too large for its own good. There were just too many tons of metal moving back and forth to hold the steam seals.

Under Captain Horatio Hall and successors, it had avoided inclusion in the Morse empire, and the Maine Central Railroad affiliates. In the 1880s and 1890s, the route featured an intermediate stop at Cottage City on Martha's Vineyard. By 1906, the line featured the steel-hulled steamers *North Star* and *Horatio Hall*, aided by the older wooden-hulled *Manhattan* (I). It was another extension of NYNH&H influence, this time into the heart of Charles Morse's home territory. As noted, Stevenson Taylor handled the details in his customary independent manner, and the Maine Steamship Company became part of the United States Transportation Company.

---

The engraved flyer from Maine Steamship Co. in 1897 shows Pier 38 East River, the New York terminus of the company's Portland Line. Alongside, apparently, is *Cottage City* again. By this time, most of Maine Steamship's work was being done by larger steel-hulled vessels such as *Horatio Hall*, *North Star*, and *John Englis*.

*Manhattan*, shown under construction below, was a sister ship to *Cottage City*, shown at lower right. While relegated to spare boat service, largely in winter when demand was lower, *Manhattan* remained on the roster through the first years of the century. The larger vessels such as *North Star*, upper right, also reduced the travel time between Portland and New York from about 30 hours to just under 24. The Martha's Vineyard stop at Cottage City (Oak Bluffs) was popular in the 1890s, but was discontinued around the turn of the century; it slowed down the run too much.

### Yale and Harvard

*Yale* and *Harvard* made their debuts on the all-water line between New York and Boston in September 1907, toward the end of the season. They were an immediate success. Reports were that *Yale* and *Harvard* were averaging 750 passengers per voyage, profitable despite the high cost of operating such fast vessels over a relatively short season.

For the first time, the Fall River Line's premier status was clearly threatened by equal or superior equipment. *Harvard* and *Yale* were faster than anything the NYNH&H owned (except its legislative rumor mill), and the early-morning transfer to a railroad train to Boston was not necessary. Whether *Yale* and *Harvard* were more comfortable than the Fall River Line paddlewheelers was a matter of opinion, which the partisans of both lines were not reticent to express.

The Fall River boats did have the edge in spaciousness and service amenities, and of course in the Line's well-deserved reputation for elegance. But thanks to their turbine powerplants, *Yale* and *Harvard* had lower vibration levels; there was less large ponderous rumbling machinery aboard. Despite increased advertising and improved passenger amenities, *Priscilla* and *Puritan* were losing Boston patronage to the collegiate speedsters.

From any angle, the triple-screw *Yale* (and, of course her twin *Harvard*) were beautiful vessels, although the wide-angle lens used by the photographer in Bath ME exaggerates the sharpness of her bow in the photo at the left. For years, people on the west coast wondered why these boats were named for eastern Ivy League colleges.

## Exit Mr. Morse

But the Metropolitan's master was not able to savor his leadership status, because of events which had occurred on and near Wall Street late in 1907. Collectively, these became known as the Panic of 1907. In October, rumors about the possible insolvency of one of Mr. Morse's banks caused a run on that institution; depositors were clamoring for their money, now. The rumor was well-founded; Mr. Morse had indeed borrowed far too much from the bank to finance his steamboat acquisitions, leaving it in a weakened condition. The Panic spread to other Morse banks, and then to all of Wall Street.

The story of J. P. Morgan's leadership in saving the banking community has been often told. He acted as virtually a one-man central bank, whipping recalcitrant financiers into line and stopping the Panic. Pertinent to our narrative are two details. One: the Morse-controlled banks by and large were allowed to go under, mostly because Mr. Morgan had no love for, nor reason to help, Charles Wyman Morse. Two: the sudden lack of cash caused the Consolidated Steamship Company to disintegrate, its component parts reverting to former owners or to trustees in receivership.

The Enterprise Line too went under at that time and suspended all operations. At the end, David Whitcomb confirmed that his own loss had not been too great, because he had not been financially involved in the line "for some time." No one doubted the Morse connection after that, but neither documentary proof nor confession surfaced.

The Neptune Line continued a while longer. The final acts of the United States Transportation Company as directed by the NYNH&H before its dissolution were these: in October 1907, it became the owner of the Joy Line, as the NYNH&H directors became more nervous about possible government curiosity regarding the Joy Line's real or imagined independence. *Connecticut* was replaced by *Tennessee* and *Rhode Island* by *Kennebec* on the Neptune Line to Fall River; the two smaller steamers were all that was needed, and in particular, *Tennessee* was more reliable than *Connecticut* which never turned a wheel in service thereafter.

Neptune Line service lasted until January 1908. Then, in March 1908, the United States Transportation Co., including the Maine Steamship Company and the Joy Line, were sold in turn to the Hartford & New York Transportation Co., which became the last of the "independent" lines. The United States Transportation Co. passed into history, its task completed.

For his part, Mr. Mellen later admitted that the United States Transportation Company had been a New England Navigation project from its inception; its sole initial purpose was to fight the Enterprise line to a finish. It should perhaps be noted

*Harvard* is shown at the upper right in July 1908 at Rowe's Wharf in Boston, looming behind *Myles Standish* and *South Shore*. The latter two vessels were owned by a New York firm, but operated out of Boston. They are included here because they were chartered by the NYNH&H a few years after this photograph was taken, for service to Martha's Vineyard.

*Tennessee* was a H&NYTCo. (Joy Line) boat which spent most of her life operating between New York and Providence on the Bay State Line. She had been built for the Old Bay Line in 1898, and came to the Sound in 1906, where she ran until 1931.

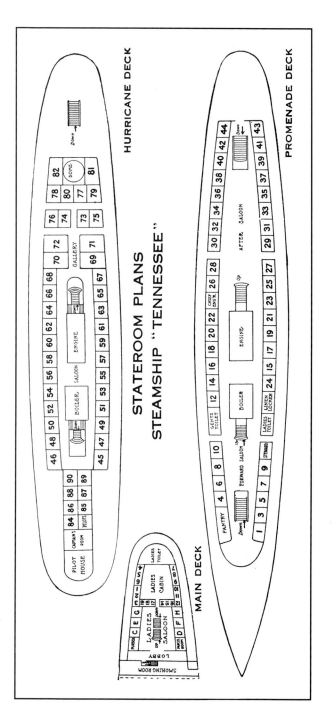

STATEROOM PLANS
STEAMSHIP "TENNESSEE"

that the United States Transportation Co. effort, which operated for less than a year, cost the NYNH&H at least $487,000 in losses ($287,000 to recondition steamers, and at least $200,000 in operating losses and other writeoffs), after factoring out as many of the intercompany transfers as could be identified. But in the end, Mr. Morse did himself more harm through extravagance than the NYNH&H ever inflicted upon him with fighting ships.

In 1908, worse was to come for the onetime "Ice King;" he was indicted for banking law violations, tried, convicted, and sentenced to fifteen years in Atlanta's federal penitentiary. Crowds with vivid memories of ice prices gathered to cheer the verdict and to jeer the prisoner. Appeals exhausted, he began serving the sentence in January 1910. He would not serve his full term.

The H&NYTCo was now established as NESS's alter ego, maintaining the veneer of a separate operation while both remained firmly in NYNH&H control. Under the H&NYTCo umbrella were the lower rate second lines to Providence and Bridgeport, the Connecticut River service, and the Maine steamboats. These were in fact operated independently of the "old line" routes of the New England Steamship Company. And it was on the "old lines" that the battle would now take place.

### The 1908 Season

It was the 1908 season that provided the battle royal between the two clashing interests. Mr. Mellen fielded the Boston Merchants' Line for round-the-Cape freight service in January, with *Massachusetts*, *Bunker Hill* and *Old Colony*. The Morse-less Metropolitan Line, now led by the capable Calvin Austin as Receiver, put *Yale* and *Harvard* on for their first full season in the spring; and Mr. Mellen returned fire by replacing *Puritan* with the new *Commonwealth*, the last of the Fall River Line passenger boats built, and unquestionably the largest. At 456 feet long, she immediately became known as "Mellen's Boarding House."

As the season progressed, the NYNH&H's Boston Merchants' Line with its three new freight steamers was making inroads into the Metropolitan freight boats' market share, but in the first-line passenger carriage department, the victory looked as if it were going to the Metropolitan. Adventurous folk risked the raised eyebrows of their friends of the Fall River Line faithful by informing them that the new boats were vessels for which the habit of a lifetime was worth breaking.

Other attitudes were changing too, notably those about social justice and undue monopolistic power. After the coal strike of 1902, public attitudes toward "the trusts" became less indifferent and less tolerant. The laissez-faire atmosphere in which J. P. Morgan had operated all of his life was eroding.

This was the era of the "muckraker" journalists, exposing to public view the excesses of certain people at or near the heads of major corporations. An increasing number of elected officials were becoming sensitive to this growing public curiosity and indignation. And other people were to turn this public feeling to their advantage.

To add injury to insult, *New Hampshire* figured in an accident in September 1908. While inching down the East River in a dense fog, she rammed a yacht. Not just any yacht, but J. P. Morgan's *Corsair*. Considerable damage was done to both vessels and, quite likely, the careers of everyone involved, although Mr. Morgan was not reported to be aboard at the time. (However, given Mr. Morgan's penchant for privacy, and his largely unreported but whispered-about dalliances with members of the Opposite Sex, reports would have been suspect either way.)

### A Different Type of Opponent

Early in 1908, a Boston lawyer voiced his suspicions in a speech about the NYNH&H and its steamboat lines, saying, "There is not a single independent line of steamers between Massachusetts and New York except the Metropolitan Line; now it has passed into the hands of a receiver. May we not expect to see as the next step its fine steamers *Harvard* and *Yale* flying the New Haven flag, and the last vestige of steamship competition disappear?"

The speaker was Louis D. Brandeis, Esq., then 51 years old, who had developed a reputation as a tenacious and ingenious attorney with an eye for highly publicized attacks on the Financial Establishment. These forays had the effect of increasing his marketability and clout. Politically, he was a progressive Republican until 1912, when he threw his support to the Democrat Woodrow Wilson. In 1916, President Wilson named Mr. Brandeis to the Supreme Court of the United States.

But that was in the future. In 1907, Mr. Brandeis was representing a client who had a grievance against the Boston and Maine Railroad. At the time, the rumor was flying that the New Haven Railroad had just purchased, surreptitiously, a large block of Boston and Maine Railroad stock. The rumor happened to be true, but since the transaction violated an 1874 Massachusetts law and (if anyone cared) the Sherman Anti-trust Act, the less said publicly about it the better.

The New Haven's purchase of some 110,000 shares of Boston and Maine Railroad stock came about when a stockbroker encountered Charles Mellen on a train and mentioned that a 55,000-share block, owned by the American Express Company, was for sale. From the New Haven's standpoint, that meant two kinds of possible trouble.

Either the Grand Trunk might buy it and threaten the NYNH&H's strength in northern New England, or (and this was far worse in the eyes of the Master of 23 Wall Street), the despised Edward H. Harriman might purchase the stock and threaten the Morgan structure. Morgan and the NYNH&H purchased what became a controlling interest in the Boston and Maine, convinced in their own minds that it was a purely defensive measure.

But Louis Brandeis' style in representing a client was not merely to sue on the merits of the case; he searched for any fact or condition, relevant or not, that might hurt an opponent. He attacked in the press, he played on public opinion, he badgered legislators with draft reform bills, he formed citizens' committees, he demanded investigations by Federal, State and local agencies, he interviewed disgruntled employees and other enemies. He tirelessly assembled facts and prejudices, and clubbed his opponents into submission with the accumulated weight of evidence and public opinion. He summed up his motto in a letter to his brother: "The man with the hatchet is the only one who has a chance of winning in the end."

And, seizing upon the shocking and unpleasant fact of the Connecticut-based NYNH&H owning a large part of the Massachusetts-based Boston and Maine, Mr. Brandeis did all of these things, playing upon the Bay State people's fear of "outside" control. Throughout 1907, he painstakingly assembled a mosaic of the NYNH&H finances in spite of large gaps in the publicly reported figures, particularly in the reporting of possibly interesting and questionable transactions of its subsidiaries such as New England Navigation.

The result was a slim volume entitled "Financial Condition of the New York, New Haven and Hartford Railroad and of the Boston and Maine Railroad," which, in fewer than 100 pages, struck the New England financial community with the impact of a mortar shell.

Conventional wisdom up to that time had been that the NYNH&H was the financial equivalent to

**This aerial view engraving of Boston harbor shows the NYNH&H terminal and port facilities, which grew up over the years to handle the Hub City's coastal and oceangoing traffic. South Station, from whence the Boat Train and other passenger flyers departed, is shown at right, but the focus is on the piers and quays that were the locus of rail and boat freight movements.**

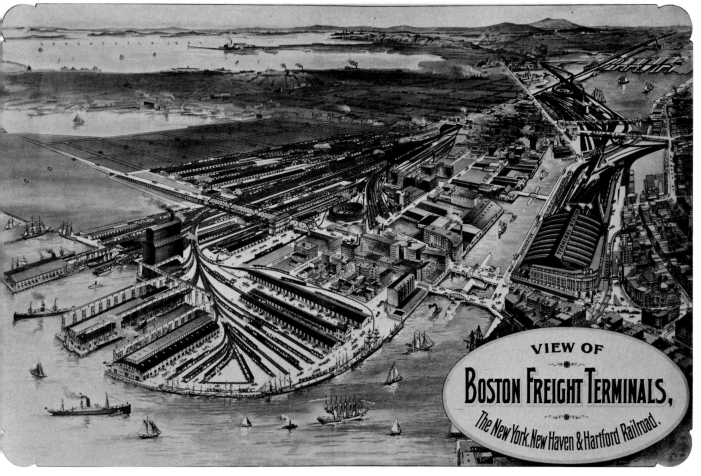

VIEW OF
BOSTON FREIGHT TERMINALS,
The New York, New Haven & Hartford Railroad.

the Rock of Gibraltar, while the Boston and Maine was on hard times and in need of rescue by the friendly giant to the south. Why, NYNH&H securities were the classic examples of safe investments, ideal for "widows and orphans," and for conservative financial institutions. Now here was this attorney saying that the NYNH&H was all but insolvent, that the NYNH&H's income was not sufficient to cover dividend payments, that a large percentage of the profits were generated through bookkeeping magic rather than operating effort; in short, that NYNH&H securities were so unsound that they were not legal investments for such institutions as savings banks. And more than 90 per cent of the savings banks in Massachusetts held NYNH&H securities.

Despite the predictable publicity blitz refuting Mr. Brandeis' statements, the seeds of doubt had been sown, and in time, his analysis would be shown to be largely correct. Between 1901 and 1907, gross earnings were up less than 40 per cent, but liabilities increased by more than 350 per cent. The railroad was not earning enough money to cover the 8 per cent dividend on its vastly increased number of shares outstanding; shares that had been issued to purchase all those trolley lines and other enterprises at high prices.

Trolley lines? Certainly. The NYNH&H had bought up most of the trolley lines in Connecticut, operating them as The Connecticut Company and The Rhode Island Company. In Massachusetts, the purchase of trolley lines had to be carried out with more discretion, because such purchases by a Connecticut railroad corporation violated Massachusetts law. The New England Navigation Company, as we have noted, had a broad holding company charter, so the NYNH&H made the Navigation Company the owner of its trolley lines. This provided at least one layer of concealment from prying eyes, and at least came within hailing distance of the letter of the law.

The Massachusetts Legislature, caught between an outraged public and a supportive platoon of railroad lobbyists, ordered the NYNH&H to divest itself of the Boston and Maine stock, and the Massachusetts trolley lines, by July 1, 1910. This they did, selling the B&M stock to a Meriden coalyard owner named John Billard for $13.7 million. John Billard didn't exactly have $13.7 million in his safe at the time, but the National City Bank of New York (to whose officers he was introduced by NYNH&H people) loaned him $11 million. Further, the New England Navigation Co. obligingly took his note for $2.7 million. Not a dime of Mr. Billard's money went into the transaction, but all concerned stoutly denied that he was a "dummy," a safe receptacle for the stock. Still, there was something about Mr. Billard; Charles Mellen later said, "trading with Mr. Billard, I always looked him straight in the eye."

A new firm, the Boston Railroad Holding Company, was formed a bit more than a year later, to provide a legal framework for NYNH&H control, within limits. The Boston and Maine Railroad stock was purchased from Mr. Billard at a profit to him of $2.9 million.

It was at this point that Mr. Billard proved that he was no dummy in any sense of the word; he kept the $2.9 million, despite polite requests from the NYNH&H that he return it. The NYNH&H directors had solemnly assured the Massachusetts legislature that the sale transaction was at arm's length; that there was no connection or collusion with Mr. Billard. They could hardly attempt to enforce return of the money without leaving themselves open for criminal indictments, and Mr. Billard lived happily for the next few years.

## The 1911 Realignment

At the close of the 1909 season, the "other" owners of the Metropolitan Line, that is, Charles Morse's former partners, had a problem. With Mr. Morse now convicted, sundry creditors would likely attempt to enforce their liens, and large liens were outstanding against *Harvard* and *Yale*. It made sense to sell the two boats at a good price if possible, and to satisfy claims before the sheriff descended upon the pier. That it made good sense to sell was probably reinforced during meetings with knowledgeable steamboat men like the independent and unbiased Stevenson Taylor.

But for the NYNH&H to participate in, or even to facilitate such activities would be illegal and outrageous; Mr. Mellen well knew that the resulting firestorm would be unbearable. But in a short time, two new Metropolitan Steamship Companies were formed, one in New Jersey and one in Maine. Metropolitan (New Jersey) bought *Harvard* and *Yale*, then chartered them to Metropolitan (Maine) for operation between New York and Boston for the 1910 season. Did the NYNH&H have a hand in this? Again, there were stout denials all around; there were even Mellen memos saying "We want nothing to do with this."

But there is some evidence to show that the NYNH&H owned a portion of the Metropolitan Steamship Co. of New Jersey. Whatever connection there was, it was decidedly not made public. One hint that the NYNH&H had *Harvard* and *Yale* under control was the sudden cessation of the Boston Merchants' Line (*Massachusetts*, *Bunker Hill*, *Old Colony*) by the NYNH&H in March 1910. It was apparently no longer "needed," and the New York to Boston all-water route was left to the Metropolitan company.

For *Harvard* and *Yale* to "fly the New Haven Railroad flag" would have been a clearly intolerable violation of federal and state laws. The next best solution was to remove them from the arena.

Here are the three freighters built by the NYNH&H to counter the Morse threat. In the top photo, *Bunker Hill* is shown in the white paint scheme that was later replaced by black; she is flying the Boston Merchants' Line flag, indicating her use in competition with C. W. Morse's direct Boston service.

The center photo shows another member of the trio, *Massachusetts,* at Providence, next to *Block Island.* She's wearing a less expensive half-and-half black and white paint scheme, and the New England Navigation Company name rather than that of the New England Steamship Company..

The photo below shows *Old Colony* in the black-hull scheme. *Old Colony* was turbine-powered, and therefore not quite identical to the other two boats.

*Old Colony* was christened by the daughter of Boston's Mayor, Miss Rose Fitzgerald, who later married one Joseph P. Kennedy.

*Massachusetts*, *Bunker Hill*, and *Old Colony* were built as freighters. In 1911, they were reconstructed as passenger and freight vessels. When they said "reconstruction," they meant it. The two photos this page taken seven days apart in the early stages of rebuilding *Massachusetts* and *Bunker Hill*. Essentially, the process involved stripping the boats down to the hull and building entirely new superstructures for these two vessels, and for *Old*

*Colony*. At the top of next page, we see *Massachusetts* and *Bunker Hill* together, at a later stage in the rebuilding. At bottom right, a view of the boats' saloon deck, looking upstairs; inasmuch as this work was done four years after *Commonwealth* was built, it (and not *Commonwealth*) represents the last of this kind of luxurious saloon–gallery deck construction and decorating done by the NYNH&H-controlled lines.

At the end of the 1910 season, *Harvard* and *Yale* were suddenly sold for a new Pacific coastal service from San Francisco to Los Angeles and San Diego. The two boats traveled together around the Cape (there was no Panama Canal at that time) to their new home. The Los Angeles Steamship Company and the Pacific Navigation Co. operated the boats in overnight service, changing neither their names nor their New England collegiate decor.

---

**Above left, the new dining room of the rebuilt *Massachusetts* and *Bunker Hill*, on the gallery deck forward, which brought food and the diners into the light, up from below decks, as was the case on *Commonwealth*. Below left, the new look of *Massachusetts*.**

**Above right, the return of Frank Dunbaugh, exemplified by Colonial Line's *Lexington*, which had been *Washington* on the run between Washington and Norfolk VA. Along with *Concord*, she provided an alternate steamboat line between New York and Providence.**

With *Harvard* and *Yale* gone, *Bunker Hill*, *Massachusetts*, and *Old Colony* were converted into passenger liners in 1911, and placed under Maine Steamship Line (H&NYTCo) control. *Massachusetts* and *Bunker Hill* operated on the Boston-New York outside route as the Metropolitan Line, while *Old Colony* entered New York-Portland service.

Late in 1911, the NYNH&H sold the Maine Steamship Company to the Eastern Steamship Co., which was the company headed by Calvin Austin that pieced together segments of the former Morse empire. The NYNH&H received in return about one-third of Eastern's stock, a minority position which enabled the railroad's executives stoutly to deny that they "controlled" Eastern.

The H&NYTCo was thus left with the Joy Line (renamed the "Bay State Line" in 1912) to Providence, as well as its Connecticut River service.

## The Colonial Line

Frank Dunbaugh, one of the Joy Line's former owners, re-entered the Sound Steamboat arena in 1910 with the Colonial Navigation Company, which began operating between New York and Providence on May 18. A number of former Joy Line officials went with him, but Mr. Dunbaugh was the sole owner.

At that time, NESS was operating the Providence Line passenger service for the summer season only, and freight service year round. H&NYTCo was operating the Bay State Line (old Joy Line) all year. Colonial set its passenger fares and freight rates above those of the Bay State Line and below those of the Providence Line. Providence was again happy to see an independent competitor (although one imagines that they may have been a touch suspicious after the number of times they had been led down the path).

The Colonial Line's advertising slogan was borrowed from William Gibbs McAdoo of the Hudson and Manhattan Railroad (Hudson Tubes): "The Public be Pleased." *Lexington* and *Concord* (which had been the *Norfolk* and *Washington* on the Norfolk and Washington Line) were the Colonial Line boats. The grey-hulled liners were smaller than the NESS steamers, having about 120 staterooms and 15-knot speed. They were, however, quite comfortable, with running water (cold) in all of the staterooms, a convenience the Fall River Line boats didn't have.

## The Grand Trunk's Grand Plan

The Central Vermont charter for connecting service by *Mohawk* and *Mohegan* from its New London railhead expired in July 1909, and the Central Vermont rebuffed all NYNH&H advances and suggestions for its modification or continuance. The Central Vermont brought in two new boats of its own, named *New London* and *New York*. For its part, the NYNH&H reassigned *Mohawk* and *Mohegan* to Providence freight service, moving *Pequonnock* and *New Haven* to the New Bedford run.

Just how independent the Grand Trunk combine intended to be was shown in 1912, when the Grand Trunk Railway, which controlled the Central Vermont, announced a future new rail extension to Providence, to be named the Southern New England Railway. Of course, it would have a connecting steamer service to New York. The extension was a pet project of GTR President Charles M. Hays. The City of Providence was jubilant at the news, and Mr. Mellen was combative. The right of way was mapped out, two steamers were actually built, and named *Manhattan* and *Narragansett*. The NYNH&H threatened to, and did, reduce interchange tonnage with the Central Vermont Railroad, a Grand Trunk affiliate. Messrs. Hays and Mellen seemed to be entering upon mortal combat.

Charles Hays and his family were returning from a European trip; Mr. Hays was wary of the competition on the ocean and what he perceived as the recklessness it fostered; he asserted to a fellow passenger, "The time will come when this will be checked by some appalling disaster." He was tragically correct; when he made the comment quoted here, he was on board the White Star liner *Titanic*, making her tragic maiden half-voyage. His listener survived; Mr. Hays did not.

Mr. Hays' successors were less willing to tangle with the NYNH&H. The final blow for the Southern New England project came on the day the Canadian Government folded the Grand Trunk into its Canadian National system. The Canadian sentiment was, if new railroads were going to be built, let them be built in Canada, not America.

But two tangible results of Mr. Hays' excursion into New England remained: the *Manhattan* and the *Narragansett*, delivered by Harlan and Hollingsworth in 1913 for a service that never happened. The two boats were moored, unused, at the Central Vermont docks in New London until World War I. *Narragansett* became *USS Narragansett* and *Manhattan* became *USS Nopatin* in January 1918. Both became troop carriers. After the war, *USS Narragansett* became Canada Steamship Lines' *Richelieu*; *USS Nopatin* (*Manhattan*) became the Hudson River Day Line's *DeWitt Clinton*.

The seas had thus been swept almost clean of competitors; the NYNH&H, through its New England Navigation Company and Hartford and New York Transportation Company subsidiaries, controlled virtually all of the Sound services, and enjoyed good relations with the managers of the Eastern Steamship Co., even if there was no perceptible ownership interest.

In 1907, the NYNH&H created the New England Steamship Company (NESS) to take over operation of the New England Navigation Co. vessels. During the next five years this included ownership of some vessels and property for a period of time. By 1912, the situation had stabilized, and the New England Steamship Co (NESS) was the owner and operator of the NYNH&H "first line" boats and services.

Also by 1912, there were the first signs that the marketplace in general was beginning to move away from the steamboats as the premier means of travel to and from New England. Through train service had improved in comfort and speed; and the automobile was beginning to have its impact. But before considering the decline and end of the Sound steamers, let us indulge ourselves in a loving look at the splendor that sailed the Sound.

---

Here, in two varieties of Central Vermont livery, are the hard-working freighters *Mohegan* (top right) and *Mohawk* (bottom right). *Mohawk* is being loaded from a sailing lighter, the boom of which was used both as a sailing mast and as a derrick pole. The Boyers tug *Amelia* is nudging the lighter into place alongside the freighter.

Many cities have annual events which serve as cultural focal points, bringing people together from all points for a few hours or days. In the case of New London, the races on the Thames River provided the NYNH&H and NESS with considerable patronage in bringing the throngs to the event, and even providing seating.

The photo above shows New London's main street in July 1907, at the height of the season. If you wonder where the term "lunch wagon" came from, look at the wagon near the center of the photo.

Below, *Chester W. Chapin* has arrived at the dock, and passengers are waiting to disembark after a hard day's watching. As we noted earlier, the bar was open and well-stocked during these events before and after Prohibition.

Above right, a NYNH&H I-2 class Pacific steams into New London's waterfront rail station with a trainload of spectators. Rail-boat connections were nothing unusual, but this one was a bit different.

Below right, the white-hooded cars were the railroad's unique contribution to the event, for those spectators not on board *Chapin* or her sisters. Since the race was run in the Thames, and the railroad's tracks ran at the water's edge, "grandstand cars" were specially constructed with lengthwise bench seating and over-head awnings. The train was paced to stay abreast of the action on the river.

Above, a summer day in New York finds *Nashua* (the freighter with the successful oscillating engine) passing Montauk Steamboat Company's Pier 13 East River on her way toward the Battery. Sights such as this delighted the eye every day. The hog-framed *Nashua* was retired in 1907, when the larger freighters *New Haven* (III) and *Pequonnock*, black, ugly, and efficient, replaced her.

In chilling contrast, the photo of *Pilgrim* below is in the dead of winter, under gray skies, and surrounded by ice. Obviously, *Pilgrim* had seen better days by the time of this photo; she became redundant in 1905 when *Providence* joined the fleet. An extension of her life came about when *Plymouth* burned, but after the newer vessel was rebuilt, *Pilgrim* was returned to retirement at Stonington.

# THE STEAMER COMMONWEALTH

The largest and longest of the Sound steamers was *Commonwealth*, placed in service July 9, 1907. She was the floating masterpiece of J. Howland Gardner, who designed her; and of C. S. Mellen, under whose administration she was built, at a cost of $2 million. Mr. Mellen's daughter Kathryn christened her.

"Mellen's Boarding House" featured 421 staterooms with 826 berths, and another 460 free berths. Visible differences included no masts, and a complete fourth deck, which included the dining room. She was designed to carry up to 2,000 passengers at a time, served by a crew of more than 200 on busy days. More than half of these were waiters and other members of the Chief Steward's department.

When *Commonwealth* entered service, usually sailing between May and November, *Puritan* became a spare boat along with *Pilgrim*. The older, more expensive beam-engined boats were phased out.

An October 1908 collision with the Norwegian freighter *Voland* in fog near The Race resulted in the sinking of the freighter and only slight damage to *Commonwealth*. *Voland*'s crew was saved, and no one on board *Commonwealth* was hurt.

July 7, 1912, another foggy morning, was the date of *Commonwealth*'s most serious mishap; she indeed picked on a boat her own size and then some, ramming the *U. S. S. New Hampshire,* a Navy battleship visiting Narragansett Bay, anchored off Newport. The Navy and NESS sued each other, the claim hinging on whether *New Hampshire* was anchored in the channel, or whether *Commonwealth* was moving too quickly for conditions. The legal wrangle went on for years; the final settlement gave NESS just over $10,000, about 40% of the damage costs. But that final settlement from the government did not come until 1925, thirteen years later.

The role that *Commonwealth* played in her best-known mishap was that of rescuer, not afflicted. In July 1924, the new Eastern liner *Boston* collided with the tanker *Swift Arrow* off Hen and Chickens lightship at the west end of Buzzards Bay. *Commonwealth* was one of the liners responding to the SOS call from the crippled *Boston*. *Priscilla* picked up *Boston*'s surviving passengers. Then Captain Edward Geer eased *Commonwealth* alongside *Boston*, and ordered the boat lashed together. Geer was going to tow the foundering competitor into Newport!

One problem: *Boston*'s metallic mass was affecting *Commonwealth*'s compass. So Capt. Geer asked *Plymouth*, newly arrived on the scene, to precede him to port. *Plymouth* provided the "eyes", *Commonwealth* the muscle. Once again the Fall River Line emergency training had paid off; the crews and Capt. Geer in particular, were hailed as heroes. Less than a month later, Capt. Geer was dismissed by NESS for pursuing a salvage claim. He later was Superintendent of the Cape Cod Canal and harbormaster at New London.

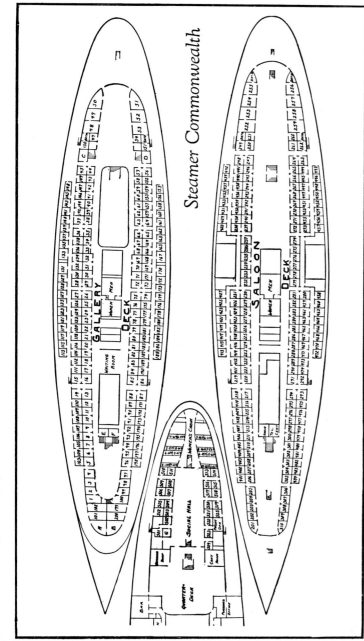

Steamer Commonwealth

The bow and stern photos taken in drydock show *Commonwealth*'s size. The transAtlantic *Great Eastern* had been larger, as were four later Lake Erie sidewheel boats, but when she was built, *Commonwealth* was the largest side-wheel steamer in existence, larger than any other steamer in service on the Sound.

The use of "older" technology, i.e. the inclined engine and side wheel propulsion, in the face of turbine propeller developments such as those on *Harvard* and *Yale*, was stoutly defended by the designers before the Society of Naval Architects and Marine Engineers as the best way to build a "six-story floating hotel with 15-foot depth," and to make it safe against collision and fire on a route where fog was prevalent, and sea routes restricted. As to the turbine, listen for a moment to Capt. Jacob Miller: "Our experience thus far with *Massachusetts* and *Old Colony*, the latter a turbine, has not shown that *Old Colony*'s engines are in any way superior economically to those of *Massachusetts*. As a commercial proposition, it is exceedingly doubtful whether the turbine is economical on short daily routes on which a number of miles has to be made under slow speed."

Not that *Commonwealth* was a laggard; her 11,000-horsepower four-cylinder double-expansion engine (a larger version of *Priscilla*'s) coupled to 33-foot wheels could move her at 20 knots (23 statute miles per hour). Further, her sidewheels made her sufficiently maneuverable that Capt. Geer regularly docked her without the aid of tugboats.

*Commonwealth*'s interior differed a bit from previous Fall River liners, in that it featured a mixture of architectural styles in different areas, rather than one unifying style. That subject will be covered in the next chapter.

274

# Chapter Thirteen

# Splendor Afloat!

The Hudson-Fulton celebration of 1909, celebrating the man who "discovered" the river named for him and the man who retarded steamboat development in the early days, involved *Providence* as the flagship in the Parade down the Hudson. Second in line was *Hendrick Hudson*, then the largest Hudson River Day Line boat.

While *Priscilla*, *Commonwealth*, and others maintained their regular services, NESS and the other steamboat companies worked to arrange for their boats to participate in the celebration. Many excursion fares swelled their Pursers' cashboxes. Other NESS boats taking part in the celebration were *Chester W. Chapin* and *Plymouth*. Made available to carry spectators, at $5.00 per head, were *City of Lowell*, *Puritan*, *Richard Peck*, and *Bridgeport*. Replicas of Hudson's *Half Moon* and Fulton's *North River (Clermont)* were also constructed for the occasion, but they were lost amid the large steamboats of the day.

The old line drawing above is a pre-photographic attempt to capture the boat-train connection at the Fall River pier. It is taken from a Fall River Line brochure dating to the 1880s.

Above, an 1880s photographic comparison of two wooden boats as they sail past; the 362-foot *Bristol* from the Fall River Line, and the 216-foot long *Rosedale* of Bridgeport. *Rosedale*, built in 1877 for shorter runs and daylight cruises, is less than twelve years old, ten years younger than Jim Fisk's famous overnight liner *Bristol*.

Below, the saloon deck of *Massachusetts* (III), with gallery deck above, shows the state of the art in 1877. The free-standing steam radiator (in front of the upright piano) was an efficient heating device, and would be used on later boats as well. One wonders whether having a stateroom near the piano was a blessing or a curse.

*Pilgrim*'s dining room (above), while electrically lighted, appears a bit somber. Custom dictated the placement of dining facilities below the main deck, to keep the upper decks available for staterooms. The trend was bucked by some vessels, but not many. Note too the larger tables, set for eight or ten diners. You could never tell whom you might meet. . .

The quarterdeck, located just aft of midships on the main deck, was the entrance lobby of a Sound steamer, the first inboard space seen by a passenger. Many were utilitarian, but *Pilgrim*'s ornate decor was carried through even to this area. It doubled as a gentleman's smoking room en route. This must be a builder's photo; where are the essential spittoons?

PURITAN.

NYNH&HRR 1941    WEST SHORE R.R.    C.20556    L.S.&M.S. MIDLAND LINE    D21515

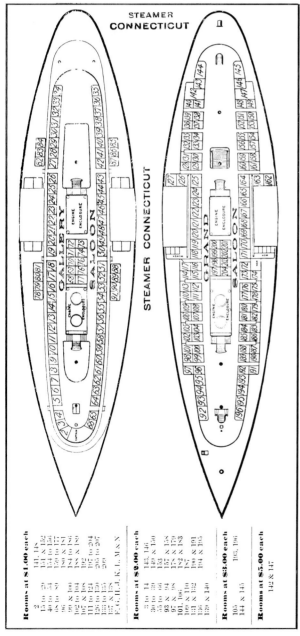

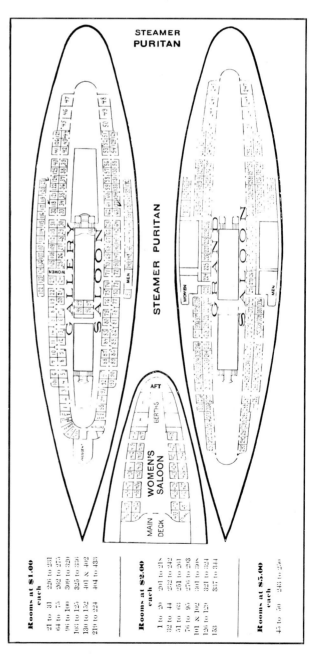

STEAMER
CONNECTICUT

STEAMER CONNECTICUT

Rooms at $1.00 each

| | |
|---|---|
| 2 | 141, 148 |
| 13 to 59 | 154 to 182 |
| 60 to 65 | 183 |
| | 184 |
| 66 | 186 |
| 89 & 106 | 187 to 189 |
| 97 | 190 |
| 101, 106 | |
| 109 & 110 | |
| 130 & 132 | |
| 126 to 135 | |
| | 209 |
| F, G, H, J, K, L, M & N | |

Rooms at $2.00 each

| | |
|---|---|
| 3 to 14 | 142, 143 |
| 30 to 59 | 149 & 150 |
| 93 & | 155 & 158 |
| 97, 96 | 178 & 183 |
| 101, 106 | |
| 109 & 110 | 190 & 191 |
| 131 & 132 | 194 & 195 |
| 139 & 140 | |

Rooms at $3.00 each

| | |
|---|---|
| 105 | 185, 196 |
| 144 & 145 | |

Rooms at $5.00 each

142 & 147

STEAMER
PURITAN

STEAMER PURITAN

Rooms at $1.00 each

| | |
|---|---|
| 21 to 31 | 226 to 251 |
| 64 to 75 | 262 to 242 |
| 96 to 100 | 251 to 261 |
| 105 to 125 | 276 to 288 |
| 130 to 152 | 301 to 402 |
| 219 to 224 | 404 to 433 |

Rooms at $2.00 each

| | |
|---|---|
| 1 to 20 | 201 to 218 |
| 32 to 44 | 252 to 242 |
| 51 to 63 | 251 to 261 |
| 76 to 95 | 276 to 288 |
| 101 to 102 | 301 to 306 |
| 126 to 129 | 321 to 324 |
| 153 | 357 to 344 |

Rooms at $5.00 each

45 to 50    243 to 250

WOMEN'S SALOON

AFT

BERTHS

MAIN DECK

280

The photo at top left is believed to date to 1896, at Newport, at the time when the Acushnet River ferry *Fairhaven* (II) (lower right of photo) was being readied for service under a court order (see Chapter 8). As she had a habit of doing, *Puritan* tended to dwarf anything else in a picture. She could hold freight equivalent to 59 of these cars.

At left, the stateroom diagrams from two contemporary vessels, the Fall River Line's *Puritan,* at that time the largest steel-hulled steamer on the Sound; and the Providence & Stonington Line's *Connecticut,* the largest wooden-hulled vessel built for the Sound. Both were from the 1888-1889 period, but their companies' design philosophies were quite different. *Puritan* was by far the more modern, and the more expensive boat in terms of capital cost. (*Connecticut* turned out to be more expensive to operate, but it wasn't intended to be that way.)

Above, two views of *Puritan*'s ornate interior, with its painstakingly carved gingerbread decorations. At the left, we are on the Gallery Deck, port side, looking aft past the Saloon Deck well and stateroom doors. Immediately in front of us is the grand staircase going down to the Saloon Deck; Governor Endecott's portrait (See Chapter 1) is just around the corner to our left.

At right above, a closeup of the carved sea creature adorning the grand stairway's newel post (did they rub its nose for luck?) and the intricate "overwrought" ironwork in the railings above and below. The staircase features the Fall River Line's patented carpet design, and at the head of the stairs is the locale on the starboard side that corresponds to the port corridor shown in the photo to the left. The small skylight windows constitute the "dome"; look carefully at the deck behind the wheelhouse in the photo at the top of Page 280.

We continue our photographic tour of *Puritan* to provide a better overall perspective of the Saloon/Gallery deck design and layout common to many vessels. The two views at the left are in the aft Gallery Deck area. The top photo is looking forward (notice Governor Endecott in the distance?), while the lower photo looks aft from the starboard corridor (see the preceding page). The brass railings mounted to the walls were helpful to uncertain passengers, or in occasionally turbulent waters. Here is further evidence that *Puritan* was a luxury vessel, the equal of any mansion or executive office *circa* 1889.

*Plymouth*, on the other hand, was slightly less opulent and more workmanlike. In the lower right photo, we see an officer ascending one of the side staircases; even here, mirrors give the illusion of greater space. Note, however, that the chandelier is guy-wired in place. This is, after all, a boat.

283

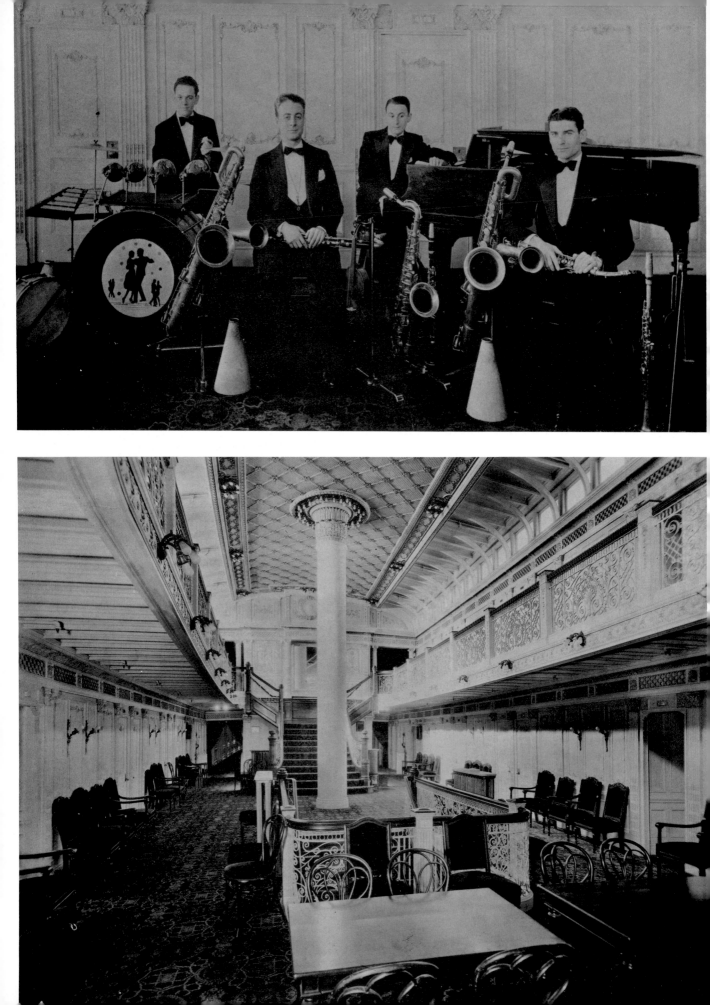

At no time did we mean to imply that *Plymouth* was a utilitarian vessel. In the photo at the lower left, we're on the Saloon Deck, in the aft saloon, looking forward. Instead of a portrait at the head of the grand staircase, Mr. Peirce settled on a mirror. The staircase in the foreground descends to the aft cabin on the Main Deck.

The lower right picture was taken on the Gallery Deck in the forward saloon, looking back toward the stern of the ship. The corridors, of course, flanked the boat's central engine compartment, allowing access on each side between fore and aft cabins.

At the top left, four stalwart musicians await the downbeat to provide entertainment. The photo is said to have been taken after 1930, which is consistent with (a) the jazz age couple design on the bass drum; and (b) the fact that there are only four musicians, versatile though they appear to be. A minimum of six had been *de rigeur* in the glory days.

Musical entertainment took the form of orchestral concerts during most of the Fall River Line's history. The programs, which were printed in the daily *Bulletin*s, contained selections familiar to concertgoers; overtures, marches, operatic highlights, and other classical gems.

The Eastern liners *Boston* and *New York* brought a different sound to the Sound in 1924: jazz, and a cabaret atmosphere. More shocking still, there was even dancing. But the Twenties were not permitted to roar aboard the Fall River Line, which continued to reflect J. Howland Gardner's conservative attitudes to the despair of passenger agents concerned about younger passengers deserting the "old fogy" boats for the seagoing cat's pajamas.

The Fall River Line's music was gradually modified to include more modern selections, but dancing was prohibited on Fall River Line boats until after Mr. Gardner's retirement in 1931.

A Parlor Stateroom

It's morning in New York City, and *Priscilla* is due at Pier 14 before 8:30 AM. Safely past the treacherous Hell Gate, she's cruising down the East River at about 57th Street (under the unfinished Queensboro Bridge) and will be around the Battery and home within the hour.

The drawing at left is of a *Priscilla* parlor stateroom. It appeared in the brochure that was distributed to dignitaries at her introduction ceremony in 1894. Now, with this kind of accommodation available, who would want to ride in a cramped Pullman berth on a sooty train?

At right, the diagram for *Priscilla*, showing the rooms and rates. As with any accommodation, larger and better-located rooms cost more than smaller and more out-of-the-way ones. The cheapest rooms were inboard, near the paddlewheels. The most expensive, the large cabins near the stern.

The crew list on the opposite page gives us some idea of the number of people involved in making the nightly voyages successful. Note that more than half of the crew reports to the Chief Steward. On *Priscilla* for many years, that was William S. Scarlett, who had started with the Providence & Stonington Line in 1874, joined *Priscilla*'s crew in 1908, and was still sailing, as Chief Steward, in the 1920s. Mr. Scarlett and his staff were widely acknowledged as major contributors to the fame of the Fall River Line; he was known to and by the wealthy and the famous.

Below, the cabin diagram for *Priscilla*, showing the rooms and rates. As with any accommodation, larger and better-located rooms cost more than smaller and more out-of-the-way ones. The cheapest rooms were inboard, near the paddlewheels. The most expensive were the large cabins near the stern. This was in the days before computerized reservations terminals; a master occupancy chart for each sailing date was prepared and updated manually as space was sold.

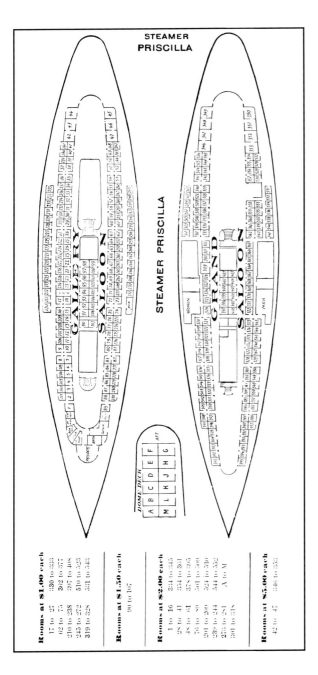

## Priscilla Crew - 1914

| Command/Deck | | Steward's Dep't. | |
|---|---|---|---|
| Captain | 1 | Chief Steward | 1 |
| First Pilot | 2 | Ass't. Steward | 1 |
| Quartermaster | 2 | Night Ass't. Steward | 1 |
| First Mate | 1 | Cashier | 1 |
| Second Mate | 1 | Checker | 2 |
| Third Mate | 1 | Bartender | 1 |
| Bow Watchman | 2 | Saloon Watchman | 1 |
| Watchman | 2 | Emmigrant Stewards | 2 |
| Coxwain | 1 | First Cook | 1 |
| Deck Hand | 14 | Second Cook | 1 |
| | --- | Third Cook | 1 |
| Group Total | 27 | Fourth Cook | 1 |
| | | Fifth Cook | 1 |
| **Purser's Dep't.** | | Broiler | 1 |
| Purser | 1 | Oysterman | 1 |
| Ass't. Purser | 1 | Baker | 1 |
| Freight Clerk | 1 | Butcher | 1 |
| Asst. Freight Clerk | 1 | First Messman | 1 |
| Ticket Collector | 1 | Second Messman | 1 |
| Baggage Master | 1 | Kitchenman | 2 |
| | --- | Pantryman | 7 |
| Group Total | 6 | Coffeeman | 1 |
| | | Silverman | 2 |
| **Engineering** | | Head Waiter | 1 |
| Chief Engineer | 1 | Second Head Waiter | 1 |
| First Ass't. Engineer | 1 | First Saloonman | 1 |
| Second Ass't. Eng'r | 1 | Ass't Saloonman | 1 |
| Third Ass't. Eng'r | 1 | F'wd Cabin man | 1 |
| Electric Engineer | 1 | Coat Room Man | 1 |
| Ass't. Electric Eng'r | 1 | Captain's Waiter | 1 |
| Watertender | 3 | Waiter | 68 |
| Oiler | 4 | Porter | 1 |
| Donkeytender | 3 | Emmigrant Waiter | 2 |
| Fireman | 20 | Stewardess | 3 |
| Coal Passer | 12 | Em'gnt Stewardess | 1 |
| | --- | | ---- |
| Group Total | 48 | Group Total | 115 |

**SUMMARY:**

| | |
|---|---|
| Command/Deck | 27 |
| Purser | 6 |
| Engineering | 48 |
| Steward | 115 |
| | ---- |
| **Grand Total** | **196** |

The crew list above gives us some idea of the number of people involved in making the nightly voyages successful. Note that more than half of the crew reports to the Chief Steward. On *Priscilla* for many years, that was William S. Scarlett, who had started with the Providence & Stonington Line in 1874, joined *Priscilla*'s crew in 1908, and was still sailing, as Chief Steward, in the 1920s. Mr. Scarlett and his staff were widely acknowledged as major contributors to the fame of the Fall River Line; he was known to and by the wealthy and the famous.

Welcome to *Priscilla*'s Grand Saloon. At the right, the head of the grand staircase, with the now-familiar carpet and wrought iron railings. A mirror, rather than a portrait of Priscilla Alden, serves as the focal point, with a clock overhead. The minute hand looks a bit fuzzy; it must have been a time exposure. Note the drinking fountain and tube of sanitary paper cups below, and the thoughtfully placed wastebasket. This represented a considerable advance in travel sanitation; the old way of providing a drink involved a pitcher, drum or barrel, and a few metal cups to be shared by all on board. The individual paper cup began to improve sanitation on boats and trains around the turn of the century.

If we place our camera on the landing in the photo at the right, in front of the mirror, and point it aft, we get the picture below. Compare this with *Puritan*'s cabin (Pages 13 and 282) and you get the idea that the level of gingerbread decoration escalated quite a bit between 1889 *(Puritan)* and 1894 *(Priscilla)*, although there are family resemblances. George Peirce did not tinker with a good thing. Rows of doors on the Saloon Deck (below) and Gallery Deck (above) lead to staterooms, and upholstered chairs line the saloon walls. For warmth, a free-standing steam-heat radiator is surrounded by chairs between us and the column. The column, of course, encloses one of *Priscilla*'s masts.

At left above, some relaxation and entertainment outside on deck, to piped-in music, in later years. Many passengers preferred the outdoor environment in good weather, and some considered the electric loudspeakers an intrusion. Others found the voyage enhanced by the presence of a congenial companion of the opposite sex. One or more of the Sound steamers were fondly remembered by people of more than one generation as the scene of some of their most romantic moments.

*Priscilla*'s dining room was not in the hold, but rather was located on the main deck, aft of the quarterdeck entrance hall. In the lower left photo, we're looking aft toward the doorways which led to two private dining rooms adjacent to this main room.

The tables were smaller than those on *Pilgrim*, set for six or eight rather than eight or ten. The ornate Italian Renaissance decor lost none of its panache in the descent from the Saloon Deck. Note the carving on the chair backs.

At the lower right, the dining room (looking forward) in later years, with some people present. The chinaware and silver was auctioned off after *Priscilla* and the other Fall River Liners went out of service; these items, inscribed with the Old Colony, Marine District, Fall River Line, or New England Steamship insignias are highly prized by collectors today. The people in the photo appear to be posing, by the way; else why is there no food on the plates?

The 1905 *Providence* (IV), shown above passing the Lackawanna ferry *Ithaca* near Pier 14, was the last steamboat to be designed by George Peirce. Her mission was to replace the aging *Pilgrim*, built in 1882, as a smaller winter boat for the Fall River Line. *Pilgrim*'s walking beam engine made her expensive to operate when compared to the inclined compound engines in *Plymouth* and *Priscilla*.

*Providence*'s design was characteristically evolutionary rather than revolutionary. She contained many of the elegant decorative touches common to all of the Fall River Line vessels. *Providence*'s dining room chairs, for example (below), were similar if not identical to those on *Priscilla*, down to the carvings on their backs.

But one design element was not an improvement. Mr. Peirce placed *Providence*'s dining room back down on a lower deck in the manner of *Pilgrim* and *Puritan*, a retrogression from *Priscilla*'s main deck dining room placement. Despite an improved ventilation system, the atmosphere (air, not ambience) in the dining room was warm and not particularly comfortable, expecially in summer.

As with *Priscilla*, the plumbing aboard *Providence* was limited. Hot and cold running water were not provided to the staterooms until NESS conducted a frantic retrofit program during the winter of 1926-27 on all four of the Fall River Line's large boats. This was in response to Eastern Steamship's newer *Boston* and *New York*.

The decorative wall panel shown above measured approximately ten feet wide by three feet high; it was one of several different ones located in the smaller public cabins. The decorations alone provided employment for literally hundreds of artisans; painters, sculptors, engravers, tinsmiths, stoneworkers, and, of course, master carpenters.

The luxury boats were equipped with barber shops so that male passengers could look their best while walking down the gangplank toward the morning's business meetings. This well-equipped shop is on board *Providence*. (Don't show this photo to a fire inspector; that motor is connected to a light socket adapter in the chandelier.)

Upstairs and downstairs in *Providence*'s main saloon. While the Saloon Deck and Gallery Deck layouts were generally similar, the smaller boats necessarily had less expansive saloons. The decor, with its wrought iron and elaborate carvings in bulkheads and overheads (walls and ceilings), was no less ornate; it had come to be expected by the Fall River Line's generally upscale clientele. While many passengers picked their sailing days on the basis of which boat would be operating, the accommodations and arrangements on all four vessels were very good.

As with *Plymouth*, describing *Providence* as a "small" boat is decidedly misleading, except in relative terms. Although she was forty feet shorter than *Priscilla*, she had almost as many staterooms; more of these were placed on her upper deck. *Providence* also had something that was very new in 1905: a telephone system with an instrument in every stateroom. For some passengers, this was their first and sometimes fearful contact with Mr. Bell's invention, as telephones were not yet common in homes. This was a considerable improvement over the call bell system used on older boats.

Of course, the Fall River liners weren't the only boats with grand staircases. Here, slightly less well lit but no less ornate, is the grand staircase of Charles Morse's *Yale*, complete with the letter "Y" in the ironwork (above as well as below). *Harvard*, of course, had an "H". The two Morse boats were decorated with the trimmings of their namesake schools; *Harvard* in crimson and *Yale* in blue, with collegiate pennants and insignia throughout, even in the staterooms. As a marketing concept, it could not have been more appropriate. Whatever his financial dealings, Charles Morse understood his customers.

*Harvard* and *Yale* were two years newer than *Providence*, but they reflected a far less conservative design philosophy than that of the Fall River Line. Only one American vessel (Mr. Morse's *Governor Cobb*) preceded them as turbine-powered boats; their relative lack of vibration meant that even the glassware did not tinkle in the sideboards. The *Nautical Gazette* pronounced *Yale*'s (and by extension, *Harvard*'s) dining room design to be "one of the largest, airiest and most beautiful to be found on any vessel, ocean-going or inland." Small wonder that the NYNH&H saw these boats as a considerable threat to the Fall River Line.

Neither the boats' names nor decorations were changed when the boats went to California as transplanted easterners. That would have involved considerable expense, considering all of the places where the colleges' insignias had been emblazoned. The decor presumably pleased some passengers similarly transplanted to California. Some of the satisfied customers on the Pacific coastal route delighted in writing "guess where I am" letters on the liners' stationery to friends in New England while en route between Los Angeles and San Francisco.

Everything about the new (in 1908) Fall River boat *Commonwealth* was massive. While she was shorter than the ocean-going Cunarder *Lusitania*, *Commonwealth* was actually wider, and could carry almost as many passengers and just as much freight. This new boat, with its upper-deck dining room and spacious social and sleeping accommodations, recaptured some of the glory (and the passengers) lost to *Yale* and *Harvard*.

*Commonwealth* was a ponderous command for her first captain, George Williamson. In the photo below, note her steering wheels. The two wheels closest to the camera would be used only if the steam steering gear were to malfunction, and are normally disconnected from the main shaft and blocked in place. But note how much of the wheels' circumference is below the pilothouse floor level. Those are large wheels.

298

The main dining room on *Commonwealth* was decorated in the classical Louis XVI style. Three domelike ceiling recesses contained indirect lighting fixtures, but the most spectacular feature regarding lighting, and indeed a view, was that the dining room was four decks above the water, rather than in the hold or on the Main Deck.

The designers had learned that passengers preferred to eat and relax in a windowed room. The dining room location on *Providence* had been a mistake; those on *Yale* and *Harvard* had outclassed the Fall River Line. But George Peirce's successors, led by J. Howland Gardner and Stevenson Taylor, would have the last word here.

*Commonwealth* main dining room, 50 feet above the waterline, was large enough to seat 300 people at one time. There were other lounges at which other passengers could be served and, of course, room service was available.

Another change in facilities from the past was the installation of smaller tables. The earliest steamboats had dining facilities that would remind us of jails or orphanages; Spartan, with long tables. As the amenities improved, the size of tables gradually shrank. The smaller tables also reflected changing tastes; there were more smaller parties desiring privacy. Of course, the tables could be joined for a large party.

*Commonwealth*'s silver service contained approximately 5,300 pieces. Glassware numbered 3,500 pieces. 17,500 pieces of china were aboard.

Her linen closets contained 3,750 cloth napkins, 4,150 towels, 5,500 pillow cases, 8,040 sheets and 1,834 blankets. 40,000 pieces of laundry were done each week.

For each trip, *Commonwealth*'s kitchen staff received a ton of roasts, steaks and chops; 200 lbs. of poultry, 240 dozen eggs, 500 loaves of bread, 100 gallons of milk, 300 lbs. of butter, 300 lbs. of fresh fish, 150 lbs. of salt fish, and 100 lbs. of coffee.

The photos on this page show some of the dining room activities; they happen to be aboard *Commonwealth*, but they are not atypical of the first-line boats.

At the upper left, a martini is under construction at the bar. Behind the scenes, the photo at lower left shows the large kitchen needed to do justice to a 300-seat dining room. At the upper right, a cook (Broiler?) is caught in the act of preparing a chicken, while, at right below, the Coffeeman (see Page 287) fills the small coffeepots that will be delivered to the tables shortly.

The service and equipment compared favorably with any first-class large restaurant of the day.

As we noted earlier, *Commonwealth*'s interior was a mixture of decorative architectural styles. At top right, her library or "Social Hall," aft of the quarterdeck, was done in Louis XVI style. Her grand saloon was done in a modified Venetian style, while the forward saloon and some other rooms, one of which is shown in the photo below, was decorated in a mahogany-and-gold scheme that was called "Napoleonic" because it allegedly mirrored the French designs *circa* 1810. Other rooms ranged in decor from Italian Renaissance to English (note the Grill Room, below right, adjacent to the Dining Room) to more Louis XVI. Architectural critics of the time disappointed and enraged J. Howland Gardner and her other designers by sniffing at the design "hodgepodge" and bemoaning the lost architectural opportunity to do something "really grand," in a unified manner.

The complainers didn't appreciate the splendor that was theirs until it was gone forever.

# Chapter Fourteen

# The Era Ends

J une 1, 1912 marked the beginning of the New
England Steamship Company's continuous
management of the Sound steamboat lines
until their demise, a management interrupted only
by the two-year period during which the United
States Railroad Administration took control of all
railroads in America. It may seem incongruous, but
that June 1912 date, when the steamboat operations finally settled down after much financial and
organizational turmoil, also marks the beginning of
the NYNH&H's decline into bankruptcy.

### A Mushrooming Investigation

In May, Interstate Commerce Commission
Chairman Charles Prouty had ordered an investigation into the NYNH&H and its control of the Boston

Lest anyone underestimate the effects of winter,
we offer this view of *Richard Peck* crunching
through the Hudson toward Pier 14 while a tug is
having similar difficulty. The larger boats often "ran
interference" for smaller ones, making it possible for
all to navigate. The gray skies were also symbolic of
NESS' overall condition, and that of the NYNH&H.
After the 1920 discontinuance of regular New Haven
service, *Richard Peck* was used on excursions and
fill-in assignments.

and Maine Railroad; that investigation would begin in the fall. Louis Brandeis had finally gotten a response to his five-year series of exhortations.

The ICC accountants arrived in New Haven for a routine look at the New Haven's accounts, to look into services and freight rates. What they found was a confusing maze of transactions between the NYNH&H subsidiaries. By the time they penetrated that maze, what had started as a routine rate inquiry became a full-scale investigation of NYNH&H finances, organization, and policies. Their report was issued early in 1913, and Mr. Brandeis pounced upon the first copies like a terrier. Now, at long last, his 1907 document charging virtual insolvency — the private report that had been all but shouted down by the NYNH&H publicists — would be proven right or wrong.

It was right. After the ICC accountants waded through the cascades of paper that concealed complex transactions among 336 identified subsidiaries, it was ascertained that between 1903 and 1913, the NYNH&H capitalization had grown from $93 million to $417 million. Of the $324 million increase,

approximately $204 million had been spent on trying to acquire "everything that moved" in New England; spent on sundry items designed to lubricate the political machinery that it might permit such transactions; and spent on fueling the public press with information designed to ensure a favorable image.

The bottom line was that the NYNH&H was in serious financial trouble. One of Mr. Brandeis' contentions in particular was borne out: that for years, the NYNH&H had been shuffling cash to its subsidiaries that they immediately returned to the parent company as dividends, i.e., "income." The NYNH&H indeed had not legitimately earned enough income to cover its bond obligations and pay out what it had been paying. The NYNH&H shocked the world by omitting its dividend in 1914; it paid no dividends at all thereafter until 1928.

Coincident with all of this investigative activity, J. P. Morgan (I) passed away, in March 1913. It was said that his death had been hastened by his appearance before the Congressional "Pujo committee on Money Trusts" in 1912. The elder Morgan had been saved from further personal appearances in matters pertaining to the NYNH&H by Mr. Mellen, who volunteered himself to appear in Morgan (I)'s place. It was another example of Mr. Mellen's loyalty to The Boss.

The man who had controlled the NYNH&H was now succeeded by his son, J. P. Morgan (II). The Boss was dead, and the younger Morgan lost very little time in trying to show the investigators and the public that (a) his father had nothing whatsoever to do with the NYNH&H's secret activities, which were now all laid to the doorstep of Mr. Mellen; and that (b) changes would swiftly be made to take care of the situation and to counteract the public heat. Mr. Morgan (II) asked for and received Mr. Mellen's resignation, in return for a consulting contract at $30,000 per year. Mr. Mellen agreed, and it was done in August. Interviews disclosed that a majority of the Board had wanted to retain Mr. Mellen, but he agreed to go, to smooth out conflicts. The new president was to be Howard Elliott, who had succeeded Mr. Mellen as President of the Northern Pacific.

And then, to give you an idea of the manner in which Morgan (II) rewarded Mr. Mellen's loyal service, the Board cancelled the consulting contract two weeks later, apparently at the strong suggestion of Morgan (II). The Morgan family was apparently attempting to rewrite history; "Mellen did it all; we never knew." About all of this craven backing and filling one Board member was privately heard to say, "The Old Man wouldn't have done that." Mr. Mellen was loudly and publicly heard to say that the Board had "welched."

That betrayal proved to be a costly mistake for the Board, because of another 1912 event which

---

### Table 14-1

## Steamboat Assignments, 1912

### New England Steamship Co.
**Passenger:**
Bridgeport Line: *Naugatuck, Bridgeport*
New Haven: *Richard Peck*
New London: *Chester W. Chapin, City of Lowell*
Providence Line: *Providence, Plymouth* (summer)
Fall River: *Priscilla, Commonwealth* (summer);
    *Providence, Plymouth* (winter)
New Bedford: *Maine, New Hampshire*
**Freight:**
Providence: *Mohawk, Mohegan*
Fall River: *City of Fall River, City of Taunton*
New Bedford: *Pequonnock, New Haven*

### Hartford & New York Trans'n. Co.
Hartford: *Hartford, Middletown*
Bridgeport (Merchants Line): *Seaboard*
Providence (Bay State Line): *Tennessee, Georgia*

### Maine Steamship Co.
Portland: *North Land, North Star, Old Colony*

### Metropolitan Line
Boston: *Massachusetts, Bunker Hill*

---

*Bridgeport* and *Naugatuck,* once known as *William G. Payne* and *Allen Joy* respectively, provided the NESS service between Bridgeport and New York until 1920. H&NYTCo. also operated *Seaboard* on what had started as the competitive Merchants' line, whose founders unknowingly turned it over to the very interests they were fighting.

*Bridgeport* was sold in 1913 to the McAllister Steamboat Co. and renamed *Highlander* for operation to Bear Mountain. Burned in 1924, she was rebuilt in 1925 and returned to the Hudson as *Bear Mountain.* She also operated to Coney Island in the late 1930s before being sold to a Potomac River firm in 1943. Above, she sails up the East River toward the partially completed Queensboro Bridge and Hell Gate beyond.

*Naugatuck* operated as a freighter on an irregular basis after 1920; for example, she was called to fill in when *Sankaty* burned at her New Bedford dock while on Nantucket-Martha's Vineyard runs in June 1924. She was sold to Sound Steamship Lines in 1935, and for a time operated between Providence and Block Island as well as providing assorted excursion services. The photo below shows her before her modification to an excursion boat.

Table 14-1 shows the normal, or standard, vessel assignments in 1912. Obviously, there were variations, based on maintenance schedules and mishaps. Further, some of the spare boats, particularly smaller boats used as freighters, might be assigned as "extras" during the summer season to handle heavy patronage.

affected them: the election of Democrat Woodrow Wilson, who immediately ordered an even more thorough investigation into the NYNH&H's finances. Malefactors of great wealth had become fair game in the political arena, and the name of Morgan rightly or wrongly had become synonymous with "oppressive secret wealth and power used against the Common Man." Morgan (I) had died before Brandeis' supporters could nail him; they would try for Morgan (II). It was not coincidental that 1914 was a Congressional election year, and that Congressmen nationwide were preparing to ride to re-election on the New Haven Railroad.

The mood of the public, particularly that segment of the public interested in law enforcement, was not made happier by Charles Wyman Morse who, you remember, had been consigned to jail in 1910 for what everyone had confidently believed would be a 15-year term. In 1911, Mrs. Morse and other friends began a campaign to get Mr. Morse out of jail; the reports were that he was ill, and would not live more than a few months. Doctors concurred, and William Howard Taft pardoned Mr. Morse in January 1912. President Taft was immediately assailed for softheadedness; and each day that Mr. Morse remained alive (thus failing to do the honorable thing) brought Mr. Taft closer to defeat in his 1912 re-election bid. Mr. Morse, by the way, remained alive until 1923; it was later said that he had drunk soapsuds and other chemicals to simulate acute kidney disease.

And now, Charles Sanger Mellen, ousted President and former consultant, was granted immunity from prosecution in exchange for his testimony, which was given with some spice if not relish. When asked his future plans, Mr. Mellen answered; "I'm going to retire to my farm and raise goats. There seems to be a growing demand for goats." He went on to relate many of the events which had theretofore been secret. The NYNH&H treasurer, Hiram Kochersperger, was taken ill; doctors advised him to travel to Europe for a rest, rendering him regrettably unable to testify. Mr. Mellen, when asked how long Mr. Kochersperger had been ill, replied, "Since the Commission began to get after the New Haven's accounts."

---

*Maine* and *New Hampshire* proved to be useful boats for services requiring medium-sized vessels to many of the NYNH&H ports. Through the 'teens, the sister ships served New Bedford with clockwork regularity. The team was quite literally broken up on Execution Rocks when *Maine* ran aground and was destroyed there in 1920.

*New Hampshire* finished her career operating to New London; on her last trip in November 1934 she carried just 60 passengers. Laid up at New London until June 1937, she was towed to Baltimore and scrapped five weeks before the end of all NESS Sound service.

Most of the revelations of the investigation did not relate to the steamboats; the full story of the hearings is fascinating, but it is far beyond the scope of this volume. One tale, however, proved the lengths to which the NYNH&H was willing to go to conceal its role in the removal of the sleek *Harvard* and *Yale* from the Sound. A young and innocent workman named Grover Richards had been bought a suit of clothes and transported to New York in March 1910, where he met three wealthy-looking gentlemen, and for the next few days was put up at a hotel, gawked at the wonders of the big city, and signed a few papers he could not comprehend before going home. Two of the people who squired Mr. Richards around were John L. Billard of Meriden, and E. D. Robbins, the latter being a Vice-president of the NYNH&H. The investigators were later seeking the Treasurer of the Metropolitan Steamship Co. who had signed the transfer papers and checks for *Harvard* and *Yale*: Grover Richards. He obviously did not work in the Yellow Building.

The ICC report was issued July 11, 1914, to the outrage of concerned Americans and the delight of those who might profit politically. Also in that year, an antitrust suit resulted in a Federal Court decree that forced the NYNH&H to sell its interest in Merchants & Miners Transportation immediately, and to sell its minority interest in Eastern Steamship within three years. The New England Navigation Co. sold its interest in Merchants and Miners Transportation Co., in December 1914, at an unconcealable loss of $3.6 million.

## Criminal Charges and Stockholders' Suits

A Federal Grand Jury returned criminal indictments against 21 of the captains of American industry who had been on the NYNH&H Board; the indictments were handed down November 2, 1914, two days before the Congressional election. Trial began about a year later, and none of the 21 were convicted. Six were acquitted, and the jury could not agree on the rest, who were never retried. The immune Mr. Mellen had been on the witness stand for 31 days.

The next question was, could the NYNH&H recover from its former directors some of the corporate assets that were alleged to have been wasted? The directors in 1915 recommended against it, but a minority of stockholders, led by one Edwin Adams, filed suit in August 1916 to recover about $150 million alleged to have been negligently or illegally wasted. The former directors, aided by the present directors and the NYNH&H, succeeded in delaying a trial for more than five years. A trial date was set at last, for January 1921; whereupon the suit was settled for $2,500,000 in December 1920.

Public exposure of their transactions did allow the NYNH&H directors partially to settle an old score. The helpful John L. Billard had, in 1911, kept the $2.9 million profit on the sale of Boston

## Freight Service

We have noted elsewhere that freight service, while unglamorous, was the more profitable side of the steamboat business. For the NYNH&H, the key was coordinated scheduling of boats and connecting railroad trains to inland points.

*Pequonnock* (shown in two photos on this page) and her sister *New Haven* (III) date back to 1906 and 1907, but were overshadowed by *Massachusetts*, *Bunker Hill*, and *Old Colony*, the trio of larger freighters built for the outside service to Boston.

For contrast, consider *Pequot*, (top, right) built in 1865 as *Thetis* for the Providence and Stonington Line. She was an ideal vessel for off-seasons and fill-in work.

*Boston* (II), built in 1904, shown at the right lying in her East River slip, was larger than *Pequonnock* yet smaller than *Bunker Hill.* She received many heavy assignments, including runs from New York to her namesake city. Note too the presence of an unusual vessel at the right of the photo: a Pennsylvania Railroad self-propelled lighter, looking something like a tugboat with a cargo deck. The NYNH&H and PRR were New York harbor's largest rail "trading partners."

And here again is *City of Brockton*, largest of the Peirce-era freighters; she and her walking-beam engine survived until 1929.

And of all these vessels, which one survived longest? Of course: the oldest and smallest, *Pequot*, scrapped in 1943.

and Maine Railroad stock which had been "parked" with him. The outraged directors had expected Mr. Billard to return most of the money as part of the alleged "deal," but they had then been prevented from seeking recovery in the courts because to do so would have revealed their illegal scheme. Once the affair was revealed anyway, they sued Mr. Billard, recovering $1,250,000 and reducing his gain to a mere $1,650,000.

One other old score, this one against the Board, was at least partially settled in 1917 when an arbitrator awarded Charles Mellen $95,000 to reimburse him for legal expenses he had incurred by defending himself in all of the legal proceedings regarding the NYNH&H. As part of their post-employment betrayal of Mr. Mellen, the Board had refused to pay any of these, in spite of their promise to do so.

But the steamboats sailed on regardless of these activities; the operating people were not directly affected by the machinations of financiers and politicians. The "main line" route assignments for the companies owned by or friendly to the NYNH&H in 1912 are shown in the table on Page 306. It reflects the beginning of traffic decline, particularly to the smaller ports.

**The Panama Canal Act Problem**

Another investigation, this one specific to the steamboat lines, was conducted by the ICC in 1914. The Panama Canal Act of 1912 made it unlawful for a railroad to own or operate steamship lines. While the focus of this law was on the Panama Canal, it applied to all railroads. The effect would have been to force the NYNH&H to sell off all of its steamboat operations except the Island services and ferries at New Bedford and Wickford-Newport.

Even as the NYNH&H was being flogged for improprieties, New England came to its defense. Literally hundreds of shipping and business firms as well as state and local governments showed up in support of the NYNH&H's continuing ownership of the Sound lines. There was good reason; the integrated Sound steamer and rail service was far better than either one would be alone in a "competitive" situation. The ICC ruled in July 1918 that the NYNH&H could continue to operate the Sound lines. Similar exemptions were secured by the Central Vermont and Maine Central railroads for their steamboat operations.

Of course, this happened in part because we were at war. The United States Railroad Administration (USRA) had taken control of America's railroads on December 26, 1917, and maintained it until March 1, 1920. That 796-day period proved to be a lifesaver for the NYNH&H, as the federal government upgraded not only the NYNH&H physical plant, but also that of its primary connec-

tion, the Pennsylvania Railroad. It probably does not come as a surprise that a uniform accounting system was imposed on the railroads during USRA days, and continued by the ICC thereafter. No longer would a railroad be able to cloud their finances as the NYNH&H had done.

The USRA had come into being because of delays in movement of war materiel, particularly at the Port of New York. Loaded and empty freight cars from the midwest clogged New Jersey yards, there were car shortages elsewhere, and loading of goods aboard ships was bogged down. One of the few bright spots in this distressing and dangerous picture was the NYNH&H's coordinated Sound

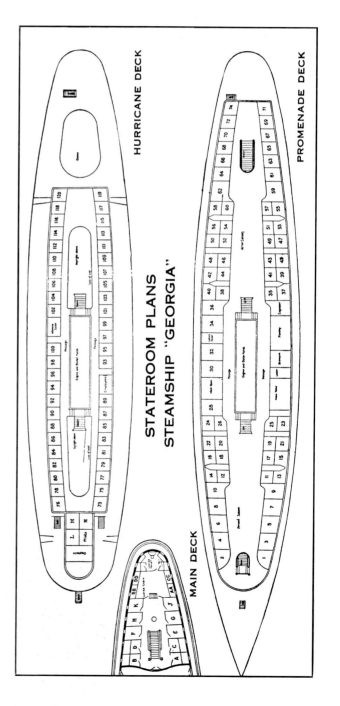

STATEROOM PLANS
STEAMSHIP "GEORGIA"

312

Operating as a second service, the Hartford & New York Transportation Co. used a small fleet of secondhand refugees from Chesapeake Bay. Perhaps the most interesting of these was the pioneer iron screw steamer *Georgia*, built in 1887 for the Old Bay Line's main line Baltimore-Norfolk route. The Old Bay Line was reducing its fleet in 1909 as a result of a competitive agreement between the owning railroads, which resulted in reduction of overall service on the Bay.

Like her larger Fall River cousins, she was built with electric lights, steam steering gear, and an ornate interior. H&NYTCo bought her in 1909, and used her mainly on the NewYork-Providence Joy Line/Bay State Line along with the smaller *Tennessee*. That service was stopped in 1931, and until 1937 *Georgia* suffered the ignominity of being a gaudy floating anchorage in New Haven.

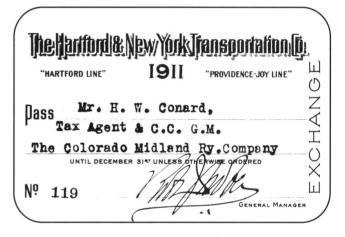

The Hartford & New York Transportation Co.

"HARTFORD LINE"    1911    "PROVIDENCE-JOY LINE"

Pass    Mr. H. W. Conard,
         Tax Agent & C.C. G.M.
    The Colorado Midland Ry.Company
         UNTIL DECEMBER 31ST UNLESS OTHERWISE ORDERED

Nº 119                          GENERAL MANAGER

EXCHANGE

---

steamer and connecting railroad operation, bringing the massive and vital flow of munitions (by Remington, Colt and others) and textiles (uniforms, blankets, etc.) to New York piers with a minimum of fuss and feathers. But another transportation mode, the motor truck, was also developing in response to the clogged rail system.

The New England Navigation Company which had functioned mainly as a holding company for securities of all kinds, went out of business on November 30, 1917, with all liabilities taken over by the NYNH&H. At that time, $3 million of NESS bonds (held by NYNH&H) were written off to adjust for the inflated value at which the Navigation company had sold the steamship assets to NESS back in 1908. Any attempt to summarize gross financial figures for the New England Navigation Company would be meaningless for our purposes because of the diversity of companies involved.

## Through the Twenties and Thirties

The operating pattern between New York and Narragansett Bay after *Commonwealth* came on line in 1908 called for *Priscilla* and *Commonwealth* to operate to Fall River in the summer, while *Providence* and *Plymouth* operated summer-only service to Providence. During the winter season, the larger *Priscilla* and *Commonwealth* were pulled out of service; *Providence* and *Plymouth* were switched to the Fall River run while "first-line" passenger service to Providence was suspended until Spring.

A second passenger service between New York and Providence was provided year-round by what had been the Joy Line, operated by the Hartford and New York Transportation Company. The Joy Line name had disappeared in 1912; the New York Providence service was now called the Bay State Line. *Tennessee* and *Georgia* provided the basic service, which continued until 1931. The H&NYTCo. also operated the Portland (ME) Line and, of course, its Hartford Line.

The Providence Line (*Providence* and *Plymouth*) summer service was terminated during USRA control in 1918, with the two boats moved to provide year-round service between New York and Fall River. Beginning with the summer season of 1919, *Priscilla* and *Commonwealth* were added to the Fall River run, reinstating the four-boat service pattern. The normal assignment was for *Priscilla* and *Providence* to run together from each port on alternate days, while *Commonwealth* and *Plymouth* operated in the opposite direction.

With the 1920 return of the NYNH&H property to private management by the USRA, operating changes were under consideration, in response to changing market conditions. In particular, passenger traffic from New York to the relatively nearby ports of Bridgeport and New Haven had switched to train and automobile in great numbers. By contrast, the New Bedford service was attracting more passengers, owing to the buildup of the area and the Islands.

One event, occurring at about the time of the return of control by the USRA, suddenly made changes mandatory. On February 4, 1920, ice forced *Maine* onto Execution Rocks near Huntington NY; she was destroyed. Remembering the *Maine*, J. Howland Gardner shuffled the fleet. New Haven passenger service was discontinued about a month after *Maine* sank, and *Richard Peck* was moved to the New London route, running opposite *Chester W. Chapin*. *City of Lowell* was moved from New London to the New Bedford service where *Maine* had been, opposite *New Hampshire*. Later that year, Bridgeport Line passenger service was discontinued. *Bridgeport* and *Naugatuck* were replaced for freight by *City of Brockton*. The H&NYTCo Merchants' Line to Bridgeport was unaffected.

Continuing increases in New Bedford Line ridership led to one other switch, in 1922; *City of Lowell* and *Chester W. Chapin*, being larger steamers, were moved to the New Bedford route, while the smaller *New Hampshire* joined *Richard Peck* in the lesser-travelled New London service.

## The Colonial and Eastern Competition

When NESS stopped its Providence Line in 1918, it was in part because the Colonial Line had become popular, as the Colonial's *Lexington* and *Concord* outclassed the Bay State Line's *Georgia* and *Tennessee*. Frank Dunbaugh had done well; he insisted on safety first, and instructed his officers to treat the passengers in a friendly manner. That human touch paid off in the decade of the Twenties, because the NESS captains tended toward lordliness at times, in the old tradition.

Frank Dunbaugh's safety emphasis resulted in an outstanding record for the Colonial Line, in sharp contrast to the bumpity-bump tendencies of the old Joy Line. The only serious accident to befall a Colonial Line vessel happened to *Lexington*, on Jan 2, 1935, when she collided with the freighter *Jane Christensen* in the East River.

The Colonial Line had its competitive problems from the beginning, though; the NYNH&H refused to allow through tickets or through bills of lading, as they had routinely denied them to all previous competitors. But people rode the train that NYNH&H ran to connect with Providence Line, then walked the block to the Colonial Line wharf. Mr. Dunbaugh went to ICC in 1916 asking that the railroad be compelled to maintain through passenger ticket rates. It is testimony to the great change in public and government attitudes that the ICC decided in favor of the Colonial Line. Note that it is less than two years after this that the NESS Providence Line was discontinued, with *Plymouth* and *Providence* moved to the Fall River Line.

## The Cape Cod Canal

The Eastern Steamship Company's New York to Boston service was still operating, even after *Harvard* and *Yale* migrated to California. *Massachusetts* and *Bunker Hill* went to war, and Eastern used *Camden*, *Belfast*, *North Land* and other vessels in the service. When the Cape Cod Canal opened to passenger steamboats in 1916, the 337-mile "out-

side route" around Cape Cod was cut to the "canal route" of 264 miles.

The canal started as a private project. In June 1909, August Belmont turned over the first shovelful of Massachusetts soil. (History does not record whether he used an Ames shovel.) The Chief Engineer was William Barclay Parsons, who had been chief engineer of the first New York subway, and who had served on the Panama Canal Commission. Captain Jacob Miller left NESS to manage the completed Cape Cod Canal operations; he was replaced by Capt. Henry O. Nickerson (senior captain of Fall River fleet). When Capt. Nickerson retired in 1931, the position went to J. Howland Gardner.

The Cape Cod canal opened to smaller boats on the Fourth of July 1914. The first steamboat through was the former freighter *Massachusetts*, in May 1916. She and *Bunker Hill* operated through the Canal between New York and Boston almost every night thereafter. There were some occasions when fog forced the boats to the outside route instead of the canal.

But Eastern Steamship did not do well financially, and the company sold its two leading vessels for a good price in 1918. The U. S. Navy bought *Massachusetts* and *Bunker Hill* for service as minelayers; *Massachusetts* became *USS Shawmut*, and *Bunker Hill* became *USS Aroostook*.

By 1924, the Eastern Steamship Co. was financially strong enough to introduce two new steamers to the New York – Boston service through the Cape Cod Canal. The new boats were named *Boston* and *New York*. As was common for the time, the season was between April and November. Eastern also bought the Old Dominion Line's route to Norfolk, an action that made one of Charles Mellen's bad dreams come true. Shipments between Boston and Chesapeake Bay via the former Old Dominion routes cut directly into NYNH&H freight revenues.

*Boston* and *New York* had hot and cold running water in each stateroom, yet another escalation in creature comfort which caused all to marvel. A competitive response was called for, and the NESS

| Table 14-2 |
| --- |

## Steamboat Assignments, 1922

### New England Steamship Co.
**Passenger:**
New London: *Richard Peck, New Hampshire*
Fall River: *Priscilla, Commonwealth* (summer);
*Providence, Plymouth* (all year)
New Bedford: *Chester W. Chapin, City of Lowell*
**Freight:**
Bridgeport: *City of Brockton*
Fall River: *City of Fall River, City of Taunton*
Providence: *Mohawk, Mohegan*
New Bedford: *Pequonnock, New Haven*

### Hartford & New York Trans'n. Co.
Hartford: *Hartford, Middletown*
Providence (Bay State Line): *Tennessee, Georgia*
Bridgeport (Merchants Line): *Seaboard*

The Cape Cod Canal was something of a wonder in the years after it opened to passenger boats in 1916. The contemporary Panama Canal might have been the more massive project, but the Cape Cod Canal was easily accessible, and the site of many excursion boat runs. How many people on *Block Island* (lower left) fantasized about Panama as they left Buzzard's Bay?

No fantasy was *Belfast*, operated along with her sister *Camden* by the Eastern Steamship Co. on a canal-aided all-water route that competed with the Fall River Line to Boston. *Belfast* later became Colonial Line's *Arrow*, destined for a special if somber place in Sound history.

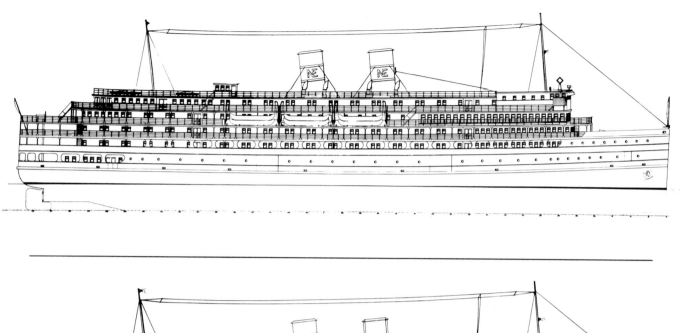

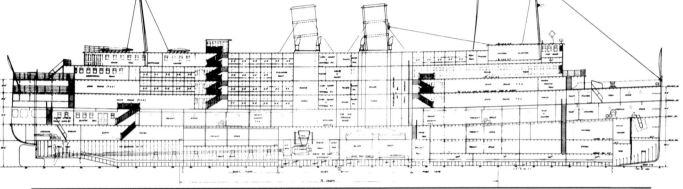

people were soon at work on plans for new Fall River Line boats. These were to be four-deck vessels with all modern conveniences, outshining *Boston* and *New York*.

Fiscal reality soon interrupted the planning process; the market size was declining, for reasons that had nothing to do with service quality. The decision was evidently made that the last thing NESS needed was two new large steamboats; the new boats never got off the drawing boards. Instead, NESS made a 1926 investment in refitting the four Fall River Line boats with hot and cold running water in every stateroom. This modification was no small task, involving as it did wholesale tearing out and replacement of bulkheads, decks and woodwork. Other minor decorative and equipment modernization was carried out.

NESS did build new boats, however, but the company chose to put its capital into four vessels that would serve the most likely market as it looked in the 1920s. That, of course, was the Island service, which had its geographic immunity from auto competition.

*Boston* and *New York* had been operating during the summer seasons only. Now, in 1927, Eastern extended the service to year 'round, using *Robert E. Lee* and *George Washington*, chartered from the Old Dominion Line. In later years, Eastern used *Acadia* and *St. John* on the winter run.

It was in 1928 that a problem which had been a negative factor for Sound steamboat passengers was solved as well as it could be. The problem was that whenever a morning fog shrouded the west end of the Sound, the steamers bound for New York dropped anchor and waited for the fog to burn off before attempting to navigate Hell Gate. When visibility returned, the small squadron of steamers that had accumulated would resume their journeys. Of course, passengers were delayed, and missed many morning meetings. While this had been a problem since the first sailboat, such unreliability could no longer be tolerated in the modern world of the 1920s; the all-rail alternative was becoming more attractive.

NESS leased a small dock adjacent to Long Island Rail Road tracks at Whitestone Landing in Queens. NESS also arranged with the LIRR to have a special train there upon receipt of a wireless message from one or more of the steamboats, to carry passengers by rail to Pennsylvania Station in New York. The "fog dock" was first used in December 1928. The passengers got to Penn Station by 8:00 AM, although *Priscilla* herself didn't dock until about Noon. For the first time, NESS could

Above left, the NESS ship that never got off the drawing board, a 7-deck turbine-screw vessel. The plan dates to 1930, apparently a response to *Boston* and *New York*. Historians are uncertain as to whether NESS was going to use these boats via Fall River or direct to Boston through the canal.

Two samples of actual canal travelers are shown on this page; *Old Colony*, above, gingerly picking her way through a narrow section; and Eastern's *Boston* gliding past the bascule bridge that preceded the giant vertical lift bridge at Buzzard's Bay. Note the passengers viewing the wonder of the canal.

If you can't lick the rubber-tired motor vehicle, why not join it? Here (upper left) is a bus-and-boat combination featuring *City of Lowell* and a United Railways (Rhode Island) coach, both part of the NYNH&H empire. The photo of the vehicles and their masters was probably taken to promote the town-to-dock feeder service, and it's hard to tell who looks more uncomfortable. The freight side of the partnership, that is, trucks and freight interchange, proved to be much more successful.

New Shoreham is not on Long Island's North Shore, but is a small community on Block Island. In fact, the town paid to have *New Shoreham* built in 1901, and contracted with NESS to operate her to and from the island. She was scrapped in 1954.

*Sankaty,* (below right) was the first propeller-driven Island boat, built in 1911. She burned rather spectacularly in New Bedford harbor in 1924, and was sold for salvage, then raised and rebuilt by her new owner, one John Snow. Mr. Snow sold her to the ferry that then operated between Stamford CT and Oyster Bay NY. In 1940 she went to new owners in Nova Scotia.

The ticket at right is one of many thousands that passed over company counters; we reproduce it here in part to show yet another version of the NYNH&H's famous "N-script" logo as applied to subsidiaries.

guarantee early morning arrival on Manhattan Island, and the advertising copy read, "Gets you there." Eastern Steamship countered with a small boat and connecting bus.

Beginning with the summer of 1928, the Fall River Line reverted to a two-boat pattern, with the larger *Priscilla* and *Commonwealth* operating in summer, while *Plymouth* and *Providence* carried the winter trade. But *Plymouth* and *Providence* were not to be idle; they entered summer service to New Bedford, where they were able to handle the increasing traffic to that resort area (which included Martha's Vineyard and Nantucket).

*City of Lowell* and *Chester W. Chapin,* which had been holding down the New Bedford run, went into the shops for an overhaul. Said overhaul included reboilering, from which the two boats emerged with only one smokestack apiece. The

In consideration of the reduced fare at which it is sold,
THIS SPECIAL LIMITED TICKET is Good Only for ONE
FIRST CLASS CONTINUOUS PASSAGE from

New Bedford Marthas Vineyard and Nantucket STEAMBOAT CO.

**VINEYARD HAVEN to WOODS HOLE**
ON STEAMER LEAVING VINEYARD HAVEN

AUG 1 5 1918

**And must be surrendered on demand.**

Baggage valuation is limited to One Hundred Dollars for an adult and Fifty Dollars for a child, unless purchaser hereof declares a greater valuation at time baggage is presented for transportation and pays excess valuation charges according to tariff rates, rules and regulations.

The company reserves the right to abandon the trip, as a whole or in part, on account of weather, accident or other cause, and in acceptance of this ticket the holder hereof expressly agrees that said company shall not be responsible in the event of said abandonment.                    8 N20                                      1938

**Form SL 32      A     174**

SANKATY

In sharp contrast to the draftsmen's dreams shown on Page 316, here is the first of four new steamboats which were actually built for the NYNH&H in the 1920s. The new boats reflected the realities of the twentieth century. They were not ornate luxury liners designed to reach Gotham, but rather a quartet of utilitarian, functional steamers scheduled to serve the only large and growing New England travel market in which the motor car could not directly compete, Nantucket and Martha's Vineyard. The boats were the only way to get there (commuter airline service to the islands was years in the future).

*Islander* was the first of the Island steel "White Fleet," built at Bath ME in 1923. In the photo at left we see *Islander* at Woods Hole MA. The photograph is technically flawed, but it is worth sharing as a rare picture of rail-boat connecting facilities with tracks running out onto the steamboat pier. When the Old Colony Railroad engineers built the facilities at Woods Hole, they drew on their experience at Fall River, Stonington and other older transfer ports. But auto loading facilities for the likes of the sedan being loaded aboard (first drained of all gasoline) were added later.

Above, the only known photo of *Transford II*, a vessel specifically designed for carrying Ford autos from a New Jersey assembly plant to New England coastal ports. NESS purchased her in 1929 as part of a contract freight service.

Below, more conventional freight haulage in the 1920s is shown on West Street; the truck in the foreground has been identified as a Graham. There are few horses left.

*Uncatena* shows more of the wave of the future in the photo above; carrying automobiles to and from the Islands on her main deck. Particularly on Nantucket, the auto was not welcome, and the drive for laws to prevent motor vehicles persisted well into the 'teens. *Uncatena*, *Islander*, and *Sankaty* maintained the service, for a year.

After *Islander* came in 1923 and *Sankaty* burned in 1924, NYNH&H invested in the trio of new steel steamers on these pages. The result was a well-regarded quartet of steel steamers, appropriate to their mission.

*Nobska* was second of the four Island vessels, built in a hurry to replace *Sankaty* in 1924. We see her at the upper right being launched at Bath ME.

*New Bedford*, at lower left, came third, in 1928; in this photo she is surrounded by wooden "erector set" scaffolding prior to launch. When *New Bedford* came on line, the names of her two older sisters were changed to reflect more prominent place names: *Islander* became *Martha's Vineyard* (II) and *Nobska* was renamed *Nantucket*.

*Naushon* was the fourth and last of the fleet, new in 1929. She was significantly larger than the other three vessels. The Navy requisitioned her, along with *New Bedford*, for wartime service in 1942.

The NYNH&H sold the service in 1945.

estimated cost was $300,000. Their new role soon became clear; NESS re-started its Providence service for the 1929 season, using the freshened-up *Chapin* and *Lowell*. In the case of *Chester W. Chapin* it was a homecoming of sorts; her last regular port was Providence, and it was Providence service for which she had been built.

But now the figurative dent appeared in Frank Dunbaugh's Colonial Line office ceiling, and he was quick to respond to this competition in three ways. In July 1929 Colonial started a New York to New Bedford service using *Concord* and *Lexington*, charging a $3.00 fare as opposed to NYNH&H $6.00 fare. Colonial chartered *State of Virginia* from the Old Bay Line, to run to Providence with *Cambridge*. The Colonial Line also purchased a truck line to give direct delivery to inland New England points. This was considerably more of a threat in 1929 than the Joy Line's earlier purchase of a drayage company, for in the 1920s, trucks were beginning seriously to encroach on the railroads' freight business, including that on the steamboats.

Mr. Dunbaugh's third move in 1929 was to petition the ICC to demand that the Panama Canal Act be enforced, and that the NYNH&H be compelled to discontinue its Providence Line service. This was the second go-around for the NYNH&H on the Panama Canal Act. In 1930, the legal battle ended with a decision in favor of the Railroad, but Mr. Dunbaugh had made his point. The Colonial Line was a viable and respected competitor in the region thereafter.

But for all three of the steamboat companies, NESS, Eastern and Colonial, the Depression was increasing the rate of passenger decline to all ports. The Colonial Line ended its New Bedford service after the 1931 season. In the same year, the NYNH&H dissolved the H&NYTCo, discontinuing the Bay State Line to Providence (steamers *Georgia* and *Tennessee*) and the Hartford Line (steamers *Hartford* (II) and *Middletown*). Also in 1931, NESS removed *Plymouth* from the New Bedford run, leaving *Providence* to operate three days a week. *Richard Peck* was removed from the New London route, leaving *New Hampshire* to run solo. But the service remained a daily one; *New Hampshire* operated from New York to New London in the daytime, and returned to New York on an overnight schedule. It was a compromise at best. New London service ended in November 1934.

1931 was also the year in which a faraway mishap destroyed a former Sound denizen. With almost 500 passengers aboard, *Harvard* grounded in a fog north of Point Arguello, California, near Santa Barbara. The passengers and crew were saved, but the boat was a total loss. *Yale* sailed on in the West until World War II, when she was requisitioned by the Navy.

For the NYNH&H, 1935 was the year of the inevitable; the railroad filed for bankruptcy. The federal court and its appointed trustees now became a party to all management policies and strategies, eliminating whatever vestige of sentiment or desire for prestige that might have remained.

Except for the Island boats, NESS concentrated on rebuilding present vessels rather than building new boats. As noted elsewhere, much of this reconstruction was to install more modern plumbing and electrical/communications facilities in the aging liners, including safety provisions. Some of these renovations were dictated by the Coast Guard. while others were a part of maintenance. Reboilering, for example, occurred when old boilers reached the end of their service life.

Below left, we're entering the slip at Pier 14, and there is the refurbished single-stack *Chester W. Chapin*, thus configured after her 1928 reboilering. *City of Lowell* underwent similar treatment before the two boats were placed (for one season) on a new Providence route. Thereafter they filled in as needed.

*Plymouth* is shown below in her later years, as rebuilt after her 1906 fire. While she looks similar to her old self, her superstructure was almost entirely rebuilt. She also received a full sprinkler system and other conveniences, becoming in essence a new boat in 1907. Visible clues to help distinguish old from new are there; for example, count the number of four-pane windows on her main deck between the words "Fall River Line" and the first cargo door. As originally built, *Plymouth* had six windows; when rebuilt, she received seven. Compare with the photos in Chapter Seven.

Hard times were affecting the entire coastal steamboat industry. The Colonial Line was able to improve its service in 1936, when it bought *Belfast* and *Camden* from the bankrupt Boston-Bangor line, renaming them *Arrow* and *Comet*. Another sale involved NESS; in April 1937 it sold the honored *Richard Peck* to the Meseck Line. She later served as a dormitory ship in World War II, and then lasted until 1953 as the Pennsylvania Railroad's *Elisha Lee*, operating between Norfolk VA and Cape Charles MD. Of the "major" Sound boats, she turned out to be the last survivor.

NESS trimmed service in response to the lower demand. At the start of 1937, the Federal Court had given permission to shut down the Providence and New Bedford freight operations to and from New York. Only two Sound lines remained: the Fall River Line and a freight steamer to New Haven. To the east, the New Bedford, Martha's Vineyard and Nantucket service continued. Word had it that a heavy advance ticket sale was booked for the summer; there was optimism about the season to come.

But two rival unions were engaged in jurisdictional combat for the right to represent the maritime workers employed by New England Steamship, Eastern Steamship, and other carriers. Occasional wildcat strikes delayed departures.

# COORDINATED FREIGHT SERVICES
## in Southern New England
### Via THE NEW HAVEN R. R. or NEW ENGLAND TRANSPORTATION CO.

Fast and dependable schedules to and from ports in connection with the New York, New Haven & Hartford Railroad and New England Transportation Company assure overnight service. Pick up or delivery can be arranged if desired. ❦ Our Traffic Representatives or local agents will be only too glad to explain our service to you at any time.

It was Wednesday, June 30, 1937; the evening sailing time was approaching, and the labor leaders had twin nasty surprises planned for the New England Steamship Company. *Priscilla* was at Fall River and *Commonwealth* at New York. *Commonwealth* in particular was heavily booked; more than nine hundred passengers expected to be rounding the Battery on the way to New England in less than an hour. Three warning blasts from the whistle and then — wait; some of the crew members aren't at their stations!

The scene was similar at Fall River; at both ends of the line, a sitdown strike was under way. Passengers were removed from both boats and carried to their destinations on special NYNH&H trains. *Commonwealth* and *Priscilla* sailed later that evening and early morning, virtually empty.

The American Federation of Labor local represented part of the workers, and a Congress of Industrial Organizations unit represented another faction. This was long before the AFL-CIO merger, in a time when the two unions fought each other tooth and nail. Negotiations between management and labor were carried on during the next few days, but both unions threatened shutdowns if they were not recognized as opposed to the other. The Sound steamboats had become the latest in a series of labor movement battlegrounds. Management also indi-

Above, an advertisement for the NYNH&H boat-rail-truck coordinated freight service, including the railroad's truck subsidiary, named the New England Transportation Co.

How little the natural part of the Connecticut River had changed in all the years since the first (in fact, the *very* first) steamboats touched her waters.

*Hartford* (II) (above right) and *Middletown* (below right) continued their course through that bucolic land until 1931, when the H&NYTCo abandoned its remaining scheduled passenger and freight services to Hartford and Providence.

cated that further sitdown strikes would result in abandonment of the service. This was dismissed as an idle threat; workers convinced each other that the NYNH&H Trustees would never abandon the 90-year old Fall River Line.

The boats sailed on schedule for the next two weeks. Then on July 12, trouble erupted on the Nantucket line; crews refused to operate the service between New Bedford and the Islands. Freight piled up, and during the next six days island residents ran low on food. In sympathy with the island boat crews, crew members on the Fall River

and New Haven passenger and freight boats also stayed in port, with crews remaining aboard but not working.

July 18 was the day that the New England Steamship Co. suspended service; the trustees had not been kidding after all. All of the crew members were paid to date and ordered off the vessels. Their jobs had been abolished, the representative said. In Fall River, *Commonwealth*'s crew of almost 200 received the news with shock; they had been assured that the Company would never shut down. In New York, some of the *Priscilla*'s people refused to leave for up to three days; but when food and hope ran out together, the last of them departed the famous old liner. *Priscilla* left Pier 14 North River on the end of a towing hawser, bound for layup in Providence, pending developments.

The NYNH&H Trustees petitioned the Federal Court at New Haven, which was directing the affairs of the bankrupt railroad, for immediate

These three aerial views of New York Harbor, specifically the area around Pier 14 North River, bear much study. At the upper right, note the aircraft carefully; they're not helicopters, but autogyros, a popular aviation toy of the 1930s. Rail and boat commerce goes on beneath the aircraft.

The two photos on the opposite page represent two different days in the four-boat service. At the top, *Plymouth* and *Commonwealth* flank the pier, as they did every other day. a smaller freighter and lighter share the facilities for the moment. Note the two-track center-platform car floats at the left and right edges of the photo; they are described more fully in Chapter 15.

On another day, we find *Priscilla* and *Providence* in residence on the Hudson, taking on coal and provisions from lighters during the day, while a Lackawanna ferry leaves for Hoboken. A smaller steamboat is at Pier 19. Note the foundations for the World-Telegram building, being constructed in 1924.

abandonment of the Fall River and New Haven lines, leaving only the New Bedford, Martha's Vineyard and Nantucket service. The hearing took place on July 27. In spite of a flood of impassioned pleas for retention of the Fall River service, and urgent offers of a truce by the labor unions, Judge Carroll C. Hincks granted the petition, and ordered the sale of the remaining Sound fleet. The financial evidence, the red ink, overwhelmed sentiment. It was clear that there was now nothing that the boats could do that trains and automobiles could not; except perhaps to provide "little voyages of enchantment," a mode of transportation of unparalleled elegance; and to stir recollections of many pleasant hours aboard the grand vessels.

But it is also clear that the service operated during the 1930s was a pale reflection of the grand manner in which these boats had captured America's heart. The orchestras were smaller, the food a bit less elegant, the carpeting and upholstery worn, the paint faded in spots. There is some evidence to show that the average level of the clientele's social standing had slipped as well; there was talk of a group of businesswomen who traveled almost every night, turning some of the staterooms into places of discreet negotiable affection.

That the termination of service was a surprise, not planned by the railroad, is verified by two facts.

First, the NYNH&H had just upgraded *Priscilla*'s safety features pursuant to a Coast Guard order. Second, there had been heavy advance sales of tickets for trips in early August for the International Yacht Races at Newport. Perhaps these actions emboldened the labor unions to take their actions. The Trustees, however, sacrificed the recent costs and the proximate revenue for what they perceived as a far larger long-term reduction in costs; the Judge agreed.

Nine ships were on the NESS roster at the end (other than those in Martha's Vineyard/Nantucket service). The "Big Four," *Priscilla, Commonwealth, Plymouth* and *Providence,* were sold as scrap to the Union Shipbuilding Co. of Baltimore, for $88,000.

*Chester W. Chapin* was sold to the Colonial Line, and renamed *Meteor. City of Lowell* was sold to an auto transport company; the projected service that would use her never started. Her former Captain, Philip Ollweiler, committed suicide. *Lowell* went to war in 1943, to be used as a training ship in Brooklyn Navy Yard, and was scrapped in 1946.

*New Haven* (III) was destroyed while berthed at Fall River in the famous September 1938 hurricane that devastated parts of Long Island and New England. *Pequonnock* was destroyed at Newport in the September 1938 hurricane. *Mohawk* was sold to the Central Vermont RR for $20,000.

*Priscilla* had by now become the Dowager Queen of the Sound, despite periodic upgrading of amenities such as running water. Many of her passengers in the 1920s and 1930s saw her beauty more in the eye of remembrance than in actuality. At top left, she is passing through the Cape Cod Canal on her way to be refurbished in the off season, just months before service was stopped.

Above, this scene in her Grand Saloon, while posed, was typical of the day. The occasion of the photo was the installation of a Western Electric sound system, evidenced by the horn-type loudspeakers flanking the clock at the top of the bulkhead. While the use of such equipment began by carrying the sounds of a live orchestra to all parts of the boat, not too much imagination is required to see that the next step might be recorded music, at considerably lower cost. Hoppe's orchestra and their brethren could not survive the Depression. Neither, for that matter, could *Priscilla*.

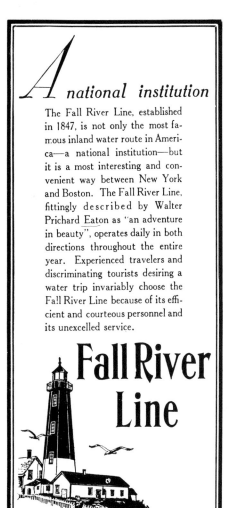
### Last Gasps

Some aficionados believe that cessation of NESS steamer service to Fall River in 1937 was the "real" end of the era, and for the purposes of this volume, it was. The NYNH&H was now merely a railroad. Two vestiges of the once-proud services remained for a time. Eastern Steamship Lines continued their "outside" service between New York and Boston for another four years; it ceased in November 1941.

The coming of World War II and Nazi submarines offshore forced changes on the Colonial Line as it maintained its New York-Providence service. The schedule was changed so that the boats operated in the daytime. But wartime hazards and wartime requirements also ended this last surviving service. On March 29, 1942, *Arrow* made the last Sound Steamer trip, from Providence to New York.

The days of scheduled splendor on the Sound were over.

---

Read the ad at the left, and then ponder the photo below. The photo shows some of the striking *Commonwealth* crew members immediately after their expulsion from the boat in July 1937.

Above, a last look at *Commonwealth*. Below, *Arrow* in
New York. To this Colonial Line vessel fell the distinction
of being the last scheduled passenger steamer on the Sound.

# THE FRIENDS OF NOBSKA BRING HER HOME

In July 1975, a small group of steamboat enthusiasts, Robert Cleasby, Bill Ewen and Ross Hudson, founded the Friends of *Nobska* (FON), for the purpose of acquiring and restoring that vessel. *Nobska* had been functioning as a floating restaurant in Baltimore. Even while she was still there, members of FON began initial preservation activities aboard *Nobska*, while announcing their intention to purchase the vessel.

The overall history of fan groups formed to preserve transportation relics is less than spectacular; too often their collective dreams far outrun their abilities to make them come true.

FON attracted more than 500 members in its first three years of operation. Two years later, the group numbered 800, due to the tireless efforts of these three men and others who joined them.

In 1979, *Nobska* became available for sale, but FON was discouraged when she was sold to Alan Spiegel, a local restauranteur, who gutted the boat while remodeling her. Then, around 1980, came the possibility of purchasing *Martha's Vineyard* from the Bridgeport and Port Jefferson Steamship Co., and even operating her in regular service between New Bedford and the Islands.

While FON's planning had been meticulously done, negotiations for financing arrangements took on the aspects of a roller-coaster ride; on again, then off again. Experience for operations, if they could ever begin, was gained when three FON stalwarts founded the New England Steamship Co. of Mass., to run steamboat fan trips using chartered vessels.

This second restaurant venture also ended in a wave of red ink. Baltimore wanted the vessel out, and after much negotiation, Mr. Spiegel donated *Nobska* to FON at the end of 1987. At that point, Mr. Cleasby quoted Winston Churchill: "It is the end of the beginning."

Funds were raised for the transfer and initial restoration, and *Nobska* was brought "home," to Fall River MA, arriving May 14, 1988. Restoration work began almost immediately, with a target completion date in 1995.

It is difficult to overstate the combination of hard work and faith that brought FON to this stage of its project, from the early days when the organization was dismissed as a bunch of dreamers, to culmination of its effort to bring home one of the last survivors of the NYNH&H Sound steamer fleet.

---

Below, *City of Lowell* in her last days.

At right above, the twin-screw *Naushon* passes in review. *Naushon* served in World War II as a hospital ship during the Normandy invasion.

At right below, *Nobska* approaches Fall River under tow, May 14, 1988. A celebration was shortly to follow.

Part of *Nobska* 's historic value derives from her engine. Unlike *Martha's Vineyard*, the steam engine in *Nobska* had never been replaced by a diesel, and even survived the "rebuildings" in Baltimore. The Friends of Nobska believe that it is the last quad-cylinder triple-expansion steam engine still in existence.

# Chapter Fifteen

# Tugs and Transfers

W e noted in Chapter Nine that railroad freight service to New York City required great effort and cost to approach adequacy, given that only the New York Central had a direct-service freight rail line on Manhattan Island. This was the west side freight line coming south from The Bronx.

Lined up along the New Jersey shore of the Hudson River were the New York Central's West Shore line at Weehawken, the Delaware Lackawanna & Western at Hoboken, and the Erie Railroad at Pavonia (Jersey City). A bit further south, there were the Central Railroad of New Jersey, Lehigh Valley Railroad, Baltimore and Ohio Railroad, and two Pennsylvania Railroad facilities at Harborside (Jersey City) and Greenville (Bayonne). In addition, the Baltimore and Ohio conducted waterfront activity on the north shore of Staten Island. Across the Upper Bay to the east, the Long Island Rail Road maintained a large waterfront freight facility at Bay Ridge, Brooklyn.

---

New York's harbor displayed a great diversity in terms of watercraft. While transAtlantic liners got the publicity, most of the day-to-day activity involved the railroads in some way.

At left above, a 1924 aerial view of lower New York, taken from a position above the Hudson River. The East River is in the background. While *Priscilla* and *Providence* appear at the left, the more common vessels are railroad-related. The passenger ferries belong to the Pennsylvania, New York Central and Jersey Central railroads; as to the lighters and car floats, it's anyone's guess. Note the floats with two tracks separated by a covered high-level platform. This provided a most efficient arangement for loading and unloading using electric carts, a system pioneered by the NYNH&H. Note too, in the lower right corner of the photo, lighters moored to the seaward side of two floats to allow transfer of cargo directly from the cars on the float to the lighter. Waste movement was to be avoided!

Below, left, a view taken at ground level roughly underneath the aerial vantage point for the photo above. The transfer steamer *Express* carries a group of passenger cars to New Jersey and the PRR.

At right, *Maryland* is framed by the Williamsburg Bridge as she moves down the East River.

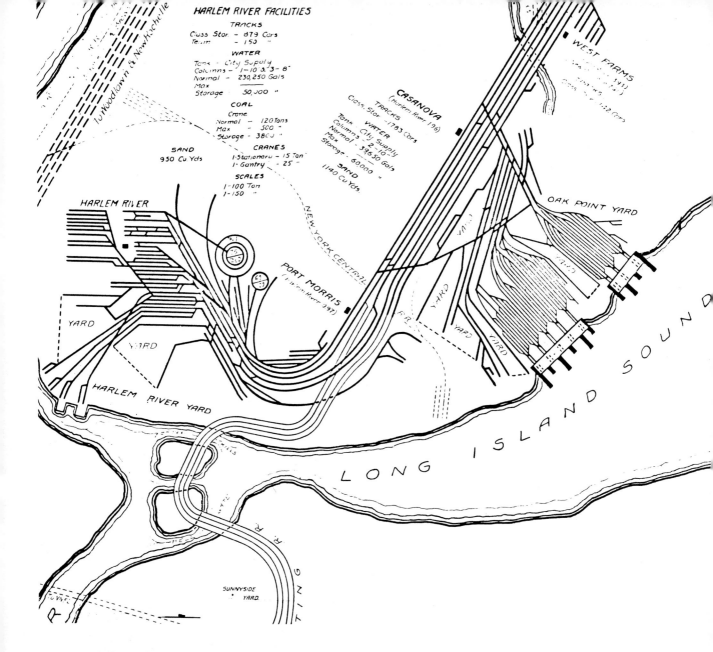

# HARLEM RIVER FACILITIES

## TRACKS
Class Stor. - 879 Cars
Team - 150 "

## WATER
Tank - City Supply
Columns - 1 - 10 & 3 - 8"
Normal - 230,250 Gals
Max
Storage - 50,000 "

## COAL
Crane
Normal - 120 Tons
Max - 500 "
Storage - 3800 "

## SAND
950 Cu Yds

## CRANES
1 - Stationary - 15 Ton
1 - Gantry - 25 "

## SCALES
1 - 100 Ton
1 - 150 "

# CASANOVA
(Harlem River 196)

## TRACKS
Class. Stor. - 1783 Cars

## WATER
Tank - City Supply
Columns - 2 - 10"
Normal - 39650 Gals
Max
Storage - 60000 "

## SAND
1140 Cu Yds.

WEST FARMS

OAK POINT YARD

HARLEM RIVER

PORT MORRIS
(Harlem River 297)

NEW YORK CENTRAL

R.R. YARD

YARD

YARD

YARD

YARD

YARD

YARD

HARLEM RIVER YARD

HELLS

SUNNYSIDE YARD

TUNNEL

TING

L O N G    I S L A N D    S O U N D

To Woodlawn & New Rochelle

NEW HAVEN

The track schematic at left shows the relative positions of the NYNH&H's Harlem River and Oak Point yards in The Bronx. Their combined storage capacity was more than 2650 cars, but of course the goal was not storage but movement. Hell Gate and its four-track bridge are shown at the lower left corner of the map. From the two yards, tugs nudged car floats carrying freight cars (and, as noted, sometimes passenger cars) to all points of the harbor.

At left, one of the less glamorous boats in the harbor, *Refuge*, believed to be a Ward's Island ferry for live humans and those who had passed away. The photo, however, shows the NYNH&H Harlem River terminal and float bridges in the background, hence its inclusion here.

Below, a New Haven tug pushes car floats *No. 41* and *No. 50* down the East River. These were three-track floats, built without the center platform, used for moving cars between waterfront yards rather than to and from a waterfront freighthouse. Note the shanties at the bow of each float, to protect the floatmen from the elements. The tug was fitted with a tall stack to improve the natural draft (rather than installing blowers), and to reduce the risk of setting wooden freight cars on fire. Judging from the age and design of the freight cars, the photo probably dates back to the time around World War I.

The lighter at right is apparently self-propelled, but close inspection shows tow ropes leading out of the photo to the right, presumably to a powered vessel.

To move freight from the New Jersey railheads to New York and New England required movement on water; there were and are no railroad bridges across the Hudson at New York City. The Pennsylvania Railroad tunnel tracks were built for passenger train use. Before the 1889 opening of the Poughkeepsie Bridge (see Chapter Nine), there were no railroad bridges across the Hudson River south of Albany NY, 150 miles to the north. With the Poughkeepsie Bridge closed due to deterioration as this volume is published, the southernmost Hudson River rail crossing is at Castleton NY, just south of Albany.

For purposes of describing how it was to be handled, railroad freight reaching New York City was classified as follows:

(a) freight consigned to or originating at New York City destinations;

(b) freight consigned for export or movement by water carrier from New York harbor; or

(c) freight moving through or beyond New York.

A further distinction was made on the basis of whether the shipment was a carload lot or less than carload (LCL).

To meet their customers' varying needs, the railroads operated their own fleets of transfer vessels to move freight across water. Two types of barges were employed: car floats, which were flat-topped scows with two or three railroad tracks on them, which could be used for moving loaded or empty freight cars; and lighters, which were open or enclosed barges used to transfer freight between terminals or piers. Some lighters were equipped with cranes to facilitate transfer of the freight carried on them.

Very few of these barges were self-propelled. It was far less expensive to use a smaller number of tugboats as waterborne "locomotives" to move unpowered car floats or lighters. Thus the Hudson and East Rivers, and to a lesser extent the Harlem River, swarmed with railroad tugboats shepherding one or two floats or lighters upstream and down between the riverside freight terminals and piers in all of New York City's boroughs and New Jersey.

The NYNH&H was a principal player in all three types of freight movement, and was particularly strong in receiving shipments of type (c) above, destined for New England points. Thus the NYNH&H maintained the second largest railroad marine transfer fleet in New York harbor, exceeded only by that of the Pennsylvania Railroad (which also controlled the Long Island Rail Road).

Note that the Long Island Sound steamboats delivered and picked up goods at their piers without such transshipment delays and costs, at Manhattan piers convenient to the industrial area. Therein lay part of their competitive advantage.

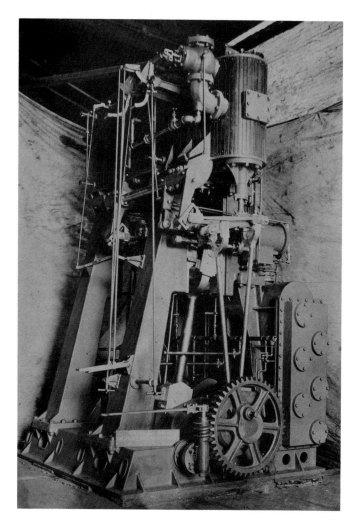

Above, a closeup of a 750-horsepower tugboat engine before installation in a hull. This example went into the NYNH&H's *Transfer No. 12*.

### Lighterage

It is axiomatic in the transportation business that each time you handle the contents of a shipment, your costs rise and there is a time delay. Thus, lighterage was not an efficient process. For example, a shipment arriving at the Pennsylvania Railroad yards in Jersey City would have to be:

1. Unloaded from its boxcar.
2. Loaded onto a lighter at Jersey City.
3. Floated across the Hudson to its destination pier.
4. Unloaded from the lighter, loaded onto a boat, ship, wagon or truck.

In the case of Type (c) shipments, for example one destined for Lowell, MA, the lighter's destination would be Pier 14 North River, and the shipment would be transferred to a Fall River Line boat. These steps would be added:

Tall stacks and raised pilothouses characterized the railroad tugs. As noted earlier, the tall stacks improved draft and reduced risks of fire on the freight cars. The taller pilothouses provided visibility over the tops of the freight cars being towed. *Transfer No. 3* was typical of early railroad tugs.

Below, *Transfer No. 11* in an early construction stage before her launch in 1898 at Wilmington DE, with only part of her superstructure in place. Tugboats had proportionately large rudders and propellers, design elements which gave tugs their maneuverability and pushing or pulling power.

5. Carried by steamer to Fall River.
6. Unloaded at Fall River.
7. Loaded into a boxcar.
8. Carried by train to Lowell.
9. Unloaded at Lowell.

Even with this handling, the NYNH&H's steamboat-and-rail coordinated service, as refined by Charles Mellen in 1903, generally got shipments to their destinations faster than the all-rail alternative. For that reason, the steamboats were used for merchandise or package freight, the value of which was great enough to justify premium rates.

Lighterage was more useful for Types (a) and (b) freight. The lighters were brought to the side of a pier or to the water side of a ship being loaded for export, and goods directly transferred.

**Car Floats**

A reduction in handling costs is effected if a boxcar or other freight car is moved by water without first being unloaded. Car floats serve this purpose; railroad cars are loaded and unloaded across float bridges connected to railroad tracks on land at one end. Car floats were also tied up alongside ships, with Type (b) or (c) cargo loaded or unloaded directly between ship and railroad car.

The railroads maintained waterfront railroad yard terminals of varying complexity. The NYNH&H's two facilities in the South Bronx, Harlem River and Oak Point, were comparable to the Hudson shore facilities of the Jersey roads. Every day, two-track and three-track car floats would ferry freight cars on the 15-mile journey between the NYNH&H facilities in The Bronx and the railroads on the New Jersey shore.

Both before and after the opening of the Hell Gate Bridge in 1916, the largest freight interchange traffic volume in New York harbor was between the Pennsylvania and the NYNH&H railroads. From the standpoint of car floatation, the Hell Gate meant that cars were floated from the Pennsylvania a shorter distance to Bay Ridge in Brooklyn, instead of to Harlem River or Oak Point. Freight trains were not operated through the Pennsylvania's Hudson River and East River tunnels.

Most of these cars were loaded cars, with about three quarters of them going north/eastward from Pennsylvania to NYNH&H. The NYNH&H apparently tried wherever possible to deliver empty cars to the New York Central Railroad on land, rather than incur the expense of floating empty cars across the harbor.

**East River Terminal**

For Type (a) freight consigned to Manhattan destinations, the NYNH&H maintained a freight terminal on the East River at Governeur St., just

*Transfer No. 11* when brand new, being towed from Wilmington to her new home in New York harbor. We deduce her condition from the condition of her paint, the fact that her hull is unscarred, and from the absence of fenders on her hull. Fenders (and scars) were to come in due time. The fenders in the era when *Transfer No. 11* was new were oak timbers, hung with lines. Rope fenders did not come into use until the 'teens; old auto tires later still.

On the next page, the side elevation and plan views of a tugboat design that was never built in that period. The plans date to the 1920s, and are likely to have been improvements upon *Transfer No. 20* and *Transfer* No. *21*, built in 1908 and 1909. But the next new boats after *Transfer No. 21* came in the 1950s.

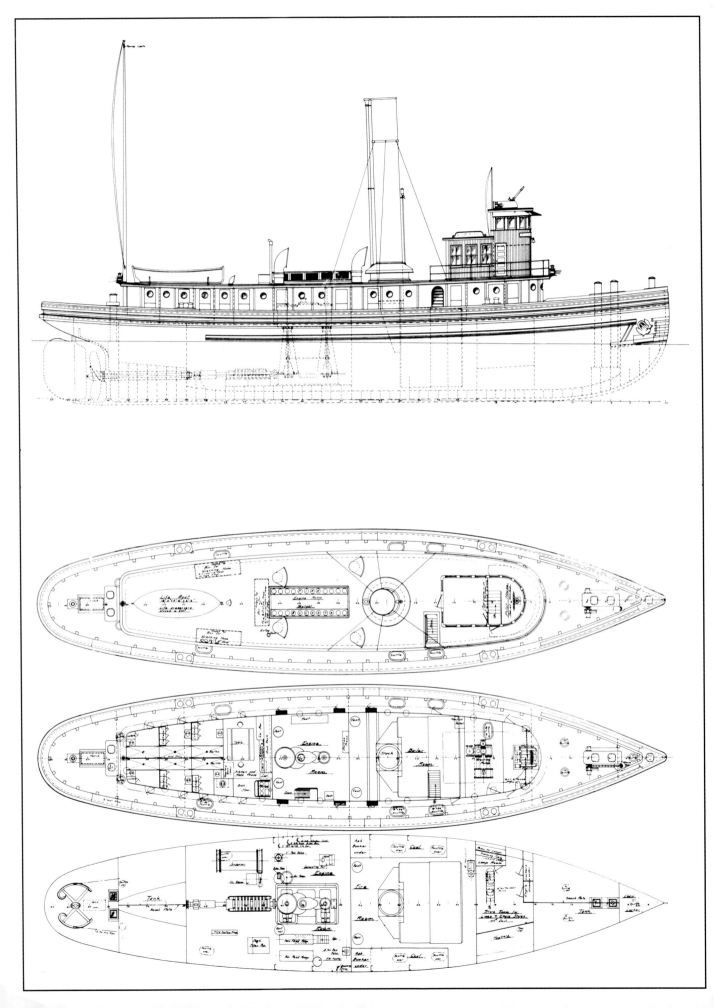

Above, the NYNH&H train ferry *Maryland* (II) with freight cars aboard. The signpainting custom of adding periods after boat and company names was still in vogue, which dates this photo to the time before World War I.

Below, *Transfer No. 15*, known as *Transfer No. 13* when she was new in 1900. Superstition likely dictated her renumbering. *Transfer No. 14* and *Transfer No. 15* were the only double-stacked tugs in the fleet, longer, heavier, and fitted with more powerful engines than the other tugs. They also had orders never to go through Hell Gate without a float on each side (double tow). Their narrow beam put them in danger of rolling under with just one float.

Above right, *Transfer No. 21* shortly after her entry into service in 1909, and before 1913. Note the windows in the lower level of the pilothouse and, like *Transfer No. 15* at left below, the relatively small upper "boot heel" pilothouse section.

Below, right, *Transfer No. 21* in the early 1950s with a remodeled pilothouse, metal "N H" letters on her stack, and something new: the first tugboat radar installation in New York, identified by the small scanning antenna. Radar provided the breakthrough that made navigation significantly less heartstopping.

north of the Hartford Line and New Haven Line piers. The terminal was of an ingenious and efficient design, in that the freight cars never budged from their floats.

The NYNH&H used a special car float design which, instead of a center third track, had a raised platform, at car door height, between the two rows of cars. The floats were moored perpendicular to the shoreline, and the ends of their center platforms butted against a corresponding platform on the pier. Freight handlers using small electric trucks would then unload and load the cars very quickly, as if the entire terminal were on land. A similar arrangement was used at Pier 14 North River.

This gave the NYNH&H a considerable advantage over those railroads with riverside team track yards at which cars were removed from the floats by switching locomotives, then unloaded on land.

The railroad tugboats were not radically different in design from their cousins that pushed and pulled ocean liners around the harbor. Their car float transfer function necessitated two design differences that instantly identified a railroad tug even at a distance. The pilothouses on railroad tugs were higher than on the general-service tugs, to allow the pilot to see over the tops of the freight cars on the floats. Most railroad tugs also had no crew bunks aboard; they operated as day boats, with crew changes every eight hours.

Car float accidents were rare en route; very few freight cars rolled off the floats into the river, despite the lack of heavy bumpers on the float tracks. Where accidents did happen in the early days was at the float bridges, most often when a switcher pushed a string of cars against a bumper,

pushing the car float away from the bridge, snapping the lines and opening a gap between the float bridge and car float. A car could then fall between float and bridge. For this reason, the car floats ceased to be equipped with heavy bumpers.

## The Transfers

The NYNH&H got into the harbor transfer business when it purchased the Harlem River and Port Chester Railroad, completing it as a branch from Port Chester to the southeast Bronx facilities at Oak Point and Harlem River. In 1878, the NYNH&H ceased total reliance on contract boat operators, and purchased its first steam tugboat.

Whereas other railroads named their tugboats, usually with names of on-line cities, the New Haven (like the New York Central) displayed no creativity whatsoever; they numbered the tugs. That first 1878 tug was "named" for the type of service performed, *Transfer No. 1*. In fact, the

---

Two veterans of the drab end of Sound steamboat service, cargo vessels *Pequot* and *New England*, appear in this rare photo. Frankly, it is not hard to see why photos of these vessels were rare.

On the other hand, *Transfer No. 17*, above right, yielded joy to the photographer with the proper vantage point. Here she's moving up the Hudson, with a Lackawanna ferry and Hoboken Terminal in the background.

At right below, a relatively unusual sight: one of the modern steel lighters built in 1953 in the new New Haven image to go with orange and green locomotives.

railroad called all of these vessels "transfers" rather than "tugboats." The later transfers were numbered consecutively, with a couple of exceptions. *Transfer No. 9* was a self-propelled lighter. *Transfer No. 13* was renumbered to become *Transfer No. 15*, apparently because of superstitions.

By 1887 there were four transfers; ten more, plus a self-propelled lighter (*Transfers No 5* through *15*) were added to the fleet during the Clark years (1887-1900), reflecting the increase in harbor traffic. Seven transfers, the last to be steam-powered, were purchased during the Mellen presidency; *Transfer No. 16, Transfer No. 17* and *Transfer No. 18* in 1904, *Transfer No. 19* and *Transfer No. 20* in 1905, and *Transfer No. 21* in 1908 and *Transfer No. 22* in 1909.

And that was that. Twenty transfers and one self-propelled lighter met the NYNH&H's needs until 1917, when *Transfers No. 21* and *No. 22* were requisitioned by the Government for the war effort. That in itself was tribute to the effectiveness of the NYNH&H under the USRA; they could do the job and meet wartime needs with two fewer tugs. Transfer 21 returned to the NYNH&H in 1926; Transfer 22 was gone forever, reappearing on the Hudson under New York Central ownership (NYC Tug *No. 15*).

The first retirement was *Transfer No. 1*, in 1924, just after conversion of *Transfers* numbered 11 and up to oil fuel. Because of the differing draft requirements of oil-fired boilers, and the lessened danger of fire from oil burners (no cinders), the stacks on these vessels could be lowered to fit under the Harlem River drawbridges without the necessity to open the spans.

(But one of your authors remembers only too well childhood days in which "bombsight" marks-manship was demonstrated by the number of potatoes or similar vegetables one could drop into those smokestacks from an unopened Harlem River drawbridge; some of the crews may have preferred the taller stacks after all.)

The decline in railroad freight traffic during the Depression of the 1930s was reflected in reduced harbor traffic. By the beginning of World War II, fifteen *Transfers* remained. The roster was down to nine by 1952, and those nine ranged from 42 to 55 years in age. The last coal-burning *Transfers* were *Nos. 7, 8* and *10*, retired in 1950.

The land facilities attendant to harbor freight operations featured the float bridges that provided the transition between the floats and land. New York harbor is, after all, subject to tidal action; the water level rises and falls. The adjustable bridges are raised and lowered at the seaward end to compensate for that variance in water level at the shoreline.

At top left, we're looking across the land end of the larger group of five float bridges at Oak Point on a summer day. The water is to the left. In the superstructure are the mechanical hoists for the bridges. Oak Point had the more extensive float facilities, compared to Harlem River.

The Harlem River float bridges, shown at left center, were fewer in number, and also structurally less imposing. Here we're looking from a tug's pilothouse toward shore, with floats containing mixed freight car loads on either side.

At left below, a deckhand and a floatman are beginning to bring and lash together two car floats into their familiar Vee configuration prior to heading for Jersey City and the PRR yard. Our vantage point is that of the Captain in the pilothouse. When approaching the bridge with two floats, the bow lines of the floats would be released at the right time and each float would glide into the bridge. That maneuver was called "splitting the rack."

At the upper right, we get another view of a similar operation, as *Transfer No. 14* pulls two floats from their slips. The floats will be lashed together and the unit will go on its way. The floatman on the bow is no doubt speculating on the sanity of the camera bug on the superstructure of the bridge. The current has begun to move the whole works to the left.

The NYNH&H's most common color scheme for its *Transfers* was dark green for the superstructure, with black hulls and smokestacks. Nameboards were black with gold lettering. At least some of the tugs had red-trimmed window sashes.

At right below, back on land, a closeup of the interface between car float and float bridge, and the turnout that allows access to all three car float tracks from only two tracks on the bridge.

At far right, Alco S-1 switcher No. 0967 moves a cut of cars toward a float. Empty flat or gondola cars were used as idler or "reach" cars to keep the weight of the locomotive off the float bridge.

348

In 1953, two new Transfers joined the roster, but these were diesel-electric powered, built to a post-war design used by most of the railroads around New York. The architect was Tippett-Arthur-McCarthy-Stratton, and the 1600-horsepower powerplant was by the Electro-Motive Division of General Motors; very similar to that of GP-7 diesel locomotives. The two newcomers departed from tradition; they were named *Cordelia* and *Bumble Bee* when they were delivered. Late in 1954, the two boats were renamed — that is, renumbered — *Transfer No. 23* and *Transfer No. 24*.

Plans for more diesel tugs were cancelled by the new management of Patrick McGinnis; the justification was that motor trucks were able to provide more flexible transshipments. In fact, motor trucks were eclipsing the railroads' ability to handle much of this freight at all, and business went into a sharp decline.

Above, we're standing on the edge of a car float during an open house (note the "civilians" walking on the car float at the left), getting an unusual close-up of *Transfer No. 21*. The radar antenna dates the photo to the postwar period. The matted rope bumpers have seen a great deal of wear.

Above right, *Transfer No. 24* is framed in a float bridge aperture at Bay Ridge in Brooklyn, where the float bridges were jointly owned by the NYNH&H and the Long Island Rail Road. A Long Island Alco S-4 is doing the honors. Compare the bridge construction with that of Oak Point, shown on Page 348.

Below, *Transfer No. 10* shows us the rope and crew arrangement as she moves two floats toward the bridge. (See also Page 348.) We also get a bit better view of the track arrangement on the floats.

In 1957, the NYNH&H leased three new tugs from the Dalzell Harbor Corp.; they were named *Dalzell 1*, *Dalzell 2* and *Dalzell 3*. These tugs were equipped with diesel–mechanical drives, rather than diesel–electrics, powered by 1800-hp Fairbanks-Morse engines. The three tugs were renamed *Lacey 1, 2,* and *3* in 1966, to conform to a change in ownership, but the NYNH&H lease remained in force unchanged.

The last steam Transfers were retired in 1960; the five diesel-powered tugs carried on until the NYNH&H was assimilated into the Penn Central in 1969. *Transfer No. 23* and *Transfer No. 24* continued with those names under PC ownership.

Railroad lighterage and carfloating has virtually ceased to exist in New York, because there is now only one railroad, Conrail, and therefore no "interchange". Through car movement to and from New England is via the Castleton bridge near Albany. More importantly, increasing shipment of freight in containers that can be carried on ship, truck, or rail car has all but eliminated the need for the old-fashioned lighters and floats.

On this page, we share the railroad's first views of two Dalzell tugs. At top left, the bulbous nose of *Dalzell 3* looms prior to launch. Above, *Dalzell 1* splashes into the water. The smooth and rounded hull was an improvement over the earlier tugs' longitudinal hulls with multiple ribbed guards.

(Note: "Guards" are longitudinal structural ribs that protect the tug's hull; "Fenders" are cushions that protect the float being towed.)

It was people who made the tugs perform. On the next page, a captain poses for posterity. The instructional sign above his head is not entirely frivolous; on some vessels, the helm was indeed "backwards". We believe that the Coast Guard required such a sign on steam vessels. At the far right, the two-man engine crew on a diesel tug. No stokers, no coal passers. The engine would be almost equally at home in an EMD locomotive.

Below right, the classic tugboat photo in New York, as diesel-powered *Transfer No. 23* (built as *Cordelia*) heads for a New Jersey connection.

## CONNECTICUT RIVER TUGS

On the Connecticut River, the Hartford & New York Transportation Co. operated a smaller tug fleet in a more bucolic setting.

The first Connecticut River towboats were used to tow sailing vessels upriver from Saybrook. This service materially increased the dependability of water transport, theretofore hampered by tides and (lack of) wind. These towboats were not likely to be sidewheelers, because they often operated alongside the vessels they were towing, in the manner of a tug working one rail car float. Towing of barges carrying any imaginable cargo was a natural extension of the service, and the river soon teemed with watercraft under tow, between Hartford and Saybrook.

An example of these early towboats was the obviously all-wood *A M Smith*, new in 1871 and not retired until 1930. She is shown, above right, on the river; we assume that is Captain James Alger in the pilothouse. Uniform requirements were not as strict here as on the Fall River Line.

A prominent towboat operator was Charles Goodrich. As recounted in Chapter Four, his

arrangement with the NYNH&H to operate the Hartford and New York Transportation Co. included not only the passenger boat service provided in later years by *Hartford* (II) and *Middletown*, but also the continuation of towboat service.

*Mabel*, which Mr. Goodrich named for his daughter, came on line in 1882. Local experts regarded her as the prettiest of the Connecticut River tugs; note the inlaid wooden paneling of her superstructure in the photo below. Reports are that she was well-varnished and maintained at least until World War I. No one wanted Mr. Goodrich's daughter's namesake to appear frowsy. By her retirement in 1930, however, she had lost her luster.

Two of the H&NYTCo tugs, *Sachem* and *Spartan*, were significantly larger than the rest of the fleet. They were used to haul coal barges from New York to Saybrook, a vestige of the old Hartford and Connecticut Valley service which had come under NYNH&H control in 1882. The 1912-vintage *Spartan*, newest member of the H&NYTCo fleet, is shown at the lower right.

# The Sound Steamer Fleet

Boats in the NYNH&H fleet (owned or controlled) are shown in **bold face** type.

| Vessel Name | Registry Number | Builder | Where Built | Year Built | Year Ret'd | Hull Type | Length | Beam | Depth | Gross Tons | Net Tons | Pass Cap'y | Freight Cap'y (cars) |
|---|---|---|---|---|---|---|---|---|---|---|---|---|---|
| Acushnet | | RFJ | Fairhaven MA | 1833 | 1855 | St.PDEW | | 26 | | 70 | | | |
| Agnes | | | Greenpoint NY | 1852 | 1862 | St.P.W. | | | | 299 | | | |
| Albatross | 429 | GG | Mystic CT | 1852 | 1915 | St.Sc.W. | 150 | 30 | 9.1 | 433 | 414 | | |
| **Allan Joy** | 127281 | ROH | **Chester PA** | 1898 | 1956 | St.Sc.S. | 220.7 | 37.2 | 14 | 1308 | 739 | | |
| Ansonia | 862 | | Brooklyn NY | 1848 | 1892 | St.P.W. | | | | 412 | | | |
| **Aransas** | 105749 | HH | **Wilmington DE** | 1877 | 1905 | St.Sc.I. | 241 | 35.5 | 16.5 | 1156 | 678 | | |
| Arrow | 206266 | DIW | Bath ME | 1909 | 1947 | St.Sc.S. | 320.6 | 40 | 16.1 | 2157 | 1147 | | |
| **Artisan** | 806 | CR | **New York NY** | 1865 | 1910 | St.Sc.W. | 133.2 | 24.2 | 6.5 | 310 | 249.76 | | |
| Atlantic | | BS | New York NY | 1846 | 1846 | St.P.W. | 320 | 36 | 10 | 1300 | 1112 | | |
| Barnet | | BB | | 1826 | | St.P.W | 75 | 14.5 | 2 | | | | |
| Bay State | | SS | New York NY | 1846 | 1864 | St.P.W. | 317 | 39 | 8 | 2200 | 1554 | | |
| Belfast | 206266 | BIW | Bath ME | 1909 | 1947 | St.Sc.S. | 320.6 | 40 | 16.1 | 2157 | 1147 | | |
| Belle | 2641 | GS | New York NY | 1837 | 1897 | St.P.W. | 220 | 29 | 9.6 | 434 | 303 | | |
| Benjamin Franklin | | BB | New York NY | 1828 | 1842 | St.P.W. | 144 | 21 | 10 | 410 | | | |
| **Block Island** | 3201 | RDS | **Noank CT** | 1882 | 1929 | St.P.W. | 187.25 | 33 | 11.1 | 757.2 | 566 | 1200 | 19 |
| Bolivar | | | New York NY | 1825 | 1850 | St.P.W. | | | | 153 | | | |
| Boston (I) | | BB | New York NY | 1831 | 1857 | St.P.W. | 150 | 28.3 | 9.9 | 380 | | | |
| **Boston (II)** | 200941 | FRS | **Quincy MA** | 1904 | 1938 | St.Sc.S. | 318 | 60.6 | 22.6 | 3626 | 2466 | 50 | 170 |
| **Boston (III)** | 223749 | BSC | **Sparrows Pt MD** | 1924 | 1942 | St.Sc.S. | 385.3 | 72.5 | 20.9 | 4989 | 2703 | | |
| Bridgeport (I) | 2166 | SS | New York NY | 1857 | 1886 | St.P.W. | 230 | 34 | 10.5 | 1062 | 930 | | |
| **Bridgeport (II)** | 81809 | HH | **Wilmington DE** | 1902 | 1953 | St.P.S. | 243.3 | 36.9 | 14.6 | 1310 | 854 | 1769 | 36 |
| Bristol | 2108 | WHW | New York NY | 1867 | 1889 | St.P.W. | 362 | 48 | 16.6 | 2962.2 | 2064.4 | 1200 | |
| Bunker Hill (I) | | | New Haven CT | 1835 | 1841 | St.P.W. | | | | 310 | | | |
| **Bunker Hill (II)** | 204264 | WM | **Philadelphia PA** | 1907 | 1947 | St.Sc.S. | 375 | 52.2 | 31.6 | 4029 | 1724 | 50 | 194 |
| **C. H. Northam** | 125177 | JE | **Brooklyn NY** | 1873 | 1907 | St.P.W. | 312 | 44 | 10 | 1436.82 | 1179.97 | 1000 | |
| C. Vanderbilt | | | New York NY | 1847 | 1896 | St.P.W. | 300 | 35 | 10 | 1041 | | | |
| Camden | 204087 | | Bath ME | 1907 | 1947 | St.Sc.S. | 320.5 | 40 | 16.1 | 2153 | 1143 | | |
| **Cape Charles** | 126278 | HH | **Wilmington DE** | 1885 | 1918 | St.Sc.I. | 252.5 | 36.1 | 13 | 940.83 | 648.68 | | |
| Capital City | | SS | Greenport NY | 1852 | 1896 | St.P.W. | 259.7 | 33.7 | 11.2 | 1306 | 1204 | 977 | |
| Capt. A. H. Bowman | 4418 | | New York NY | 1854 | 1871 | St.Sc.W. | | | | 361 | | | |
| Cataline | | HL | New York NY | 1845 | 1861 | St.P.W. | 184 | 25.4 | 8.9 | 391 | | | |
| Champion | | | New York NY | 1834 | 1843 | St.P.W. | | | | 241 | | | |
| Chancellor Livingston | | HE | New York NY | 1817 | 1842 | St.P.W. | 165 | 32 | 10 | 494 | | | |
| Charter Oak | | | Hartford CT | 1838 | 1850 | St.P.W. | 200 | 50 | 9.6 | 439 | | | |
| Chesapeake | 5022 | | Wilmington DE | 1864 | 1896 | St.Sc.W. | 72 | 16.5 | 9.1 | 66 | 33 | | |
| **Chester W. Chapin** | 127379 | MSC | **Sparrows Pt MD** | 1899 | 1948 | St.Sc.S. | 312 | 64 | 16.9 | 2868 | 1822 | 1014 | 64 |
| Chief Justice Marshall | | TW | New York NY | 1825 | 1836 | St.P.W. | | | | 314 | | | |
| City of Boston | 5270 | SS | Brooklyn NY | 1861 | 1898 | St.P.W. | 301 | 40 | 12.5 | 1577 | 1457 | | |
| City of Bridgeport | 126376 | BS | Pt. Jeff. NY | 1886 | 1922 | St.Sc.W. | 144.8 | 28.4 | 10 | 500 | 340 | | |
| **City of Brockton** | 126386 | MA | **Chelsea MA** | 1886 | 1929 | St.P.W. | 271.2 | 43.4 | 18.1 | 2771.42 | 1911.8 | 40 | 115 |
| **City of Fall River** | 126088 | MH | **Chelsea MA** | 1882 | 1923 | St.P.W. | 262 | 42.4 | 17.3 | 2533.19 | 1722.7 | 50 | 107 |
| **City of Fitchburg** | 125258 | JBV | **Williamsb'g NY** | 1874 | 1907 | St.Sc.W. | 188.3 | 33.4 | 13.5 | 1087.07 | 821.55 | | 50 |
| City of Hartford | | SS | Greenpoint NY | 1852 | 1852 | St.P.W. | 259.7 | 33.7 | 11.2 | 1306 | 1204 | 977 | |
| **City of Key West** | 5020 | NEE | **Athens NY** | 1865 | 1908 | St.P.W. | 224 | 30.4 | 10 | 879.01 | 600 | | |
| **City of Lawrence** | 5243 | HH | **Wilmington DE** | 1867 | 1907 | St.P.I. | 235 | 40 | 11.9 | 1678.06 | 1351.03 | 400 | 60 |
| **City of Lowell** | 127035 | BIW | **Bath ME** | 1894 | 1946 | St.Sc.S. | 322.3 | 49.7 | 17.7 | 2975.04 | 1877.28 | 1000 | 95 |
| **City of New Bedford** | 125254 | JVB | **Brooklyn NY** | 1874 | 1906 | St.P.W. | 181.3 | 33.3 | 14 | 1085.93 | 820 | | |
| City of New London | 5269 | JE | Greenpoint NY | 1863 | 1871 | St.P.W. | 219 | 36 | 12.4 | 1203 | 990 | | |
| City of New York | 5271 | SR | Greenpoint NY | 1861 | 1896 | St.P.W. | 301 | 40 | 12.6 | 1591 | 1497 | | |
| City of Newport | 5033 | SC | New York NY | 1863 | 1915 | St.P.W. | 177.5 | 28.5 | 8.85 | 561.73 | 468.86 | | |
| City of Norwich (I) | 5272 | JE | Greenpoint NY | 1862 | 1871 | St.P.W. | 200.7 | 36 | 13.2 | 997 | 498 | | |
| **City of Norwich (II)** | | | | 1881 | | | | | | | | | |
| City of Richmond (I) | 5020 | NEE | Athens NY | 1865 | 1908 | St.P.W. | 224 | 30.4 | 10 | 879.01 | 600 | | |
| City of Richmond (II) | 125850 | | Philadelphia PA | 1880 | 1904 | St.P. | 238.9 | 35.8 | 12.2 | 614.99 | 327.52 | | |
| City of Springfield | 22571 | | Brooklyn NY | 1867 | 1898 | St.P.W. | 286 | 36 | 9.6 | 1417.03 | 1047.39 | | |

## Notes:

**Aransas:** Hull & Engine: Harlan & Hollingsworth #163; Designer, Herman Winter; Launched Oct. 27, 1877

**Bay State:** Rebuilt 1848, Lengthened to 252 ft.. in 1854

**Boston (II):** Hull & Engine: Fore River Shipbldg #114; Launched Mar 2, 1904

**Bristol:** Cost $1,250,000

**Bunker Hill (II)_:** Rebuilt, Wm. Cramp & Sons 1911

**Chester W. Chapin:** Designer, A. Cary Smith; Launched July 11, 1899; 146 Staterooms, 204 Berths

**C. H. Northam:** John Englis #71; Launched Oct 19, 1892; Cost $500,000; 112 staterooms, 500 berths. Rebuilt, John Englis #82 L 315 X B 46 X D 17.

**City of Brockton:** Designer, George Pierce; Launched July 1, 1886

**City of Bridgeport:** Launched August 12, 1886

**City of Fall River:** Launched Oct 12, 1882

**City of Fitchburg:** Launched April 1, 1874; Christened by Miss Fannie Delamater

**City of Lawrence:** Harlan & Hollingsworth #102; Cost $150,000; Rebuilt, 1983 77 Staterooms, 123 Berths

**City of Lowell:** Designer, A. Cary Smith; 146 Staterooms, 129 Berths

**City of New York:** Designer, Charles W. Copeland

# Sound Steamer Ports/Engines

| Vessel Name | Registry Number | Radio Call | Ports Served | Engine Builder | Engine Type | Horse-power | Bore and Stroke | No. of Boilers | Pressure | Type |
|---|---|---|---|---|---|---|---|---|---|---|
| Acushnet | | | NB | | | | | | | |
| Agnes | | | | | | | | | | |
| Albatross | 429 | | FR | | | | | | | |
| **Allan Joy** | 127281 | | BP BI | ROH | TE | 1200 | 17, 31, 48, X 28 | 2 | | SES |
| Ansonia | 862 | | BP NH | | | | | | | |
| **Aransas** | 105749 | | BO | | | 650 | | | | |
| Arrow | 206266 | LBCQ | BO | | T | 4000 | | | | |
| **Artisan** | 806 | | BP MY | | VD | 250 | 26 X 26 | | | |
| Atlantic | | | NO | | | | | | | |
| Barnet | | | | | | | | | | |
| Bay State | | | FR | AIW | VB | 1500 | 76 X 144 | 2 | | RT |
| Belfast | 206266 | LBCQ | BO | | T | 4000 | | | | |
| Belle | 2641 | | NH NO | | | 400 | | | | |
| Benjamin Franklin | | | PR | | | | | | | |
| **Block Island** | 3201 | | NL BI NO | WAF | VB | 800 | 46 X 120 | 2 | | RT |
| Bolivar | | | NH | | | | | | | |
| Boston (I) | | | ST | | 2 VB | | | | | |
| **Boston (II)** | 200941 | LOMV | NB BO | FRS | 2TE | 5500 | 24, 37, 63, X 42 | 8 | | SES |
| Boston (III) | 223749 | KTDG | PO | | | 2680 | | | | |
| Bridgeport (I) | 2166 | | BP | | | | 56 X 144 | 2 | | |
| **Bridgeport (II)** | 81809 | | BR | HH | IC | 2000 | 35 X 72 | 4 | 140 | SES |
| Bristol | 2108 | HCMS | BR FR NE | EIW | VB | | 110 X 144 | 3 | 18 | RT |
| Bunker Hill (I) | | | HF PR | | | | | | | |
| **Bunker Hill (II)** | 204264 | KWDT | BO PR FR | QIW | 2 TE | 7500 | 26, 43, 51, 51X42 | 8 | 185 | SES |
| **C. H. Northam** | 125177 | | NH PR | QIW | VB | 2200 | 80 X 144 | 2 | 40 | RT |
| C. Vanderbilt | | | PR ST | | | | | | | |
| Camden | 204087 | KWCG | BO BA | | T | 4000 | | | | |
| Cape Charles | 126278 | | OB WP HR | | VB | | 22 X 20 | | | |
| Capital City | | | HF | MIW | VB | | 60 X 144 | | | |
| Captain A. H. Bowman | 4418 | | BP | | | | | | | |
| Cataline | | | BP | | | | | | | |
| Champion | | | | | | | | | | |
| Chancellor Livingston | | | PR | | | 75 | | | | |
| Charter Oak | | | HF NO | | | | | | | |
| Chesapeake | 5022 | | | | | 37 | | | | |
| **Chester W. Chapin** | 127379 | | NH PR | MSC | TE | 4200 | 24, 38, 60, X 30 | 6 | 170 | SES |
| Chief Justice Marshall | | | HF NO | | | | | | | |
| City of Boston | 5270 | | NO | NIW | VB | | 80 X 144 | 2 | | RT |
| City of Bridgeport | 126376 | | BR PR BO | NL | C | 500 | 20, 34, X 26 | | | |
| **City of Brockton** | 126386 | | FR | WAF | C | 2250 | 44X96H, 68X144L | 2 | 110 | RT |
| **City of Fall River** | 126088 | | FR BP | WAF | B | 2000 | 44X96H; 68X144L | 2 | 110 | RT |
| **City of Fitchburg** | 125258 | JPKH | NB FR | DIW | S | 600 | 36 X 36 | | | |
| City of Hartford | | | HF | MIW | VB | 1200 | 60 X 144 | 2 | | |
| **City of Key West** | 5020 | HDVW | NL | FHC | VB | 350 | 46 X 144 | | | |
| City of Lawrence | 5243 | HTML | NO NL HF BP | HH | VB | 1200 | 65 X 132 | 2 | 40 | |
| **City of Lowell** | 127035 | KLWV | NO | BIW | TE | 4500 | 26, 49, 64, X 36 | 6 | 165 | SES |
| **City of New Bedford** | 125254 | JPHR | NB FR | | | | | | | |
| City of New London | 5269 | | NO | AIW | VB | | 54 X 132 | | | |
| City of New York | 5271 | HTWJ | NO | NIW | VB | 1800 | 80 X 144 | 2 | | RT |
| City of Newport | 5033 | HDWK | PR | AG | VB | 250 | 40 X 96 | | | |
| City of Norwich (I) | 5272 | | NO | AIW | VB | | 52 X 120 | | | |
| **City of Norwich (II)** | | HTMK | NO | | | | | | | |
| City of Richmond (I) | 5020 | HDVW | NL | FHC | VB | 350 | 46 X 144 | | | |
| City of Richmond (II) | 125850 | JTVL | PR HF | | | | | | | |
| City of Springfield | 22571 | HQWP | HF | | | | | | | |

## Notes:

**Block Island:** W&A Fletcher #103; Boilers, Delameter; New Boilers 1915

**Boston:** Speed 14 knots avg.

**Bristol:** Speed 17 Knots; Wheels 38.8 ft. diam, 12 ft. width, 4 ft. dip; stepped buckets (to prevent jarring and; shaking)

**C. H. Northam:** Speed 13.5 mph.; Wheels 38 ft. 6 in. diam, 11 ft. width; coal consumption per hour, 3 tons approx.; Engine built 1853 Morgan Iron Works, originally in *Crescent City* (Lake Erie), then *Morning Star*. Reboilered, Hepershaussers 1896; engine rebuilt 1898

**Chester W. Chapin:** Speed 20 mph (Maximum); coal consumption per hour:

3-1/2 tons approx.; New boilers 1928, one stack removed.

**City of Fitchburg:** Rebuilt 1902 w/engine from s/s *Dessoug* (Built 1885 by Wm Cramp); Boilers from *Nutmeg State*

**City of Lawrence:** Speed 16 mph (Maximum); Feathering Paddle Wheels 26.2 ft. diam. (outer ring); 9 ft. width; 3.4 ft. depth; coal consumption per hour: 2-1/2 tons appox.

**City of Lowell:** Speed 20 mph (Maximum); Coal consumption per hour: 3 tons appox.; 2 propellers, pitch 16 ft. Dia. 11 ft. New boilers 1929, one stack removed.

**City of Richmond (I):** New boilers 1907 at Red Bank

| Vessel Name | Registry Number | Builder | Where Built | Year Built | Year Ret'd | Hull Type | Length | Beam | Depth | Gross Tons | Net Tons | Pass Cap'y | Freight Cap'y (cars) |
|---|---|---|---|---|---|---|---|---|---|---|---|---|---|
| City of Taunton | 126875 | MH | Chelsea MA | 1892 | 1929 | St.P.W. | 283 | 43 | 18.2 | 2881.82 | 1998.95 | 47 | 119 |
| City of Worcester | 125941 | HH | Wilmington DE | 1881 | 1915 | St.P.I. | 328 | 46 | 14.5 | 2489.85 | 1921.83 | 700 | 69 |
| Cleopatra | | BS | New York NY | 1836 | 1852 | St.P.W. | 193 | 23 | 8.11 | 402 | | | |
| Cocoa | 127271 | | Philadelphia PA | 1879 | 1913 | St.Sc.I. | 205.4 | 36 | 25 | 1241 | 941 | | |
| Columbia | 12559 | JE | Greenpoint NY | 1877 | 1926 | St.P.W. | 260.6 | 39 | 12.6 | 1468 | 1098 | 1000 | |
| Comet | 204087 | | Bath ME | 1907 | 1947 | St.Sc.S. | 320.5 | 40 | 16.1 | 2153 | 1143 | | |
| Commodore | | | New York NY | 1848 | 1866 | St.P.W. | 275 | 32 | 11 | 948 | | | |
| Commonwealth (I) | | LF | Greenpoint NY | 1855 | 1865 | St.P.W. | 330 | 42 | 13.6 | 1732.76 | | 600 | |
| Commonwealth (II) | 205149 | WM | Philadelphia PA | 1908 | 1938 | St.P.S. | 437.9 | 55 | 19.3 | 5980 | 2500 | | |
| Conanicut | 126369 | | Wilmington DE | 1886 | | St.PDEFW | 125.5 | 28 | 10 | 353 | 241 | | |
| Concord | 81310 | NJBV | Chester PA | 1891 | 1931 | St. S. | 246 | 46 | 15.5 | 1248 | 697 | | |
| Connecticut (I) | | | New York NY | 1816 | 1836 | St.P.W. | 150 | 26 | | 351 | | | |
| Connecticut (II) | 4897 | | New York NY | 1848 | 1894 | St.P.W. | 303 | 26 | 8 | 723.8 | 512 | | |
| Connecticut (III) | 126559 | RPS | Noank CT | 1889 | 1913 | St.P.W. | 345.5 | 48.8 | 17 | 3399.67 | 1872.98 | 650 | |
| Continental | 4631 | | New York NY | 1861 | 1902 | St.P.W. | 282 | 36 | 11 | 686 | | | |
| Cottage City | 126631 | NES | Bath ME | 1890 | 1911 | St.Sc.W. | 233.1 | 40.6 | 23.3 | 1885 | 981.9 | | |
| Crystal Wave | | | Greenpoint NY | 1874 | 1889 | St.P.W. | 203 | 22 | 10 | 777 | 588 | | |
| Cumberland | 126281 | NES | Bath ME | 1885 | 1907 | St.P.W. | 252.2 | 37 | 14.8 | 1605 | 1188 | | |
| Curlew | | | New York NY | 1856 | 1863 | St.Sc.W. | | | | 343 | | | |
| Dirigo | 6368 | | Cape Eli'bethNJ | 1866 | 1873 | St.Sc.W. | 184 | 31 | 15 | 941.65 | | | |
| Doris | 6373 | JVB | New York NY | 1865 | 1898 | St.Sc.W. | 213 | 35 | 15 | 1360 | | | |
| Dover | 80390 | HH | Wilmington DE | 1873 | 1912 | St.Sc.I. | 165 | 28 | 12 | 617 | 397 | | |
| Eagle(I) | | GB | Norwich CT | 1817 | 1824 | St.P.W. | 92 | 17.8 | 6.8 | 80 | | | |
| Eagle (II) | 8503 | | Mystic CT | 1861 | 1908 | St.Sc. | 102.4 | 28 | 7.7 | 170.57 | 114.10 | | |
| Eagle's Wing | | SS | Greenpoint NY | 1854 | 1861 | St.P.W. | 173 | 27 | 9 | 439 | | 80 | |
| Edgemont | 115856 | NES | Bath ME | 1882 | 1924 | St.P.W. | 241 | 37 | 14.6 | 1409.99 | 1145.74 | | |
| Eleanor F. Peck | 135755 | JE | Brooklyn NY | 1884 | 1923 | St.Sc.W. | 105 | 30 | 8 | 357.72 | 218.43 | 0 | 6 |
| Eleanora | 135015 | JE | Greenpoint NY | 1874 | 1899 | St.P.W. | 186.4 | 35 | 16 | 988.29 | 582.24 | | |
| Electra | 7921 | JBV | New York NY | 1864 | 1886 | St.Sc.W. | 240 | 40 | 17 | 1300 | | | |
| Elm City | 7563 | SS | New York NY | 1855 | 1897 | St.P.W. | 245 | 32 | 10 | 760 | | | |
| Empire State | 7607 | SS | New York NY | 1848 | 1887 | St.P.W. | 305 | 40.3 | 13 | 1691.53 | 1578.79 | | |
| Enterprize | | | Hartford CT | 1819 | 1823 | St.P.W. | | | | 105 | | | |
| Eolus | 7814 | TM | New York NY | 1864 | 1894 | St.P.W. | 144 | 25 | 10.2 | 371.24 | 275.55 | | |
| Erastus Corning | 8449 | | Brooklyn NY | 1857 | 1938 | St.Sc.W. | 176 | | | 441 | | | |
| Eudora | | | Philadelphia PA | 1844 | 1854 | ST.P.W. | 155 | 28 | 9 | 252 | | | |
| Experiment | | | Middletown CT | 1822 | 1828 | St.Sc.W. | | | | 62 | | | |
| Express | 136079 | HH | Wilmington DE | 1889 | 1938 | StScDEFI | 272 | 44.1 | 12.6 | 945.04 | 538.45 | | |
| Fairfield | 110174 | BX | Bulls Ferry NJ | 1874 | 1907 | St.P.W. | 203 | 33 | 10 | 892.35 | 673.71 | | |
| Fairhaven (I) | | | Philadelphia PA | 1835 | 1860 | StScDEFW | | | | 57 | | | |
| Fairhaven (II) | 121013 | MH | Chelsea MA | 1876 | 1934 | St.PDEFW | 95 | 26.2 | 10 | 279 | 227 | | |
| Falcon | 9053 | | Mystic CT | 1861 | 1881 | St.Sc.W. | | | | 457 | | | |
| Falmouth | 120019 | JE | Greenpoint NY | 1872 | 1884 | St.P.W. | 232 | 35.4 | 10 | 1156.31 | 849.88 | | |
| Fanny | | | New York NY | 1825 | 1844 | St.P.W. | | | | 126 | | | |
| Firefly | | | New York NY | 1812 | 1821 | St.P.W. | | | | 47 | | | |
| Frances | 9313 | HH | Wilmington DE | 1865 | 1899 | St.P.I. | 222.7 | 32.8 | 10 | 988.18 | 717.82 | | |
| Frances (motorboat) | | | | | | | 57.9 | 20.2 | 6.3 | | 44 | | |
| Franconia | 2511 | | Kennebunk ME | 1873 | | St.Sc.W. | 179 | 30 | 17.5 | 674.87 | 445.07 | | |
| Frank E. Garnett | 226234 | | Camden NJ | 1927 | 1955 | El.Sc.DEFS | 145.6 | 37.1 | 12.7 | 405 | 268 | | |
| Frank Jones | 120903 | NES | Bath ME | 1892 | 1918 | St.P.W. | 253.2 | 36.3 | 13.8 | 1634 | 1078 | | |
| Franklin | | | New York NY | 1819 | 1850 | St.P.W. | | | | 193 | | | |
| Fulton | | | New York NY | 1813 | 1838 | St.P.W. | 133 | 29 | 9 | 327 | | | |
| Galatea | 10614 | JBV | New York NY | 1864 | 1885 | St.Sc.W. | 240 | 40 | 17 | 1301 | | | |
| Gay Head | 86151 | BGH | Philadelphia PA | 1891 | 1931 | St.P.W. | 203 | 34 | 11.6 | 701.92 | 443.32 | | |
| General | 86056 | CIW | Brooklyn NY | 1889 | 1934 | St.Sc.S. | 130 | 25.1 | 9.4 | 332.44 | 201.64 | | |
| General Jackson | | | New York NY | 1829 | 1849 | St.P.W. | 114 | 22 | | 174 | | | |
| General LaFayette | | | New York NY | 1824 | 1832 | St.P.W. | | | | 92 | | | |
| George Law | 10044 | | New York NY | 1852 | 1894 | St.P.W. | 147.6 | 27.7 | 7.2 | 266.8 | 228.2 | | |

**City of Taunton:** Launched May 28, 1892

**City of Worcester:** Harlan & Hollingsworth #196; Launched March 12, 1881; 159 Staterooms, 116 Berths

**Columbia:** Designer, John A. Connolly; John Englis #80; Launched May 29, 1877; Cost $220,000.

**Connecticut (III):** Designer, George B. Mallory; Joiner work, William Rowland; Launched November 16, 1887; Frames of white oak and hackmatack; floor timbers filled in solid for 180 feet of the length of the vessel; keelsons and ceilings of yellow pine; bottom planking of white oak.

**Commonwealth (I):** Designer, Alexander Hawkins; Joiner Work, Reed, Tice & Hamilton (NY); Cost $250,000; 163 Staterooms

**Commonwealth (II):** Wm. Cramp & Sons #348

**Eleanora:** John Englis & Sons #74; Launched May 23, 1874; Cost $275,000; 40 Staterooms

**Eleanor F. Peck:** John Englis & Son #89; Launched Nov 14, 1883

**Elm City:** Launched Nov 2, 1854

**Empire State:** Rebuilt, 1849

**Express:** Launched August 10, 1889; Alterations: Morgan Iron Works; Engine room shorten, upper deck stanchions shifted, stern modified, and side platforms shortened. Rebuilt, 1914 Morse Dry Dock & Repair Co.

**Frances:** Harlan & Hollingsworth #95

**Gay Head:** 10 Staterooms

**General:** Launched May 21, 1889

| Vessel Name | Registry Number | Radio Call | Ports Served | Engine Builder | Engine Type | Horse-power | Bore and Stroke | No. of Boilers | Pressure | Type |
|---|---|---|---|---|---|---|---|---|---|---|
| City of Taunton | 126875 | | FR | WAF | CVB | 2500 | 47X8H, 71X12L | 2 | 120 | RT |
| City of Worcester | 125941 | JVLM | NL | HH | VB | 3500 | 90 X 144 | 4 | 60 | |
| Cleopatra | | | PR HF | WPF | VB | | 44 X 132 | | | |
| Cocoa | 127271 | KNMV | BO PR | | | 700 | | | | |
| Columbia | 12559 | JSKG | HF SA | QIW | VB | 1200 | 66 X 132 | 2 | | |
| Comet | 204087 | KWCG | BO | | T | 4000 | | | | |
| Commodore | | | NO PR ST | | | | | | | |
| Commonwealth (I) | | | NO ST GO | MIW | VB | | 76 X 144 | 2 | 25 | RT |
| Commonwealth (II) | 205149 | KWPJ | FR BO | WM | CI | 11000 | 50, 96, 96, X 144 | 10 | | SES |
| Conanicut | 126369 | | NE | | | 225 | | | | |
| Concord | 81310 | | PR NB | | | 1700 | | | | |
| Connecticut (I) | | | NH PR HF | | SQ | | 75 X 144 | | | |
| Connecticut (II) | 4897 | | NH NO PO | | | | | | | |
| Connecticut (III) | 126559 | | PR | WM | CO | 4000 | 56.25x132H104x132L | 6 | 120 | |
| Continental | 4631 | | NH | | | | | | | |
| Cottage City | 126631 | KGWT | PO | BIW | TE | 1300 | 22, 54, 55 X 56 | 4 | | |
| Crystal Wave | | | BP | | | | | | | |
| Cumberland | 126281 | KCWL | PR | PC | VB | 1200 | 60 X 144 | | | |
| Curlew | | | PR | | | | | | | |
| Dirigo | 6368 | | PO | | VB | | 42 X 60 | 2 | 44 | RT |
| Doris | 6373 | | FR | EIW | VB | | 50 X 40 | | | |
| Dover | 80390 | JNMS | PR | HH | HH | 492 | 34 X 34 | | | |
| Eagle(I) | | | NL NA HF | | | | | | | |
| Eagle (II) | 7716 | | FR | | | | | | | |
| Eagle's Wing | | | NA | NIW | B | 200 | 40 X 120 | | | |
| Edgemont | 115856 | | PR | PC | VB | 1200 | 60 X 144 | 2 | | RT |
| Eleanor F. Peck | 135755 | | NH | JWS | | 300 | 20 X 24 | 1 | | RT |
| Eleanora | 135015 | JPNH | PO BO | DIW | VB | | 42 X 60 | | | |
| Electra | 7921 | | PR | ROH | | | 44 X 36 | | | |
| Elm City | 7563 | | NH | NNW | VB | | 65 X 144 | 2 | | RT |
| Empire State | 7607 | HFTW | FR | AIW | VB | 1522 | 76 X 144 | 2 | | |
| Enterprize | | | HF SA | | | | | | | |
| Eolus | 7814 | | WI NP | WIW | VB | 285 | 40 X 96 | | | |
| Erastus Corning | | | HF SA NL | | | | | | | |
| Eudora | | | NO FR | | | | | | | |
| Experiment | | | SA NL HF | | | | | | | |
| Express | 136079 | KGNP | JC WP HR | HH | C | | 26, 48, X 36 | 2 | | |
| Fairfield | 110174 | | BP | DIW | VB | 1200 | 50 X 144 | 2 | | |
| Fairhaven (I) | | | NB | | | | | | | |
| Fairhaven (II) | 121013 | | NB | WAF | VB | 250 | 30 X 72 | 1 | | RT |
| Falcon | 9053 | | FR | | | | | | | |
| Falmouth | 120019 | JLNG | SO NO NL | QIW | VB | | 54 X 132 | 2 | | RT |
| Fanny | | | | | | | | | | |
| Firefly | | | NE PO | | | | | | | |
| Frances | 9313 | HGPS | PR ST | HH | VB | | 50 X 132 | | | |
| Frances (motorboat) | | | NB FH | | | 100 | | | | |
| Franconia | 2511 | HGTS | PO | | | 250 | | | | |
| Frank E. Garnett | 226234 | | NB MV | BIW | DE | 700 | | | | |
| Frank Jones | 120903 | KLHQ | FR | | | 1200 | | | | |
| Franklin | | | | | | | | | | |
| Fulton | | | NH NO NL SA | | | | | | | |
| Galatea | 10614 | | PR | ROH | | | 44 X 36 | | | |
| Gay Head | 86151 | KSCG | NA | PJ | VB | 1000 | 50 X 120 | 2 | 50 | RT |
| General | 86056 | | WI NP | WAF | C | 380 | 17, 32, X 24 | 2 | | RT |
| General Jackson | | | NO | | | | | | | |
| General LaFayette | | | BP | | | | | | | |
| George Law | 10044 | | NA | | | 460 | | | | |

---

**City of Worcester:** Speed 15 mph (Maximum); Coal Consumption per Hour: 4-1/2 tons approx.; Straight paddle wheels, 36.6 ft. diam, 11 ft. width, 4.8 ft. depth

**Columbia:** Speed 15 mph; Wheels: 32' 10" diam, 11 ft. width, 22 in. depth, 28 buckets; Engine: Rebuilt from "Santiago de Cuba"; Reboilered 1909

**Commonwealth (I):** Wheels:, 38 ft. diam, 10 ft. 6 in. width; at 8 ft. 4 in. draft buckets dip 3 ft 4 in.; 28 Buckets. Reboilered 1859

**Commonwealth (II):** Reboilered 1929

**Connecticut:** Speed 17 mph; Feathering type wheels, 28 ft. diam, 12 buckets per wheel, buckets 14 ft. long, 4 ft. wide, and 6 in. deep. Dip: App. 6 ft. Extensive engine modification done in 1902 at W & A Fletcher Co.; Cost $696,000

**Empire State:** Wheels 38 ft diam, 10 ft 3 in wide

**General:** Engine W & A Fletcher #132; Speed 10 knots cruising

| Vessel Name | Registry Number | Builder | Where Built | Year Built | Year Ret'd | Hull Type | Length | Beam | Depth | Gross Tons | Net Tons | Pass Cap'y | Freight Cap'y (cars) |
|---|---|---|---|---|---|---|---|---|---|---|---|---|---|
| Georgia | 85961 | HH | Wilmington DE | 1887 | 1936 | St.Sc.I. | 280 | 40 | 15 | 1749.28 | 1188.54 | | |
| Glaucus | 26066 | | New York NY | 1864 | 1894 | St.P.W. | 240 | 40 | 17 | 1244 | | | |
| Globe | | | New York NY | 1842 | 1851 | St P.W. | | | | 481 | | | |
| Granite State | 10332 | SS | Greenpoint NY | 1853 | 1883 | St.P.W. | 246.10 | 32 | 19.7 | 887 | | | |
| Groton | | | Greenpoint NY | 1877 | 1889 | St.DEFW | 253.6 | | 13.6 | 1420.52 | | | |
| Hartford (I) | 96172 | NL | Philadelphia PA | 1892 | 1960 | St.Sc.I. | 220 | 40 | 13 | 1337.99 | 985.69 | | |
| Hartford (II) | 96472 | CXW | Baltimore MD | 1899 | 1938 | St.Sc.I. | 243.3 | 45.7 | 12.5 | 1488 | 1012 | 350 | |
| Harvard | 204372 | ROH | Chester PA | 1907 | 1931 | St.Sc.S | 376 | 61.3 | 20.2 | 3737 | 2317 | | |
| Helen Augusta | 11331 | | Clinton NJ | 1863 | 1878 | St.Sc.W. | 82.7 | 21.2 | 6.6 | 71 | | | |
| Henry Eckford | | | New York NY | 1824 | 1841 | St.P.W. | | | | 153 | | | |
| Hero | 11476 | HL | New York NY | 1845 | 1870 | St.P.W. | 205.4 | 26.6 | 8.9 | 462 | | | |
| Horatio Hall | 96401 | DRI | Chester PA | 1898 | 1909 | St.Sc.S. | 296.8 | 46 | 17.2 | 3167 | 2007 | | |
| Hudson | | BB | New York NY | 1824 | 1848 | St.P.W. | 108 | 23 | 6.5 | 170 | | | |
| Huntress | | | New York NY | 1858 | 1862 | St.P.W. | | | | 333 | | | |
| Island Home | 12141 | SW | Greenpoint NY | 1855 | 1901 | St.P.W. | 184 | 29.6 | 11 | 484 | 330.2 | | |
| Islander | 223089 | BIW | Bath ME | 1923 | | St.Sc.S. | 204.4 | 36.1 | 13.1 | 1089 | 456 | 1960 | |
| James B. Schuyler | 12825 | | Jersey City NJ | 1865 | 1897 | St.P.W. | 195 | 29 | 9 | 597 | 525 | | |
| James T. Brady | 13170 | JS | Brooklyn NY | 1864 | 1869 | St.P.W. | 212 | 30.4 | 9.5 | 1402 | 923.32 | | |
| John Brooks | 13452 | | New York NY | 1859 | 1868 | St.P.W. | 250 | 34 | 11 | 780 | | | |
| John Englis | 77240 | DRI | Chester PA | 1896 | 1955 | St.Sc.S. | 290.8 | 46 | 21 | 3094 | 1987 | | |
| John H. Starin | | | | 1870 | | St.P.W. | | | | | | | |
| John M. Worth | 201699 | ACB | Tottenville NY | 1905 | 1938 | St.Sc.W. | 139.7 | 30 | 10.8 | 442 | 379 | 0 | 12 |
| John Sylvester | 13185 | | Jersey City NJ | 1866 | 1931 | St.P.W. | | | | 495 | | | |
| John W. Richmond | | | Providence RI | 1838 | 1843 | St.P.W. | 200 | 24 | 12 | 487 | | | |
| Josephine | 13167 | | New York NY | 1853 | 1892 | St.P.W. | | | | 552 | | | |
| Kennebec | 14484 | | Bath ME | 1898 | | St.P.W. | 256 | 37.6 | 13.6 | 1652 | 1271 | | |
| Kentucky | 141499 | NES | Bath ME | 1897 | 1910 | St.Sc.W. | 203.4 | 37.9 | 12.6 | 996.57 | 532.24 | | |
| Kingfisher | | | Mystic CT | 1863 | 1866 | St.Sc.W. | | | | 441 | | | |
| Knickerbocker | | | New York NY | 1843 | 1865 | St.P.W | 291.6 | 31.6 | 9.6 | 858 | | | |
| Lafayette | | | New York NY | 1824 | | St.P.W. | | | | 92 | | | |
| Larchmont | 126281 | NES | Bath ME | 1885 | 1907 | St.P.W. | 252.2 | 37 | 16 | 1605 | 1188 | | |
| Laura | 15261 | HH | Wilmington DE | 1867 | 1891 | St.P.I. | 225 | 34 | 11 | 1098 | 946 | | |
| Lexington (I) | | BS | New York NY | 1835 | 1840 | St.P.W. | 205 | 22 | 11.6 | 488 | | | |
| Lexington (II) | 130526 | NJBV | Chester PA | 1891 | 1931 | St. S. | 246 | 46 | 15.5 | 1248 | 697 | | |
| Lincoln | 141499 | NES | Bath ME | 1897 | 1910 | St.Sc.W. | 203.4 | 37.9 | 12.6 | 996.57 | 532.24 | | |
| Linnaeus | | | New York NY | 1824 | 1852 | St.P.W. | | | | 92 | | | |
| MacDonough | | | New York NY | 1826 | 1839 | St.P.W. | 132 | 26 | | 272 | | | 1 |
| Maine | 92391 | HH | Wilmington DE | 1892 | 1920 | St.Sc.S. | 308.7 | 44 | 17.5 | 2395 | 1505 | 600 | 88 |
| Manhattan (I) | 92280 | NES | Bath ME | 1891 | 1910 | St.Sc.W. | 233.9 | 40.9 | 24.5 | 1892.13 | 982.34 | | |
| Manhattan (II) | 211737 | | Wilmington DE | 1913 | | St.Sc.S. | 320.2 | 48.1 | 22 | 3439 | 2134 | | |
| Marco Bozzaris | | | New York NY | 1826 | 1833 | St.P.W. | | | | 129 | | | |
| Martha's Vineyard (I) | 90288 | LF | Williamsb'g NY | 1871 | 1917 | St.P.W. | 171.18 | 28 | 9.35 | 515.62 | 363.40 | | |
| Martha's Vineyard (II) | 223089 | BIW | Bath ME | 1923 | | St.Sc.S. | 202.4 | 36.1 | 13.1 | 1089 | 456 | 1960 | |
| Maryland (I) | 17794 | HH | Wilmington DE | 1853 | 1889 | St.PDEFI | 220 | 36 | 10 | 1395.44 | 1150 | | |
| Maryland (II) | 92156 | HH | Wilmington DE | 1890 | 1913 | StScDEFI | 238 | 38 | 13 | 859.52 | 542.83 | | |
| Massachusetts (I) | | BB | New York NY | 1836 | 1859 | St.P.W. | 202 | 29 | 12 | 713 | 676 | | |
| Massachusetts (II) | 16109 | SS | New York NY | 1842 | 1881 | St.P.W | 161.2 | 23.10 | 8.4 | 308 | | | |
| Massachusetts (III) | 90973 | HS | Greenpoint NY | 1877 | 1903 | St.P.W. | 323.8 | 42.5 | 15.9 | 2606.83 | 2171.01 | | 55 |
| Massachusetts (IV) | 204012 | WM | Philadelphia PA | 1907 | 1972 | St.Sc.S. | 386.7 | 52.252 | 15.7 | 4029 | 1724 | 50 | 194 |
| Metacomet | | | New York NY | 1854 | 1858 | St.P.W. | 170 | 26 | 9 | 395 | | | |
| Meteor (I) | 91527 | NL | Philadelphia PA | 1883 | | St.Sc.I. | 162 | 23 | 8.7 | 423 | 338 | | |
| Meteor (II) | 127379 | MSC | Sparrows Pt MD | 1899 | 1948 | St.Sc.S. | 312 | 64 | 16.9 | 2868 | 1822 | 1014 | 64 |
| Metis | 17058 | JVB | New York NY | 1864 | 1872 | St.Sc.W. | 213 | 35 | 15 | 1359 | 1238 | | |
| Metropolis | 16760 | SW | Greenpoint NY | 1854 | 1877 | St.P.W. | 327.9 | 44.4 | 15 | 2210 | 2108 | | 33 |
| Middletown | 92699 | NL | Philadelphia PA | 1896 | 1938 | St.Sc.S. | 243.3 | 45.6 | 14 | 1554.28 | 1164.64 | | |
| Miles Standish | 92656 | MH | Chelsea MA | 1895 | 1936 | St.P.W. | 197.8 | 33.6 | 10.9 | 700 | 339 | | |
| Miramar | 203183 | | Noank CT | 1906 | 1935 | St.P.W. | 103.3 | 24.3 | 9.4 | 181 | 99 | | |
| Mohawk | 92698 | DRI | Chester PA | 1896 | 1948 | St.Sc.S. | 265 | 43 | 16.8 | 2783.53 | 2150.83 | 0 | 190 |

**Georgia:** Harlan & Hollingsworth #227; Launched March 21, 1887; Cost $252,263; Christened by Miss Lota Robinson

**Granite State:** Launched Nov 29, 1852; Lengthened 1875: L 265 X B 35 X D 11

**Horatio Hall:** Delaware River Company #293; Launched March 23, 1889

**Hartford (I):** Launched July 27, 1899

**Harvard:** Roach Shipyard #334; Launched Jan 30, 1907; Cost $1,250,000

**Island Home:** Launched July 2, 1885; Converted to Coal Barge c1925

**Islander:** Launched July 19, 1923; Completed August 2, 1923; Passengers: Winter 456; Summer 1960

**Larchmont:** Launched December 16, 1884

**Laura:** Harlan & Holl. #103

**Maine:** Harlan & Holl. #263; Launched Oct. 31, 1891; 102 Staterooms, 62 Berths

**Maryland (I):** Harlan & Hollingsworth #17; Remodeled & rebuilt, lengthened; L 294.3 X B36.5 X D10.2; Gross Tons: 1093 Net Tons: 881

**Maryland (II):** Launched October 23, 1889; Cost $235,000

**Massachusetts (III):** Joiner work, William Rowland; Launched Sept 6, 1876

**Massachusetts (IV):** Launched January 29, 1907; Rebuilt, Wm. Cramp & Sons 1911; 4779 Gross Tons, 2575 Net Tons

**Martha's Vineyard (I):** Launched April 10, 1871

**Metropolis:** Launched April 20, 1854; 304 Berths

**Middletown:** Neafi & Levy #888

**Mohawk:** Designer, Frank E. Kirby (Detroit MI); Delaware River Co. #284

| Vessel Name | Registry Number | Radio Call | Ports Served | Engine Builder | Engine Type | Horse-power | Bore and Stroke | No. of Boilers | Pressure | Type |
|---|---|---|---|---|---|---|---|---|---|---|
| Georgia | 85961 | | PR BO PO | HH | C | 1950 | 34, 64, X 42 | | | |
| Glaucus | 26066 | | FR | | | | | | | |
| Globe | | | HF | | | | | | | |
| Granite State | 10332 | | HF | MIW | VB | | 52 X 144 | 1 | | |
| Groton | | | NL GO | | | | | | | |
| Hartford (I) | 96172 | KIGP | HF | NL | | | | | | |
| Hartford (II) | 96472 | | HF | CXW | 2C | 1000 | 20, 40, X 28 | 4 | | SES |
| Harvard | 204372 | KWDG | BO | WAF | T | 10,000 | | 12 | | SES |
| Helen Augusta | 11331 | | | | | | | | | |
| Henry Eckford | | | HF | | | | | | | |
| Hero | 11476 | | HF | | | | | | | |
| Horatio Hall | 96401 | KNJL | BO | DRI | TE | 4000 | 28, 48, 75, X 54 | 6 | 180 | SEBRO |
| Hudson | | | | | | | | | | |
| Huntress | | | | | | | | | | |
| Island Home | 12141 | HKJR | NA HI | MIW | VB | 487 | 34 X 132 | 1 | | |
| Islander | 223089 | WCFA | NB MV NA WO | BIW | TE | 1200 | 16, 26, 30, 30X24 | 2 | | RT |
| James B. Schuyler | 12825 | | BP | | VB | | | | | |
| James T. Brady | 13170 | HLGP | | | | | | | | |
| John Brooks | 13452 | | BP | Mor | VB | | 56x144 | | | |
| John Englis | 77240 | KMBW | PO | | TE | 4000 | 30, 48, 75 X 54 | 6 | 180 | |
| John H. Starin | | | NH | | | | | | | |
| John M. Worth | 201699 | | BO | | SC | 500 | 11, 29, X 14 | 2 | | WT |
| John Sylvester | | | | | | | | | | |
| John W. Richmond | | | PR | | | | | | | |
| Josephine | 13167 | | BP | | | | | | | |
| Kennebec | 14484 | KGJP | | | VB | 1400 | 60 X 30 | | | |
| Kentucky | 141499 | KNDC | FR PR | | 2TE | 1600 | 15, 26, 39, X 28 | 2 | | SES |
| Kingfisher | | | FR | | | | | | | |
| Knickerbocker | | | ST | | | | | | | |
| Lafayette | | | NA NB | | | | | | | |
| Larchmont | 126281 | KCWL | PR | PC | VB | 1200 | 60 X 144 | | | |
| Laura | 15261 | | BR HF | HH | VB | | 50 X 144 | | | |
| Lexington (I) | | | PR | | | | | | | |
| Lexington (II) | 130526 | | PR NB | | | 1700 | | | | |
| Lincoln | 141499 | KNDC | PO | NF | 2TE | 1600 | 15, 26, 39. X 28 | 2 | | SES |
| Linnaeus | | | NH | | | | | | | |
| MacDonough | | | HF | | | | | | | |
| Maine | 92391 | KLDB | ST | HH | TE | 2500 | 28, 45, 51, 51X42 | 4 | 160 | RT |
| Manhattan (I) | 92280 | KJHR | PO | BIW | TE | 2500 | 22, 34, 55 X 36 | | | |
| Manhattan (II) | 211737 | LDFT | None | | T | 4000 | | | | |
| Marco Bozzaris | | | NB NC | | | | | | | |
| Martha's Vineyard (I) | 90288 | JKNG | MV NA | HW | VB | 724 | 46 X 120 | | | |
| Martha's Vineyard (II) | 223089 | WCFA | NA | BIW | TE | 1200 | 16, 26, 30, 30X24 | 2 | | RT |
| Maryland (I) | 17794 | JFMH | JC HR | HH | HI | | 40 X 96 | | | |
| Maryland (II) | 92156 | | JC HR | HH | 2CH | | 24, 44, X 180 | | | |
| Massachusetts (I) | | | PR FR | | 2 VB | 2900 | 44 X 96 | | | |
| Massachusetts (II) | 16109 | | NA | AIW | CH | | | | | |
| Massachusetts (III) | 90973 | | PR ST | ROH | | 2800 | 90 X 168 | 6 | | SES |
| Massachusetts (IV) | 204012 | KWBM | BO NB BP | QIW | 2 TE | 7500 | 26, 43, 51, X 42 | 8 | 185 | SES |
| Metacomet | | | NA NB FR | | | | | | | |
| Meteor (I) | 91527 | | FR | | | 32 | 28 X 28 | | | |
| Meteor (II) | 127379 | | NH PR | MSC | TE | 4200 | 24, 38, 60, X 30 | 6 | 170 | SES |
| Metis | 17058 | | FR | EIW | | | 50 X 40 | | | |
| Metropolis | 16760 | | FR | NIW | VB | | 105 X 144 | 4 | 24 | |
| Middletown | 92699 | KMQF | HF | NL | C | 1000 | 20 40, X 28 | 4 | | SES |
| Miles Standish | 92656 | KMHG | NB MV NA | | TE | 1350 | | | | |
| Miramar | 203183 | KVLQ | NB MV | | C | 400 | | | | |
| Mohawk | 92698 | KMQC | NL | DRI | TE | 1600 | 21, 34, 56, X 42 | 2 | 165 | SES |

**Granite State:** Cobanks & Theall 1870 New Boiler and rebuilding; engine with a 60 inch Cyl. When lost her boiler was sold to the Cornell Steamboat Co. for the new Austin.
**Harvard:** Engines: W & A Fletcher, 3 Parsons Turbines; Converted to oil 1910
**Horatio Hall:** Speed 16 knots; Propeller 15 ft. 6 in. diam
**Laura:** Engine: Originally from Magnolia; Boiler: New 1879 Cobanks & Theall
**Islander:** Boilers: Babcock & Wilcox; Speed 14-1/2 Knots
**Maine:** Speed 18 mph (Maximum); coal consumption 3 tons per hour approx.; Propeller, 60 sq. ft. area, 18 ft. 6in. pitch, 13 ft. 6 in. diam.

**Metropolis:** Speed; 20 mph; Reboilered 1860; Iron Paddle Wheels 41 ft. diam, 13 ft. width
**Mohawk:** Speed 15 mph (Maximum); coal consumption per hour: 2 tons approx.; 2 Boilers, Lake Erie Boiler Works (Buffalo NY); Reboilered 1924, 3 Babcock and Wilcox; 1650 IHP; Propeller: Wheel sectional blades cast of iron and steel, 50 sq. ft. area, 12 ft. diam, 14 ft. pitch; Rebuilt 1905
**Mohegan (II):** Speed 15 mph. (Maximum); Coal consumption per hour: 2 tons approx.; 3 Boilers, W&A Fletcher, (Hoboken NJ); Propeller, sectional blades iron and steel cast, 49 sq. ft. area, 12 ft. diam, 14 ft. pitch

| Vessel Name | Registry Number | Builder | Where Built | Year Built | Year Ret'd | Hull Type | Length | Beam | Depth | Gross Tons | Net Tons | Pass Cap'y | Freight Cap'y (cars) |
|---|---|---|---|---|---|---|---|---|---|---|---|---|---|
| Mohegan (I) | | | New York NY | 1839 | 1856 | St.P.W. | | | | 399 | | | |
| **Mohegan (II)** | 92705 | DRI | **Chester PA** | 1896 | 1939 | St.Sc.S. | 265 | 43 | 16.8 | 2783.53 | 2150.83 | 0 | 190 |
| Monohansett | 16795 | WTC | New York NY | 1862 | 1904 | St.P.W. | 176.65 | 27.11 | 9.11 | 465.61 | 347 | | |
| Mount Hope | 92004 | MH | Chelsea MA | 1888 | 1936 | St.P.W. | 193.1 | 58.8 | 11.5 | 880 | 440 | | |
| **Nantucket (I)** | 130354 | BGH | **Camden NJ** | 1886 | 1919 | St.P.W. | 190 | 33 | 9 | 629.02 | 468.51 | | |
| **Nantucket (II)** | 224501 | BIW | **Bath ME** | 1925 | | St.Sc.S. | 202.4 | 36.1 | 13.3 | 1082 | 428 | 2000 | |
| Narragansett (I) | | | New York NY | 1836 | 1847 | St.P.W. | 212 | 27 | 10 | 576 | | | |
| Narragansett (II) | | JS | New York NY | 1866 | 1880 | St.P.W. | 253 | 40 | 15 | 1634 | 1246 | | |
| Narragansett (III) | 210653 | | Wilmington DE | 1913 | | St.Sc.S. | 320.2 | 48.1 | 22 | 3539 | 2134 | | |
| **Nashua** | 130340 | RPS | **Noank CT** | 1884 | 1913 | St.P.W. | 291.6 | 43 | 16.1 | 2554.65 | 1800.97 | 40 | 102 |
| **Naugatuck** | 127281 | DRI | **Chester PA** | 1898 | 1956 | St.Sc.S. | 220.7 | 37.2 | 14 | 1308.24 | 739 | 500 | 34 |
| Naushon (I) | 18286 | WTC | New York NY | 1845 | 1880 | St.P.W. | 134.1 | 22 | 8.6 | 285 | 240.16 | | |
| **Naushon (II)** | 228531 | BSB | **Quincy MA** | 1929 | 1974 | St.Sc.S. | 240.1 | 45.2 | 14 | 1978.79 | 936 | 2850 | 5 |
| Neptune | | | New York NY | 1863 | 1865 | St.Sc.W. | 228 | 40 | 18 | 1244 | | | |
| Nereus | 22099 | | New York NY | 1863 | 1865 | St.Sc.W. | 228 | 40 | 18 | 1244 | | | |
| **New Bedford** | 227565 | BSC | **Quincy MA** | 1928 | 1968 | St.Sc.S. | 202.6 | 36.2 | 13 | 1116.91 | 451 | | |
| New Champion | 18574 | | New York NY | 1842 | 1887 | St.P.W. | 215 | 26 | 8 | 571 | | | |
| New England (I) | | | New York NY | 1833 | 1869 | St.P.W. | 153 | 23.6 | 8 | 261 | | | |
| **New England (II)** | 20464 | FRS | **Quincy MA** | 1907 | 1952 | St.Sc.S. | 118 | 31.4 | 11.3 | 341.24 | 232 | | |
| **New Hampshire** | 130581 | HH | **Wilmington DE** | 1892 | 1943 | St.Sc.S. | 303.7 | 44 | 17.5 | 2395.07 | 1505.37 | 600 | 88 |
| New Haven (I) | | LS | New York NY | 1835 | 1869 | St.P.W. | 178 | 22.8 | 9 | 342 | | | |
| New Haven (II) | 18189 | | East Haven CT | 1866 | 1895 | St.Sc.W. | 175 | 32 | 10 | 467.9 | 417.4 | | |
| **New Haven (III)** | 204200 | DRI | **Chester PA** | 1907 | 1938 | St.Sc.S. | 275.7 | 45.1 | 16.7 | 2930 | 1986 | | |
| New London | 641 | GG | Mystic CT | 1859 | 1910 | St.Sc.W. | 125 | 25 | 7.8 | 221.77 | | | |
| **New Shoreham** | 130934 | WMC | **East Boston MA** | 1901 | 1954 | St.Sc.S. | 151.9 | 28.1 | 11.8 | 503 | 317 | 500 | 0 |
| New York (I) | 18657 | LS | New York NY | 1836 | 1867 | St.P.W. | 212 | 20.1 | 5 | 524 | | | |
| New York (II) | 223901 | BSC | Sparrows Pt MD | 1924 | 1942 | St.Sc.S. | 385.3 | 72.5 | 20.9 | 4989 | 2703 | | |
| Newburgh | 130350 | NL | Philadelphia PA | 1886 | 1955 | St.Sc.I. | 200 | 32 | 11 | 1033 | 741 | | |
| Newport | 18221 | JE | Greenpoint NY | 1865 | 1890 | St.P.W. | 342 | 43.3 | 14.2 | 2151 | 1862 | | |
| Niagara | 18577 | | New York NY | 1845 | 1897 | St.P.W. | 251 | 30 | 9 | 511 | 352 | | |
| Nimrod | | | New York NY | 1834 | 1858 | St.P.W. | 175 | 20 | 8 | 432 | | | |
| **Nobska** | 224501 | BIW | **Bath ME** | 1925 | | St.Sc.S. | 202.4 | 36.1 | 13.3 | 1082 | 428 | 2000 | |
| **North Land** | 207282 | HH | **Wilmington DE** | 1910 | 1935 | St.Sc.S | 304.4 | 47.2 | 19.85 | 3282 | 1973 | | |
| **North Star** | 130924 | DRI | **Chester PA** | 1901 | 1919 | St.Sc.S. | 298.8 | 46 | 17.2 | 3159 | 1999 | | |
| Northampton | 18190 | | East Haven CT | 1866 | 1872 | St.Sc.W. | 178 | | | 450 | | | |
| Norwich | 18578 | LS | New York NY | 1836 | 1924 | St.Sc.W | 160 | 25.3 | 9 | 346.5 | | | |
| Nutmeg State | | RPS | Noank CT | 1890 | 1899 | St.Sc.W. | | | | | | | |
| Oceanus | | JVB | New York NY | 1865 | 1868 | St.Sc.W. | 240 | 40 | 17 | 1996 | 1301 | | |
| Old Colony (I) | 19009 | JE | Greenpoint NY | 1865 | 1874 | St.P.W. | 310 | 42 | 14 | 1958 | 1714 | | 27 |
| **Old Colony (II)** | 204528 | WM | **Philadelphia PA** | 1907 | 1922 | St.Sc.S. | 375 | 52.2 | 31.6 | 4029.24 | 1564 | 50 | 194 |
| **Old Dominion** | 19350 | HH | **Wilmington DE** | 1872 | 1937 | St.P.I. | 255.5 | 42.5 | 20.7 | 2222 | 1775 | | |
| Oliver Ellsworth | | | New York NY | 1824 | 1853 | St.P.W. | 112 | 24 | 8 | 227 | | | |
| Oregon | | | New York NY | 1845 | 1861 | St.P.W. | 318 | 35 | 10 | 1004 | | | |
| Osceola | | | Brooklyn NY | 1848 | 1861 | St.Sc.W. | 177 | | | 177 | | | |
| Osprey | 19097 | | Greenpoint NY | 1854 | 1880 | St.Sc.W. | | | | 341 | | | |
| **Owana** | 202692 | | **Tottenville NY** | 1905 | 1936 | St.Sc.S. | 113 | 28.8 | 9.1 | 356.45 | 242.39 | | |
| Pelican | 19995 | | Kensington PA | 1851 | 1875 | St.Sc.W. | | | | 250 | | | |
| P   uin | 9434 | | Mystic CT | 1860 | 1884 | St.Sc.W. | | | | 389 | | | |
|   bscot | 150253 | ST | East Boston MA | 1882 | 1918 | St.P.W. | 255 | 38 | 13 | 1414 | 1244 | | |
| ι  uonnock | 202939 | DRI | **Chester PA** | 1906 | 1938 | St.Sc.S. | 275.7 | 45.1 | 17 | 2930 | 1986 | 0 | 159 |
| Pι  juot | 24449 | JBV | **New York NY** | 1865 | 1943 | St.Sc.W. | 219 | 35 | 16.3 | 1360.25 | 946.8 | 0 | 72 |
| Petrel | 19899 | | Kensington PA | 1851 | 1866 | St.Sc.W. | | | | 267 | | | |
| **Pilgrim** | 150280 | ROH | **Chester PA** | 1882 | 1924 | St.P.I. | 372 | 50 | 15.6 | 3483.66 | 2512.9 | 1200 | 53 |
| **Plymouth** | 150502 | ROH | **Chester PA** | 1890 | 1938 | St.P.S. | 352 | 50 | 18.8 | 3770.89 | 2280.13 | 1500 | 75 |
| Plymouth Rock | 20151 | JS | New York NY | 1854 | 1887 | St.P.W. | 330 | 40 | 13 | 1810 | 1752 | | |
| President | | BB | New York NY | 1829 | 1842 | St.P.W. | 160 | 32.4 | 11 | 518 | | | |

**Mohegan (II):** Designer, Frank E. Kirby (Detroit MI); Delaware River Co. #285; Launched April 9, 1896

**Monohansett:** Launched March 8, 1862

**Nashua:** Joiner work, William Rowland; Cost $150,000

**Naugatuck:** Delaware River Co. #296; Launched July 6, 1898; 38 Staterooms, 126 Berths

**Newport:** John Englis #52; Launched Dec 3, 1864; Rebuilt, Barge 1890

**Naushon (II):** Designer, Bethlehem S. B. Corp.; Launched May 7, 1929; Passenger Capacity: (Day) 2000

**New Bedford:** Launched May 5, 1928

**New Hampshire:** Harlan & Hollingsworth #264; Launched January 16, 1892; 113 Staterooms (later 117), 62 Berths

**New Haven (III):** Launched May 5, 1907; Christened by Miss Sarah Long

**New Shoreham:** Launched April 20, 1901

**North Land:** Launched January 10, 1912

**North Star:** Launched May 7, 1901

**Old Colony (I):** John Englis #55; Launched August 8, 1865

**Old Colony (II):** Launched June 26, 1907; Mrs. Isabel Taylor Ball

**Old Dominion:** Designer, Herman Winter; Harlan & Hollingsworth #132; Launched February 24, 1872

**Pequot:** Cost $100,000

**Pequonnock:** Delaware River Co. #331; Launched February 21, 1906

**Penobscot:** Cost $200,000

**Pilgrim:** Designer, George Pierce; Launched July 22, 1882

**Plymouth:** Designer, George Peirce; Delaware Iron Shipbuilding & Engine Works #257; Cost $800,000; Joiner work, William Rowland; Launched April 3, 1890; Rebuilt, 1902 John N. Roberts; Joiner work, William Rowland

**Plymouth Rock:** Launched May 30, 1854

| Vessel Name | Registry Number | Radio Call | Ports Served | Engine Builder | Engine Type | Horse-power | Bore and Stroke | No. of Boilers | Pressure | Type |
|---|---|---|---|---|---|---|---|---|---|---|
| Mohegan (I) | | | NO | | | | | | | |
| **Mohegan (II)** | 92705 | KMRC | NL | DRI | TE | 1650 | 21, 34, 56, X 42 | 2 | 165 | SES |
| Monohansett | 16795 | | NB MV NA | NIW | VB | | 40 X 120 | 1 | | |
| Mount Hope | 92004 | KFBM | BR | | VB | | 46 X 120 | 2 | 50 | RT |
| **Nantucket (I)** | 130354 | KDJN | NB MV NA | PJ | VB | 745 | 48 X 120 | 1 | | |
| **Nantucket (II)** | 224501 | WBFZ | NB MV NA | BIW | TE | 1000 | 16, 26, 30, 30X24 | 2 | 200 | RT |
| Narragansett (I) | | | PR | | | 300 | | | | |
| Narragansett (II) | | | ST | DIW | VB | | 62 X 144 | | | |
| Narragansett (III) | 210653 | LCQF | None | | T | 4000 | | | | |
| **Nashua** | 130340 | | NB WH MV | ROH | COI | 2000 | 42, 78, X 124 | 4 | 100 | SES |
| **Naugatuck** | 127281 | KNQL | BP BI | DRI | TE | 1200 | 17, 31, 48, X 28 | 2 | | SES |
| Naushon (I) | 18286 | | NB MV | JEC | CH | | 34 X 96 | 1 | | |
| **Naushon (II)** | 228531 | WODS | NB MV NA | BSB | 2TE | 2400 | 16, 26, 30, X 30 | 2 | 200 | RT |
| Neptune | | | FR | | | | | | | |
| Nereus | 22099 | | FR | | | | | | | |
| **New Bedford** | 227565 | WBFY | NB MV NA | BSC | 2TE | 1200 | | | | |
| New Champion | 18574 | | HF | WPF | VB | 175 | | | | |
| New England (I) | | | HF | | | 120 | | 2 | | |
| **New England (II)** | 20464 | KWJH | BO | | TE | 400 | 26 X 26 | 2 | | RT |
| **New Hampshire** | 130581 | KLFC | ST NH NB | HH | TE | 2500 | 28, 45, 51, X 42 | 4 | 160 | SES |
| New Haven (I) | | | NH | AIW | VB | | 47 X 120 | | | |
| New Haven (II) | | | NH | | C | | 34x38 | | | |
| **New Haven (III)** | 204200 | KWDL | ST NB NL | DRI | | | | | | |
| New London | 641 | | PO NB NL | CHD | VD | | 34 X 30 | 1 | | RT |
| **New Shoreham** | 130934 | KRCH | PO BI | | C | 847 | 16.5, 41, X 30 | 2 | | |
| New York (I) | 18657 | | NH | | | | | | | |
| New York (II) | 223901 | MFNL | PO | | | 2680 | | | | |
| Newburgh | 130350 | KDJQ | PR | | | | | | | |
| Newport | 18221 | | FR BO NE | NIW | VB | | 85 X 144 | 4 | | |
| Niagara | 18577 | | BP | | | | | | | |
| Nimrod | | | BP | | VB | | 40x108 | | | |
| **Nobska** | 224501 | WBFZ | NB MV NA | BIW | TE | 1000 | 16, 26, 30, 30X24 | 2 | 200 | RT |
| **North Land** | 207282 | LBJT | BO PO YA | HH | TE | 4000 | 28.5, 46, 75, X 54 | 2 | | SES |
| **North Star** | 130924 | | BO PO YA | DRI | TE | 4200 | 25, 48, 75, X 54 | 6 | | SES |
| Northampton | 18190 | | NH | | | | | | | |
| Norwich | 18578 | | NO | JWS | TE | | 18, 27, 42, X 28 | | | |
| Nutmeg State | | | BR | | | | | | | |
| Oceanus | | | FR | EIW | | | 44 X 36 | | | |
| Old Colony (I) | 19009 | | FR NE | AIW | VB | | 80 X 144 | 2 | | |
| **Old Colony (II)** | 204528 | KWHQ | BO | QIW | T | 7500 | | 8 | 185 | SES |
| **Old Dominion** | 19350 | JLKN | PR BO | HH | VB | | 75 X 132 | 2 | | RT |
| Oliver Ellsworth | | | HF | | | | | | | |
| Oregon | | | PR NO | | | | | | | |
| Osceola | | | HF NL NA | | | | | | | |
| Osprey | 19097 | | PR | | | | | | | |
| **Owana** | 202692 | | NL MK | | | 425 | | | | |
| Pelican | 19995 | | PR | | | | | | | |
| Penguin | 9434 | | FR | | | | | | | |
| Penobscot | 150253 | JWDL | PR | AW | VB | 1200 | 58 X 144 | | | |
| **Pequonnock** | 202939 | KVGT | BP NB PO | DRI | TE | 1700 | 20 34, 56, X 42 | 4 | | SES |
| **Pequot** | 24449 | HSBD | PO NB ST NH | EIW | VD | 325 | 50 X 40 | 2 | | |
| Petrel | 19899 | | PR | | | | | | | |
| **Pilgrim** | 150280 | KBDK | FR | MIW | VB | 5300 | 110 X 168 | 12 | 50 | RT |
| **Plymouth** | 150502 | KHQS | PR FR | WAF | DIC | 5500 | 2- 47, 75, 81.5X99 | 8 | 170 | SES |
| Plymouth Rock | 20151 | | ST PR NL GO | | VB | | | 2 | | |
| President | | | PR | | | | | | | |

**Nashua:** Reboilered 1895, W & A Fletcher
**Naushon:** Speed 14-1/2 knots
**New England:** Speed 8-1/2 knots; converted 1931 to oil burning tanker; L 118 X B 31.4 X D 11.3, 341.24 Gross tons, 232 Net Tons
**New Hampshire:** Speed 14 knots; coal consumption per hour, 3 tons approx.; Reboilered 1929 with Return tube; 4-blade propeller (left hand) 13 ft. diam, 10 ft 6 ini pitch
**New Haven (II):** Reboilered New York Iron Works 1885
**New Shoreham:** Speed 14 knots; Rebuilt 1918
**Nobska:** Speed 14 mph.; Boilers, Babcock & Wilcox (Alert type); Return tube
**Old Colony (I):** Speed 14 knots; Engine from "Bay State"; Paddle wheels 36 ft. diam; Extensive Repairs, 1874 at Newport, Hull recaulked and substantial planking put on where needed to the water line. Then to New York for underwater work and general repairs to hull and joiner work. Hog frames renewed, and fastened with 40,000 spikes.

**Old Colony (II):** Speed 20 knots; coal consumption per 24 hours, 159 tons; Engine: Parsons Turbines constructed by I. P. Morris Co. (This was the first to be built.); Overhaul, 1913; Rebuilt, 1910 Wm. Cramp & Co.
**Old Dominion:** Radial wheels; Rewheeled 1890, W & A Fletcher with Morgan's patent iron feathering wheels with steel buckets. Converted 1910 into 3 masted schooner barge.
**Pequot:** Rebuilt 1883-84, Noank CT; Engine, Compound 28, 53 X 48; New boilers 1884, 2 Scotch; Converted to schooner 1923; L 22.2 X W 35.7 X D 14.3; 705 gross tons, 662 net tons
**Pilgrim:** Speed 14 mph (Maximum); Wheels, Stationary Buckets 40 ft. diam, 14 ft. width 2 ft. 2 in. depth; Reboilered 1901
**Plymouth:** Speed 16 knots; W & A Fletcher #153; Rebuilt 1905, Quintard Iron Works; 4 cyl.; double inclined compound 50, 75, 81,; 81 x 99., 5550 IHP; Reboilered 1920, Babcock & Wilcox RT's; Wheels: Feathering 30 ft. diam (12 curved steel buckets) 13 ft. width, 4 ft. depth
**Plymouth Rock:** Wheels: 37 ft. diam, 10 ft. width, 2 ft. depth (30 buckets)

| Vessel Name | Registry Number | Builder | Where Built | Year Built | Year Ret'd | Hull Type | Length | Beam | Depth | Gross Tons | Net Tons | Pass Cap'y | Freight Cap'y (cars) |
|---|---|---|---|---|---|---|---|---|---|---|---|---|---|
| Priscilla | 150666 | DRI | Chester PA | 1894 | 1938 | St.P.S. | 425.8 | 52.3 | 18.3 | 5292.27 | 2673.37 | 1500 | 67 |
| Providence (I) | | | Newport RI | 1823 | 1843 | St.P.W. | 100 | | | 135 | | | |
| Providence (II) | 19612 | WHW | New York NY | 1867 | 1901 | St.P.W. | 360 | 48 | 16.6 | 2962 | 2064 | | 40 |
| Providence (III) | 201732 | FRS | Quincy MA | 1905 | 1938 | St.P.S. | 379.4 | 50 | 18.6 | 4365.34 | 2502 | 1500 | 900 |
| Puritan | 150471 | DRI | Chester PA | 1888 | 1920 | St.P.S. | 420 | 52.5 | 21 | 4593 | 3075 | 1500 | 59 |
| Rhode Island (I) | | BB | New York NY | 1836 | 1850 | St.P.W. | 211 | 28 | 10 | 588 | | | |
| Rhode Island (II) | | HS | Greenpoint NY | 1873 | 1880 | St.P.W. | 325 | 45.6 | 15.6 | 2742 | | | |
| Rhode Island (III) | 110519 | RPS | Noank CT | 1882 | 1919 | St.P.W. | 332.2 | 46.2 | 16.4 | 2888.20 | 2386.72 | 600 | 70 |
| Richard Borden | 110174 | BX | Bulls Ferry NJ | 1874 | 1908 | St.P.W. | 203 | 33 | 10 | 785.35 | | | |
| Richard Peck | 110971 | HH | Wilmington DE | 1892 | | St.Sc.S. | 303.0 | 48 | 17.9 | 2906 | 1819 | 1000 | 80 |
| River Queen | 21455 | BCT | Keyport NJ | 1864 | 1911 | St.P.W. | 181 | 28.5 | 9 | 536.12 | 426 | | |
| Roger Williams | | | Brooklyn NY | 1845 | 1853 | St.P.W. | | | | 447 | | | |
| Rosalie | 126376 | BS | Pt. Jeff. NY | 1886 | 1922 | St.Sc.W. | 144.8 | 28.4 | 10 | 518.27 | 274.02 | | |
| Rosedale | 110329 | NS | Norfolk VA | 1877 | 1922 | St.P.W. | 216 | 34.2 | 10 | 928.65 | 677.88 | 1200 | 22 |
| Sankaty | 208399 | FRS | Quincy MA | 1911 | 1940 | St.Sc.S. | 187.5 | 38.2 | 11.3 | 677.93 | 342 | | |
| Santiago | 115662 | ROH | Chester PA | 1879 | 1924 | St.Sc.S. | 269 | 39.1 | 22.4 | 2358.78 | 1695.64 | | |
| Scout (Motorboat) | | | | | | | | | | | | | |
| Sea Gull | 22098 | | Mystic CT | 1863 | 1893 | St.Sc.W. | 147 | 33.1 | 12 | 346.51 | 200.37 | | |
| Seaboard | 115348 | HH | Wilmington DE | 1874 | | St.Sc.I. | 184.5 | 28.4 | 12.3 | 662.07 | 563.18 | | |
| Shaumpishuh | 23348 | JW | New York NY | 1852 | 1866 | St.P.W. | 116 | 42 | 10 | 414 | | | |
| Shinnecock | 116712 | HH | Wilmington DE | 1896 | 1947 | St.Sc.W | 234 | 35 | 14.3 | 1250 | 706 | | |
| Shore Line | 23349 | GG | Mystic CT | 1858 | 1890 | St.PDEFW | 125 | 34 | 11 | 400 | | | |
| South Shore | 203001 | FRS | Quincy MA | 1906 | 1928 | St.P.S. | 200 | 32.5 | 11.5 | 874 | 516 | | |
| Splendid | | SDC | New York NY | 1832 | 1856 | St.P.W. | 130 | 21 | 8 | 209 | | | |
| St. Johns | 115633 | | Wilmington DE | 1878 | | St.P.W. | 250 | 38 | 12.5 | 1098.03 | 667.03 | | |
| Stamford | 22430 | | Brooklyn NY | 1863 | 1900 | St.P.W. | 168 | 28 | 8 | 483 | 326 | | |
| State of Maine (I) | | BS | New York NY | 1848 | 1871 | St.P.W. | 236 | 32 | 11 | 806 | | | |
| State of Maine (II) | 115856 | NES | Bath ME | 1882 | 1925 | St.P.W. | 241 | 37.1 | 14.6 | 1410 | | | |
| State of New York | 22571 | CR | Greenpoint NY | 1867 | 1898 | St.P.W. | 286 | 36 | 9.6 | 1417.03 | 1047 | 800 | |
| Stonington | 23371 | JS | New York NY | 1866 | 1890 | St.P.W. | 253 | 40 | 15 | 1633 | 1246 | | |
| Sunshine | 22573 | | East Haddam CT | 1864 | 1864 | St.P.W. | 156 | 26 | 9.2 | 420 | | | |
| Superior | | SDC | New York NY | 1831 | 1859 | St.P.W. | 130 | 21 | 7.6 | 194 | | | |
| Surprise | 125258 | JEV | Williamsb'g NY | 1874 | 1907 | St.Sc.W. | 188 | 33.4 | 13.5 | 821 | 433 | 50 | 107 |
| Telegraph (I) | | LS | New York NY | 1832 | 1870 | St.P.W. | 120 | 20 | 8 | 171 | | | |
| Telegraph (II) | | LS | New York NY | 1837 | 1870 | St.P.W. | 147.8 | 21.8 | 7.1 | 243 | | | |
| Tennessee | 145783 | HH | Wilmington DE | 1898 | 1938 | St.Sc.S. | 245 | 38 | 15.8 | 1240 | 743 | | |
| Thames River | 24870 | HS | Greenpoint NY | 1871 | 1909 | StPDEFW | 183.2 | 39.7 | 13 | 950.14 | 882.10 | | |
| Thetis | 24449 | JBV | New York NY | 1865 | 1943 | St.Sc.W. | 213 | 35 | 15 | 1360 | | | |
| Tockwogh | 145523 | SSY | Baltimore MD | 1889 | 1892 | St.P.W. | 166 | 30 | 8.6 | 457.38 | 343.82 | | |
| Transford II | 223068 | BSB | Elizabeth NJ | 1920 | 1939 | St.Sc.S. | 245 | 40.1 | 17.7 | 1625 | 962 | | |
| Traveler | 24269 | | New York NY | 1845 | 1873 | St.P.W. | 225 | 29 | 9.6 | 584 | 494 | | |
| Tremont | 145336 | JE | Greenpoint NY | 1883 | 1904 | St.P.W. | 260 | 37 | 12.3 | 1427.67 | 1023.68 | | |
| Uncatena | 25351 | PS | Wilmington DE | 1902 | 1937 | St.P.S. | 178 | 31 | 12 | 652.66 | 370 | | |
| Union | 25052 | EW | Greenpoint NY | 1854 | 1854 | StPDEFW | | | | 244 | | | |
| United States | | | New York NY | 1821 | 1849 | St.P.W. | | | | 180 | | | |
| Virginia | 25955 | HH | Wilmington DE | 1879 | 1927 | St.P.I. | 251 | 34.7 | 7.9 | 990 | 665 | | |
| Vulcan | 25674 | | New York NY | 1842 | 1908 | St.Sc.W. | 121.6 | 23 | 7.9 | 250 | 223 | | |
| Washington | | | New York NY | 1825 | 1831 | St.P.W. | 137 | 30.9 | 10 | 339 | | | |
| Water Witch | | BB | New York NY | 1831 | 1862 | St.P.W. | 134.2 | 21.1 | 7.5 | 207 | | | |
| Waterbury | 15261 | HH | Wilmington DE | 1867 | 1891 | St.P.W. | 225 | 34 | 11 | 1098 | 948 | | |
| Weetamoe | 26274 | | Fall River MA | 1859 | 1907 | StPDEFW | | | | 79 | | | |
| William G. Payne | 81809 | HH | Wilmington DE | 1902 | 1953 | St.P.S. | 243.3 | 36.9 | 14.6 | 1310 | 854 | 1736 | 36 |
| William T. Hart | 80866 | NL | Philadelphia PA | 1881 | 1910 | StPDEFI | 281 | 42 | 10.4 | 971.05 | 922.50 | | |
| Winifred | 206380 | | Islip NY | 1909 | 1954 | Ga.Sc.W. | 44.9 | 13 | 5 | 14 | 9 | | |
| Winthrop | 81141 | | Bath ME | 1887 | | St.Sc.W. | 195.2 | 38.8 | 23.3 | 1442.87 | 1019.34 | | |
| Worcester | | | New York NY | 1841 | 1861 | St.P.W. | 219 | 28.6 | 10 | 605 | | | |
| Yale | 204047 | ROH | Chester PA | 1907 | 1949 | St.Sc.S. | 376 | 61.3 | 20.2 | 3737 | 2317 | | |

**Priscilla:** Designer, George Peirce; Delaware Iron Shipbldg & Eng. Works #270; Joiner work, Wm. Rowland; Cost $1,500,000; Launched Aug. 10, 1893

**Providence (II):** Cost $800,000; Launched July 28, 1866

**Providence (III):** Fore River Shipyards #115; Launched July 16, 1904

**Rosedale:** Launched May 19, 1877; 1 Stateroom

**Rhode Island (I):** Lengthened 1845, L 286 X B 28 X D 10.1; 818.7 Gross Tons. A suite of staterooms added to upper deck in 1843.

**Rhode Island (III):** 165 Staterooms, 126 Berths

**Richard Peck:** Designer, A. Cary Smith; Harlan & Hollingsworth #265; Launched April 28, 1892; 113 Staterooms (with 210 Berths), 153 Berths in cabins

**Sankaty:** Launched February 2, 1911; Rebuilt 1929 Tebo Yacht Basin Co.

**Santiago:** John Roach & Sons #186; Launched March 22, 1879

**Seaboard:** Harlan & Hollingsworth #147; Cost $72,852; Launched November 28, 1874; Retrofit: Staterooms added; Rebuilt, 1934 Motor Barge; Cargo: Oil  L 184.5 X W 28.2 X D 12.3; 514 Gross Tons, 390 Net Tons

**Stonington:** 177 Staterooms, 381 Berths

**Tennessee:** Launched July 9, 1898; Cost $250,000; Christened by Miss Henrietta Hoffman

**Tremont:** John Englis #87; Launched March 1, 1883

**Uncatena:** Launched June 25 1902; Pusey & Jones #898

**Virginia:** Harlan & Hollingsworth #171; Launched October 15, 1878; Cost $211,479

**Yale:** John Englis #105; Launched December 1, 1906

| Vessel Name | Registry Number | Radio Call | Ports Served | Engine Builder | Engine Type | Horse-power | Bore and Stroke | No. of Boilers | Pressure | Type |
|---|---|---|---|---|---|---|---|---|---|---|
| Priscilla | 150666 | KLWJ | FR PR | WAF | DIC | 8500 | 2- 95, 51, X 132 | 10 | 150 | SES |
| Providence (I) | | | | | | | | | | |
| Providence (II) | 19612 | HPNS | BR FR | EIW | VB | 2900 | 110 X 144 | 3 | | |
| Providence (III) | 201732 | KTQP | PR FR | FRS | DIC | 6500 | 44, 83, X 108 | 6 | | WT |
| Puritan | 150471 | KGJQ | FR BO | WAF | CVB | 1500 | 75, 110 X 108 | 8 | 110 | |
| Rhode Island (I) | | | PR ST | AIW | CH | 350 | 60 X 132 | 2 | | |
| Rhode Island (II) | | | PR | MIW | VB | | 90 X 168 | | | |
| Rhode Island (III) | 110519 | | PR FR | MIW | CVB | 800 | 90 X 168 | | | |
| Richard Borden | 110174 | | FR PR | BX | VB | 1200 | 50 X 144 | 2 | | |
| Richard Peck | 110971 | KLGF | NH NO BP | HH | TE | 4200 | 24, 38, 60, X 30 | 6 | 160 | SES |
| River Queen | 21455 | HQJS | NA NB | | VB | 400 | | | | |
| Roger Williams | | | | | | | | | | |
| Rosalie | 126376 | KDMB | PR NL NO | NL | C | 500 | 20, 34, X 26 | | | |
| Rosedale | 110329 | | BP | JBX | VB | 800 | 50 X 144 | 2 | 35 | |
| Sankaty | 208399 | LBTK | MB MV NA | FRS | TE | 1460 | 16, 25, 42, X 27 | 4 | | WT |
| Santiago | 115662 | JTKB | PR | ROH | C | 1376 | 36, 68, X 54 | 4 | | |
| Scout (Motorboat) | | | NB FA | | | | | | | |
| Sea Gull | 22098 | HQMN | FR | | | 999HP | | | | |
| Seaboard | 115348 | JQRK | PO BO BP | HH | S | 693 | 34 X 42 | 1 | | |
| Shaumpishuh | 23348 | | SA LY | | | | | | | |
| Shinnecock | 116712 | | PR | NE | C | 1600 | 28, 56, X 102 | 4 | 170 | WT |
| Shore Line | 23349 | JBVW | | | | 170 | | | | |
| South Shore | 203001 | KVHF | MV | | | 1200 | | | | |
| Splendid | | | NH | | VB | | 37 X 84 | | | |
| St. Johns | 115633 | JTDQ | | | VB | | | | | |
| Stamford | 22430 | | | | VB | | | | | |
| State of Maine (I) | | | FR | | VB | | 54 X 132 | | | |
| State of Maine (II) | 115856 | JWGK | | | | | | | | |
| State of New York | 22571 | HQWP | | CR | VB | | 65 X 144 | 2 | | |
| Stonington | 23371 | JBWH | ST | FHC | VB | 800 | 62 X 144 | 2 | | |
| Sunshine | 22573 | | HF | | | | | | | |
| Superior | | | NH | | VB | | 36 X 96 | | | |
| Surprise | 125258 | JPKH | PR | | | | | | | |
| Telegraph (I) | | | NB NA | CH | | 160 | | | | |
| Telegraph (II) | | | NH | | | | | | | |
| Tennessee | 145783 | WOJT | PO BO FR | HH | 2TE | 2100 | 18, 28, 45, X 30 | 4 | 160 | SES |
| Thames River | 24870 | | NL GO | MIW | VB | 250 | 37 X 144 | 2 | | |
| Thetis | 24449 | HSBD | FR | EIW | VDA | | 50 X 40 | | | |
| Tockwogh | 145523 | | WI NE | | VB | 500 | | | | |
| Transford II | 223068 | | BA PR | | 2 TE | 700 | | | | |
| Traveler | 24269 | | HF NO | | | | | | | |
| Tremont | 145336 | | PR | QIW | VB | | 56 X 144 | 1 | 45 | RT |
| Uncatena | 25351 | KRWJ | NB MV NA | PS | VB | 1000 | 42 X 120 | 2 | | RT |
| Union | 25052 | | NB FH | | | | | | | |
| Virginia | 25955 | | PO | HH | VB | 800 | 60 X 132 | | | |
| Vulcan | 25674 | | BP | | | | | | | |
| Washington | | | PR | | | | | | | |
| Water Witch | | | HF NL | | | | | | | |
| Waterbury | 15261 | | BR HT | HH | VB | | 50 X 144 | | | |
| Weetamoe | 26274 | | NB FH | | | | | | | |
| William G. Payne | 81809 | | BP | HH | IC | 2000 | 35 X 72 | 4 | 140 | RT |
| William T. Hart | 80866 | | NB FL | | 2 H | | 46 X 96 | | | |
| Winifred | 206380 | | NB FH | | | 25 | | | | |
| Winthrop | 81141 | KDAL | PO | | | | | | | |
| Worcester | | | NO | | | | | | | |
| Yale | 204047 | KWBR | BO | WAF | T | 10500 | NA | 12 | | RT |

**Port Abbreviations:**

| | | | |
|---|---|---|---|
| BR | Bay Ridge NY | PR | Providence RI |
| BI | Block Island NY | NP | Newport RI |
| FL | Fishkill NY | WI | Wickford RI |
| HR | Harlem River NY | AY | Allyn's Point Ct |
| NB | Newberg NY | BP | Bridgeport CT |
| OP | Oak Point NY | GO | Groton Ct |
| OY | Oyster Bay NY | LY | Lyme CT |
| MK | Montauk NY | HF | Hartford CT |
| BO | Boston MA | MY | Mystic CT |
| NB | New Bedford MA | NH | New Haven CT |
| FA | Fairhaven MA | NL | New London CT |
| FR | Fall River MA | NO | Norwich CT |
| MV | Martha's Vineyard MA | SA | Saybrook CT |
| NA | Nantucket MA | ST | Stonington CT |
| WO | Woods Hole MA | WP | Wilson's Point CT |
| PO | Portland ME | JC | Jersey City NJ |

**Priscilla:** Speed 21 mph (Maximum); W & A Fletcher #270; coal consumption per hour, 8 tons approx.; Feathering wheels 35 ft. diam, 14 ft. width, 5 ft. depth. Reboilered 1923, 8 Water Tube

**Providence (II):** Wheels, 38 ft. 8 in. diam, 12 ft. width, 4 ft depth

**Rhode Island (II):** Wheels: 24 ft. diam, 11 ft. width, 30 in. depth

**Rhode Island (III):** Speed 16-1/2 mph (Max); Engine from Rhode Island (II) 1872; New engine in 1890, Morgan Iron Works, Compound Beam; 64, 84 X 144, 4000 IHP; Boilers: 5 (3 double ended, 2 single ended), 100 psi.; Radial paddle wheels 34 ft. diam, 6.8 ft width, 28 in. depth.

**Richard Borden:** Designer, Samuel Sneeden; Baxter's Shipyard, Bulls Ferry NJ

**Richard Peck:** Speed 18 mph (Max); coal consumption 4 tons/hr.; Reboilered 1925, B&W 4 Water Tube; 2 Propellers 10 ft. 6 in. diam, 15 ft. 6 in. pitch

**Santiago:** Speed 13 Knots

**Seaboard:** Re-engined 1934, Worthington Diesel 450 hp

**Stonington:** Engine, 1872 new Cylinder of 72 in.

**Yale:** Speed 22.4 knots; Engines, W & A Fletcher 3 Parsons Turbines; Converted to oil 1910

# The NYNH&H Harbor Fleet

## NYNH&H Transfers (Tugboats)

| Vessel Name | Registry Number | Builder | Where Built | Year Built | Year Ret'd | Hull Type | Length | Beam | Depth | Gross Tons | Net Tons | Radio Call | Ports |
|---|---|---|---|---|---|---|---|---|---|---|---|---|---|
| Transfer 1 | 145167 | | Phila. PA | 1877 | 1924 | St.Sc.W. | 94 | 21.3 | 10.4 | 136.16 | 68.08 | | NH |
| Transfer 2 | 145218 | NL | Phila. PA | 1880 | 1945 | St.Sc.I. | 92.2 | 22 | 11 | 101.13 | 50.57 | | NH |
| Transfer 3 | 145426 | NL | Phila. PA | 1886 | 1948 | St.Sc.I. | 92.7 | 22 | 10 | 130 | 65 | | NH |
| Transfer 4 | 85637 | NL | Phila. PA | 1880 | 1928 | St.Sc.I. | 92.3 | 21 | 8.8 | 102.75 | 51.38 | | NH |
| Transfer 5 | 145475 | | Wilmington DE | 1888 | 1936 | St.Sc.I. | 91.1 | 20 | 9.5 | 142 | 71 | | NH |
| Transfer 6 | 145476 | | Wilmington DE | 1888 | 1941 | St.Sc.I. | 91.1 | 20 | 9.5 | 142 | 71 | | NH |
| Transfer 7 | 145581 | | E'port NJ | 1891 | 1950 | St.Sc.I. | 90.1 | 22.2 | 10.5 | 129.69 | 64.85 | | NH HR |
| Transfer 8 | 145585 | | E'port NJ | 1891 | 1950 | St.Sc.I. | 90.1 | 22.2 | 10.5 | 131.23 | 65.62 | | NH HR |
| Transfer 9 | 145587 | | E'port NJ | 1891 | 1945 | StScl.Lgt | 101.7 | 29 | 10.9 | 196.84 | 98.42 | | NH OP |
| Transfer 10 | 130444 | HH | Wilmington DE | 1888 | 1950 | St.Sc.I. | 114 | 23.6 | 11.6 | 217 | 108 | KGLD | NH HR |
| Transfer 11 | 145764 | PJ | Wilmington DE | 1898 | 1955 | St.Sc.S. | 110 | 25 | 14 | 248 | 109 | | NH OP |
| Transfer 12 | 145770 | PJ | Wilmington DE | 1898 | 1953 | St.Sc.S. | 110 | 25 | 14 | 249 | 110 | | NH OP |
| Transfer 13 | 145837 | BIW | Bath ME | 1900 | 1953 | St.Sc.S. | 119.9 | 26.1 | 15.8 | 322 | 189 | | NH |
| Transfer 14 | 145839 | | Bath ME | 1900 | | St.Sc.S. | 120 | 26 | 15.8 | 322 | 189 | | NH OP |
| Transfer 15 | 145837 | BIW | Bath ME | 1900 | 1953 | St.Sc.S. | 119.9 | 26.1 | 15.8 | 322 | 189 | | MH HR |
| Transfer 16 | 200761 | WMC | Phila. PA | 1904 | 1959 | St.Sc.S. | 112 | 26.2 | 14 | 268 | 182 | KLBB | NH BR |
| Transfer 17 | 200799 | WMC | Phila. PA | 1904 | 1954 | St.Sc.S. | 112 | 26.2 | 14 | 268 | 182 | KTBJ | NH BR |
| Transfer 18 | 200844 | WMC | Phila. PA | 1904 | 1955 | St.Sc.S. | 112 | 26.2 | 14 | 268 | 182 | KTBV | NH HR |
| Transfer 19 | 202631 | WMC | Phila. PA | 1905 | 1959 | St.Sc.S. | 112 | 26.2 | 14 | 270 | 183 | KVDB | NH |
| Transfer 20 | 202634 | WMC | Phila. PA | 1905 | 1957 | St.Sc.S. | 112 | 26.2 | 14 | 270 | 183 | KVDC | NH BR |
| Transfer 21 | 204859 | FRS | Quincy MA | 1908 | 1959 | St.Sc.S. | 110.9 | 27.9 | 13.5 | 267.79 | 155 | | NH |
| Transfer 22 | 206133 | FRS | Quincy MA | 1909 | | St.Sc.S. | 110.9 | 27.6 | 13.5 | 267 | 155 | | NH HR |
| Transfer 23 | 266145 | | Oyster Bay NY | 1953 | | DE.Sc.S | 100.3 | 27 | 12.6 | 262 | 178 | | NH HR |
| Transfer 24 | 265688 | | Oyster Bay NY | 1953 | | | 106 | 26 | 14 | 262 | 178 | | NH HR |
| Dalzell 1 | 273952 | | Camden NJ | 1957 | | D.Sc.S. | 96.3 | 26.7 | 13.1 | 214 | 146 | | HR OP JV |
| Dalzell 2 | 274443 | | Camden NJ | 1957 | | D.Sc.S. | 96.3 | 26.7 | 13.1 | 214 | 146 | | HR OP JV |
| Dalzell 3 | 274845 | | Camden NJ | 1957 | | D.Sc.D. | 96.3 | 27.7 | 13.1 | 214 | 146 | | HR OP JV |

## Barges, scows and other craft

| Vessel Name | Year Built | Year Ret'd | Hull Type | Ports |
|---|---|---|---|---|
| Americus | | 1898 | Scow, W. | |
| NH 1 | | | Car Fl.W. | HR |
| NH 2 | | 1956 | Car Fl.W. | HR |
| NH 3 | | 1956 | Car Fl.W. | HR |
| NH 3 | | 1956 | Car Fl.W. | HR |
| NH 4 | | 1956 | Car Fl.W. | HR |
| NH 4 | | 1956 | Car Fl.W. | HR |
| NH 5 | | 1956 | Car Fl.W. | HR |
| NH 6 | | 1956 | Car Fl.W. | HR |
| NH 7 | | 1949 | Car Fl.W. | HR |
| NH 7 | | 1949 | Car Fl.W. | HR |
| NH 8 | | 1949 | Car Fl.W. | HR |
| NH 8 | | 1949 | Car Fl.W. | HR |
| NH 10 | | 1949 | Car Fl.W. | HR |
| NH 11 | | 1954 | Car Fl.W. | HR |
| NH 12 | | 1953 | Car Fl.W. | HR |
| NH 14 | | 1953 | Car Fl.W. | HR |
| NH 15 | | 1953 | Car Fl.W. | HR |
| NH 16 | | 1953 | Car Fl.W. | HR |
| NH 18 | | | | |
| NH 40 | | 1952 | Car Fl. | OP |
| NH 41 | | 1952 | Car Fl. | OP |
| NH 42 | | 1949 | Car Fl. | HR |
| NH 43 | | 1952 | Car Fl. | OP |
| NH 44 | | 1949 | Car Fl. | HR |
| NH 45 | | | | |
| NH 46 | | 1953 | Car Fl. | HR |
| NH 47 | | 1953 | Car Fl. | HR |
| NH 48 | | 1953 | Car Fl. | HR |
| NH 49 | | 1953 | Car Fl. | HR |
| NH 50 | | | | HR |
| NH 52 | | 1954 | Car Fl. | HR |
| NH 53 | | 1953 | Car Fl. | HR |
| NH 55 | | 1954 | Car Fl. | HR |
| NH 56 | | 1954 | Car Fl. | HR |
| NH 57 | | 1953 | Car Fl. | HR |
| NH 58 | | 1954 | Car Fl. | HR |
| NH 59 | | | | |
| NH 60 | | | | |
| NH 61 | | | | |
| NH 62 | | | | |
| NH 63 | | | | |
| NH 71 | 1957 | | Bg. | |
| NH 72 | 1957 | | Bg. | |
| NH 80 | | 1953 | Car Fl.S. | HR |
| NH 81 | | 1953 | Car Fl.S. | HR |
| NH 82 | | 1953 | Car Fl.S. | HR |
| NH 83 | | 1953 | Car Fl.S. | HR |
| NH 84 | | 1954 | Car Fl.S. | HR |
| NH 85 | | 1954 | Car Fl.S. | HR |
| NH 101 | 1906 | | Cov.Bg.W. | HR |
| NH 102 | 1906 | 1952 | Cov.Bg.W. | NH |
| NH 103 | 1906 | | Cov.Bg.W. | HR |
| NH 104 | 1906 | | Cov.Bg.W. | HR |
| NH 105 | 1907 | | Cov.Bg.W. | HR |
| NH 106 | 1907 | 1952 | Cov.Bg.W. | HR |
| NH 108 | 1907 | | Cov.Bg.W. | HR |
| NH 107 | 1907 | | Lgt.W. | HR |
| NH 109 | 1907 | | Cov.Bg.W. | HR |
| NH 110 | 1907 | 1952 | Cov.Bg.W. | HR |
| NH 111 | 1912 | 1953 | Cov.Bg.W. | HR |
| NH 112 | 1907 | 1952 | Cov.Bg.W. | HR |
| NH 113 | 1912 | 1953 | Cov.Bg.W. | HR |
| NH 114 | 1907 | 1952 | Cov.Bg.W. | HR |
| NH 115 | 1912 | 1952 | Cov.Bg.W. | HR |
| NH 116 | 1907 | 1952 | Cov.Bg.W. | HR |
| NH 117 | 1912 | 1953 | Lgt.W. | HR |
| NH 118 | 1907 | | Cov.Bg.W. | HR |
| NH 119 | 1912 | 1953 | Cov.Bg.W. | HR |
| NH 120 | 1907 | 1953 | Cov.Bg.W. | HR |
| NH 121 | 1912 | 1952 | Cov.Bg.W. | HR |
| NH 122 | 1907 | 1953 | Cov.Bg.W. | HR |
| NH 123 | 1913 | | Cov.Bg.W. | HR |
| NH 124 | 1907 | 1953 | Cov.Bg.W. | HR |
| NH 125 | 1913 | 1952 | Cov.Bg.W. | HR |
| NH 126 | 1907 | 1952 | Cov.Bg.W. | HR |
| NH 128 | | 1952 | Cov.Bg. | HR |
| NH 129 | | 1953 | Cov.Bg. | HR |
| NH 130 | | 1953 | Cov.Bg. | HR |
| NH 131 | | 1952 | Scow | HR |
| NH 132 | | 1953 | Cov.Bg. | HR |
| NH 133 | | 1952 | Scow | HR |
| NH 134 | | | | |
| NH 135 | | 1952 | Scow | HR |
| NH 137 | | 1954 | Lgt. | HR |
| NH 142 | | 1954 | Car Fl. | HR |
| NH 143 | | 1953 | GaHos.Lt. | HR |
| NH 144 | | 1954 | Car Fl. | HR |

# NYNH&H Tug Engines

| Vessel Name | Registry Number | Engine Type | HP | Bore & Stroke | Note |
|---|---|---|---|---|---|
| Transfer 1 | 145167 | | 125 | 26 X 26 | (1) |
| Transfer 2 | 145218 | | 350 | 26 X 30 | (2) |
| Transfer 3 | 145426 | C | 500 | 20, 34 X 26 | |
| Transfer 4 | 85637 | | | 30 X 30 | (3) |
| Transfer 5 | 145475 | C | 600 | 22, 40 X 26 | (4) |
| Transfer 6 | 145476 | C | 600 | 22, 40 X 26 | (5) |
| Transfer 7 | 145581 | C | 600 | 20, 40 X 28 | |
| Transfer 8 | 145585 | C | 600 | 20, 40 X 28 | |
| Transfer 9 | 145587 | C | 600 | 20, 40 X 28 | |
| Transfer 10 | 130444 | C | 600 | 22,40 X 26 | (6) |
| Transfer 11 | 145764 | C | 750 | 20, 40 X 28 | |
| Transfer 12 | 145770 | C | 750 | 20, 40 X 28 | |
| Transfer 13 | 145837 | C | 1500 | 22, 48 X 36 | (7) |
| Transfer 14 | 145839 | C | | 22, 48 X 36 | |
| Transfer 15 | 145837 | C | 1500 | 22, 48 X 36 | (8) |
| Transfer 16 | 200761 | C | 1000 | 20, 44 X 30 | |
| Transfer 17 | 200799 | C | 1000 | 20, 44 X 30 | |
| Transfer 18 | 200844 | C | 1000 | 20, 44 X 30 | |
| Transfer 19 | 202631 | C | 1000 | 20, 44 X 30 | |
| Transfer 20 | 202634 | C | 1000 | 20, 44 X 30 | |
| Transfer 21 | 204859 | | 1000 | | (9) |
| Transfer 22 | 206133 | C | 1000 | 20, 44 X 30 | (10) |
| Transfer 23 | 266145 | | 1350 | | (11) |
| Transfer 24 | 265688 | | | | (12) |
| Dalzell 1 | 273952 | DE | 1800 | | (13) |
| Dalzell 2 | 274443 | | 1800 | | (14) |
| Dalzell 3 | 274845 | | 1800 | | (15) |

## Tugboat Notes

| | | |
|---|---|---|
| 1 | (b) | Charles McAllister |
| 2 | (b) | Fred'k Lenning |
| | (c) | Hercules |
| 3 | (a) | George W. Watrous |
| | (c) | Aquadon |
| 4 | (b) | Red Ash No. 2 |
| 5 | (b) | Colonel |
| 6 | (a) | New England Terminal No. 3 |
| | (b) | Intrepid |
| 7 | (b) | Transfer 15 |
| 8 | (a) | Transfer 13 |
| 9 | (b) | USS Transfer 21 |
| | (c) | Molosse (French) |
| 10 | (b) | USS Transfer 22 |
| | (c) | New York Marine No. 6 |
| | (d) | New York Central No. 15 |
| 11 | (a) | Bumble Bee |
| 12 | (a) | Cordelia |
| 13 | (b) | Lacey 1 |
| | (c) | David McAllister |
| 14 | (b) | Lacey 2 |
| | (c) | Michael J. McAllister |
| 15 | (b) | Lacey 3 |
| | (c) | Timothy McAllister |

(1) Approx. tonnage 200
Cargo Capacity 20,000 cu ft

Tug Hulls:

| | |
|---|---|
| 1 | William Cramp & Sons No: 324 |
| 2 | William Cramp & Sons No: 325 |
| 3 | William Cramp & Sons No: 337 |

*Cordelia*, later *Transfer 24*, on the way to her next assignment shortly after her arrival in 1953.

| Vessel Name | Year Built | Year Ret'd | Hull Type | Ports |
|---|---|---|---|---|
| NH 145 | | 1954 | Lgt. | HR |
| NH 146 | | 1953 | Cov.Bg. | HR |
| NH 147 | | 1954 | Lgt. | HR |
| NH 148 | | | | |
| NH 149 | | 1952 | Ga.Hos.Lt | HR |
| NH 150 | | 1952 | Cov.Bg. | HR |
| NH 154 | | 1952 | Cov.Bg. | HR |
| NH 157 | | 1952 | Ga.Hos.Lt | HR |
| NH 159 | | | | HR |
| NH 161 | | 1954 | Lgt. | HR |
| NH 163 | | 1954 | Lgt. | HR |
| NH 165 | | | | HR |
| NH 167 | 1953 | 1952 | Ga.Hos.Lt | HR |
| NH 200 | 1953 | | Cov.Bg. | HR |
| NH 201 | 1953 | | Cov.Bg. | HR |
| NH 203 | 1953 | | | HR |
| NH 204 | 1953 | | | HR |
| NH 205 | 1953 | | | HR |
| NH 206 | 1954 | | | HR |
| NH 207 | 1954 | | | HR |
| NH 300 | 1953 | | Lgt.S. | HR |
| NH 301 | 1953 | | | HR |
| NH 302 | | | | HR |
| NH 303 | 1954 | | Lgt.S. | HR |
| NH 304 | 1954 | | | HR |
| NH 305 | 1954 | | | HR |
| NH 306 | 1954 | | | HR |
| NH M-34 | | 1949 | Car Fl. | HR |
| NH M-37 | | 1949 | Car Fl. | HR |

# Hartford & New York Trans. Co. Tugs and Barges

| Vessel Name | Registry Number | Builder | Where Built | Year Built | Year Ret'd | Hull Type | Length | Beam | Depth | Gross Tons | Net Tons | Radio Call | Ports |
|---|---|---|---|---|---|---|---|---|---|---|---|---|---|
| A. M. Smith | 105021 | | Phila. PA | 1871 | 1930 | St.Sc.W. | 69.4 | 16.4 | 6 | 36.09 | 18.5 | | HF |
| Admiral Farragut | 562 | | Phila. PA | 1862 | | St.Sc.W. | 69.2 | 16.5 | 7.5 | 31.39 | 20.51 | | HF |
| Comet | 208083 | | Baltimore MD | 1910 | 1951 | St.Sc.S. | 72.3 | 20 | 9.6 | 104 | 70 | WHPG | HF |
| J. Warren Coulston | 75381 | | | 1872 | 1874 | St.Sc. | | | | | | | HF |
| Luther C. Ward | 140596 | | Newburgh NY | 1882 | 1914 | St.Sc. | 98 | 21.5 | 9.8 | 106 | 53 | KDPC | HF |
| M. R. Brazos | 90506 | | Hartford CT | 1873 | | St.Sc.W. | 95 | 20 | 8.8 | 86.37 | 43.19 | | HF |
| Mabel | 91470 | NL | Phila. PA | 1882 | 1941 | St.Sc.W. | 82.9 | 20 | 8.6 | 84.02 | 42.01 | | HF |
| Onrust | 202812 | | Phila. PA | 1906 | 1939 | St.Sc.S. | 72.5 | 19.1 | 8.4 | 95 | 64 | | HF |
| Owl | | | | | | St.Sc. | | | | | | | HF |
| Raymond | 202779 | | Hartford CT | 1906 | 1936 | St.Sc.W. | 51.7 | 15 | 5.5 | 33 | 22 | | HF |
| Sachem | 116994 | | Baltimore MD | 1900 | | St.Sc.S. | 110.3 | 24 | 10 | 195 | 132 | | HF |
| Spartan | 210272 | | Baltimore MD | 1912 | | St.Sc.S. | 105.9 | 25.1 | 11.1 | 226 | 154 | LCMJ | HF |
| E. S. Tyler Jr. | 36731 | | Hartford CT | 1881 | | Derr.Bg | 129.6 | 32 | 9.2 | 299.78 | 284.80 | | HF |
| Frank Jones | 37489 | | Hartford CT | 1880 | | Barge | 127.5 | 32.5 | 8.8 | 274 | 260 | | HF |
| George E. Hatch | 39592 | | | | | Barge | 296.34 | | | | | | HF |
| Gracie E. Williams | 39550 | | Hartford CT | 1873 | | Barge | | | | 175.23 | 166.47 | | HF |
| Josie C. Williams | | | | | | Barge | 177.38 | | | | | | HF |
| Nauticus | 52900 | | Rocky Hill CT | 1874 | | Barge | | | | 212.23 | 201.96 | | HF |
| Seventy-six | 57806 | | Rocky Hill CT | 1878 | | Barge | | | | 268 | 255 | | HF |
| H.& N.Y.T.Co.No. 1 | 42666 | | Hartford CT | 1882 | | Barge | | | | 243.56 | 231.39 | | HF |
| H.& N.Y.T.Co.No. 2 | 42671 | | Hartford CT | 1882 | | Barge | | | | 270 | 258 | | HF |
| H.& N.Y.T.Co.No. 3 | 42676 | | Hartford CT | 1883 | | Barge | 123.5 | 28.5 | 7.4 | 213 | 202 | | HF |
| H.& N.Y.T.Co.No. 4 | 42708 | | Hartford CT | 1889 | | Barge | 136.8 | 33.5 | 12.5 | 369 | 351 | | HF |
| H.& N.Y.T.Co.No. 5 | 42720 | | Hartford CT | 1890 | | Barge | 154 | 33.7 | 9.7 | 513 | 488 | | HF |
| H.& N.Y.T.Co.No. 6 | 42727 | | Hartford CT | 1891 | | Barge | 154 | 33.7 | 9.7 | 510 | 487 | | HF |
| H.& N.Y.T.Co.No. 7 | 42728 | | Gildersl'v CT | 1891 | | Barge | 154 | 33.7 | 9.7 | 513 | 488 | | HF |
| H.& N.Y.T.Co.No. 8 | 42733 | | Gildersl'v CT | 1892 | | Barge | 157 | 36.6 | 9.7 | 526 | 500 | | HF |
| H.& N.Y.T.Co.No. 9 | 42737 | | Hartford CT | 1893 | | Barge | | | | 66 | 63 | | HF |
| H.& N.Y.T.Co.No.10 | 42752 | | Gildersl'v CT | 1896 | | Barge | 157 | 33.8 | 10 | 525 | 499 | | HF |
| H.& N.Y.T.Co.No.11 | 42764 | | Gildersl'v CT | 1896 | | Barge | 182.4 | 33.9 | 10 | 575 | 542 | | HF |
| H.& N.Y.T.Co.No.12 | 42826 | | Hartford CT | 1898 | | Barge | | | | 72 | 63 | | HF |
| H.& N.Y.T.Co.No.14 | 42795 | | Hartford CT | 1898 | | Barge | 132 | 30.6 | 9.2 | 301 | 247 | | HF |
| H.& N.Y.T.Co.No.15 | 42827 | | Hartford CT | 1900 | | Barge | 181.2 | 37.2 | 10.2 | 652 | 620 | | HF |
| H.& N.Y.T.Co.No.16 | 42844 | | Hartford CT | 1900 | | Barge | 182 | 37.5 | 12.7 | 689 | 655 | | HF |
| H.& N.Y.T.Co.No.17 | 42867 | | Hartford CT | 1901 | | Barge | 137 | 33 | 12.5 | 477 | 447 | | HF |
| H.& N.Y.T.Co.No.18 | 42885 | | Hartford CT | 1903 | | Barge | 127.5 | 32.8 | 11 | 340 | 299 | | HF |
| H.& N.Y.T.Co.No.19 | 162158 | | Hartford CT | 1904 | | Barge | 146.4 | 32.7 | 12.6 | 513 | 479 | | HF |
| H.& N.Y.T.Co.No.20 | 163120 | | Hartford CT | 1907 | | Barge | 147 | 32.8 | 12.6 | 524 | 483 | | HF |
| H.& N.Y.T.Co.No.21 | 163119 | | Gildersl'v CT | 1907 | | Barge | 147 | 32.8 | 12.6 | 521 | 481 | | HF |
| H.& N.Y.T.Co.No.22 | 163180 | | Noank CT | 1907 | | Barge | 144.5 | 32.5 | 12 | 505 | 474 | | HF |
| H.& N.Y.T.Co.No.23 | 163230 | | Noank CT | 1907 | | Barge | 148 | 32.2 | 11.1 | 489 | 458 | | HF |
| H.& N.Y.T.Co.No.24 | 163275 | | Noank CT | 1907 | | Barge | 148 | 32.2 | 11.1 | 489 | 458 | | HF |
| H.& N.Y.T.Co.No.25 | 163305 | | Noamk CT | 1907 | | Barge | 148 | 32.2 | 11.1 | 489 | 458 | | HF |
| H.& N.Y.T.Co.No.26 | 163198 | | Gildersl'v CT | 1907 | | Barge | 147 | 32.8 | 12.6 | 522 | 481 | | HF |
| H.& N.Y.T.Co.No.27 | 163775 | | Hartford CT | 1909 | | Scow | 82 | 30.5 | 5.7 | 146 | 82 | | HF |
| H.& N.Y.T.Co.No.28 | 163988 | | Hartford CT | 1909 | | Barge | 147 | 32.2 | 12.5 | 514 | 479 | | HF |
| H.& N.Y.T.Co.No.29 | 164362 | | Hartford CT | 19ll | | Barge | 145.7 | 32 | 12.5 | 5l5 | 475 | | HF |
| H.& N.Y.T.Co.No.30 | 164578 | | Gildersl'v CT | 1911 | | Barge | 157.5 | 32.6 | 12.5 | 550 | 513 | | HF |
| H.& N.Y.T.Co.No.31 | 164728 | | Hartford CT | 1912 | | Barge | 157.5 | 32.6 | 12.5 | 551 | 513 | | HF |
| H.& N.Y.T.Co.No.32 | 165127 | | Hartford CT | 1913 | | Barge | 157.5 | 32.6 | 12.5 | 551 | 513 | | HF |
| H.& N.Y.T.Co.No.33 | 166694 | | Hartford CT | 1917 | | Barge | 157.5 | 32.6 | 12.5 | 550 | 511 | | HF |
| H.& N.Y.T.Co.Pile 1 | 162453 | | Hartford CT | 1904 | | Scow | 60 | 22.5 | 4.3 | 101 | 49 | | HF |

# H&NYTCo Tug Engines

| Vessel Name | Registry Number | Engine Type | HP | Bore & Stroke | Note |
|---|---|---|---|---|---|
| A. M. Smith | 105021 | Single | 135 | 17 X 17 | |
| Admiral Farragut | 562 | | | | |
| Comet | 208083 | | | | (16) |
| J. W. Coulston | | | 50 | | |
| L. C. Ward | 140596 | | 275 | | |
| M. R. Brazos | 90506 | | | | |
| Mabel | 91470 | C | | 15, 26 X 22 | |
| Onrust | 202812 | | 300 | | (17) |
| Owl | | | | | |
| Raymond | 202779 | | | | |
| Sachem | 116994 | | 500 | | |
| Spartan | 210272 | | 800 | | |

**Notes:**
| 16 | (b) | Eileen McAllister |
|---|---|---|
| 17 | (b) | Thomas F. O'Brien Jr. |
| | (c) | Russell 2 |

---

## Abbreviations for hull & propulsion

| | |
|---|---|
| DE.Sc.S. | Diesel-electric, Screw, Steel |
| DM.Sc.S. | Diesel-mechanical, Screw, Steel |
| St.P.W. | Steamer, Paddle, Wood |
| St.P.I. | Steamer, Paddle, Iron |
| St.P.S. | Steamer, Paddle, Steel |
| St.Sc.W. | Steamer, Screw, Wood |
| St.Sc.I. | Steamer, Screw, Iron |
| St.Sc.S. | Steamer, Screw, Steel |
| StScLgt.I | Steamer, Screw, Lighter, Iron |
| St.PDEFW | Steamer, Paddle, Double-End, Ferry, Wood |
| St.PDEFI | Steamer, Paddle, Double-End, Ferry, Iron |
| St.PDEFS | Steamer, Paddle, Double-End, Ferry, Steel |
| StScDEFW | Steamer, Screw, Double-End, Ferry, Wood |
| StScDEFI | Steamer, Screw, Double-End Ferry, Iron |
| StScDEFS | Steamer, Screw, Double-End, Ferry, Steel |
| IHP | Indicated Horse Power |
| NHP | Nominal Horse Power |
| VB | Vertical Beam |
| I | Inclined |
| IC | Inclined Compound |
| C | Compound |
| CH | Cross Head |
| T | Turbine |
| TE | Triple Expansion |
| DE | Diesel Electric |
| DM | Diesel Mechanical |
| R.T. | Return Tube |
| W.T. | Water Tube |
| SES | Single-Ended-Scotch |
| Car Fl | Car Float |
| Car Fl.W. | Car Float, Wood |
| Car Fl. S. | Car Float, Steel |
| Cov. Bg. | Covered Barge |
| Cov. Bg.W. | Covered Barge, Wood |
| Cov. Bg. S. | Covered Barge, Steel |
| DerrBg. | Derrick Barge |
| Lgt. | Lighter |
| Lgt.W. | Lighter, Wood |
| Lgt.S. | Lighter, Steel |
| Ga.Hos.Lt. | Gas, Hoist, Lighter |

---

## Largest Vessels, Ranked by Gross Tonnage

| Vessel Name | Year Built | Hull Type | Length | Beam | Depth | Gross Tons | Net Tons |
|---|---|---|---|---|---|---|---|
| Commonwealth (II) | 1908 | St.P.S. | 437.9 | 55 | 19.3 | 5980 | 2500 |
| Priscilla | 1894 | St.P.S. | 425.8 | 52.3 | 18.3 | 5292. | 2673 |
| Boston (III)/New York | 1924 | St.Sc.S. | 385.3 | 72.5 | 20.9 | 4989 | 2703 |
| Puritan | 1888 | St.P.S. | 420 | 52.5 | 21 | 4593 | 3075 |
| Providence (III) | 1905 | St.P.S. | 379.4 | 50 | 18.6 | 4365 | 2502 |
| Bunker Hill /Mass. | 1907 | St.Sc.S. | 375 | 52.2 | 31.6 | 4029 | 1724 |
| Old Colony (II) | 1907 | St.Sc.S. | 375 | 52.2 | 31.6 | 4029 | 1564 |
| Plymouth | 1890 | St.P.S. | 352 | 50 | 18.8 | 3771 | 2280 |
| Harvard/Yale | 1907 | St.Sc.S. | 376 | 61.3 | 20.2 | 3737 | 2317 |
| Boston (II) | 1904 | St.Sc.S. | 318 | 60.6 | 22.6 | 3626 | 2466 |
| Narrag/Manh'tn | 1913 | St.Sc.S. | 320.2 | 48.1 | 22 | 3539 | 2134 |
| Pilgrim | 1882 | St.P.I. | 372 | 50 | 15.6 | 3483 | 2512 |
| Connecticut (III) | 1889 | St.P.W. | 345.5 | 48.8 | 17 | 3399 | 1873 |
| North Land | 1910 | St.Sc.S | 304.4 | 47.2 | 19.85 | 3282 | 1973 |
| Horatio Hall | 1898 | St.Sc.S. | 296.8 | 46 | 17.2 | 3167 | 2007 |
| North Star | 1901 | St.Sc.S. | 298.8 | 46 | 17.2 | 3159 | 1999 |
| John Englis | 1896 | St.Sc.S. | 290.8 | 46 | 21 | 3094 | 1987 |
| City of Lowell | 1894 | St.Sc.S. | 322.3 | 49.7 | 17.7 | 2975 | 1877 |
| Bristol/Providence | 1867 | St.P.W. | 362 | 48 | 16.6 | 2962 | 2064 |
| New Haven /Pequonn'k | 1907 | St.Sc.S. | 275.7 | 45.1 | 16.7 | 2930 | 1986 |
| Richard Peck | 1892 | St.Sc.S. | 303.0 | 48 | 17.9 | 2906 | 1819 |
| Rhode Island (III) | 1882 | St.P.W. | 332.2 | 46.2 | 16.4 | 2888. | 2387 |
| City of Taunton | 1892 | St.P.W. | 283 | 43 | 18.2 | 2882 | 1999 |
| Chester W. Chapin | 1899 | St.Sc.S. | 312 | 64 | 16.9 | 2868 | 1822 |
| Mohawk/Mohegan | 1896 | St.Sc.S. | 265 | 43 | 16.8 | 2784 | 2151 |
| City of Brockton | 1886 | St.P.W. | 271.2 | 43.4 | 18.1 | 2771 | 1912 |
| Rhode Island (II) | 1873 | St.P.W. | 325 | 45.6 | 15.6 | 2742 | |
| Massachusetts (III) | 1877 | St.P.W. | 323.8 | 42.5 | 15.9 | 2607 | 2171 |
| Nashua | 1884 | St.P.W. | 291.6 | 43 | 16.1 | 2555 | 1801 |
| City of Fall River | 1882 | St.P.W. | 262 | 42.4 | 17.3 | 2533 | 1723 |
| City of Worcester | 1881 | St.P.I. | 328 | 46 | 14.5 | 2490 | 1922 |
| New Hampshire/Maine | 1892 | St.Sc.S. | 303.7 | 44 | 17.5 | 2395 | 1505 |
| Santiago | 1879 | St.Sc.S. | 269 | 39.1 | 22.4 | 2359 | 1696 |
| Old Dominion | 1872 | St.P.I. | 255.5 | 42.5 | 20.7 | 2222 | 1775 |
| Metropolis | 1854 | St.P.W. | 327.9 | 44.4 | 15 | 2210 | 2108 |
| Bay State | 1848 | St.P.W. | 317 | 39 | 8 | 2200 | 1554 |
| Belfast (Arrow) | 1909 | St.Sc.S. | 320.6 | 40 | 16.1 | 2157 | 1147 |
| Camden (Comet) | 1907 | St.Sc.S. | 320.5 | 40 | 16.1 | 2153 | 1143 |
| Newport | 1865 | St.P.W. | 342 | 43.3 | 14.2 | 2151 | 1862 |

---

## Longest Vessels, Ranked by Length

| Vessel Name | Year Built | Hull Type | Length | Beam | Depth | Gross Tons | Net Tons |
|---|---|---|---|---|---|---|---|
| Commonwealth (II) | 1908 | St.P.S. | 437.9 | 55 | 19.3 | 5980 | 2500 |
| Priscilla | 1894 | St.P.S. | 425.8 | 52.3 | 18.3 | 5292 | 2673 |
| Puritan | 1888 | St.P.S. | 420 | 52.5 | 21 | 4593 | 3075 |
| Boston/New York | 1924 | St.Sc.S. | 385.3 | 72.5 | 20.9 | 4989 | 2703 |
| Providence (III) | 1905 | St.P.S. | 379.4 | 50 | 18.6 | 4365 | 2502 |
| Harvard/Yale | 1907 | St.Sc.S | 376 | 61.3 | 20.2 | 3737 | 2317 |
| Bunker Hill / Mass. | 1907 | St.Sc.S. | 375 | 52.2 | 31.6 | 4029 | 1724 |
| Old Colony (II) | 1907 | St.Sc.S. | 375 | 52.2 | 31.6 | 4029 | 1564 |
| Pilgrim | 1882 | St.P.I. | 372 | 50 | 15.6 | 3484 | 2513 |
| Bristol/Providence | 1867 | St.P.W. | 362 | 48 | 16.6 | 2962 | 2064 |
| Plymouth | 1890 | St.P.S. | 352 | 50 | 18.8 | 3771 | 2280. |
| Connecticut (III) | 1889 | St.P.S. | 345.5 | 48.8 | 17 | 3399 | 1873 |
| Newport | 1865 | St.P.W. | 342 | 43.3 | 14.2 | 2151 | 1862 |
| Rhode Island (III) | 1882 | St.P.W. | 332.2 | 46.2 | 16.4 | 2888 | 2387 |
| Commonwealth (I) | 1855 | St.P.W. | 330 | 42 | 13.6 | 1733 | |
| Plymouth Rock | 1854 | St.P.W. | 330 | 40 | 13 | 1810 | 1752 |
| City of Worcester | 1881 | St.P.I. | 328 | 46 | 14.5 | 2490 | 1922 |
| Metropolis | 1854 | St.P.W. | 327.9 | 44.4 | 15 | 2210 | 2108 |
| Rhode Island (II) | 1873 | St.P.W. | 325 | 45.6 | 15.6 | 2742 | |
| Massachusetts (III) | 1877 | St.P.W. | 323.8 | 42.5 | 15.9 | 2607 | 2171 |
| City of Lowell | 1894 | St.Sc.S. | 322.3 | 49.7 | 17.7 | 2975 | 1877 |
| Belfast (Arrow) | 1909 | St.Sc.S. | 320.6 | 40 | 16.1 | 2157 | 1147 |
| Camden (Comet) | 1907 | St.Sc.S. | 320.5 | 40 | 16.1 | 2153 | 1143 |
| Narrag./Manh'tn | 1913 | St.Sc.S. | 320.2 | 48.1 | 22 | 3539 | 2134 |
| Atlantic | 1846 | St.P.W. | 320 | 36 | 10 | 1300 | 1112 |
| Boston (II) | 1904 | St.Sc.S. | 318 | 60.6 | 22.6 | 3626 | 2466 |
| Oregon | 1845 | St.P.W. | 318 | 35 | 10 | 1004 | |
| Bay State | 1848 | St.P.W. | 317 | 39 | 8 | 2200 | 1554 |
| C. H. Northam | 1873 | St.P.W. | 312 | 44 | 10 | 1437 | 1180 |
| Chester W. Chapin | 1899 | St.Sc.S. | 312 | 64 | 16.9 | 2868 | 1822 |
| Old Colony (I) | 1865 | St.P.W. | 310 | 42 | 14 | 1958 | 1714 |
| New Hampshire/Maine | 1892 | St.Sc.S. | 308.7 | 44 | 17.5 | 2395 | 1505 |
| Empire State | 1848 | St.P.W. | 305 | 40.3 | 13 | 1692 | 1579 |
| North Land | 1910 | St.Sc.S | 304.4 | 47.2 | 19.85 | 3282 | 1973 |
| Connecticut (II) | 1848 | St.P.W. | 303 | 26 | 8 | 1129 | |
| Richard Peck | 1892 | St.Sc.S. | 303.0 | 48 | 17.9 | 2906 | 1819 |
| City of Boston/N. York | 1861 | St.P.W. | 301 | 40 | 12.5 | 1577 | 1457 |
| C. Vanderbilt | 1847 | St.P.W. | 300 | 35 | 10 | 1041 | |

# Vessel Name Changes

| | | |
|---|---|---|
| Albatross | (b) | USS Albatross |
| Allen Joy | (b) | Naugatuck |
| Artisan | (b) | Renovator |
| Augusta | (b) | Transmotor |
| Bridgeport | (a) | William G Payne |
| | (c) | Highlander |
| | (d) | Bear Mountain |
| Bunker Hill | (b) | USS Aroostook |
| | (c) | Bunker Hill |
| Chester W. Chapin | (b) | Meteor |
| City of Bridgeport | (b) | Rosalie |
| | (c) | Henry C. Rowe & Co. |
| City of Fitchburg | (b) | Surprise |
| | (c) | Warren |
| City of Richmond | (b) | City of Key West |
| City of Springfield | (a) | State of New York |
| Cocoa | (a) | Cuba (Spanish) |
| | (b) | Argonauta (Spanish) |
| | (d) | M. F. Plant |
| | (e) | Yukon |
| Cumberland | (b) | Larchmont |
| Dover | (a) | Westover |
| Edgemont | (a) | State of Maine |
| | (c) | Cape May |
| Eleanor F. Peck | (b) | Philip J. Kenny |
| Empire State | (a) | Plymouth Rock |
| Express | (b) | Mandalay |
| Fairfield | (a) | Richard Borden |
| Fairhaven | (b) | Mohican |

| | | |
|---|---|---|
| Frank Jones | (b) | Fenimore |
| Gay Head | (b) | Pastime |
| Hartford (I) | (b) | Charles H. Hackley |
| | (c) | Carolina |
| Harvard | (b) | USS Charles |
| | (c) | Harvard |
| Islander | (b) | Martha's Vineyard (II) |
| John Englis | (b) | USS Relief |
| | (c) | USS Repose |
| | (e) | Hai Ning (Foreign) |
| | (f) | Mindanao (Foreign) |
| | (g) | Lanao (Philippine) |
| Kennebec | (b) | Iroquois |
| Kentucky | (a) | Lincoln |
| | (b) | Martinique |
| Larchmont | (a) | Cumberland |
| Martha's Vineyard (I) | (b) | Keyport |
| Martha's Vineyard (II) | (a) | Islander |
| Massachusetts (II) | (b) | John W. D. Pentz |
| Metacomet | (b) | Pulaski |
| Meteor | (b) | Brazoria |
| Miramar | (a) | Gosnold |
| | (b) | USQM Gosnold |
| | (d) | W. S. White |
| | (e) | Caribbean |
| Naugatuck | (a) | Cape Charles |
| | (b) | Allen Joy |
| Naushon | (b) | Hospital Ship 49 |
| | (c) | Naushon |
| | (d) | John A. Meseck |

| | | |
|---|---|---|
| New England | (b) | Sarah Pinser |
| New London | (b) | Acushnet |
| New Shoreham | (b) | Myrtle II |
| | (c) | Priscilla Alden |
| Newburgh | (b) | Nantasket |
| Nobska | (b) | Nantucket |
| | (c) | Nobska |
| Neptune | (b) | USS Neptune |
| | (c) | Alleghany |
| Owana | (a) | Thomas C. Millard |
| Pequot | (a) | Thetis |
| Penobscot | (b) | Mohawk |
| | (c) | Allene (Schooner) |
| Rhode Island (III) | (b) | Dovrefjeld (Schooner) |
| Richard Borden | (b) | Fairfield |
| Richard Peck | (b) | Elisha Lee |
| Sankaty | (b) | HMS Sankaty |
| | (c) | Charles A. Dunning (Can.) |
| State of New York | (b) | City of Springfield |
| Surprise | (a) | City of Fitchburg |
| | (c) | Warren |
| Tennessee | (b) | Romance |
| Stonington | (a) | Grampus |
| Thames River | (b) | John R. King (Schooner) |
| | (c) | Virginia Hudson (Schooner) |
| Transford II | (a) | Aquidaban |
| Uncatena | (b) | Pemberton |
| Virginia | (b) | Tadousac (Can. #112267) |
| Yale | (b) | USS Greyhound |
| | (c) | Yale |

---

## Shipbuilders

| | |
|---|---|
| ROH | John Roach & Son |
| DRI | Delaware River Iron Shipbldg. Co. |
| WHW | William H. Webb |
| JS | Jeremiah Simonson |
| HS | Henry Steers |
| NES | New England Shipbldg Co. |
| SS | Samuel Sneeden |
| SW | Sneeden & Witlock |
| JE | John Englis & Son |
| HH | Harlan & Hollingworth |
| CH | Charles Hillman & Sons |
| BGH | B. G. Hillman & Co. |
| CXW | Columbia Iron Works |
| BIW | Bath Iron Works |
| BS | Bishop & Simonson |
| TM | Thomas Marvel |
| BB | Brown & Bell |
| EW | Eckford & Webb |
| RPS | Robert Palmer & Son |
| WM | William Cramp |
| MSC | Maryland Steel Co. |
| MH | Mongomery & Howard |
| JBV | J. B. VanDeusen |

| | |
|---|---|
| SC | Samuel Collyer |
| NEE | N. E. Edmonds |
| LS | Lawrence & Sneeden |
| JW | Jacob Westerveldt |
| GG | George Greenman |
| SDC | Smith, Dimon & Comstock |
| CR | C. & R. Poillon |
| BX | Baxter Shipyard |
| CIW | Continental Iron Works |
| ACB | A. C. Brown & Sons |
| LF | Lawrence & Foulks |
| NL | Neafie & Levey |
| WTC | William & Thomas Collyer |
| BSB | Bethlehem Shipbuilding Corp. |
| FRS | Fore River Shipbuilding Co. |
| WMC | William McKie |
| SSY | Skinner Shipyard |
| SR | Sneeden & Rowland |
| BS | Bayles & Son |
| RFJ | Ruben Fish & Joshua Delano |
| GB | Gilbert Bruster |
| NS | Norfolk Shipbuilding (Atlantic City Shipbuilding & Iron Works) |

## Enginebuilders:

| | |
|---|---|
| MIW | Morgan Iron Works |
| WAF | W. & A. Fletcher Co. |
| AIW | Allaire Iron Works |
| SA | Stillman Allan & Co. |
| NIW | Novelty Iron Works |
| DIW | Delamater Iron Works |
| FHC | Fletcher Harrison & Co. |
| JWS | J. W. Sullivan |
| PJ | Pusey & Jones |
| PC | Portland Co. |
| HW | Hubbard & Whittaker |
| JEC | Joseph E. Coffee |
| EIW | Etna Iron Works |
| QIW | Quintard Engine Works |
| WIW | Washington Iron Works |
| NNW | Neptune Iron Works |
| NRI | North River Iron Works |
| CXW | Columbia Iron Works |
| JBX | E. J. Belknap |
| CH | Cunningham & Hall |
| CT | Cobanks & Theall |
| AG | Arch Guion |
| NS | Norfolk Shipbuilding (Atlantic City Shipbuilding & Iron Works) |

## NEW ENGLAND STEAMSHIP COMPANY TERMINAL PROPERTY

(Adapted from ICC Report, 1929)

| LOCATION<br>*Property in Connecticut* | AREA<br>(Sq Ft) | DESCRIPTION OF BUILDINGS AND EQUIPMENT | Traffic<br>Handled | Type of<br>Title | Investment<br>in Terminal |
|---|---|---|---|---|---|
| 1. Stonington (Pearl St.) | 128,415 | Steamboat dock 603' south side, 365' north side, 140' front, irregular width. No Buildings. Rail Connection. | N | O | $ 38,940 |
| 2. New London (Monument Sq.) | 75,446 | Wharf 490' east side, 450' west side, 105' front, irregular width. Frame shed 1 story 378' x 94' containing office. Equipment-scales, hand trucks, Electric Portables, Fire Alarm Box (50%),Gas Tank etc., Rail Connection. | FP | O | 127,557 |
| 3. Norwich, (Market St.) | 2,936 | Section of pier-150' x 25'. No Buildings. Not used in 1929. | N | L | --- |
| 4. Bridgeport (Water St. & Union Sq.) | 61,133 | Pequonnock Dock, extends 930' alongside harbor. Freight shed 1 story frame 50' x 150'. Freight shed 1 story frame, 36' x 500'. Equipment-Electric Ramps, Fire Alarm System, Automatic Scales, Hand Trucks, Rail Connection. | F | O | 191,650 |
| 5. New Haven (Bridge St.) | 19,838 | Belle Dock Wharf, extends 345' alongside harbor with land U.W. Cover shed 65' x 26'. Equipment-Hand Truck, Scales, Truck Conveyor, Elevated Runway, etc. Rail Connection. | F | O | 81,216 |
| 6. New Haven (Meadow St.) | -- | General Office Building, Office Equipment | N | O | 3,854 |
| 7. Hartford (State St.) | 46,174 | Wharf 250' long containing Freight House two story wood 200' x 87' includes Offices and Gangway to upper level, office equipment. | FP | L | * 556 |
| 8. Middletown (Water St.) | 35,690 | Wharf 280' long containing Freight House two story wood 70' x 90' containing offices. | FP | L | 000 |
| 9. East Haddam (Highway) | 4,052 | Wharf 80' long with adjoining Freight Shed 32' x 33' | FP | L | 000 |
| 10. Saybrook Point (Cottage St.) | 50,000 | Wharf 615' long containing one story frame Freight House 50' x 252' containing offices. | FP | L | 000 |
| 11. Deep River (Highway) | NA | Not available. | FP | R | 000 |
| *Property in Rhode Island* | AREA<br>(Sq Ft) | DESCRIPTION OF BUILDINGS AND EQUIPMENT | Traffic<br>Handled | Type of<br>Title | Investment<br>in Terminal |
| 12. Newport (Washington St.) | 220,000 | Briggs Wharf 480' long x 44' x 45'. Hydrants. No Bldgs. Equipment. Area includes 145,000 sq. ft. land under water. | N | O | $ 69,647 |
| 13. Newport (Washington St.) | 283,792 | Repair Shop, Wharves and Dock; area includes 63,000 sq. ft. land under water. Property contains Repair Shops, Power Plant, Storehouses and Offices including Office Equipment. Heavy Machinery. Electric Tractive Equipment, etc. Rail Connection. | N | L | 101,591 |
| 14. Newport (Washington St.) | 772,215 | Steamboat Dock 670' x 210' area includes 85,850 sq. ft. land under water north of dock, 550,740 sq. ft. south of dock. Dock contains 2-story frame Pass. Station 110' x 25', Freight Shed 240' x 42', Freight Shed 90' x 60'. Equipment-Hand Trucks, Scales, Hydrants, Gas Tank etc. Rail Connection. | FP | L | 1,319 |
| 15. Providence (India & So. Water Sts.) | 132,266 | Wharf 415' along Providence River, 555' along Seekonk River, solid fill. Open Platforms 80' x 50' and 80' x 40'. Triangular open platform 125' long by 25' average width. One-story transite on steel frame Freight House 380' x 38', one story transite on steel frame covered platform 380' x 40', one story frame covered platform 125' x 30', Two wharf drops, electrical escalators. Two-story brick Office and Passenger Facilities, 30' x 50'. Equipment-Hand Trucks, Scales, Truck Conveyor, Charging Station, Gas Tanks, etc. Four-track Rail Connection. | FP | O | 725,907 |
| 16. Wickford Landing (Beach St.) | 8,712 | Wharf 329' long alongside harbor including Coal Pocket 100' x 21'. | N | O | 11,550 |

# NEW ENGLAND STEAMSHIP COMPANY TERMINAL PROPERTY (Cont'd.)

| LOCATION<br>*Property in Massachusetts* | AREA<br>(Sq Ft) | DESCRIPTION OF BUILDINGS AND EQUIPMENT | Traffic<br>Handled | Type of<br>Title | Investment<br>in Terminal |
|---|---|---|---|---|---|
| 17. Fall River (Water St.) | 226,164 | Fall River Line Pier 445' x 250'. Stone Freight House 1 story 300' x 62'. Two 1 story frame freight houses 200' x 65' and 300' x 55'. Train Shed 500' x 60'. Rail Connection. | FP | L | $ 6,774 |
| 18. New Bedford (Front & Commercial Sts.) | 74,000 | Steamboat Wharf 555' long, 113' wide on outer end. Freight House 100' x 50' Freight Shed 380' x 85', Waiting Room 60' x 15' and covered platforms. Equipment-Hand Trucks, Scales, Truck Conveyor, Gas Tank, Office Equip., etc. | FP | L | 8,494 |
| 19. New Bedford (Front & School Sts.) | 29,400 | NBMV&N Steamboat Line Wharf 285' x 60' and 30' x 140'. Wharf Shed 58' x 270'. Open Coal Bin 30' x 100' fitted with electric coal handling gear. Adjoining Cover Shed 40' x 58'. Property contains Office Building of brick 2 stories 30' x 49' - 1 story 14' x 39. Frame Storehouse 25' x 50'. Covered Platform 7' x 50'. Shelter 10' x 140'. Garage 8' x 8'. Mail Automobile, Office Equipment, etc. | FP | L | 110,446 |
| 20. Woods Hole (Depot Ave.) | 38,000 | Wharf, 132' front, irregular dimensions, includes frame Freight House 35' x 18' Waiting Room and Ticket Office 14' x 27', Office Equipment. Wharf used by mutual agreement. | FP | N | 10,013 |
| 21. Gay Head | 126,740 | Water front and rear land. No wharf or Buildings. | N | O | 50 |
| 22. Vineyard Haven | NA | Landing Privileges, use of facilities, Storehouse, Waiting Room, etc. | FP | L | 000 |
| 23. Oak Bluffs (Oak Bluffs & Sea View Aves.) | 219,165 | Water front property with Wharf 440' long, 172' wide at outer end 42' wide inshore. Connecting Wharf and Shelter 90' x 10'. Wharves have frame Shelter 182' x 10', frame Freight House 140' x 80' with canopy 100' x 10', frame Freight Office 28' x 20', Covered Shed 120' x 72' containing baggage room, Covered Shed 80' x 26'. Wharf fitted with five (5) wharf drops. Passenger facilities 1-story brick 25' x 50' located on shore. | FP | O | 160,065 |
| 24. Edgartown (Front & Wharf) | 18,731 | Wharf 142' long by 102'6" wide has Open Shelter 100' x 29', Freight House 28' x 24'6" and Portable Ticket Office 12' x 12' x 10'. | FP | O | 923 |
| 25. Nantucket (Broad St.) | 87,900 | Wharf 614' long on north side, 513' long on south side, 182' wide on outer end, wharf has frame Freight House 140' x 80' with canopy 110' x 10', frame Freight House 38' x 20', frame Baggage Room 40' x 28', Ticket Office and Waiting Room 28' x 20', Covered Platforms 148' x 28' and 130' x 10', Shelter with concrete platform 112' x 28', Open Shed 124' x 18', Fish House 100' x 28', Wharf fitted with four (4) wharf drops. | FP | O | 170,805 |

| LOCATION<br>*Property in New York* | AREA<br>(Sq Ft) | DESCRIPTION OF BUILDINGS AND EQUIPMENT | Traffic<br>Handled | Type of<br>Title | Investment<br>in Terminal |
|---|---|---|---|---|---|
| 26. New York City (Fulton St.) | 108,784 | Pier 14-N.R.N.Y. 718' x 125' with adjoining one-half bulkheads north & south of Pier, 1 story iron Pier Shed 654' x 121', South Bulkhead Shed 1 story iron, 145' x 46', Headhouse 2 story iron 118' x 66'. North Bulkhead Shed, iron, 2 story 182' x 48' between Piers 14 & 15. Sheds contain Offices, Cold Storage and Refrigerating Plant, Charging Station, Steel Canopy over entrance. Equipment-Automatic Scales and Platforms, Hoisting Engines, Office Equipment, etc. | FP | L | $ 106,708 |
| 27. New York City (Vesey St.) | 39,043 | Pier 15-N.R.N.Y. 714' x 45' with adjoining one half bulkhead south of Pier. 1 story Iron Pier Shed 645' x 48'6". Headhouse 2 story iron 50' x 55' Steel Canopy over entrance. Contents of Pier Sheds, Piers 14 & 15 mentioned above. | (incl. with Pier 14) | | |
| 28. New York City (Catherine St.) | 29,428 | Pier 27-E.R.N.Y. 461' long x 50' wide outer end, 98' wide shore end with 79' adjoining bulkhead east of Pier. 1 story iron Pier Shed 193' x 47'6", 1 story iron pier shed 220' x 47'6" x 89'. 2 story Iron Pier Shed 41'6" x 89' x 96'6". Pier had office and Miscellaneous Equipment. | FP | L | 1,796 |
| 29. New York City (Market St.) | 36,385 | Pier 28-E.R.N.Y. 460' x 79'. 1 story Iron Pier Shed 412' x 78'. 2 story Iron Pier Shed 38' x 78' with Offices. Equipment-Hand Trucks, Automatic Scales, Office Equipment etc. | (incl. with Pier 27) | | |
| 30. New York City (Clarkson St.) | 79,029 | Pier 40-N.R.N.Y. 815' x 75' with adjoining one half bulkheads north and south of Pier. 1 story Iron Pier Shed 740' x 72. Shed 90' x 48', 2 story Iron Pier Shed 45' x 72'. 1 story Iron Headhouse 257' x 50', Pile Platform 10' x 76' south of Pier. Steel Canopy over entrance. Pier has offices. Equipment-Office, Hand Trucks, Automatic Scales, Charging Stations, Gas Tank, etc. | FP | L | 20,761 |
| 31. Queens (Whitestone Ldg) | 23,275 | Wharf 399.5' long x 52' wide, outer end 99.8' wide, contains covered platform 130'6" x 10'8" wood frame. roof and side corrugated iron. Cover shed over ramp 24' x 15' similar construction. Watchman's Shed 7' x 10' similar construction. Three Flood Lights and eight outlets. Two Electric Howlers on top Watchman's Shed. Rail Connection on Wharf, tracks electrified. | P | L | 20,314 |
| 32. New York City (Various) | -- | This Company's proportion of Office Equipment in Consolidated Ticket Offices Brooklyn, N.Y. and N.Y. City, N.Y. | -- | -- | 1,007 |
| 33. New York City | -- | Freight Handling Equipment, electric Trucks, Tractors, Trailers and Re Bo bodies for handtrucks used at various terminals. | -- | O | 221,859 |
| | | | | | ------------- |
| | | | | | $2,193,802 |

Investment totals by state: Conn. $443,773 (20%); Rhode Island $910,014 (42%); Mass. $467,570 (21%); New York $372,445 (17%)
Symbols: N = None; F = Freight; P = Passenger; O = Owned; L = Leased; R = Rented

**Two closeups of *Transfer 24* as she begins a double tow run.**

# Glossary of
# Relevant Terms

**Abaft:** Astern of, or toward the stern. Opposite of "forward."

**Abeam:** Directly to either side of the vessel.

**Able seaman:** an experienced sailor, with sufficient skill and experience to hold a certificate identifying him as such.

**Adrift:** Floating, at the mercy of the action of wind and water. Unmoored.

**Afterdeck:** That part of any deck abaft of the vessel's midships.

**Aground:** Condition in which a vessel rests on a solid surface other than in a dry dock or shipyard. Caused by lowering tide or errant navigation. Embarrassing, and possibly dangerous.

**Altar Steps:** The stepped tiers in the floor and sides of a drydock, against which the hull supporting timbers are braced.

**Astern:** Toward the stern, or abaft of the boat. (Never "behind.")

**Athwart:** At right angles to the fore-and-aft line of the vessel.

**Auto ferry:** A ferryboat designed to transport automobiles. (Possible confusion: see **Car ferry**)

**Baggage:** Articles taken along on a trip by a passenger for his personal use during the trip or at his destination.

**Bar: (1)** A buildup of material, usually silt or sand, at the mouth of a river, impeding entrance from or exit to open water.

**(2)** A significant source of revenue from dispensation of beverages on passenger vessels. Do not confuse with **Saloon**.

**Barge:** flat-bottomed boat adapted for the transportation of bulky freight (coal, sand, stone). Cargo is carried in the hull.

**Beam:** The width of a ship's hull; also called breadth. Sometimes used to describe width over guards.

**Beam Engine:** See **Walking Beam**.

**Bilge:** space at the bottom of a boat's hold wherein water collects, and from which such water is pumped.

**Bill of Lading:** The contract between shipper and carrier for transport of the shipper's goods.

**Boat:** A waterborne craft, usually small, propelled by oars, sails, or some form of engine. Also applied to larger vessels built to navigate rivers and inland waters; but in this context is most often used as part of a compound word, e.g., "ferryboat," "steamboat," "riverboat."

**Boatswain** ("Bosun"): A petty officer who is the first-line supervisor of all deck hands.

**Boat train:** A train operated to terminate at or near a steamboat dock, coordinated with the schedule of a steamboat, to provide a through transportation service.

**Boiler:** An apparatus for generating steam, consisting of a furnace, a heat exchanger to transfer heat from burning fuel to water, and pipes for circulation of water and steam. May be a fire-tube or a water-tube boiler.

**Bow:** The forwardmost part of a vessel, particularly the point above the waterline at which the sides come together.

**Bowsprit:** On a sailboat, a spar projecting forward from the top of the bow to anchor the foresail. On a steamboat, the forwardmost vertical structural member. The part that first makes contact with other ships in collisions.

**Breakwater:** A ridge, wall, or other structure (including a sunken hulk or pile of automobile bodies) that serves to protect a harbor from the action and force of waves.

**Bulk cargo:** A homogenous cargo stowed in a ship's hold without being enclosed in any boxes, bags, or other containers. Oil, grain, coal and lumber are examples.

**Bulkhead:** A vertical partition separating spaces on a ship. On land, it would be known as a "wall."

**Bunker:** A compartment for fuel storage, usually below decks.

**Buoy:** An anchored floating aid to mark the navigable limits of channels, danger areas, or the position of a sunken object.

**Captain:** Popularly, the commander or master of a vessel. In commercial steamboating, a person possessing a Captain's license, whether or not currently in command of a vessel.

**Car ferry:** Possible confusion; could be a ferry designed for railroad cars (**train ferry**), or for automobiles (**auto ferry**).

**Car float:** A harbor scow fitted with a deck and railroad tracks, used for ferrying railroad cars between waterfront railroad facilities.

**Cargo:** Goods or merchandise transported for payment.

**Cast off:** Releasing the lines holding a vessel to a wharf.

**Chandler:** A merchant who deals in supplies for ships; canvas, rope, fittings, etc.

**Channel:** The deeper part of a river, harbor entrance or other body of water, with depth sufficient for navigation. May be formally marked.

**Charter:** An agreement whereby a ship's owner leases the entire vessel to another party for a period of time or for a number of trips.

**Chief Engineer:** The senior licensed officer responsible for the upkeep and performance of a ship's propulsion and auxiliary machinery and systems.

**Chief Steward:** The senior officer responsible for service to, and comfort of, passengers. Supervises all food and beverage service and housekeeping personnel.

**Coaster:** A vessel engaged regularly in relatively short sea passages between ports along a coast, e.g., New York - Baltimore, or Los Angeles - San Francisco.

**Commander:** Person in overall charge of a vessel; in commercial shipping, a licensed officer. Often called "Captain."

**Commodore:** A courtesy title given to the senior captain of a line of ships, usually passenger ships.

**Common carrier:** A person or firm engaging in the transport of freight or passengers for hire, not exclusively engaged by one customer.

**Compound engine:** A steam engine in which the same steam is used more than once, in successive cylinders.

**Contract carrier:** A person or firm engaging in the transport of freight or passengers, whose vessel or vehicle is exclusively engaged by one customer.

**Cooperage:** A charge made by a carrier for repair of damaged barrels, boxes or shipping containers inadequately packed by the shipper.

**Crankshaft:** A shaft turned by cranks, the purpose of which is to turn reciprocating motion into circular motion. In a sidewheel steamboat, a large transverse shaft with a paddlewheel on each end, turned by cranks attached to the engine.

**Crosshead:** In a steam engine, the pivoting link connecting the cylinder's piston rod to the main rod that transmits power to the crankshaft. The piston rod is thus kept straight in the cylinder, minimizing "wobble" and steam leaks; while the main rod moves from side to side as the crankshaft turns.

**Dead reckoning:** A means of navigation that determines the position of a vessel by calculation based on the last known measured position of the vessel and the running time since that measurement was made.

**Deck:** An approximately horizontal surface structure extending between a ship's sides. Serves as a floor or working surface, and divides the ship horizontally. On a steamboat, from the bottom up, decks include the lower deck, main deck, saloon deck, gallery deck and dome or hurricane deck.

**Deck officer:** Officers who assist the commander in navigation and passenger/cargo operations; distinguished from engineering officers.

**Derrick lighter:** A harbor lighter fitted with hoisting apparatus to handle cargo.

**Dome deck:** The uppermost deck of a steamboat fitted with a dome or clerestory windows to provide light to the saloon on the deck below.

**Double-expansion engine:** A reciprocating steam engine with two cylinders, the first of which is a smaller, high-pressure cylinder. Steam exhausted from this cylinder goes to a larger, low pressure cylinder and is used again.

**Double-hull:** A ship design featuring two interconnected watertight hulls, one inside the other, separated by spaces.

**Draft:** The minimum water depth a ship needs to float freely.

**Dry dock:** An enclosed basin fitted with a watertight gate, used for repairs to that part of a ship which is normally underwater. The ship is floated in and braced, the gate closed, and water pumped out.

**Fantail:** The overhanging rounded stern section of a vessel from waterline up to the first exposed deck.

**Fathom:** A nautical measure; six feet. Used to measure depth of water and length of lines.

**Feathering paddle wheel:** A wheel in which the paddles are mounted with a mechanism that tilts each blade or bucket as the wheel turns, to provide maximum force and minimum resistance as the bucket enters or leaves the water. The increase in efficiency means that the wheel may be smaller, or may turn faster, than a fixed paddle wheel.

**Fighting ship:** A vessel engaged in a low-fare service designed to drive out a competitor.

**Firetube Boiler:** A boiler in which combustion gases flow through large tubes around which water circulates. Also called a Scotch boiler.

**Float bridge:** A floating or hanging structure attached to a wharf at one end, with provision for mooring a barge or ferry at the other end. Facilitates loading and unloading. May have railroad tracks for use with car floats.

**Flotsam:** That portion of a jettisoned cargo which floats on the surface of the water. See **Jetsam**.

**Fog:** Small globules of moisture floating in the air, obscuring visibility. Comparable to a cloud, but on the surface of water or land. Caused by moist warm wind passing over colder water, or vice versa.

**Foredeck:** That part of a deck forward of the vessel's midships.

**Forward:** Ahead of, or toward the bow. Opposite of "abaft."

**Free lighterage:** Harbor lighterage service performed by a railroad to move cargo between the railhead and another part of the port. Included in the freight rate.

**Freight:** The price paid for transportation of goods (not passengers). Also used to describe the goods being transported.

**Gallery deck:** If present, the deck on a steamboat above the saloon deck, with a cutout above the central space providing a "second story" for the public room below, and access to a second tier of staterooms from longitudinal balconies.

**Gangway:** A narrow portable ramp placed between ship and pier, for passenger and freight access.

**Geared Turbine:** The mechanism by which the power generated by a high-speed turbine is transmitted to a lower-speed shaft to turn a propeller or other driving device.

**Gross ton:** Unit of capacity used for registering vessels, equal to 100 cubic feet. Has nothing to do with weight, and doers not include the entire cubic capacity of a vessel. Based on the arbitrary assumption that 100 cubic feet is taken up by the typical ton of cargo.

**Guard:** Longitudinal structures fastened to the sides of a ship at deck level, serving as fenders or outboard supports for the superstructure.

**Harbor:** An area of water which provides reasonable shelter or haven for ships from sea and wind. A place where ships are loaded and unloaded. See **Port**.

**Harbor tug:** A small tugboat used for towing ships and lighters to and from mooring places in a harbor.

**Hatch:** An opening in a deck allowing access to the space below. Usually covered.

**Hawser:** A heavy fiber or wire rope used for towing or docking.

**Hog:** A condition of buoyancy in which the vessel arches up amidships. Opposite of sag.

**Hog frame:** A bridge-type truss above the hull, forming part of a wooden-hulled vessel's structural framing. Designed to counteract sag.

**Hold:** Name for the spaces between the lowest deck and the ship bottom; generally, spaces below deck.

**Hull:** The body of a vessel exclusive of machinery, equipment, masts and rigging.

**Hurricane deck:** An upper deck on a vessel, unroofed.

**Icebound:** A condition in which a vessel is surrounded by ice and unable to move.

**Idler flat:** A railroad flat car coupled between a locomotive and the cars being loaded or unloaded from a car float. Used to keep the weight of the locomotive off the float bridge. More than one idler flat may be used to reach all cars.

**Inboard:** Toward the longitudinal center line of the vessel; within the limits of a deck.

**Indicated horsepower:** A calculated measurement of the power delivered by the pistons of a reciprocating engine.

**Inside cabin:** A cabin separated from a ship's side by another space; without porthole or window to the sea.

**Jetsam:** That portion of a jettisoned cargo which does not float on the surface of the water. See **Flotsam**.

**Jetty:** A man-made structure projecting into the water at the mouth of a river or harbor to narrow and concentrate the channel, thus increasing its depth.

**Keel:** The main centerline structural member of a ship, running fore and aft along the bottom.

**Knot:** Unit of speed; velocity in nautical miles per hour.

**Ladder:** Any stairway aboard ship (even including *Priscilla*'s grand staircase.)

**Launching:** Sliding of a ship by its own weight down an inclined plane into the water.

**Lay up:** To tie up a vessel in an inactive state for a period of time, as for the winter.

**Lee:** The side toward which the wind is blowing; the leeward side is sheltered from the wind.

**Lighter:** a flat-bottomed barge used in a harbor to transport cargo between a vessel and the shore, or between vessels.

**Lighthouse:** A building on a conspicuous part of the coast from which a light is displayed at night to aid navigation. May also have an audible signal. Lighthouses have different constant or flashing light patterns and colors to aid in identification.

**Lightship:** An anchored vessel fitted with lighting, sound and radio equipment, serving the same purpose as a lighthouse.

**Long ton:** 2,240 pounds. Also called "English ton."

**M. V.:** Letters designating a Motor Vessel.

**Main deck:** The principal deck on a vessel. On steamboats, the deck with large side cargo doors, just below the superstructure and the Saloon deck.

**Mast:** A vertical wood or metal pole or post set up to support sails, pennants, navigation lights, booms, or derricks.

**Master:** The commanding officer of a vessel; the person in general charge of a ship. Often called a "Captain." The term "master" usually refers to the person in charge of a cargo or fishing vessel rather than a passenger ship.

**Midships:** The transverse line of the vessel at its widest part. Generally, the middle part of the vessel.

**Nautical mile:** Unit of length: 6,080 feet. Equivalent to a one-minute arc of longitude.

**Navigation:** The science and art of guiding a ship from one place to another, involving determination of the vessel's present position and calculation of a course which will move the ship to the desired position.

**Net tonnage:** A calculated measurement of a ship's capacity for registry purposes. Based on deducting from gross tonnage the spaces not available for cargo according to a formula.

**Officer:** A licensed member of the ship's staff who assists the commander in operation and navigation of the ship. Regulations dictate minimum numbers of officers required, based on the size of the ship.

**Oiler:** Member of the engine operating crew.

**Opposite:** See **Running Opposite**

**Opposition Line:** a service started in competition with an established steamboat line, usually at cut-rate fares. Intrusion of an opposition line usually meant a few months of fare wars, followed by withdrawal of opposition service after a financial settlement or purchase by the established company.

**Outboard:** Away from the longitudinal center line of the vessel; outside of the limits of a deck.

**Outside cabin:** A cabin having a porthole or window in the side of the ship.

**Paddle box:** Structure enclosing the upper part of the paddle wheel. May be ornately decorated.

**Paddle wheel:** A large rotating propulsion wheel, most of which is above the waterline, with paddles or buckets that transmit power to the water. May be one paddle wheel at the stern (usually riverboats) or two paddle wheels located amidships at the sides (usually lakes and bays).

**Passageway:** A narrow corridor giving access to passenger or crew accommodations.

**Passenger:** One who travels on a vehicle or vessel by contract with the carrier, and who pays a fare.

**Perishable cargo:** Goods or products which are subject to decay or deterioration during the time of transit; they may or may not be refrigerated.

**Pier:** A landing place for vessels projecting out from the shore-line. The vessel docks perpendicular to the shoreline.

**Pilot:** A person with knowledge of local waters who is qualified and licensed to conduct a ship through a certain area, or into and out of a port. Not just "someone who steers."

**Pilothouse:** The room or structure from which the ship is controlled while under way. Usually located at the forward edge of the topmost deck.

**Port: (1)** A place where ships are loaded, unloaded and repaired. Includes a harbor and the associated maritime structures; wharves and warehouses.

**(2)** The left side of a vessel as you look forward.

**Power steering gear:** A mechanism which amplifies the human effort applied to the steering wheel to move the rudder or to hold it firmly in place. May be powered by steam or electricity, and may be hydraulic or mechanical.

**Propeller:** An underwater propulsion wheel, usually at the aft end of the vessel, with angled blades that, when turned, translate propulsion power into forward or reverse movement of the ship.

**Public room:** A room in a passenger vessel for use of all passengers, such as a grand saloon, dining room, or lounge.

**Purser:** The officer on a ship who supervises all accounting and clerical activity relating to crew, passengers and cargo.

**Quarter deck:** The after part of the saloon deck; usually the part of the ship from which the passenger gangway reaches the wharf. Place from which passengers board and alight; contains the Purser's office at which payment for passage and state-rooms is received and accounted for.

**Quartermaster:** Crewmember who actually steers the boat.

**Quay** (often pronounced "key"): A landing place for ships, usually a solid wall rather than a wooden structure. Unlike a pier, ships at a quay are parallel to the shoreline.

**Race:** A strong current of water at a coastline, marked by the interaction of two tides. The Race is a specific location at the eastern end of Long Island Sound.

**Radar:** RAdio Detection And Ranging; an electronic aid to navigation.

**Registry:** Enrollment of a vessel at its home port to secure the protection and privileges of the federal government. Each ship has a unique registry number. Analogous to an automobile license plate.

**Rudder:** A vertical pivoted wood or steel underwater paddle mounted longitudinally at the ship's stern. When pivoted, it deflects water and causes the ship to turn.

**Run aground:** To drive a ship accidentally into an area of insufficient depth, usually stranding her. Negative influence on the careers of all involved.

**Running Opposite:** A service using two boats on the same schedule, with each boat making one one-way trip per day. Each vessel, therefore, makes a round trip in two days. Not to be confused with "Opposition line."

**Saloon:** Corruption of the term "Salon;" a large public room inboard of staterooms on a steamer. The room may be two decks high if a gallery deck exists, providing access to a second tier of staterooms.

**Saloon deck:** The deck immediately above the main deck, containing the saloon.

**Scotch boiler:** See **Firetube boiler**.

**Scow:** A flat-bottomed boat with square sloping ends fore and aft. Cargo is carried on deck. See Barge, Lighter. Also used to describe any vessel owned by a competing carrier.

**Screw:** See **Propeller**.

**Seaman:** A man engaged on a ship, below the rank of officer.

**Sheer:** The longitudinal sweeping curvature of a deck from high points at bow and stern to low point amidships; part of the design, and not a sagging condition.

**Ship:** A vessel of considerable size, suitable for navigation.

**Shoal:** Any part of the sea bottom that comes within six fathoms (36 feet) of the surface. Includes sand banks.

**Short ton:** Unit of weight: 2,000 lbs. Also called "American ton."

**Silt:** A deposit of mud or fine soil sediment, placed by action of water, accumulated in banks and at river mouths.

**Single bottom:** A hull design with no inner hull plates; more vulnerable to damage than double-hulls.

**Slip:** The area of water between two piers or wharves.

**Sound:** An arm of the sea sufficiently shallow that depth soundings may be taken over its entire area. Called a firth in Scotland.

**Sponson:** A small solidly braced platform on the side of a paddlewheel steamboat, supporting the bearing through which the paddle wheel shaft emerges from the hull.

**Stack:** A metal cylinder through which combustion gases are led from the boilers to the open air. Also called a funnel.

**Starboard:** The right side of a vessel as you look forward.

**Steamboat:** A mechanically propelled vessel with its motive power derived from expanding steam. Also called steamship.

**Steerageway:** The lowest speed at which the ship will respond to movement of the rudder.

**Stem:** The central upright structural piece at the bow. Usually the foremost part of the ship.

**Stern:** The aftermost part of the ship.

**Stevedore:** A dockworker who loads and unloads ships, or a company employing same.

**Steward:** One who attends to the food, beverage and housekeeping needs of passengers and crew on a vessel. In the dim past, female stewards were called "Stewardesses."

**Stoker:** A member of the engine room crew who feeds and tends the boiler furnaces. Also called a fireman.

**Strait:** A narrow waterway connecting two large bodies of water. For example, New York's East River is actually a strait.

**Superstructure:** Any structure above the main deck.

**Tender** (boat): A small boat whose function is delivery of supplies to a larger boat.

**Tender** (railroad): A car carrying water and fuel for a steam locomotive, and semipermanently coupled to the locomotive.

**Through Bill of Lading:** A shipping contract document calling for movement by more than one carrier or type of carriage. The issuing carrier is usually liable for the entire shipment. Example: a single Bill covering shipment from New York to Worcester MA; by boat to New London, and rail to Worcester.

**Through ticket:** A passenger carriage document covering more than one carrier or type of carriage. Example: the ticket from New York to Boston on the Fall River Line contained a coupon for steamboat passage, and another coupon for the fare on the Boat Train.

**Tide:** variations in ocean and coastal water levels, caused by the combined gravitational pull of the sun and the moon. Tidal effects are felt in bays, harbors, sounds, straits and lower parts of rivers, all of which are considered tidal waters even though they may be fresh rather than salt water.

**Traffic pool:** An agreement among carriers apportioning traffic according to agreed-upon percentages, to control competition and rates.

**Train ferry:** A ferry with tracks on its deck, designed to move railroad freight or passenger cars across a body of water.

**Triple-expansion engine:** A reciprocating steam engine with three cylinders, the first of which is a small, high-pressure cylinder. Steam exhausted from this cylinder goes to a larger, medium pressure cylinder where it is used again and exhausted to a third, even larger, low pressure cylinder to be used for the third time before exhausting to the atmosphere.

**Triple-screw:** A vessel fitted with three propellers.

**Truss:** A frame consisting of interlocked triangles, used to strengthen a structure.

**Tugboat:** A mechanically propelled vessel with little or no cargo capacity, used for towing or pushing unpowered vessels, or assisting powered vessels in confined areas. Contains a powerful engine and a large rudder for this purpose.

**Turbine:** A high-speed rotating engine in which steam jets directly turn rotary vanes. More powerful than a reciprocating engine (one with pistons, cranks, etc.) of equal weight. Power from a turbine is transmitted through speed-reducing gears to propulsion and auxiliary drive shafts.

**Twin-screw:** A vessel fitted with two propellers.

**Vessel:** General term for all craft capable of floating on water and larger than a rowboat, whether powered or unpowered.

**Wake:** The agitated water caused by the movement of a powered ship. Most visible (and perceptible) behind the vessel.

**Walking Beam Engine:** An old steam engine design used with sidewheel boats. The beam (often a steel rhombic or diamond-shaped truss) is pivoted at the center and rocks or "walks" when the engine os operating. At one end of the beam is connected a rod from the steam cylinder; at the other end is a rod connecting to the crank.

**Watch:** A designated period of the day during which specified members of the crew are on duty. Normal maritime practice is based on being at sea 24 hours a day, and divides the day as follows:

> 8 PM - 12 Mid: First Watch
>
> 12 Mid - 4 AM: Mid Watch
>
> 4 AM - 8 AM: Morning Watch
>
> 8 AM - Noon: Forenoon Watch
>
> Noon - 4 PM: Afternoon Watch
>
> 4 PM - 6 PM: First Dog Watch
>
> 6 PM - 8 PM: Second Dog Watch

The two two-hour Dog Watches are designed to rotate the duty so that each day, a given segment of the crew stands the next earlier watch. In overnight Sound steamboat service, the watches were geared to level of activity, placing the most qualified officers on duty at the critical times of navigation (e.g., casting off, Battery through Hell Gate, The Race, Point Judith, docking.)

**Watertube boiler:** A boiler in which water flows through large tubes heated by hot combustion gases. A more efficient design than the firetube boiler.

**Way:** A vessel's movement or progress through the water.

**Wharf:** A wooden or steel structure built on the shore of a harbor, extending out into the water. Also called a pier.

**Wheelhouse:** See **Pilothouse**.

**White water:** Water coursing over shallow sand banks or rocks.

**Windward:** The direction from which the wind is blowing. Opposite of **Leeward**.

**Wireless:** An early name for radiotelegraph and radiotelephone facilities and equipment.

**Yacht:** A ship used exclusively for pleasure. ("If you have to ask how much they cost to operate, you can't afford one." — attributed to J. P. Morgan.)

# Bibliography

Allen, Frederick Lewis, *The Great Pierpont Morgan*; New York NY, Harper & Bros., 1949

Baker, George Pierce, *The Formation of the New England Railroad Systems*; Cambridge MA, Harvard University Press, 1937

Bradlee, Francis B. C., *Steam Navigation in New England*; Salem MA, The Essex Institute, 1920

Campbell, E. G., *The Reorganization of the American Railroad System, 1893-1900*; New York NY, Columbia University Press, 1938

Corey, Lewis, *The House of Morgan*, New York NY, AMS Press, 1930, 1969

DeKerchove, Rene, *International Maritime Dictionary*; New York NY, D. Van Nostrand Co., 1948

Droege, John A., *Freight Terminals and Trains*; New York NY, McGraw-Hill Book Co., Inc., 1925 (2nd Ed.)

Droege, John A., *Passenger Terminals and Trains*; New York NY, McGraw-Hill Book Co., Inc., (Reprint, Milwaukee WI, Kalmbach Publishing Co., 1972)

Dunbaugh, Edwin L., *The Era of the Joy Line*; Westport CT, Greenwood Press, 1982

Farnham, Elmer F., *The Quickest Route*; Chester CT, Pequot Press, 1973

Farson, Robert H., *The Cape Cod Canal*; Middletown CT, Wesleyan University Press, 1977

Flexner, James Thomas, *Steamboats Come True*; Boston MA, Little, Brown & Co., 1944, 1978

Hager, Louis P. and Handy, Albert D., *History of the Old Colony Railroad*; Boston MA, Hager & Handy, 1893

Harlow, Alvin F., *Steelways of New England*; New York NY, Creative Age Press, 1946

Hilton, George W., *The Night Boat*; Berkeley CA, Howell-North, 1968

Hough, Henry Beetle, *Martha's Vineyard*; Edgartown MA, Avery's, Inc. 1966

Hungerford, Edward, *Men of Erie*; New York NY, Random House, 1946

Kirkland, Edward Chase, *Men, Cities and Transportation*; Cambridge MA, Harvard University Press, 1948

Jacobus, Melancthon W., *The Connecticut River Steamboat Story*; Hartford CT, Connecticut Historical Society, 1956

McAdam, Roger Williams, *The Old Fall River Line*; New York NY, Stephen Daye Press, 1937

McAdam, Roger Williams, *Salts of the Sound*; New York NY, Stephen Daye Press, 1939, 1957

McAdam, Roger Williams, *Priscilla of Fall River*; New York NY, Stephen Daye Press, 1947

McAdam, Roger Williams, *Commonwealth, Giantess of the Sound*; New York NY, Stephen Daye Press, 1959

McAdoo, William G., *Crowded Years*; Boston MA, Houghton Mifflin Co., 1931

McCullough, David, *The Great Bridge*; New York NY, Simon & Schuster, 1972

Morris, Paul C. and Morin, Joseph F., *The Island Steamers*; Nantucket MA, Nantucket Nautical Publishers, 1977

Morrison, John H., *History of American Steam Navigation*; New York NY, Stephen Daye Press, 1959

Satterlee, Herbert L., *J. Pierpont Morgan, an Intimate Portrait*; New York NY, Macmillan Company, 1939

Sinclair, Andrew; *Corsair*; New York NY, Little, Brown & Co. 1981

Swanberg, J. W., *New Haven Power*; Medina OH, Alvin F. Staufer, 1988

Taylor, William Leonhard, *A Productive Monopoly*; Providence RI, Brown University Press, 1970

Turner, Gregg M. and Jacobus, Melancthon W., *Connecticut Railroads*; Hartford CT, The Connecticut Historical Society, 1986

Wheeler, George, *The Anatomy of a Myth*; Englewood Cliffs NJ, Prentice-Hall, Inc., 1973

Weller, John L., *The New Haven Railroad*; New York NY, Hastings House, 1969

# General Index

(Boat index on next page)

# Boat/Photo Index

**(Bold face type** indicates photograph on that page)

**George H. Foster**, a native of Long Island, has had a lifelong love of transportation. In his career of marketing, financial management and administration, he has been able to interweave railroads, busses, helicopters and aircraft, while developing an interest in steamboats that led to more than 2,000 hours and 10,000 miles of research and accumulation on America's railroads and steamboats for this project.

His previously published works include *Steel Rails to the Sunrise*, a history of the Long Island Rail Road, and *Steam in the '60s*, a story of locomotive survival. Both of these works were co-authored with Ron Ziel.

Mr. Foster is a life member and past director of the Steamship Historical Society of America, and holds membership in the New Haven Technical Information Society and the Railway & Locomotive Historical Society.

A graduate of the New York University School of Commerce, Accounts and Finances, Mr. Foster is a marketing consultant, residing with his wife Helen in Tucson, Arizona, where they are both active in community affairs.

George is still, at this writing, waiting for *Trains* magazine to correct its erroneous report (Jan '87, p. 37) of his death. There is a sizeable body of evidence, now including this volume to support the contention that he is still alive.

**Peter C. Weiglin** grew up in New York City and on the south shore of Long Island Sound, graduating from high school in Port Jefferson NY and from Fordham University four years later. His youth included many hours riding, photographing and modeling the NYC, NYNH&H, PRR, LIRR and other railroads. He also holds an MBA degree from the University of Pittsburgh.

His career has included work in radio, television, publishing, and advertising, as a writer, editor, producer, performer and manager. During the 1970s he played an active role in the revitalization of America's public transportation industry as a manager and consultant. He has published a book and numerous articles on transportation, management, marketing, computers and model railroading.

Peter and Jeanne Weiglin reside in San Mateo CA. They have two grown children, Dawn and Glenn. Mr. Weiglin currently divides his time between a computer supplies and software firm, and a marketing and management communications consulting practice.

Peter's classes in Marketing, Management and Communications at the University of California at Berkeley, the University of Santa Clara, and National University have been well-received. His weekly radio program, *That Was America*, a lighthearted look at our nation's past with words and music, is being readied for syndication.

**E(lizabeth) Tone** recalls an early memory of her mother pointing across New Haven harbor, saying, "There goes the *Richard Peck*!" Betty never forgot; steam locomotives and steamboats became natural subjects for an artist descended from railroaders on both sides of the family.

Betty Tone went to Boston to study art, and was invited into a roundhouse, to walk around, to look at and to feel the various locomotive parts, which she credits with enabling her to impart a three-dimensional feel to her drawings and paintings. In New York, during a long career as an outstanding commercial artist and art director, she spent some time on car float trips around the harbor, sketching everything from the Statue of Liberty to the *Queen Mary*. She has become one of America's foremost artists on transportation themes. She has long served the Railroad & Locomotive Historical Society as Art Editor of its periodical, *Railroad History*.

Elizabeth's eleven-year marriage and partnership with railfan and printer Herb Summers ended with his untimely death. Today Betty Tone lives and works in a Yonkers NY home and studio filled with railroad artifacts, fulfilling freelance art commissions on transportation and other subjects. Her knowledge and talent have contributed immeasurably to the pictorial quality of this volume, including the color rendition at its beginning.

# Photo Credits

Credits for photographs not from the authors' collections are as shown below. We thank them all.

**Roger Arcara:** 166

**Brooklyn Public Library:** 51

**Joseph Caprilozzi:** 71

**Norton D. Clark:** 151, 266b

**Connecticut Historical Society:** 60, 85

**William King Covell** (Collection now in Fall River Maritime Museum): 12, 14, 17, 32t, 76, 86, 99t, 102b, 106t, 108b, 109, 111, 114b, 129t, 143, 144, 146, 152, 190, 191b, 228, 230, 231, 238, 247, 273, 274, 278t, 283, 284b, 285, 338b, 331, 332b, 333t, 346

**Eleutherian Mills Historical Library:** 180, 181, 340, 341, 342

**Essex Institute:** 120

**Fall River Historical Society:** 280t, 284t, 298t, 299, 300, 301, 325

**Frank Goldsmith:** 28

**R. Loren Graham:** 222b, 320, 321b

**Charles Gunn:** 345b, 347b, 348, 349, 352, 353, 367

**Miss Faith Jennings:** 68, 75

**Keystone-Mast Collection, California Museum of Photography, University of California at Riverside:** 38, 210, 239, 243, 337

**Steven Lang:** 338b, 344b

**Paul E. Levasseur:** 183

**Library of Congress:** 10t, 31, 33, 32b, 37, 62, 63, 116

**Mariners' Museum:** 8, 23, 25b, 27, 35, 36t, 44, 52, 53, 61, 78, 80, 83, 84, 88b, 89b, 91, 113, 115t, 121t, 129b, 132, 136, 138t, 155, 167t, 179b, 197, 203, 222t, 232, 244t, 245b, 249, 256, 257, 262t, 266t, 276, 296, 297b, 304, 307, 308, 309, 311t, 318t, 330, 339

**Conrad Milster:** 350

**National Archives:** 134, 160t, 162t, 222, 318, 328, 329, 336

**New Bedford Public Library:** 182

**New Haven Railroad Historical And Technical Association:** 107t, 135, 338t

**New York Historical Society:** 43

**Henry R. Palmer:** 71, 103, 104t, 146t

**Railroad and Locomotive Historical Society:** 106, 194, 198, 199, 200, 208

**Alice Ramsdell:** 19, 47, 74, 99b, 101, 121, 137b, 145, 204

**Charles Sayle:** 15, 161, 163b, 172b, 174b, 176b, 177b, 178

**Smithsonian Insitution:** 66b, 79, 95t, 96, 97, 98t, 100, 104t, 117, 137, 139, 147, 159, 162, 170, 237, 240, 254t

**Society for the Preservation of New England Antiquities:** 45, 80, 102t, 162b, 229, 253, 255b, 259t, 336b

**The Steamship Historical Society of America:** 13, 41, 54t, 57, 67, 83, 94t, 107b, 108t, 153, 160b, 191t, 196t, 206b, 215, 216, 217, 229, 236t, 237t, 241, 242, 244b, 250, 254b, 255t, 259b, 262, 278b, 279, 281r, 282, 290b, 292b, 293, 294, 295, 299b, 313, 316, 317t, 322b, 333, 321t, 327b, 332b, 343, 351, 355t, 372, 373

**Stanford University:** 24, 34, 55, 58, 89t, 105, 118, 131, 211, 224, 251

**Thomas Stevens:** 327, 355b

**University of Arizona:** 84, 141, 142, 149, 252

**The Whaling Museum, New Bedford MA:** 163t, 164

**David Witbeck:** 335b

**World Ship Society, England:** 347t

**Vineyard *Gazette*:** 156, 169, 171t, 172b

**Ron Ziel:** 207